Also by Anne Chambers

Biography
Granuaile: Grace O'Malley – Ireland's Pirate Queen (1530-1603)
Shadow Lord: Theobald Bourke – Lord Viscount Mayo (1567–1629)
Pirate Queen of Ireland (children)
Eleanor Countess of Desmond (1545–1638)
La Sheridan: Adorable Diva (1887–1958)
Ranji: Maharajah of Connemara (1872–1933)
T.K. Whitaker: Portrait of a Patriot (1916–2017)

Other
At Arm's Length: Aristocrats in the Republic of Ireland
The Geraldine Conspiracy (a novel)
Finding Tom Cruise (short stories)

The Great Leviathan

The Great Leviathan

The Life of Howe Peter Browne
2nd Marquess of Sligo
1788–1845

Anne Chambers

NEW ISLAND

THE GREAT LEVIATHAN
First published in 2017 by
New Island Books
16 Priory Hall Office Park
Stillorgan
County Dublin
Republic of Ireland

www.newisland.ie

Print ISBN: 978-1-84840-639-1
Epub ISBN: 978-1-84840-640-7
Mobi ISBN: 978-1-84840-641-4

British Library Cataloguing Data.

A CIP catalogue record for this book is available from the British Library.

Typeset by JVR Creative India
Cover design by Mariel Deegan

New Island Books is a member of Publishing Ireland.

Jeremy

In memoriam

Contents

Author's Note

Located in Westport House, a collection of manuscripts and papers survived four hundred years of war, rebellion, famine, fire, rodents and damp. During the course of my research among these remarkable relics for biographies of Ireland's sixteenth-century Pirate Queen, Grace O'Malley, and her son, Lord Mayo, I came across the correspondence of their descendant, Howe Peter Browne, 2nd Marquess of Sligo.

Brimful with incidents and historic events, with a cast of famous and infamous personages, the story of the 2nd Marquess of Sligo brought me on a journey from Ireland to England, France, Greece, Italy, America, the West Indies and many places in between. Like his enormous portrait by Sir William Beechey, which overshadows those of his ancestors and descendants in the Long Gallery at Westport House, Sligo was truly larger than life. The portrait of him as a student in Cambridge exudes all the youthful exuberance, confidence and foibles of an aristocratic Regency dandy. In a discreet corner in Westport House, however, a more modestly sized portrait of him in middle age shows a face lined with experience, ill-health, worries and responsibilities. As I subsequently discovered, the two portraits are, in effect, visual depictions of his journey from a youth of wealth, privilege and hedonistic self-indulgence to a mature reforming, indebted and well-intentioned landlord, statesman and family man.

The range of Lord Sligo's undertakings, the sheer volume of his correspondence scattered in archives throughout the world, as well as the geographical scope of his travels, initially made his biography a prohibitive undertaking. And yet I could not quite ignore him. On visits to Westport House his portrait loomed even larger and beckoned even more. A visit to Jamaica in 1996, in the company of his great-great-grandson the late 11th Marquess of Sligo, to commemorate his contribution to the abolition of slavery on the island in the nineteenth century, was revealing of a man somewhat at odds with the modern-day perception of a nineteenth-century West Indian plantation owner. Researching the Jamaican side of his life for an exhibition in Westport House to commemorate the bicentenary of the abolition of slavery in 2007, I finally realised there was no escape. Howe Peter Browne, 2nd Marquess of Sligo had me hooked.

His relatively short lifespan of fifty-six years was crammed with a diverse and extensive range of activities as a Regency buck, an embattled Irish landlord, a peer of the realm, a West Indian plantation owner, Custos Rotulorum, Lord Lieutenant of County Mayo, Knight of St Patrick, militia colonel, governor general of Jamaica, privy counsellor, legislator, intrepid traveller, political commentator, favoured guest at the court of successive kings of England, as well as in the courts of Napoleon's family and in the fashionable salons of Mayfair and Paris, an antiquarian, a patron of the arts, a successful horse breeder, founder and steward of the Irish Turf Club, an emancipator, a friend and fellow traveller of Byron, a spy, sailor and jailbird, as well as the father of fifteen children – each role seemed to warrant a biographical treatment in its own right.

A prolific letter writer, Sligo left behind a vast collection of letters, including copies of his own correspondence with others, which, in turn, was further complicated by his atrocious handwriting! This unique and hitherto unpublished archive throws new light on historical events in Ireland, England, Europe and the West Indies and on the people who shaped them in a period of fundamental political and social change, from the French Revolution, to the abolition of slavery, to the Great Irish Famine.

Unable to resist Sligo's magnetic appeal, or to choose one aspect of his chequered life over another, I decided, like his portrait in the gallery at Westport House, on the big picture – a portrait of his life and times.

*

I am deeply grateful for the assistance and cooperation I received from the many institutions referred to in the reference and source pages. For additional information and material, I am especially indebted to the late 11th Marquess of Sligo, to whom this book is dedicated, and to the Staff at Westport House, especially Sheelyn Browne, Eileen Fahy and Biddy Hughes; the late Lord John Brabourne; Valerie Facey, Kent Reid and Jackie Ranston in Jamaica; and to the late Peter Cochran of the Byron Society.

My thanks to my agent, Jonathan Williams; editor, Emma Dunne; and Edwin, Daniel and staff at New Island. To Martina Chambers Farah and Therese Chambers for their translation assistance, and, as ever, to Tony, family and friends for their encouragement and patience.

Anne Chambers
Dublin 2017

LORD SLIGO'S TRAVELS

Gottenburg

Ystad

Bergan

Berlin
Spandau
Potsdam

Leipzig
Gotha Weimar

Frankfurt
am Main
Darmstadt
Hockenheim
Stuttgart

Munich   Vienna

Konstanz Kempten

asle

Vengen

rig

Lecco

Bracca

ortofino Milan

Turin

Genoa   Piacenza

Sestri   Parma   Bologna

Lerici   Florence

Lucca   Siena

Pisa

Elba   Viterbo

Livorno

Rome

Candida

Naples

Istanbul

Pera
Sestos

Abydos
Hellespont Troad
Marathon

Kastri   Thebes
Lividia
Delphi   Cape of
Sunium   Smyrna
(Izmir)

Patras   Corinth   Kea (Zea)   Ephesus

Monreale Palermo

Milo   Messina

Eleusis

Tripolitsa   Athens   Patmos

Argos   Pireaus

The
Morea

Malta

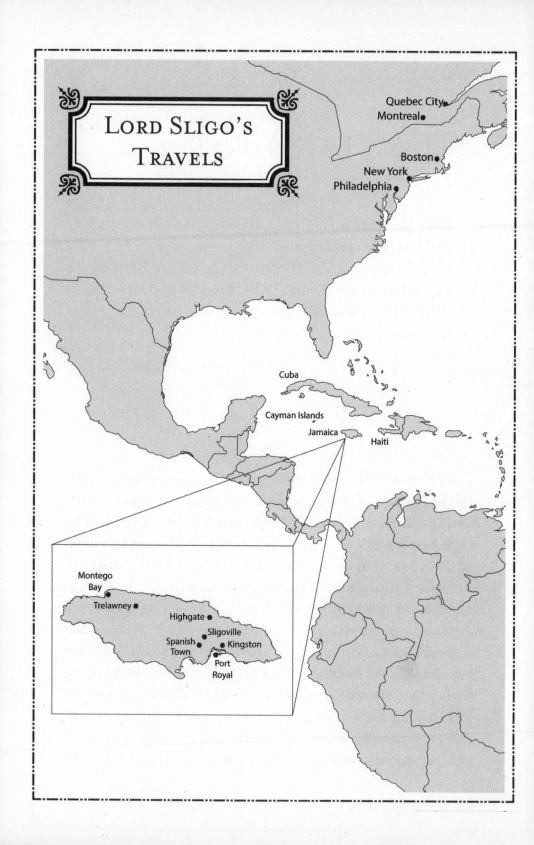

Chapter 1

Little Westport

Little Westport is improving. His teeth tease him a good deal but he is considered as cutting them favourably. His conversation is exceedingly entertaining but not very intelligible, being a mixture of English, French and Portuguese, all of which he understands but sometimes in conversation he blends them a little together.

Earl of Altamont, November 1790

This reference to his two-year-old son and heir was written by John Denis, 3rd Earl of Altamont, to his brother-in-law, Ross Mahon, Castlegar, County Galway, from Lisbon where John Denis and his English-born wife, Louisa Catherine Howe, were temporarily resident. At thirty-four years of age, the earl had suffered a mild stroke and found the benign climate of Lisbon more beneficial than the chill and dampness of his west of Ireland estate. 'My feet continue quite well and I walk about with my crutches very stoutly … Every day of rain or wind I have a fresh supply of rheumatism; fortunately they occur but seldom in this climate.'[1] An only child of the marriage, inheriting the title Lord Westport, Howe Peter Browne was born in London on 18 May 1788. He was named after his maternal grandfather, Admiral Richard Howe, British hero of the American War of Independence, and his paternal grandfather, Peter Browne, 2nd Earl of Altamont.

At two years old he had embarked on the first of many journeys that would make him one of the most travelled men of his time.

His father owned one of the largest estates in Ireland, comprising almost 200,000 acres in counties Mayo and Galway, plantations on the island of Jamaica, and a mansion house in Dublin's Sackville Street. Westport's ancestry was an intriguing mix of Gaelic Irish and Elizabethan English. Among his Irish ancestors was the redoubtable 'Pirate Queen' Grace O'Malley (Granuaile), 'the most notorious woman' of Elizabethan Ireland. Perhaps it was from this remarkable grande dame that Westport inherited his lust for adventure, as well as the individualism, dash and confidence that marked his early life; from his less flamboyant Browne ancestry perhaps his adaptability and pragmatism.

The Browne family acquired their estate by methods other than confiscation and initially shared the same religion as the majority of their Irish neighbours. In 1669 John Browne, a successful lawyer, married Maud Bourke, daughter of the 3rd Viscount Mayo and great-great-granddaughter of Grace O'Malley. Following the Restoration settlements of Charles II, by purchase and by mortgage, Browne acquired much of the encumbered estate of his insolvent father-in-law. He was a staunch Jacobite and colonel in the army of King James II, and the capitulation of the Jacobite cause at Limerick in 1691 heralded his financial ruin and, as a Catholic, confiscation and imprisonment.

Once the heir to the richest man in Connaught, John Browne's eldest son, Peter, found himself bankrupt and, as a Catholic, a political outcast. His son, John, however, ticked all the right boxes for advancement in the new Ireland that emerged from the ruin of the Williamite confiscations. Educated at Christ Church, Oxford, he converted to the religion of the establishment and was ambitious and able. In 1729 he married Anne (Nancy) Gore, sister of the 1st Earl of Arran. In rapid succession he became Baron Mount Eagle (1768), Viscount Westport (1770) and the 1st Earl of Altamont (1771). One of his sons, James Browne, became Prime Sergeant of Ireland. Another son, Arthur, a colonel in the British army, fought in the American War of Independence. His youngest son, Henry, a lieutenant in the Louisburgh Grenadiers, fought against the French at the battles of Louisburgh and Ticonderoga. He won fame for helping the mortally wounded General Wolfe at the Battle of Quebec on 13 September 1759. 'He was wounded as he stood a foot from me,' Henry wrote to his father. 'The poor General after I had his wounds dressed, died in my arms, before he died, he thanked me for my care of him.'[2] The incident is enshrined in the famous painting *The Death of General Wolfe* by Benjamin West.

Land, its acquisition, management and fertility, was the Earl of Altamont's abiding interest. Side by side with his agricultural endeavours, he introduced flax-growing, established a successful linen industry and built new houses for weavers in Westport. A new mansion house, designed by the German architect Richard Cassels, rose above the waters of Clew Bay as a fitting symbol of his new-found prosperity and status. In 1767 he set out to replace the original village, which had grown around the old stronghold of Cathair-na-Mart, with its thatched cabins and narrow lanes, with the splendid new town of Westport, planned by the architect William Leeson.

John's son and heir, Peter Browne, further enhanced the family's fortune. In 1752 he married Elizabeth, only child and heiress of Denis Kelly of Lisduff, County Galway, and Spring Garden, County Mayo, former Chief Justice and a wealthy plantation owner in Jamaica. The Kelly Jamaican estates were to transform the fortune and status of the Browne family.

There was a long-standing connection between the west of Ireland and the West Indies. From the early 1600s Catholic merchant families from Galway city were actively involved in trade with the Spanish- and French-controlled West Indian colonies. This connection became widespread in the early eighteenth century on the enactment of the Penal Laws, which sought to eradicate the

Catholic religion in Ireland by making it a barrier to political and financial advancement. For the younger sons of Catholic families, emigration thus became a necessary option. Many from the west of Ireland went to the island of Jamaica where some ten per cent of the island's plantations were Irish-owned. If they survived the rigours of the long sea voyage, tropical disease, despondency, cultural alienation and the 'deceitful, dreadful climate', the new arrivals found employment as bookkeepers, overseers, attorneys, agents and managers for absentee proprietors, often their own relations. They quickly became integrated into the ruling white supremacy, ever grateful for additional arrivals to swell their ranks and assuage fears of being overrun by the black slaves who outnumbered their white masters nine to one. Many of the new arrivals subsequently inter-married with the daughters and widows of plantation owners and became wealthy proprietors in their own right. A few, like Denis Kelly, also became prominent in the legislative, administrative and legal offices of state where, unlike Ireland, there was no prohibition to their advancement on religious grounds.

The Kelly name was long established in Jamaica. Denis Kelly, an Irish-born barrister, was resident in Jamaica at the close of the seventeenth century. He purchased 621 acres of fertile land west of Old Harbour Bay, which became known as Kelly's Estate. The estate consisted of sugar works, cane fields and a cattle pen (farm). He married Elizabeth Meade from County Cork and they had seven sons and three daughters. In 1716 Denis Kelly returned to Ireland and settled at Lisduff, County Galway, on lands purchased by his eldest son, Edmond.

Edmond Kelly remained in Jamaica and in 1720 acquired the moiety 'in all that plantation or sugar work in the parish of St. Dorothy's commonly known by the name of Cocoa Walk ... and also one full moiety and equal half part of all those negro, Mulatto and other slaves with their increase then living.'[3] His marriage in 1719 to Mary, daughter and heiress of Charles Fuller and Catherine

Maria Byndloss, endowed him with additional property, including outright ownership of Cocoa Walk, of which his father-in-law was co-owner. Cocoa Walk was situated some nine miles inland in a mountainous area in the parish of St Dorothy's. It produced coffee, cedar timber and plantains, as well as cattle and sheep. In 1722, by royal patent, Edward was granted an additional 1,569 acres in the parishes of St Dorothy, St Mary and St George, making him one of the largest plantation owners on the island. In 1711 he was appointed a member of the Jamaican House of Assembly for the parish of St John. From 1717 to 1723 he was Attorney General and was elected Speaker of the Jamaican House of Assembly. Despite or because of his spectacular rise in the property market, he fell into financial difficulties, left Jamaica and died in London in 1728.

His youngest brother, Denis, secured what remained of his brother's estate and served as Chief Justice of Jamaica from 1742 to 1746. In 1729 he married Priscilla Halstead, an heiress to extensive properties on the island. They had one child, Elizabeth, born in 1732. In 1747, on the death of his wife, leaving Kelly's and Cocoa Walk estates in the care of agents, Denis Kelly returned with his young daughter to the family estate at Lisduff.

The portrait of Elizabeth Kelly in the long gallery at Westport House evokes a sense of the exotic among the more conventional ancestral portraits. From the rakish slant of her feathered hat, the nonchalantly displaced pearl and ruby necklace, to the provocative display of her well-endowed bosom, this Creole heiress stares out languidly with large blackberry eyes on a world far removed from her Caribbean roots. For a young woman from the tropical, vibrant and indulgent world of Jamaican planter society, where her every wish and comfort was a priority, moving to the grey and more restrained life of the wife of a west of Ireland landowner was a challenging transition. Perhaps the appalling living standards of the multitude of Irish cottiers and landless labourers, not much removed from the condition of the Jamaican slaves, was one abject familiarity. According to tributes paid to her, Elizabeth seemed to have been affected by the plight of her husband's dependants in Mayo, as perhaps she had been by the slaves on her father's estates in Jamaica. Whether she had any say in her marriage to Peter Browne, if she fell madly in love with him or whether their union was motivated by more mercenary considerations, is unknown. As in Jamaica, Connaught society was intimate, interrelated and hospitable, providing outlets for social intercourse between the landed classes. The return of 'Jamaica Kelly' with a fortune and an only daughter opened many doors.

Peter Browne's lack of title (his father had not yet ascended the aristocratic ladder) made him a less than desirable suitor. Unimpressed by his lack of fortune and prospects, Denis Kelly insisted that he change his name to Browne Kelly before giving his consent to the marriage of his daughter. On 16 April 1752, aged twenty, Elizabeth Kelly married Peter Browne Kelly. The young couple took up residence at Mount Browne, a few miles from Westport. Notice of their marriage was carried in the *Dublin Gazette*, which described Miss Kelly as 'a young lady of great beauty with a £10,000 fortune'.[4] Their first child, Priscilla, named after her Jamaican grandmother, was born the following year but died in childhood. A son, John Denis, was born in 1756, followed by another son, inexplicably also named Denis, and three daughters, Anne, Elizabeth and Charlotte.

Denis Kelly died in 1757. By his will, dated 1 March 1754, he bequeathed his estates in Jamaica and Ireland to his daughter. In the event that she failed to produce a male heir, his property should then 'devise to my nephew John Dalton and the heirs male of his body, he and they taking upon themselves the sirname [*sic*] of Kelly'.[5] He left minor bequests to servants and relations in Galway and the sum of £500 to 'Margaret Wright, now in Jamaica ... for her maintenance until she shall arrive at that age (18 years) or marry.'[6] It appears that, like his white counterparts, Denis Kelly had had a dalliance with another woman in Jamaica. Peter Browne Kelly subsequently leased Cocoa Walk 'with Negroes, slaves, beasts and other appurtances',[7] to his relation John Daly of Carrownakelly, County Galway, and Thomas Kelly of Dublin for one year, while he busied himself with the management of his father's estate in Mayo and his wife's estate in Galway. From 1761 to 1768 he represented Mayo in the Irish parliament.

Elizabeth Browne Kelly did not live to see her husband elevated to the peerage. At Mount Browne on 2 August 1765, aged just thirty-three, 'the Lady of the Honble. Peter Browne, Esqre. whose death is universally lamented especially by the poor whom she charitably supplied with medicine and a skilful person to administer them',[8] died, leaving a family of five young children.

Peter Browne succeeded to the title as 2nd Earl of Altamont on the death of his father in 1776. His eldest son, John Denis, assumed the title 'Lord Westport', his younger son, Denis, becoming a 'Right Honourable'. The anglicisation of the Irish aristocracy had intensified since the conversion of Peter's grandfather to the established religion. Together with religious conversion, an English education was also *de rigueur* and the earl sent his heir, John Denis, to be educated at Eton. He also set about enlarging Westport House with plans drawn up by the Dublin architect Thomas Ivory, who rebuilt the south wing. He broke up his father's extensive horse-racing and breeding establishment. His tenure, however, was short-lived and he died in Westport House in December 1780.

By his will, all of forty-five pages long, he bequeathed the bulk of his property to his eldest son and heir, John Denis. To his second son, Denis, he left the sum of £5,000, 'trusting that his Elder Brother will do further for him as an elder Brother ought'. Denis was also granted a life interest in the lands and property of Mount Browne. Denis subsequently purchased the Claremont estate near Claremorris in east Mayo from Dominick Browne of Castlemacgarrett (a relation through marriage), which later became his principal residence. Peter Browne also made provision for the sum of £18,000 as marriage portions for his three daughters, set against the rents and profits forthcoming from 'the several lands, tenements, negroes and particulars in the island of Jamaica which formerly did belong to Denis Kelly'. He left the income from the Kelly estate in Galway to his eldest daughter, Lady Anne Browne, and to her future male offspring, with the proviso that 'such son when in possession taking and using the name and arms of Browne'. To Anne he also left 'all her mother's jewels and paraphernalia' and land in Mayo, and £1,000 to his illegitimate son Peter Browne, 'whom I have placed at school at Drogheda'. Peter Browne subsequently entered Holy Orders and became Dean of Ferns. The earl also acknowledged his liaison with Peter's mother, Mary Stanford of Westport, by rewarding her with an annuity of £100 for life, payable out of his estate. To circumvent the Penal Laws, he further stipulated that 'on account of her being a papist and the payment thereof shall be disputed, then and in such case I give to the said Mary Stanford the sum of one thousand pounds Irish money'.[9]

John Denis succeeded to the title and estates of his father at the age of twenty-four. From 1768 to 1772 he represented Mayo in the Irish parliament. On his father's death he became Commander of the Mayo Legion of Volunteers. In the summer of 1777 he undertook a journey through northern Europe. The trip did not merely follow the pattern of the usual Grand Tour. From the journal he wrote of his travels through Saxe-Coburg, Bohemia, Austria and Hungary, agricultural and manufacturing techniques, especially of linen, cotton, glass and porcelain, consumed his interest as much as architecture and culture.

Like his grandfather, however, John Denis's main preoccupation was agriculture and estate management. He wrote papers on agricultural innovations suited to the particular circumstances of his west of Ireland estate. He experimented with wheat seeds he had procured from Egypt and elsewhere. His estate books detail the number and breed of his livestock, even the individual names of each of his fifty-one dairy cows, as well as detailing cures for scour in cattle and broken wind in horses and the cultivation of the 'globe' turnip. A Tory in politics, he was more content at home in Westport than in the political and social whirl of the House of Lords in Dublin. He had 'a full, strong and distinct voice' and, unlike many of his contemporaries, was known to have 'disliked high living, gambling and swearing'.[10] He created the lake to the west of Westport House, which previously had been washed by Atlantic waves, and completed his father's extension, employing the notable craftsman James Wyatt to decorate his new gallery and dining room. Later in 1800 he further embellished his grandfather's new town of Westport with tree-lined boulevards on either side of the Carrowbeg River, flanked by imposing Georgian houses.

By 1780 John Denis's world as a landowner in the west of Ireland was not an enviable one. The state of the majority of his countrymen was one 'of almost unlimited submission: speaking a language that is despised, professing a religion that is abhorred and being disarmed, the poor find themselves in many cases slaves'.[11] Land was the main outlet of employment for the vast majority, whose rents were the principal source of income for their landlords. Subsistence living on minute rented holdings in mud-and-wattle single-roomed thatched cabins, lit by rushes dipped in tallow, most without chimneys, with only straw beds, rudimentary furniture and utensils, the hand-to-mouth existence gave little sense of security or any incentive to improve their lot, even for the few who managed to acquire a thirty-one-year lease, the longest allowable to a Catholic. A system known as 'canting', whereby a lease could be sold by the landlord to the highest bidder, without any regard to the former tenant, was also rife. Subdivision of land within families, or rented in common by numerous tenants by a practice known as 'rundale,' conspired to aggravate the sense of impermanency and made rents exorbitant and out of proportion with the productivity of the land. At the beginning of the nineteenth century a rising population made the common people further dependent on subdivision to provide for their expanding families. Badly led by 'fence-sitter' leaders, both aristocratic and clerical, they became 'the buffoons or the dangerous rebels caricatured by the English press and alluded to in the memoirs of the Ascendancy who despaired of the ignorance and dependence of the class they themselves had created'.[12] The imposition of tithes for the upkeep of the minority Anglican Church, to which they did not belong, further contributed to the destitution of the mass of the Irish Catholic population. With no political means to assuage their lot, their anger and sense of hopelessness were vented in occasional outbreaks of agrarian violence and on the hope of foreign intervention. Despite their disadvantaged status, however, their music, dance, storytelling and an innate hospitality, even among the poorest, set the Irish peasantry apart.

While the Earl of Altamont was acknowledged as a progressive landlord, much of his land was of poor quality and the rent was less than that forthcoming from a property of superior quality. In 1796 income rental from his estates amounted to £11,388, which by 1802, mainly owing to his improvements as well as income from his newly established town of Louisburgh, had risen to £16,126. Kelp harvesting and fishing provided an additional source of income for his tenants, as did smuggling and the making of illicit alcohol (poitín). In the early part of the nineteenth century, over two hundred fishing boats operated out of Westport harbour, as well as a fleet of six trading vessels. The town had a custom house, bonding stores, flour mills, a tannery and numerous large warehouses. The linen industry, established by his father, still flourished, while a twenty-six-loom cotton factory and two 'bleach greens' at Belclare employed a considerable number of men, women and children.

The earl was part of the Protestant ascendancy whose rule in Ireland was absolute. The anglicisation of Irish aristocrats commenced in the eighteenth century through their conversion to the reformed Church of England, their education in English public schools, marriage to the daughters of English aristocrats and adoption of English language and customs. Over time they became estranged from their own people becoming, in effect, a 'garrison' maintained in their loyalty to the English crown by the distribution of titles, patronage and political control. They presided over a parliament in Dublin which represented their own interests and from which the vast majority of their fellow countrymen were excluded.

While life for the under-classes in England and on the Continent was also unenviable, unlike their Irish counterparts, they were not obliged to labour under such onerous political, social and religious disadvantages. English society was also ruled by an aristocracy and a form of government that was both undemocratic and corrupt but there 'the landed aristocracy formed the graceful apex of a society which had grown up naturally from the soil. Landlord and tenant took each other for granted.'[13] The mass of the common people in Ireland, by contrast, were outcasts in their own country and consequently had little faith in the legislative process. While few among the Irish Protestant aristocracy were enforcers of the penal system and some, like the Brownes of Westport, were outspoken opponents of it, it was in the interest of the landlord class that the Irish parliament stayed in Protestant hands to ensure that the circle of privilege, wealth and power remained confined to the few.

As a resident landlord in a remote area of Ireland, the Earl of Altamont's interest was centred on the locality over which he held sway. He had a deep-rooted aversion to the prevailing cult of absentee landlords who lived abroad on the rent from their estates and ceded responsibility to agents and middlemen. 'Never be an Absentee from your own country,' he later advised his son. 'Support and encourage the Town of Westport it is the best possession we have,'[14] advice that was initially more honoured in the breach than in the observance by his heir. A resident landlord, the earl's finger was on the pulse of every development within his lordship. Westport House was the power base for local politics in Mayo. Appointments to local office and the selection of candidates to represent the county in parliament were decided by the Earl of Altamont. Because of their Catholic origins and marriage connections with some of Mayo's indigenous families, since their conversion to the new status quo, the Earl of Altamont was the acknowledged buffer between the government in Dublin and the neighbouring Catholic gentry, who, in turn, gave him their allegiance, while thousands of tenants and labourers were dependent on him for their very existence.

In an age when advancement in politics, administration, the military and the professions, in England and in Ireland, was through the patronage of powerful aristocrats, the earl's influence in Mayo was immense. Much like a present-day public representative, he sought to exact the maximum funding from central government to improve the infrastructure in his immediate locale, competing with his fellow parliamentarians for the limited resources available. Patriarchal and ambitious for the welfare and advancement of his extended family and adherents, through his contacts with Irish and English government officials, the earl promoted their interests in the political, legal, military, administrative and religious outlets at his disposal and expected and received their loyalty in return. From various ministers, admirals and army commanders, he competed for commissions and promotions in the British services. The poet, essayist and critic Thomas De Quincey wrote of him: 'His language is neither elegant nor animated; little adapted to command the attention, conciliate the regard or invigorate the minds of his hearers, and is alike deficient in philosophical clearness and grammatical precision,' but, he conceded, he was 'as good a scholar as a nobleman needs to be.'[15]

The earl's accession to his title and estates coincided with a remarkable period in Irish history. Fuelled by developments in the American colonies, Irish political leaders, such as Henry Grattan, campaigned for greater independence from Britain. In April 1782 the British government relinquished its right to legislate for Ireland and a new Irish parliament came into being. Albeit Protestant in orientation and ethos, it presided over a period of growth and rejuvenation which saw an upsurge in municipal building, industry, agriculture, trade, science and in the arts. The more severe edicts of the Penal Laws were abolished. On taking the oath of allegiance to the king, Catholics were permitted to inherit land on the same terms as Protestants, to avail of a 999-year lease and to bequeath their estate in its entirety to their eldest male heir. Pressure from an emerging Catholic merchant class forced the government to concede the right to vote to those Catholics with property valued above forty shillings. While still ineligible to run for parliament and debarred from the bench or from holding high public office, Roman Catholics and Protestant dissenters, such as Presbyterians (against whom the Penal Laws were also directed), began to contemplate a common political strategy.

The plantations of his Jamaican-born mother contributed an average £3,000 annually to the earl's income. The biannual crop of sugar, and its derivative rum, was shipped and sold on his behalf by an agency in Bristol. He also exported produce from his linen mill in Westport to his estates in Jamaica. 'I have received a letter from Messrs Beamish and Crawford informing me they have shipped on your Lordship's account two Bales of linen on the *Rebecca* which is safe arrived … and are very good for Negroes use.'[16]

In 1787 the income from the estates was to prove a vital asset to the earl to secure the hand of Louisa Catherine Howe, youngest daughter and co-heir (with her sisters Juliana, Mary and Sophia Charlotte, wife of Penn Assheton Curzon, son of Viscount Curzon) of Admiral Richard Earl Howe. Richard was the second son of Emanuel Scrope Howe, 2nd Viscount Howe, former Governor of Barbados; his mother was the daughter of a mistress of King George I; and his sister was married to William Augustus Pitt. His sister-in-law, a granddaughter of George I, was 'always treated by the King [George III] with extraordinary familiarity, more indeed as a relative than a common visitant'.[17] The family seat, Langar Hall, near Nottinghamshire, was mentioned in the 1086 Domesday Book. By the eighteenth century it had evolved into an imposing Georgian mansion, set in open parkland. Filled with valuable furniture, books, pictures – including a nativity by Rubens 'found in the ceiling of the Drawing Room' – and other curiosities, much of its contents were later transferred to Westport House. In 1772 Admiral Howe purchased Porter's Lodge (also known as Porter's Mansion) in Shenley, Hertfordshire, where he resided after his retirement from the navy. The family also owned a house on Grafton Street in London.

The naval achievements of Richard Howe and his brothers, George and William, made them household names in England. On leaving Eton at fourteen, Richard had entered the navy as a midshipman. Rising through the ranks, he was appointed commander of the North American fleet on the outbreak of the American Revolution. Popularly known in the service as 'Black Dick' because of his swarthy appearance, he suffered no ostentation and was solicitous of the men he commanded. Among his many naval accolades, he is credited with refining the signalling code at sea.

With his younger brother William, who commanded the British army in North America, he was commissioned by the British government in 1776 to open negotiations with the American colonists. Political intransigence and duplicity in England, however, resulted in the collapse of the negotiations. On 4 July 1776 America declared independence and all-out war with Britain commenced. Anchored off Staten Island, on board his ship *Eagle,* Richard made one final effort to meet with General George Washington, 'trusting that it may be the means of preventing further bloodshed and bring about peace and lasting union between Great Britain and America'. He planned 'to advance in a frigate as near to the town of New York as would meet with Washington's approval,'[18] but the meeting did not materialise. In August 1778 Richard Howe prevented the French fleet from taking Rhode Island. Irked by an orchestrated campaign against him in England, the muddled policies of the British Admiralty and War Office, combined with his distrust of the government of Lord North, he subsequently resigned his North American command. He was later persuaded by the government to resume command of the Channel fleet. His reinstatement was crowned by his relief of the siege of Gibraltar in 1782.

Richard became a close confidant of George III, and the king entrusted him with the naval training of two of his troublesome sons. Admiral Howe's determination not to allow his royal charges any favourable treatment elicited their disdainful complaints. 'You will have heard I asked Lord Howe for the Phaeton and that I was refused.... His lordship plans to keep me back as long as he could,' Prince William complained to his brother the Prince of Wales.[19] 'A stupid old fool eat[en] up with gout and various other bad humours ... I think his Lordship ought to be surfeited,' was the opinion of his brother, the Duke of Clarence.[20] In 1787 Richard Howe became First Lord of the Admiralty and was created earl by King George III in 1788.

Portraits of his daughter, Louisa Howe, painted by George Romney and by Opie at the time of her marriage to the Earl of Altamont, show a fine-boned face with a provocative mouth and blue eyes, framed by well-defined eyebrows. Her mother, her sister Mary and her aunt were ladies-in-waiting to Queen Charlotte. One of Louisa's wedding gifts was a fire screen embroidered by the royal princesses. 'That mild and civil little Mary,' Queen Charlotte wrote to Lady Howe, 'beat the King her sovereign at backgammon every night and when I represented that this was not the behaviour of a loyal Subject, I was answered, she did the same to Lord Howe and upon that we settled that what was respectful and dutiful to Papa, must prove towards the King.'[21] Charlotte, the Princess Royal, was particularly taken with Louisa and her sister Mary. 'I have had the pleasure to spend many evenings with dear Miss Mary Howe who I think more charming than ever,' the princess wrote to her brother Prince Augustus, 'but she is very low at the thoughts of parting with her sister, Miss Louisa, who is going to be married to Lord Altamont, an Irish peer of great fortune.'[22]

There are few clues as to how an Irish peer from the remote west coast of Ireland, socially more at home in his rural environment than in the salons of royalty, became acquainted with someone as urbane and refined as twenty-year-old Louisa Howe. There was a remote family connection between the Howe and Browne families through the 'gorgeous' Gunning sisters, Maria and Elizabeth, granddaughters of the 6th Viscount Mayo, from Castlecoote, County Roscommon. In the mid-eighteenth century the sisters had taken English society by storm. Maria married the Earl of Coventry and Elizabeth married first the Duke of Hamilton in 1752 and secondly the Duke of Argyle in 1759. The uncles of the Earl of Altamont, Henry and William Browne, fought in the Anglo-French war in America under Admiral Howe's oldest brother, Brigadier-General George, 3rd Viscount Howe.

The Earl of Altamont, however, found the pathway to love strewn with difficulties. Marriage between aristocrats involved complex and lengthy negotiations. By law, a husband had control over the property of his wife, and for a potential heiress such as Louisa Howe who, with her two sisters, stood to inherit substantial property and wealth from both her parents, adequate safeguards had to be secured. In correspondence edged with icy politeness, the Earl of Altamont found his initial advances rebuffed by his intended's wary father. His opening shot requesting Louisa's hand in marriage was deftly parried by the admiral's determination to establish the adequacy or otherwise of the suitor's fortune. His lawyers at Lincoln's Inn demanded a detailed account of the title, size and income of the earl's Irish and Jamaican estates. The financial terms proffered, however, by his potential father-in-law did not please the prospective groom, who protested that they undermined his status and impeached his character. The riposte from the admiral that he was 'under the painful necessity of being obliged to decline the honour of your alliance, and to preclude myself from the satisfaction of your future acquaintance'[23] was accompanied by the withering offer to reimburse the earl for any expense incurred at the jewellers.

The progress of the negotiations was avidly followed by the royal family. In March 1787 Princess Elizabeth informed her brother Prince Augustus that 'Louisa Howe is not as yet concluded with Lord Altamont, but will be soon. She is prettier than ever. Her sisters are miserable at the thought of parting with her, particularly Mary who has always lived with her ever since she was born and constantly slept in the same room. But they have the pleasure of thinking that she will be perfectly happy, as everybody gives him the best of characters.'[24]

Like many aristocrats of his generation, Altamont had enjoyed previous amorous liaisons, as evidenced by his will, in which he provided for two natural daughters the substantial sum of £1,500 invested in 'Government or real Securities … to pay the dividends and interest unto his natural daughter Mary Browne by Ann Walsh … during her continuance unmarried'. Should his illegitimate daughter marry after his death, the bequest was most civilly dependent on Mary Browne first obtaining the Countess of Altamont's consent as to the suitability of her prospective husband.

17

He left another 'annuity of £50 ... to his natural daughter Elizabeth Mathews for her life', which he stipulated 'is to be for her separate use independent of her Husband.'[25]

The financial wrangling between the earl and the admiral was eventually resolved. A substantial dowry of £15,000 per annum was agreed, with the customary safeguards of annuities in land and money. The marriage took place on 21 May 1787 at Porter's Lodge, Shenley, Hertfordshire. There was much misgiving and sadness on the part of her family when Louisa departed her English surroundings for the beautiful but remote west coast of Ireland. Some years later, Thomas De Quincey, who visited Westport House, described the world of the 'old Irish rural nobility' into which Louisa Howe stepped. 'Here might be found old rambling houses in the style of antique English manorial chateaux ... a comfort and "cosiness" combined with magnificence, not always so effectually attained in modern times.'[26] Regardless of the extensions, renovations and improvements lavished on the earl's home, it still retained aspects of its more ancient beginnings, including an open courtyard at its core. And perhaps symbolic of its more ancient Gaelic origins, Westport House was also home to the last of the original breed of Irish wolfhound, described by a visitor to Westport House in 1786 as 'being above three feet high, large, noble and handsome ... remarkably quiet, patient in anger till really provoked but then truly formidable at which time their hair stands erect. They hunt both by scent and by sight ... their colour is white or white with a few black or brown spots.'[27] Later in 1810 when the last surviving dog died, the 2nd Marquess of Sligo ordered the bitch to be put down, to protect the origins of the ancient breed.

The Irish aristocracy lived on less formal terms with their servants, retainers and tenants than their counterparts in England. In the west of Ireland this lack of formality was more pronounced. The earl's agent, John Gibbons, was a local man, while most of his household and estate staff were Irish-born. 'At Westport,' De Quincey observed, 'you might fancy yourself overlooking the establishment of some Albanian pasha. Crowds of irregular helpers and grooms, many of them totally unrecognised ... some half-countenanced by this or that upper servant, some doubtfully tolerated, some *not* tolerated but nevertheless slipping in by the postern doors ... made up a strange mob ....'[28] While perhaps appalled by the living conditions of his tenants, Louisa might well have admired the innovative methods her husband employed to improve agricultural practices and encourage trade through his port, as well as the pleasant appearance of his principal town of Westport. Her dowry enabled the earl in 1794 to purchase part of the Lord Mayo estate at Old Head from John Evelyn, a native of Bath in England, who had acquired it from Edmund Jordan, husband of the last dowager Countess of Mayo.

Admiral Howe maintained close contact with his daughter in Ireland, writing to her from his postings abroad, often voicing his anxiety as to her safety and health, to the annoyance of her husband. Louisa was well educated and her hobbies were many and varied. She painted and drew well and was interested in botany, natural history, chemistry and geometry, as a copy of *The Elements of Euclid* in her collection testifies. As is also evident from her extant correspondence, she was well-versed in the politics of the day. Despite her ethereal looks, she was strong-willed, independent and self-possessed. Later, during her son's extended absences abroad, her dextrous handling of his estate and of local and family issues, as well as his financial problems, drew his praise and appreciation. 'Indeed my affairs are in such able hands that I think it would be to my advantage to stay away ten or twelve years.'[29] Louisa was inordinately proud of her Howe family lineage and of her father's iconic status in England and, with her sister Mary, penned an account of his maritime career. Lest her relationship to Admiral Howe be forgotten, her last will and testament stipulated 'that the inscription on my coffin may express that I am one of the daughters of the late Earl Howe'.[30] Such was her husband's care and concern for her happiness that he agreed to her frequent and lengthy absences from her marital home in Westport to enable her to remain in contact with her family and friends in England.

Following the birth of their only child, the earl's indulgence in that regard also extended to his son.

Chapter 2

An Only Child

You will soon however have your little Treasure with you and then you will be quite happy as should I be if I could be with you both.

Lady Altamont

The birth of Lord Westport on 18 May 1788 in London was celebrated, not merely by his parents and his English grandparents, but also by the family of King George III at Windsor Castle. The news, conveyed to the Royal Family by his aunt Lady Mary Howe, provided a diversion from the repressive lifestyle endured by the royal princesses, who took a special interest in the nephew of their 'particular friend'. Their eldest brother, the Prince Regent (a lock of whose hair is preserved in Westport House), later facilitated the young Irish peer's induction into British society and even later, as king, stood godfather to his protégé's eldest son. In the town of Westport and the surrounding countryside, bonfires blazed and revellers celebrated the birth of an heir to the Westport House estate.

From the start, both parents idolised their son. The Earl of Altamont 'viewed him [Westport] with an anxiety of love that sometimes became almost too painful to witness'.[1] Somewhat embarrassed at the intensity of his affection for his son, whose 'conduct to me is that of an Angel', the earl begged the indulgence of his half-brother, Peter Browne, 'as I know you are too much interested about Him to laugh at me for it'.² The antithesis of his cautious and low-key father, Westport, despite their irregular meetings, developed a strong bond of affection, loyalty and respect with his father. Westport's relationship with his mother, as is obvious from their voluminous correspondence, is intimate and humorously affectionate. From an early age he adopted the role of her adviser, while Louisa followed his early life of constant mobility and excess with mild trepidation. And while the offspring of such adoring parents, and from such a privileged background, might well be expected to turn out a snob, pretentiousness never became part of Westport's make-up. He grew up, as one of his friends wrote of him, to be 'rather handsome and conciliated general goodwill by his engaging manners',³ characteristics later tinged with the headstrong propensity of youth, the privilege his status endowed and a determination to have his own way.

Westport's life-long addiction to travel started early. By autumn 1790, aged two, he had undertaken that first sea voyage with his parents to Lisbon. They were accompanied by a number of servants and by Mr Fitzmaurice, a naval medical doctor, whom Admiral Howe released from duty to attend his daughter and son-in-law. The earl's rheumatic ailments responded to the mild climate and, as he wrote to his cousin, he 'was gaining ground rapidly' and his 'dearest Louisa' was also doing 'tolerably well'.⁴ News of his family and estate was conveyed by the packets which sailed between Ireland, England and Lisbon. One of the first letters contained news of the marriage of the earl's younger brother, Denis, to his first cousin, Anne Mahon of Castlegar, County Galway. By return mail from Lisbon, the earl wished the happy couple 'from my soul every happiness … nor shall my efforts ever be wanting to make them happy in every way'.⁵ Remaining true to his father's last wishes, the earl supported his younger brother, financially and politically, despite the latter's participation in events that were destined to make his name akin to the devil in his native county. News of the pregnancies of the earl's two sisters, Elizabeth (Betsy), married to Ross Mahon in Castlegar, and Anne, the wife of Lord Desart in County Kilkenny, induced the earl to despatch 'a box of lemons and two boxes of oranges which my dearest Betsy desired',[6] as well as pipes of wine and sherry to his brother-in-law. His generosity extended also to his father-in-law, to whom he sent casks of wine and sherry. The sheer quality of the 'Calcavella' might well, the admiral told his son-in-law, induce him 'to become a more potent toper than you seem willing to believe'.[7] The royal princesses frequently added their own lines to Lady Mary's letters, especially with enquiries and good wishes for Louisa's 'little boy'.

In late spring 1791 the family returned to Westport where the earl became absorbed in the management of his estate and where his three-year-old son received all the attention that befitted his status. These early years were the longest uninterrupted period Westport was destined to spend in his ancestral home. The leather-bound volumes on history, politics, belle-lettres, botany, arts, sciences and theology in the library at Westport House shaped his early education. One of the oldest portraits in the house, that of Maud Bourke, the great-great-granddaughter of his remote ancestor Grace O'Malley, may well have inspired his penchant for adventure, while his future predilection for antiquities was nurtured by such tomes as Lavery's *Letters on Greece*, Stuart and Revett's *Antiquities of Athens*, Wood's *Ruins of Palmyra* and the Earl of Pembroke's *Collection of Ancient Marble Antiquities*. Their faded engravings of antiquities in distant lands fired his imagination.

The earl's sporadic attendances at parliament in Dublin helped break the isolation of their remote location. As a member of the peerage, the earl sat in the Irish House of Lords, while his brother, Denis, sat in the Lower House as MP for Mayo. Almost two hundred miles long, travelled at an average speed of twenty-five miles a day on a winding road that meandered through the middle of Ireland, punctuated by detours to the houses of relations and friends, combined with changes of horses at the few inns and hostelries en route, the journey between Westport and Dublin, via towns such as Ballinrobe, Ballinasloe, Kilbeggan, Kinnegad and Maynooth, took many days.

One of the larger European cities, Dublin had a population in excess of 150,000 citizens. Transformed from a medieval town to a modern city, by the late eighteenth century it possessed broad thoroughfares, large public gardens, imposing civic buildings, fashionable town mansions and uniform red-brick Georgian terraces. Handsome public edifices, such as the Custom House on the newly developed quays, the Law Courts, King's Inns, the Royal Exchange and the Blue Coat School in Blackhall Place further enhanced its appearance. By the 1790s the newly built mansions of the aristocracy extended from the river Liffey northwards along Sackville Street towards the Rotunda and Rutland Square. Their spacious rooms were furnished *à la* Wyatt, Adam and Chippendale by the multitude of decorative plasterwork companies that flourished in the city.

During the parliamentary term, Dublin was crowded and *en fête*. Carriages, curricles, landaus, post-chaises, carts, coaches and brightly painted sedan chairs jostled for position in the busy thoroughfares. The wheeled traffic vied with cattle drovers and their four-legged charges, haughty young bucks with duelling on their minds, beggars, shrill-voiced hawkers and hucksters, plaintive balladeers, street musicians and pickpockets. The parliamentarians socialised and partied, attended masked balls, concerts and firework displays, promenaded in the Rotunda and Ranelagh gardens, took carriage drives along the fashionable North Circular Road and farther afield to picturesque suburbs such as Blackrock and Bray. 'Nothing can be so gay as Dublin,' one visitor enthused, 'the Castle twice a week, the opera twice a week, with plays, assemblies and suppers to fill up the time.'[8] Parliamentary sessions were looked on as a financial boon to the capital and benefited all classes, from merchant to messenger.

The focal point of business, politics and pleasure centred on Dublin Castle and on the court of the Viceroy, the king's representative in Ireland. The viceregal court, fashioned on the royal court in England, was the epicentre of style and entertainment, as well as political advancement. Invitations to balls and suppers at the castle were at a premium. More significantly, however, the Viceroy had at his disposal the dispersal of Crown patronage from which every job, sinecure, favour and promotion, in both state and church, emanated. A local magnate was only as good as the patronage he might elicit to dispense within his own locality. To maintain his status in Mayo and to keep the ambitions of local rivals, such as the Earl of Lucan in Castlebar, Viscount Dillon in Costello and O'Donel in Newport, at bay, the Earl of Altamont competed for his share of government spoils.

Based in their Dublin residence at 9 Sackville Street, the earl and his countess, as an intimate of the royal family, were especially feted. More adverse than most to the incessant socialising that accompanied parliamentary sessions, with the exception of presenting Louisa at one of the castle balls, the earl's time in Dublin tended to revolve around more practical pursuits. He attended lectures at the newly established Royal Dublin Society, where the latest experiments and developments in agriculture were presented. He personally contributed for debate many articles about the innovative agricultural undertakings he employed on his estate in Mayo.

In 1789 all eyes, however, were turned towards France as the revolution moved towards its catastrophic conclusion. Initially news of the overthrow of an out-of-touch French monarchy was greeted with satisfaction by most Protestant and Catholic classes in Ireland, with the exception of the ascendancy and the Catholic clergy. Following the Reign of Terror and despite the atrocities and the usurpation of power by a military dictatorship, the French Revolution continued to inspire. Challenging the established principle of power being the exclusive preserve of hereditary monarchs, it sought to evaluate and change the social and political structure in relation to fundamental values, perceptions in the creation and usage of wealth and in religion and culture. In Ireland, with its immense social and political inequalities, such sentiments found enthusiastic adherents, as well as determined opponents.

Inspired by French revolutionary principles, the Catholic Committee, an organisation founded to elicit political reforms for Catholics and led ineffectually by members of the old Catholic aristocracy, including the Earl of Altamont, was taken over by middle-class radicals. In 1791 the committee's new secretary, Theobald Wolfe Tone, urged the introduction of religious equality in Ireland and unity between Catholic, Protestant and Dissenter. With the establishment of the Society of United Irishmen in Belfast, Dublin and other locations around the country, for the first time, a united Catholic and Protestant opposition began to emerge.

The response from the British government, under William Pitt, was to introduce a policy of conciliation and reform. This was opposed by elements in the Irish parliament adamant that Catholics should remain excluded from political power. The Williamite confiscations of the previous century still loomed large in the minds of Protestant landowners, who feared a Catholic majority in parliament a threat to ownership of their estates. In 1793, however, the Irish parliament granted Catholic freeholders the right to vote but not the right to stand for parliament or other high office. This served to further infuriate the radicals and to swell the ranks of the United Irishmen. In 1794 the outbreak of war between Britain and France threatened to plunge Ireland into revolution should France make common cause with Irish discontent. As the heads of French aristocrats tumbled daily into baskets at the foot of the guillotine and their property was confiscated, their fate was a gruesome portent to the Irish ascendancy of what might happen should France gain a foothold in Ireland.

The war, however, had a more personal significance for the family of the Earl of Altamont. Reappointed commander of the channel fleet, Admiral Howe experienced manpower shortages aboard his flag ship, the *Charlotte*. His son-in-law offered to raise a company of one hundred men in Mayo to make up the deficiency. 'They would have been esteemed very highly,' Admiral Howe assured him, 'if they had cordially engaged for the service proposed. I should have cherished them much and felt a different interest than the coldness which men impressed … urges one to profess.'[9] Events, however, overtook the earl's offer and the admiral had to make do with whatever unfortunates the press-gangs dragged from the taverns and brothels of Spithead. On the 'Glorious First of June' 1794, after a series of engagements against the French fleet off Ushant, in the first naval battle to carry the tricolour of the new French republic, in one of the bloodiest sea-battles in history, Admiral Howe emerged victorious.

From Windsor Castle King George expressed his gratitude and relief for the victory to Lady Howe, which he adjudged had been won 'by the skill and bravery of Earl Howe …. The first of June must be reckoned as a proud day for him as it will carry down his Name to the latest posterity. I will not add more than that I trust now both your own mind and that of Lady Mary will be at ease when we must soon hear of his return to Spithead.'[10] When the victorious fleet returned to port, the king and queen (in whose honour the admiral's flagship was named) with their family, together with Lady Howe and her daughter Mary, visited the admiral on board the *Charlotte*. 'My father's knees trembled with emotion when he kissed the king's hand,' Lady Mary informed her sister Louisa, 'who presented him with a most magnificent sword set in diamonds and afterwards a gold chain, to which is to be hung a gold medal struck for the occasion.'[11] The admiral conducted the king and royal family on a tour of the *Charlotte* to meet, as Mary described them, 'the brave fellows everyone of which I am certain would attend my father to the cannon's mouth and all of whom have exposed their lives for him'.[12] The admiral's decanters and his desk from the *Charlotte* were later taken to Westport House, together with his portrait by John Copley.

At the time of her father's famous victory, Louisa was on the high seas. A reoccurrence of her husband's rheumatic condition made them once more seek the beneficial climate of Lisbon. Westport, now a precocious boy of six, accompanied them. Their journey to Lisbon brought a stern rebuke from Admiral Howe. England was at war with both France and Spain. Reports of English ships taken by the enemy, and of the indignities to which women passengers, in particular, were subjected, impelled him to remonstrate with his son-in-law.

> Joining those reflections … of the resentment which would be shown to my daughter, after our pretty rough business with the French fleet and the good fortune on our side attending it, I cannot suppose that you are unconscious of it. I trust therefore that it will be totally unnecessary for me to urge you not to hazard a similar disaster by her passing back to Lisbon again pending the war.[13]

The tone of the admiral's letter and the implication that the earl had placed his wife's life in danger greatly upset Altamont. The admiral sought to reassure him that he meant merely to point out 'the great hazards to which you and your family I thought were exposed in crossing the seas on your passage to or from Lisbon in the present state of the war'.[14] Events in Ireland, particularly in his native Mayo, conspired to ensure that it was the last sojourn in Lisbon that the earl and his family were to enjoy for fifteen years.

On their return to Ireland later that year the whiff of conspiracy and revolution was in the air in Ireland. From the mud-and-wattle cabins of rural tenants to grand ascendancy drawing-rooms, from the floor of the Irish parliament to the smoke-filled backrooms of Dublin taverns and coffee houses, it permeated all conversation and debate. 'The French are on the seas says the *sean-bhean bhocht* [the poor old woman, i.e. Ireland],' the balladeers sang on Dublin street corners. Reports of French spies and of collusion between the United Irishmen and French revolutionaries grew apace. As her allies fell away and as French power in Europe and the West Indies prospered, England's military strength became stretched. The United Irishmen saw their advantage to establish an Irish republic on the French prototype. Discontent seethed and bubbled in almost every layer of Irish society. Resentment at the heavy burden of rents and taxes borne by the landless masses, combined with the political and religious discrimination perpetrated against the emerging Catholic middle class and their Presbyterian counterparts, required just a spark to ignite into flames of rebellion.

As a landlord in the west of Ireland, surrounded by thousands of disenfranchised, subsistence Catholic farmers and tenants, remote from the centre of military protection in Dublin, the Earl of Altamont viewed such developments with unease. His power base in Mayo depended on the support of local Catholic gentry, while his personal prospects for political advancement rested with the government of the day. It was a tightrope that required a judicious and careful balancing act.

Events in Ulster were the first to affect his estate. Economic rivalry between Catholic and Protestant linen-weavers in Armagh and Tyrone brought both communities into conflict. Armed Protestant gangs, the Peep O'Day Boys, conducted a campaign of violence against Catholics, wrecking homes and destroying looms. Abandoned by the authorities, debarred by law from carrying arms, Catholics formed a secret organisation known as 'the Defenders'.

On 21 September 1795, at a crossroads between Portadown and Loughgall, the Protestant force bedecked with orange-coloured cockades, both sides confronted each other in what was to become known as the Battle of the Diamond. The defeat of the 'Defenders' by the 'Orangemen' resulted in the widespread expulsion of Catholics from Ulster and the beginning of a divisive conflict that was to survive for centuries. Homeless and destitute, thousands of Catholic refugees travelled south. Over one thousand men, women and children sought succour from the Earl of Altamont in Westport. The earl's support for Catholic Emancipation, as well as his promotion of the linen industry in which they hoped to gain employment, determined their choice.

The arrival of a large body of refugees on his estate posed many problems, as the earl communicated to the government in Dublin. 'Plunder, religious prejudices, and a wish for disturbance from disaffection to the State, appear to me to have been the groundwork of the persecution .... I can see most clearly the causes and the consequences are highly dangerous to the peace and safety of the kingdom'.[15] Despite his concerns, the earl accommodated the refugees as best he could. Initially housing them in makeshift shelters, he then petitioned the government in Dublin for more permanent accommodation, offering

> ... to pay into the hands of such trustees as shall be named by the government for that purpose, the sum of one thousand pounds, provided a sum of two thousand pounds is added to it from the public funds, towards building houses for those unhappy sufferers who have been obliged to flee from their homes by a merciless and unheard of persecution.[16]

Most of the Ulster refugees were accommodated on the earl's estate and many more settled in his newly built town of Louisburgh.

As rumours of a French invasion intensified during 1796, fears that the Ulster refugees might incite rebellion in Mayo also became an issue. 'Be assured,' the earl's brother, Denis Browne, county sheriff and chairman of the Grand Jury, wrote to Thomas Pelham, the Irish Secretary of State, 'that no circumstances that has happened in Ireland for a hundred years past has gone so *decidedly* to separate the mind of this country from the government as this unfortunate and untimely business.'[17] Rumours ebbed and flowed of guns being stored, pikes being hammered into shape in rural smithies and secret oaths being administered. In mid-December a French fleet was prevented from making landfall in Bantry harbour only by adverse weather. Shaken out of its complacency, the government reacted with a policy of coercion. Local militias and yeomanry were let loose to raid, burn, torture and kill anyone suspected of United Irishmen sympathies. An attempt to introduce a reform bill in the Irish parliament was overwhelmingly defeated and Ireland drifted into chaos.

In 1797 Louisa's father, Admiral Howe, proffered his resignation, which was reluctantly accepted by the king. His 'advanced time of life and the slow progress in the re-establishment of my health', as he indicated in his resignation letter, hid a more painful and humiliating reason.[18] Differences had arisen between the admiral and Prime Minister Pitt, and when Pitt recommended that the Blue Riband, the highest decoration in the king's giving, should be bestowed on another, on a matter of principle, the admiral chose to resign. In October 1797 Admiral Howe and his family were special guests of the king and queen at Windsor Castle.

The main concern of the Earl and Countess of Altamont was centred on their son's education. Owing to the lack of a school system in Ireland, the sons of Irish aristocrats continued to be educated abroad, mainly in England. There were, however, additional considerations which made Westport's education in England a prerequisite. The prominence of his mother's family, her pride and identification with the Howe name, as well as her frequent absences in England, all determined that he should be educated there. The prevailing political unrest in Ireland and the inherent dangers it augured for the landlord class, as well as the remoteness of their west of Ireland home, augmented Louisa's resolve. Although reluctant to be parted from his only son, the earl agreed to their separation. He also prophetically noted, however, that once having left the west of Ireland, his son might 'never bear patiently the solitude of his home again'.[19]

In the eighteenth century the journey from Ireland to England was both lengthy and arduous. Sailing by packet from the Pigeon House at Ringsend to Holyhead or Beaumaris in Wales was an endurance test for adults, albeit an adventure for a nine-year-old boy destined to undertake the journey countless times during the course of his lifetime. The crossing under sail was at the whim of wind and weather and could endure from hours to weeks. Aristocrats usually travelled in their carriage, the body of which was 'unslung' from its base and left on the ship's deck for the duration of the voyage, where it served as a place of rest or refuge from the elements during the crossing. On making landfall, the road ahead, little more than a bridle-path, stretched across the lonely expanse of Anglesey towards the first natural obstacle, the wide and treacherous crossing of the Menai Straits. Until 1826, when the famous Telford suspension bridge came into use, at low tide travellers embarked from one of the designated crossing stages by ferry across the treacherous Lavan Sands. Around the intimidating Penmaenmawr, the road clung perilously to the side of high cliffs, then on through the interior of Wales via Oswestry and Shrewsbury to Birmingham, then a major terminus for carriage traffic. The bone-shattering and debilitating journey was relieved by overnight stops for refreshment, rest and changes of horses at inns and hostelries along the way. From Birmingham the main route south snaked through Oxfordshire along narrow country lanes towards London. At Porter's Lodge, like every grandfather with time on his hands, Admiral Howe entertained his young grandson with stories of his adventures at sea, and perhaps also imbued him with the spirit of seafaring, which as a young man he embraced, albeit with more notoriety than his famous grandfather.

Initially the Rev. Grace, a graduate of Trinity College Dublin, 'reserved and haughty' and possessing 'considerable pretensions as a scholar', was engaged as a tutor.[20] Westport, however, proved a reluctant student. A solitary life with a tutor for company, especially one with a pompous personality, ill-suited a pupil who, as a school friend attested, was 'out-going and thoroughly free from opinionativeness'.[21] His handwriting was of particular concern, especially to his father, whose remonstration with Grace brought about little improvement, much to the frustration of those with whom Westport later corresponded. His mother took a more indulgent view of her son's lack of penmanship: 'I care not five farthings about it, as when he leaves school, if he chooses it, he can learn.'[22] While Westport struggled to adapt to his solitary student life in England, political events in his native country prevented any possibility of his return.

On 22 August 1798 his father's worst nightmare was realised when a French invasion force from La Rochelle, numbering over 1,000 soldiers, commanded by General Humbert, made landfall on the north-west coast of Mayo. As word of the French invasion spread, tenants and labourers, motivated more by an opportunity to vent their anger on those they blamed for their wretched state than to further the lofty ideals of the French Revolution, made their way to Humbert's banner and were formed into the Mayo Legion. Leaving a Franco-Irish garrison in Killala, Humbert pressed on to Castlebar, the principal town in Mayo, where the Franco-Irish force won a spectacular victory over a superior force of militia and yeomanry commanded by General Lake. So quickly did the Crown forces flee through the town, the event became known as the 'Races of Castlebar'. John Moore, the son of a prominent local Catholic landlord, a cousin of the Earl of Altamont, was appointed

President of the Provisional Government of Connaught. After the military success in Mayo, the French and their Irish allies moved inland. On 7 September, at Ballinamuck in County Longford, after a brief engagement against the combined forces of Lord Cornwallis and General Lake, Humbert surrendered. The French were allowed to return home, honour and arms intact, abandoning their Irish allies, without terms, to face a savage retribution.

The arrival of the French, the insurrection of their fellow Irishmen and the defeat of the English at Castlebar caused consternation among the loyalist gentry in Mayo. The Earl of Altamont was in Dublin when the French forces landed. With communication between Dublin and Mayo severed, his thirty-five-year-old brother, Denis Browne, took command of the situation. Damned by history and folklore, demonised by poets, inheritor of such derogatory tags as 'the old Bear of the West' and 'Soap-the-Rope' for his alleged arbitrary hanging of rebels, like every bête noir in history Browne had both negative and positive attributes. A confirmed loyalist, for whom the future welfare of his country, as much as his own, lay firmly within the British Empire, he realised that if the French established a presence in Ireland, he and the rest of the Irish ascendancy, like their French counterparts, were likely to be swept away, their lands and possessions parcelled out to others. It was a case of survival, and in August 1798 the Right Honourable Denis Browne realised what was at stake for himself and his family.

It was not the actions of the French invaders or even those of his rebel countrymen, however, that provoked Browne's anger, but the disloyal and predatory actions of his own tenants and retainers. As sheriff of the county, Browne became a prime target on the arrival of the French and barely escaped hanging by a lynch mob in Castlebar. Forced to abandon his house at Mount Browne, he initially sought refuge for himself and his family with his Mahon relations in Castlegar. In his absence, Mount Browne was sacked by his servants. It was an unexpected development that shocked the entire Browne family, as Denis's aunt, Lady Anne Mahon, informed her daughter:

> Mount Browne is stripped of all its furniture, books, chimney pieces are destroyed, nothing but the bare shell of the house left. Granaries, cattle and even the growing crops all destroyed ... the mischief was solely done by his [Denis's] own labourers .... At Claremont [Claremorris] the servants they placed confidence in were the principals in robbing their house for it was completely pillaged.[23]

Westport House was more fortunate and, other than a brief occupation by the rebels and the loss of a few horses and cattle, remained intact. Denis Browne's wife and his young family fled to Scotland for safety. Further shock ensued when it was revealed that the Earl of Altamont's long-serving agent and confidant, John Gibbons, and members of his family, together with James McDonnell, a prominent member of the emerging Catholic merchant class in Westport, as well as several local Catholic clergymen, had joined the French. To the Browne family it smacked of betrayal and weakened the long-established bond between them and their Catholic retainers and neighbours.

On the departure of the French forces, the wrath of the government fell full-square on their Irish allies. The initial retribution was committed on the field of battle at Ballinamuck, where the English troops and yeomanry were allowed free rein to wreak their vengeance on the vanquished Irish as they attempted to escape. Military courts were hastily established in the hours and days after the battle, and prisoners were as hastily despatched on the gallows. In counties Carlow, Tipperary, Wexford and Wicklow, pitch-capping, torture, flogging, hanging, half-hanging and sentences of transportation to penal colonies across the seas were indiscriminately inflicted.

In Mayo, where Denis Browne presided as sheriff, less draconian measures were applied. Rather than wide-scale retribution, as he wrote, 'the capital punishment of a few and the banishment of others will be a measure of mercy & will correct the bad disposition of the county at a small expense of blood'.[24] Court martial was confined to convicted leaders of the rebels, some of whom, such as Edmund Gibbons, the son of the earl's agent, through the intercession of both the earl and Denis Browne, were later reprieved. Others, like John Moore, had their sentence of death commuted to transportation. Denis Browne's reputation as an ogre rests on the enmity he displayed, stemming from personal rather than political prejudice, towards individual local figures, such as Edmund Garvey of Rosmindle, for whom he harboured a personal animosity. On the intercession of the Earl of Altamont, however, Garvey's sentence of death was commuted to transportation. The most notable case that served to cement Denis Browne's negative reputation was his role in the trial and execution in September 1798 of the aged priest James Conroy. It is also probable that he was instrumental in the prosecution of another individual, hanged in Westport in April 1799 ostensibly as a rebel but more particularly for his participation in the attack on Mount Browne. In the main, however, to eject influential rebels, through banishment or transportation, from his home patch motivated Denis Browne's actions in the aftermath of the rebellion.

The actions of former trusted retainers and friends during the rebellion fractured the relationship of dependency and loyalty that existed between landlord and tenant. The owners of the 'Big Houses' thereafter tended to replace their Irish retainers and house servants with those of English or Scottish birth. George Glendenning, an able and ambitious son of the Church of Ireland rector at Westport, became estate agent to the Earl of Altamont. By the time Westport succeeded to the title and estates of his father, as political social, agrarian and religious differences intensified, the fracture between the Irish aristocracy and the rest of their fellow countrymen had widened further.

In December 1798 Westport was reunited with his father. Plagued by another bout of rheumatism, the earl sought respite in the therapeutic waters of the fashionable geothermal spa at Bath. In the graceful houses of the newly developed Royal Crescent and Circus, royalty and aristocracy, both home-grown and foreign, socialised and observed the daily ritual at the Pump Room of imbibing the efficacious waters. Ensconced in a spacious house on the Crescent with his parents and tutor, during the winter and early spring Westport attended the local King Edward's School, where he made the acquaintance of his first, if unlikely, school friend.

Thomas De Quincey, future writer and critic, friend of Wordsworth and Coleridge, notorious alcoholic and drug addict, irresponsible and improvident, first made Westport's acquaintance at the home of a friend with business contacts in the west of Ireland. Although older in years, and from a background considered inferior by society, his friendship with Westport endured for many years. The young De Quincey, a 'problem' teenager by the standards of the time, small and puny, was born plain Thomas Quincey (the 'De' was a later affectation). Bright, ambitious, well-read and conceited, the reason for his attraction to the young Irish nobleman is difficult to ascertain. An avid disciple of all things Gothic and macabre, De Quincy was already showing signs of the talent that was to elevate him onto a literary pedestal and little of the full-scale addiction that was to mar his adult life. He had mastered a schoolboy code called *Ziph* which he imparted to Westport so that that they might communicate and 'conduct a conversation in secrecy'.[25] Financial circumstances intervened to remove De Quincey from Bath to a school at Winkfield in Wiltshire, but not before he had made an impression on his Irish friend.

In early 1799 the Earl of Altamont returned to his estate in Westport, leaving his son in England with his mother and tutor.

Westport's aversion both to his tutor and to the isolation private tuition imposed adversely affected his concentration and learning. Reports on his lack of scholastic progress from the Reverend Grace made worrisome reading. 'If Grace has said ... that he had long since given up the hope of making my Howe a clever man, I should instantly look out for another,' Louisa suggested but, she astutely suspected, that 'from the moment Grace gave up the hope of success [Grace] would inevitably and probably unconsciously give up trying to succeed.'[26]

Before another tutor could be found, however, in August 1799 Admiral Howe died. His grieving widow found it difficult to cope and Louisa asked her husband's indulgence to remain with her family in England. Such was her mother's anguish at the death of 'my beloved father that she would not live six months', and 'seeing her sink under the heavy burden of misfortune I cannot bring myself to deprive her of what I firmly believe is at this moment the greatest comfort this world affords her'.[27] Legal complications relating to the admiral's will and an estrangement between her two older sisters and her mother further postponed Louisa's return to Ireland.

The solution to Westport's lack of scholastic progress and his mother's preoccupation with her family was solved by his admittance to his father's and grandfather's alma mater in October 1799. Aged eleven and signing his name 'Westport' in bold, clear letters in the college attendance book, he became a pupil at Eton College. Situated in the shadow of Windsor Castle, the college boasted King George III as patron and Eton boys had access to the terraces of Windsor by royal permission. Then, as now, one of the premier public schools in England, Eton drew students from many places. Westport's first cousin, Lord Castle Cuffe (the future Earl of Desart), was already established there, as was another relation, Dominick Browne (later 1st Baron Oranmore and Browne) from Castlemacgarrett in Mayo. Many old Etonians had taken their places on the world stage, including Admiral Howe, Arthur Wellesley, future hero of Waterloo, and the controversial Whig leader Charles J. Fox. Among Westport's fellow students and future friends were Scrope Berdmore Davies, irrepressible wit, dandy, gambler and bon viveur, Charles Skinner Matthews and Michael Bruce, with whom he was to share many adventures.

At Eton there were two student categories: King's Scholars, boys of scholastic ability but restricted means; and Oppidans, sons of the 'grandees', aristocratic and wealthy. Eton was a demanding environment, especially for the scholars, who were housed in the rat-infested Long Chamber, where they lived without adult supervision. For Oppidans, such as Westport, conditions were somewhat better. Together with their tutors, who supervised their homework, they lodged in boarding houses run by landladies known as 'dames'. For all students, some as young as seven years of age, the school regime was daunting and austere. Despite their means, the 'grandees' did not allow their sons much in the way of comfort and maintained a tight rein on fees for their lodging, board, bed, fire and candle, study, washing and mending, tutor fees and a personal allowance of £1.7.0. per half-year. Flogging on the naked back with birch canes was widespread and an accepted part of a student's 'education'. During Westport's tenure, the provost, Dr D. Davies, was noted as being particularly partial to the 'custom'. Fagging, whereby a younger student became in thrall to an older boy, running his errands to nearby 'sock shops' in the village, performing his domestic chores, being used as a 'human bed warmer' in winter, in the all-male, pubescent atmosphere, made homosexuality widespread, albeit hidden behind codes of secrecy and loyalty. Morally repugnant and legally an offence punishable by the death penalty, it was winked at by the authorities provided it remained hidden. The ethos of hero worship, patronage, protection and male bonding, endemic in public schools, was reinforced by the reading of the classics, with their tales of love between the gods and beautiful youths, such as Hyacinth and Ganymede, and the 'lightly-bounding boy' of Byron's ode. As one student noted 'at a public school every vice and every virtue which we meet with in the world is practised'.[28]

Ensconced with his tutor in local lodgings, dressed in the regulation blue coat, knee breeches, white waistcoat and ruffled shirt, Westport attended school from eight in the morning until five in the evening, with a break for dinner mid-morning. On Saturday and Sunday there was service and choir practice in the college chapel. Naturally sociable with a 'graceful self-possession',[29] Westport was popular and adapted well to his new surroundings. He studied French, in which he became fluent, Latin, drawing, writing, dancing and fencing. Gambling, drinking, bull-baiting, cockfighting in Bedford Yard in Windsor village, poaching in Windsor Home Park, fights to settle schoolboy differences in 'Sixpenny Corner', hopscotch, marbles, spinning tops, cricket, fives, football and the traditional 'wall game' – a type of rugby played between Oppidans and Scholars – occupied his free time. The annual pig fair in the village on Ash Wednesday with its fairground booths offering a shooting gallery, rings, cards, roulette wheels and toys, although out of bounds for students, was a magnet and worth the punishment if caught.

'Westport is as happy as a Prince at school,' his relieved father wrote to a relation, 'quite up to his business, in a high place in it and so pleased to get play fellows that he would undoubtedly double his business to have half an hour's play with them.'[30] His tutor, Grace, also concurred with the improvement in his student's scholastic achievements – 'he does more business now in one day than he ever got him to do in a week', his father wrote.[31] St Patrick's Day, Ireland's national holiday, was celebrated in the college when the headmaster entertained the Irish students to breakfast and donned the 'Irish badge' they presented to him.

'An Etonian is always a gentleman,' De Quincey observed, whether born, or moulded into one by the ethos of the college. As the son of one of Ireland's premier peers, Westport encapsulated an easy confidence and sense of place which emanated both from his social status and from his engaging personality. The informality that existed in the west of Ireland between the aristocrat, his tenants and neighbours endowed him with an adaptability that helped him survive the bias and rivalry of playground and classroom. He was not immune, however, from the problem that bedevilled many of the aristocracy: the opportunity their status and wealth afforded them to indulge in whatever whim took their fancy. The virtue of self-restraint, preached and practised by his sober father, found little resonance in his son. For Westport, as for many of his fellow students and friends to whom he remained close in adult life, their experience at Eton was a prequel to years of excess and debauchery. For one such friend, Scrope Berdmore Davies, 'Eton turned the simple clergyman's son into a wit, a dandy and a scholar with the entrée to the greatest drawing rooms of London. At the same time it made him a gambler, a drunkard and a spendthrift who ended his days in ruin.'[32] While the seeds of Westport's addiction to high living and excess might well have germinated in Eton, it was in the hedonistic atmosphere of his next alma mater that they were to fully bloom.

At Eton he benefited from his family's connection with the royal family, which resulted in invitations to royal social occasions, as well as affording him unrestricted access to the grounds at Windsor Castle and to nearby Frogmore, the private residence of Queen Charlotte. Few subjects ever saw, much less expected to be in proximity to the monarch or intimate with the royal family. As De Quincy observed, Westport became blasé about the privilege accorded to him and 'through his frequent admissions to the royal presence ... had lost somewhat of the awe natural to a young person in a first situation of this nature'.[33]

There was great excitement in the Howe family in February 1800, when Westport's aunt, Lady Mary, became engaged to George

Douglas, Earl of Morton. In April, however, she died suddenly at Porter's Lodge, three days prior to her wedding day. Since the death of her father, she had become depressed, a condition that her impending marriage did not appear to alleviate. When choosing her wedding dress, she had gloomily predicted that it might well serve as her shroud. Louisa wrote to her husband of her utter grief at the passing of 'my angel sister … I can hardly persuade myself that I am never again to speak to that being which I have idolised from infancy and from whom I never had a thought hid.'[34] The royal princesses expressed themselves equally shocked and saddened at losing so close a companion and confidante.

Despite making new friends at Eton, Westport had not forgotten his first friend, De Quincey, whom he invited to accompany him to Ireland for the school holidays. De Quincey linked up with his friend at Eton. Seizing every opportunity to evade Grace's supervision, the two friends roamed the streets of Windsor and the royal parklands at Windsor Castle and Frogmore, where they occasionally encountered members of the Royal Family. On one occasion, as they were 'theorising and practically commentating on the art of throwing stones' on the lake at Frogmore, Westport, who 'was practising on the peculiar whirl of the wrist with a shilling', suddenly turned the head of the coin in his hand towards De Quincey muttering the words, 'Grace of God, France and Ireland' to alert him of the king's approach.[35] Envious of the composure shown by his companion, and with some trepidation, De Quincey came face-to-face with his monarch. 'The King having spoken with great kindness to my companion,' he recorded, 'inquiring about his mother and grandmother, as persons particularly well known to himself, then turned his eyes upon me.'[36]

George III's reign was disturbed and difficult. Enduring the loss of the American colonies, the French Revolution and the savage overthrow of his French counterpart, the ongoing war with France, rebellion in Ireland and demands for Catholic Emancipation

– which from both a personal and political point of view he vehemently opposed – all marked its progress. Such events, perhaps, also contributed to the madness that in 1788 engulfed him, which made him unfit to reign and led to a constitutional crisis. Cultured in the arts and sciences, deeply religious, his preference was for simplicity and domesticity. The father of a family of seven sons and six daughters, as dysfunctional as it was numerous, his reign was further compounded by familial tribulations. His eldest son, the Prince Regent was dedicated to debauchery, high living and scandal. Estranged from his wife, Princess Caroline of Brunswick, by 1800 the prince was back in the arms of one of his mistresses (and some said his wife), Mrs Fitzherbert, who, to make matters worse in the eyes of the king, was also a Catholic. Another son, William, Duke of Clarence, was ensconced with Mrs Jordan, a celebrated comic actress. The king's daughters, with the exception of the Princess Royal, were unmarried and the king contrived in every way possible to ensure that they so remained. Windsor was referred to as 'the nunnery' so diligently did the king guard the virtue of his daughters, leading them in a crocodile procession for daily walks in the gardens.

On that spring morning in the gardens of Frogmore, the king smiled graciously on the grandson of Admiral Howe, his former trusted counsellor and friend. Then in a series of quick-fire questions, a nervous legacy from his earlier bout of dementia, he addressed De Quincy. Was he at Eton? Had he a father living? Had he a mother? Had his family come with the French Huguenots? De Quincey did his best to give as short a reply as possible to each question. When the king paused in his stream of questioning, the boys understood it as a signal to withdraw. Bowing low, they took a few paces back and stood to attention. With a smile, the king returned to his party while the boys returned to skimming stones on the lake.

An invitation to a ball given by Queen Charlotte at Frogmore followed the encounter with the king. While 'Lord Westport, young as he was, had become tolerably indifferent about such things,'[37] for his friend, who was also included in the invitation, it was of greater significance to partake in 'the splendours of a royal party'. The ballroom 'wore an elegant and festal air; the part allotted to the dancers being fenced off by a gilded lattice-work, and ornamented beautifully from the upper part with drooping festoons of flowers'.[38] But De Quincey soon discovered the reason for his friend's indifference. Despite the sense of occasion, the regal surroundings, the decorations and music, an air of staidness permeated the ball. The royal princesses were permitted to dance only with their brothers while the other guests looked on. Once the novelty of being in such august surroundings wore off, 'the peculiar circumstances attaching to a royal ball were not favourable to its joyousness or genial spirit of enjoyment'.[39] Far more interesting diversions beckoned elsewhere, and after four hours Westport indicated to De Quincey in their *Ziph* secret language that they should take their leave. On emerging onto the high-road from Frogmore, both boys 'threw up our hats and huzzaed, meaning', as De Quincey recorded, 'no sort of disrespect but from uncontrollable pleasure in recovered liberty'.[40]

Before travelling to Ireland, they were invited to visit Westport's mother and grandmother at Porter's Lodge. With Reverend Grace at the reins of their open carriage and owing to his 'non-acquaintance with the roads, both town and rural, along the whole line of our progress from Uxbridge', the journey via London took longer than expected.[41] On entering the Edgware Road, the 'one monotonous awe and blind sense of mysterious grandeur and Babylonian confusion' hit them full tilt. Traffic jams of carriages of every shape and size slowed their progress through the tumultuous streets, before the 'whole ice-bound mess' thawed and they dashed forward again in a great rush of 'flying carriages'.[42] Grace being summoned away to attend to some business of his own, for the few hours allotted to them, the boys determined to 'see London'.

Tossing a coin between Westminster Abbey and St Paul's Cathedral, they choose the latter which, for the present, had to suffice as proof of their having 'seen' the great metropolis.

At Porter's Lodge, Westport found his mother and grandmother in deepest mourning, the whole house 'painfully depressed' at the unexpected death of his aunt. Lady Mary's fiancé, Lord Morton, was also resident in the house. Having an interest in literature, he conversed at length with De Quincy, much to the aspiring writer's delight. Lady Altamont took the opportunity to also assess his suitability as a travelling companion for her son. While De Quincey met with her approval, her approbation did not, however, stretch to Westport's relation and fellow student at Eton, Dominick Browne, whom Louisa considered anything but 'a well disposed boy' and advised her husband 'that you will not allow him to see Westport one moment except in your company'.[43] After spending a number of days at Porter's Lodge, Westport and De Quincy were driven back to Eton. Grace having indicated his decision not 'to cross the seas', Louisa procured the services of a French tutor recommended by her niece, Marianne Curzon. Grace, however, agreed to accompany the boys as far as Holyhead.

On 19 July 1800 they set out from Eton, via Oxford and Stratford upon Avon, where they visited Shakespeare's house. Crossing into Wales through Shrewsbury and Oswestry, they travelled through the celebrated vale of Llangollen, negotiated the crossing of the Menai Straits, through the island of Anglesey and on to 'the *Head*'. Owing to contrary winds, they were entertained by the captain for four days. On a dark and gusty night Grace brought his charges in a small rowing boat out to the packet moored in the bay. Once satisfied that they were safely stowed, and that Lord Westport had his 'boat cloak' to hand, without further ado the Reverend Grace was rowed back to land and out of Westport's life.

Because of further contrary winds, the passage to Ireland, a distance of some seventy miles, took thirty hours to accomplish.

During the course of the voyage they encountered Lady Elizabeth Conyngham from Slane Castle, an acquaintance of the Earl and Countess of Altamont. Lady Conyngham invited them into her coach which lay unslung on deck and where they passed a few hours in conversation. As night fell, the boys forsook their cabin below to sleep, wrapped in their cloaks, on deck. During the night they were startled by a stealthy footfall and observed a man making his way towards Lady Conyngham's coach, where he remained throughout the night. On landing at the Pigeon House in Dublin, both boys watched the 'lovely lady … looking as beautiful and hardly less innocent than an angel',[44] being greeted by her husband, while her admirer of the previous night was nowhere to be seen. Lady Conyngham introduced them to her husband and invited them to Slane Castle. Although 'pressed with a weight of awe' with the knowledge of her secret tryst, the boys resolved, as gentlemen, 'to drop no hint of it in any direction'.[45]

The Earl of Altamont awaited their arrival in his house on Sackville Street. On the journey from the landing stage, De Quincey fretted lest he might be 'a freezing restraint upon that re-union, to which after such a long separation, both father and son must have looked forward with anticipation'.[46] He had no reason to worry, for the earl, as De Quincey wrote, 'in one minute, under his courteous welcome I had come to feel that, as a companion of his one darling upon earth, he also comprehended me within his paternal regard'.[47] Sitting down to a hearty breakfast, father and son renewed acquaintances and exchanged news.

The embers of rebellion still smouldered in Ireland. With Britain and France at war, rumours and hopes of another French invasion persisted. The British prime minister, William Pitt the Younger, deemed the Irish parliament inconsistent with the integrity of the empire and a threat to Britain's security and he proposed a legislative union between Ireland and Britain. This he hoped might also provide a solution to the issue of Catholic

Emancipation, as well as transforming the Irish Protestant minority into a majority in a United Kingdom. Encompassing such diverse objectives, affecting the aspirations and fears of both Catholics and Protestants, the creation of a union between the parliaments of London and Dublin divided friendships and families. For the vast majority of Catholic tenants and labourers, however, the outcome was of little significance. Whether a government resided in Dublin or London, rent and tithes still had to be paid and the struggle for survival would continue regardless.

For two years the earl agonised over Pitt's plan. As early as December 1798, he wrote of his reservations 'that the proposition of a union is, at this time, dangerous, wicked, foolish and cruel'.[48] Over the succeeding months, however, with incentives such as Catholic Emancipation and the promise of investment in trade and agriculture, issues in which he had a particular interest, as well as a deterrent to another French incursion into Ireland, his views changed. The financial and other inducements proffered by the British prime minister to persuade members of the Irish parliament to vote themselves out of office, perhaps, also counted. However, as De Quincey observed, 'he [Altamont] acted all along upon patriotic motives and in obedience to his real views (whether right or wrong) of the Irish interests .... Lord Altamont, I am certain, believed … that Ireland would be bettered by the commercial advantages conceded to her as an integral province of the empire.'[49] For his son, the enormity of his father's decision to vote for the abolition of the national parliament brought mixed feelings. As an Irish boy in Eton he endured his share of racist jibes and taunts from his English fellow students, which he resisted in the time-honoured way of fisticuffs. 'For he [Westport] had an Irish heart and was jealous of whatever appeared to touch the banner of Ireland.'[50]

Having lost his own father at an early age, De Quincey came to regard his courteous host as a father-figure substitute whom, as he wrote, he both 'loved and respected'. After his visit to Ireland, the earl continued to correspond with him 'sometimes upon the great improvements which he had made in the counties of Mayo and Sligo [*sic*], sometimes upon the merits of a Latin poet, at other times suggesting subjects on which he fancied that I could write verses myself, or breathe poetic inspiration into the mind of … his son'.[51] The earl found De Quincey to be, unlike his less scholarly son, knowledgeable not only about literature, but also on a range of issues from politics, economics and history to metaphysics and agriculture.

On a fine day in June 1800 Westport and De Quincey accompanied the Earl of Altamont to the Houses of Parliament in Dublin's College Green to attend one of the most controversial and emotive episodes in Ireland's history. As the earl's extreme lameness made it difficult for him to walk any great distance, they drove in their carriage close to the parliament buildings. A huge crowd was gathered on the green and they were obliged to dismount and make their way by foot through the throng who, on recognising the earl, showed him no antagonism, much to the boys' relief. From the gallery, Lady Conyngham gaily waved to them, oblivious of their shared secret. A tumult outside heralded the arrival of the major players in the drama, including lords Clare and Castlereagh, determined promoters of the Union, who were obliged to run the gauntlet of angry protestors outside. The Commons were summoned to witness the final act of the Irish parliament – the enactment of its own demise. The momentous event was received by the Irish parliamentarians, as De Quincey noted in amazement, 'without a muttering, or a whispering or the protesting echo of a sigh'.[52] On the dissolution of the Irish House of Lords, twenty-eight of their number, known as Representative Peers, were elected to sit in the British House of Lords, one of whom was the Earl of Altamont, then elevated as the First Marquess of Sligo.

In August the earl was invested with the distinguished Blue Riband of the Order of St Patrick in St Patrick's Cathedral. Sitting with Lord and Lady Castlereagh, Westport watched his father walk in procession up the ancient aisle and felt his embarrassment when someone in the congregation sniggered at his pronounced lameness. The ceremony concluded with a resounding rendition of 'God Save the King' and was followed by 'a grand dinner at the Castle'.[53] The earl held the national order of honour in high regard as a symbol of his Irish nationality, albeit set in a wider imperial context.

After the great events in Dublin, by 'movements as slow and circuitous as those of any royal progress in the reign of Elizabeth', in the summer heat they set out for Westport.[54] The first stage, from Dublin to Tullamore, they undertook by canal boat, staying at Charleville Castle, the home of Lord Tullamore. The journey onwards by phaeton was interrupted by many detours to visit friends and relations, while an accident to their carriage required an additional detour to a blacksmith. At Tuam they were entertained by the Protestant archbishop, Power le Poer Trench. A former captain in the militia, he had been active against the French and Irish insurgents in 1798. As De Quincy noted, Lord Sligo did not find his host's company to his liking, and 'to avoid being pressed by the Archbishop to stay another day' they left Tuam at daybreak.[55] Arriving on the outskirts of Westport, they finally laid eyes on 'that miracle of beauty', as the writer Thackeray immortalised Clew Bay, looking its majestic best in the glorious summer weather. At Westport House the young heir renewed acquaintances with the familiar faces of his childhood and introduced his friend to the pleasures and sights of his ancestral home.

Rising at four-thirty in the morning, after a breakfast of 'bread, milk and fruit', the boys rode out in the care of 'Moran the groom' who, although having 'carried a pike' in the recent rebellion, still retained his position in Westport House. To the boys' amusement, Moran insisted on referring to De Quincey as 'His Majesty'. Hunting, fishing and sailing on Clew Bay passed the summer days but schoolwork was also part of the daily routine.

'Lord Westport,' De Quincy noted, 'writes copies and ciphers', while both became 'considerably improved' in French. Westport's cousins from Kilkenny came to visit and, despite his mother's aversion, Dominick Browne, from nearby Castlemacgarrett, also came to call. Noted for his horsemanship, Browne challenged his companions to gruelling contests, bribing Moran to lead them purposely across bogs and morasses in races that became a 'regular comedy of fun'.[56]

Lady Sligo remained in England to attend her mother. In her letters to her husband – 'her ever dearest lord' – she bemoaned their continued separation and asked for his forbearance. 'I am miserable at not being with you and yet my wretched mother is in a state in which it would be barbarity to desert her. Why can I not cut myself in two and give you the best side!' She urged him to take solace in having Westport, 'his little Treasure', with him. 'How happy should I be if I could be with you both … I should like to be in Westport House and never stir from it.'[57] Despite his lengthy absence, Westport adapted well to his west of Ireland home, much to his mother's relief. 'I am delighted to see how fond he is of Ireland and especially of Westport.'[58]

In August the Countess Howe died, just four months after her daughter. The Earl of Altamont prepared to journey over for the obsequies but his wife urged him 'not to think of coming over here, that is my greatest horror as the journey is so dreadful for you particularly this hot weather'.[59] Legal complications relating to her mother's will further detained Louisa in England. As co-heiress with her surviving older sister, Sophia Charlotte (who inherited the title Baroness Howe), each was entitled to half their parents' estate. Louisa also inherited property in Nottinghamshire, Leicestershire, Derbyshire and Hertfordshire, together with the town house in Grafton Street. In a controversial codicil to her mother's will, made a few days before her death, she also inherited Porter's Lodge, with a sum equal to its value to be given to her sister. Since it was unclear from the will whether she enjoyed merely a life interest in the property, it later became the subject of legal proceedings. Some of the Howe properties were sold and Porter's Lodge rented, with much of the furniture and effects, including Admiral Howe's papers, library, plate, sea chest, writing table and chest of drawers 'with straps for lashing to the deck'[60] transferred to Westport House.

In late September the earl bid farewell to his son and De Quincey, placing them in the care of his half-brother, Peter Browne, who escorted them to Dublin. They crossed the Irish Sea and on arrival at Holyhead followed the route south through Wales. At Birmingham the friends parted: Westport returning via Oxford to Eton; De Quincey to visit relatives near Stratford upon Avon. Although they continued to correspond for some time, they were not destined to meet again. After a short stay in Manchester Grammar School, De Quincey abandoned his education to live as a wayfarer in Wales. Penniless, he attempted to use his friendship with his Irish friend, by then the Earl of Altamont and 'heir by general repute to a fortune of £30,000 per annum',[61] to guarantee money owed to loan sharks to whom De Quincey had become hopelessly indebted. Confident that his friend's generosity would resolve his predicament, his hopes were dashed when, on arriving at Eton, he learned that 'Lord Altamont was gone to Jesus College, Cambridge'.[62]

Chapter 3

Men Behaving Badly

Altamont is a good deal with me. Last night at the Opera
Masquerade, we supped with seven whores, a Bawd and a
Ballet Master, in Madame Catalani's apartment behind the
Scenes.

Lord Byron

Altamont entered Cambridge on 27 October 1802 as the 4th Earl
of Altamont, following his father's elevation as Marquess of Sligo.
The university comprised sixteen separate colleges 'that look like
workhouses', as one of its students, Samuel Taylor Coleridge, recorded.[1]
Altamont was admitted to Jesus College as a 'Fellow Commoner', an
appellation reserved for those of noble birth. Fellow Commoners paid
higher fees than the 'Commoners', enjoyed additional privileges and
were not obliged to follow any prescribed course of study. Derisorily
termed 'Empty Bottles', they enjoyed 'a kind of prescriptive right to
idleness and … an habitual contempt for discipline'.[2] Most came and
went for as long as they chose, obtaining their degree by merely fulfilling
the conditional nine terms' residence. 'Nothing was to be learned at
English Universities' was the opinion of the Duke of Bedford, whose
son was a fellow student and friend of Altamont.[3]

Fellow Commoners enjoyed comfortable rooms, a varied diet
and the services of personal servants. Their college gowns were silk

and elaborately ornamented, their cap covered in velvet instead of cloth, the tassel of which was gold-fringed. But, as Altamont was to discover to his cost, a Fellow Commoner's wealth and status could also prove to be a disadvantage. 'To meet the expectations of those around him … he must spend more and be more careless in controlling his expenditure than a moderate and prudent Commoner.'[4] Living up to expectations could be both expensive and exhausting. Charged on the double for tutorage, a Fellow Commoner also subscribed to a regular fund for wine, whether he imbibed or not, and was expected to entertain his friends to a high standard and to partake in the multitude of social and extra-curricular activities on offer.

Political upheavals such as the loss of the American colonies and the French Revolution, mass movements for social and political reform, brought new thinking to bear on academe. Classical studies were beginning to give way to political economy and travel, ending the isolation normally associated with university life. While change was in the air, in 1802 the college curricula still adhered to such arcane subjects as the Old and New Testaments, Paley's *Moral and Political Philosophy*, Church History, Euclid, and the Rules of Arithmetic, subjects unlikely to inspire independently minded young scions who signed up for Cambridge merely to fill the time until they came of age. Study, or what passed for it, took place in the morning. 'College improves everything but learning,' Byron noted of his scholastic experience at Cambridge. 'Nobody here seems to look into an Author, ancient or modern, if they can avoid it.'[5] Dinner, taken in the college hall at one o'clock, denoted the end of daily study and the start of what student life was all about – entertainment and enjoyment.

Altamont's parents, however, had other ideas. His father held education in high esteem and was determined that his son would benefit academically from his university experience, as well as improve his 'bad style and handwriting', or his 'scrawl' as Altamont unashamedly referred to it. Still resident in England, his mother was anxious, as she wrote to her husband, 'in light of our present separation and the uncertainty of our meeting', to ensure his wishes regarding their son's application to his studies.[6] To this end she appointed a private a tutor to supervise his study.

The choice of George Caldwell, 'the most excellent, the most Pantisocratic of Aristocrats ... a man deservedly loved and esteemed,' according to his friend Coleridge, led to a relationship with Altamont and his mother which lasted for twenty years. A Fellow of Jesus College and a classical scholar, twenty-eight-year-old Caldwell was the son and heir of a wealthy merchant in Macclesfield. 'Though a man of fortune, he is prudent; nor does he lay claim to the right, which wealth confers on its possessor, of being a fool,' virtues that found much favour with Altamont's father.[7] With tact and consideration Caldwell steered his young charge through his first year at college. He also became a confidant and advisor to Lady Sligo. In an early copy of her will, Louisa impulsively bequeathed Caldwell the extraordinarily generous sum of '£10,000 stock of bank annuities',[8] which she later reduced to a more reasonable sum. Caldwell's steadying influence on his pupil, however, had to compete with the world of decadence and indulgence that flourished outside academe.

While changes were afoot in the ethos and structure of university life, the town of Cambridge had little changed since Tudor times. Situated on the banks of the Cam, its streets unpaved and unlighted, Cambridge's taverns, such as the Rose Inn, the White Horse, Eagle and Child and The Hoop, and its many bawd houses provided a range of outlets for its student population. But it was London, some seven hours distant by coach, that offered the wealthy scions of the aristocracy far more fashionable outlets to indulge their every whim in the dissipation and debauchery that marked the Regency period. And the figure to whom the period owed its name, the prime participant in every scandal, debauch and controversy, was the king's son and heir, George Augustus

Frederick, the Prince Regent. It was a world to which Altamont and his Cambridge friends were to become ardent devotees.

For the first two years, however, Altamont pursued his studies under the guidance of George Caldwell, which encouraged his father to believe that his beloved son had assumed the responsibilities compatible with his status and role as his heir. Interspaced with visits to his mother in London and visits by her to his rooms at Cambridge, during which time Louisa painted many watercolours of the college, and a four-month stay at Westport in 1802, Altamont kept to his studies. In 1803, as revolution again raised its head in Ireland, his father instructed him to remain in Cambridge rather than return to Westport for the summer holidays.

By the summer of 1803, despite the signing of the Treaty of Amiens in 1802, Britain and France were once more at war. The renewal of international hostilities was taken advantage of by the proponents of revolution and reform in Ireland. While the new French leader, Napoleon Bonaparte, declined to embark on another back-door entry to Britain through Ireland, regardless of the French disinterest the rising went ahead in Ireland. 'By whom headed, by whom instigated whence drawn or whither fled *no one* has the slightest idea,' a contact in the administration in Dublin advised Lord Sligo.[9] Ill-prepared and ill-led, the rising, however, ended in an inglorious scuffle in the streets of Dublin's Liberties, while one of its leaders, Robert Emmet, paid the ultimate price and was subsequently executed.

The 1803 insurrection, coupled with the rising ambition of France under its dynamic new leader, confirmed the Marquess of Sligo's belief that Ireland's future, as much as his own, was best served within the United Kingdom. From an economic viewpoint, his decision to vote for the Union appeared to have been vindicated as, because of the war with France, Irish agriculture enjoyed a boom period of growth. On 22 November 1803, as one of the new representative peers for Ireland, the Marquess of Sligo was chosen to respond to the king's address to the Houses of Parliament.

Then in the forty-fourth year of his reign, George III was afflicted by a reoccurrence of that 'alienation of mind' that had led to the previous Regency crises and was tormented by the thought that his profligate and spendthrift son might rule in his place. The defence of the realm and the vigorous prosecution of the war must be the chief objective, he told parliament. Ireland, as ever, was proving difficult and, in light of the recent rebellion, the king indulged 'the hope that such of my deluded subjects as have swerved from their allegiance are now convinced of their error; and that having compared the advantages they derive from the protection of a free Constitution, with the conditions of these countries which are under the domination of the French Government, they will cordially concur in resisting any attempt that may be made against the security and independence of my United Kingdom.'[10]

In response, the Marquess of Sligo, while modestly admitting to being 'little in the habit of addressing you on such occasions and not, perhaps, suited to it on any', in view of the deepening threat from across the English Channel, contended that 'perfect unanimity was required to resist the threat of a determined and vindictive enemy,' of which he had personal experience in Ireland. Conscious of the effects on the majority of his fellow countrymen of the king's opposition to Catholic Emancipation, he stated that, despite such 'distinctions of religion, there are points and principles in which we shall be actuated by one mind; we will not be dictated to by anyone; we will live as an independent people as our forefathers have done, or we will not live at all.' He felt confident that any future French incursions into Ireland would be met with 'vigorous resistance from every rank and every persuasion of the inhabitants'. No admirer of the excesses of the king's son and heir, in his closing words Sligo evinced the hope that the 'unexampled virtues' of the monarch might be 'lastingly impressed on his successors'.[11] In the packed gallery of the House of Lords, Altamont listened to his father's speech with pride but, perhaps, with less attention to his criticism of the profligate lifestyle espoused by the king's son and heir, under whose influence Altamont had already been drawn.

Throughout England, patriotic fervour was heightened and people rushed to bear arms to defend the country from French aggression. 'The artisan left his day's work for drill, the tailor laid aside his goose to mount his war hobby, the shopkeeper could not attend to his customers, he had to attend parade. Pruning hooks were turned into swords, and plough shears into spears.'[12] In Cambridge, a university corps of four companies of light infantry, which included students and fellows of every rank and degree, was established. An hour each day was allotted for military manoeuvres, sham fights on Parker's Piece, an open common, parading in splendid uniforms behind a band through the streets of Cambridge and 'dons and undergraduates vied with one another in making themselves efficient volunteers'.[13]

Altamont's academic endeavours were further directed off-course by the arrival in Cambridge in 1805 of George Gordon, Lord Byron. Armed with an attitude, a reputation and an image he fastidiously fashioned to become one of the most famous if notorious celebrities of his day, the seventeen-year-old was already 'wretched at going to Cambridge instead of Oxford'.[14] Of similiar age, the two young peers became immediate friends. With Byron's companions, who included the radical John Cam Hobhouse, Scrope Davies, the 'invisible man' of Byron's later masterpiece *Don Juan*, Michael Bruce, William Banks, C.S. Matthews, Sir Godfrey Vassall Webster, William Lowther, 2nd Earl of Lonsdale, the Marquis of Tavistock, the future 7th Duke of Bedford and a fellow Irishman the Duke of Leinster, Altamont entered the murky, hedonistic demi-monde of Regency England.

Handsome, vain, cynical, hyper-sensitive, moody, secretive, often cruel and frequently sceptical, 'as fickle as the wind and as uncertain as the waves',[15] a living embodiment of Gothic depravity, determinedly self-absorbed and self-fashioning, Byron seemed the antithesis of his affable, good-natured Irish friend. The poet had developed an affinity with Ireland, his imagination fired by the rebellion of the United Irishmen in 1798, especially the part played by Lord Edward Fitzgerald, the son of the Duke of Leinster. Their mutual friend and Byron's later biographer, the Irish bard Thomas Moore, immortalised the execution of Robert Emmet in his ballad 'She is Far from the Land'. While such views may not have found favour with his father, in his rebellious youth Altamont tolerated, if not sympathised with, Byron's revolutionary leanings. As determinedly heterosexual as Byron was bisexual, Altamont's sexual adventures seem somewhat innocent in comparison to the darker and reckless depravity of his college friend. Being on the edge of society, testing moral boundaries, living a 'hair breath existence', as he gleefully boasted, fuelled the radical brilliance of the poet's writing. But for Byron, Altamont and their college friends, regardless of their orientation, sex was all-pervasive and to be indulged in at every opportunity.

While both were fascinated by Napoleon, and while Byron empathised with the injustices perpetrated against Irish Catholics, both were nonetheless conscious of the dangers posed to their aristocratic status by revolutionary reform. While proud of his Irishness, like his father, Altamont was determinedly pro-Union. His penchant for political and social reform, while greater than that of his father, was nevertheless confined by virtue of his status and inheritance. From the moment he succeeded to his estate in Ireland, he embraced his role as a landlord, his responsibilities as 'head of his house' and as a legislator in the House of Lords. While indulging his desire for travel, especially in the early years of his inheritance, he still concerned himself with the administrative minutiae of his estate, albeit from a distance. Byron's interest in *his* estate, by contrast, was merely in its value as a means to further his literary career and to maintain himself in his self-created never-never land of indulgence and irresponsibility. Altamont's respect for his father and love for his mother, his 'angel', was in sharp contrast to Byron's negative attitude to his deceased father and his troubled relationship with his mother. While swimming with Altamont some years later in the Gulf of Lepanto, pointing to his deformed foot, Byron bitterly blamed his mother's 'false delicacy at my birth ... and yet as long as I can remember, she has never ceased to taunt and reproach me with it'.[16]

While intellectually no match for Byron, Altamont's knowledge of the classics, further enhanced by his enthusiasm, turned him into an amateur archaeologist, while Byron's greater knowledge and intelligence was reserved exclusively for his literary endeavours, self-promotion and the attainment of celebrity status. Byron's blatant disregard for authority and his determination to indulge in every whim, lawful or otherwise, coupled with his magnetism and charm, kept Altamont in thrall. While Byron splashed around the money he did not have to indulge his many interests and vices, Altamont, whose means appeared infinite by comparison, followed suit. They shared a dislike of parental and college discipline. Altamont chafed at the bit of his father's control, while Byron's mother wrote of her despair at the excessive and spendthrift ways of her son. Both were reluctant scholars. Byron loftily attested that 'college life is neither conducive to my improvement nor suitable to my inclination' and, to emphasise the point, he kept a 'tame' bear, Biron, in his rooms, which he threatened to have sit for a fellowship in his place. Yet, despite their differences, it is notable how the courses of the friends' early lives ran in tandem. They were part of the same circle, enjoyed the same pastimes, were bitten by the same travel bug, entered parliament at the same time and embarked on an almost identical path of travel abroad.

Life in Byron's circle at Cambridge was energetically devoted to 'a villainous chaos of din and drunkenness, nothing but hazard, and burgundy, hunting, mathematics, and Newmarket, riot and racing

... We have several parties here and this evening a large assortment of jockeys, gamblers, boxers, authors, parsons and poets sup with us – a precious mixture, but they all go on well together.'[17] Byron's bisexuality, evident at Harrow, was even more blatantly demonstrated at Cambridge. His open relationship with his protégé, John Edleston, was balanced by his later admission of being 'given to harlots' and to living 'in a state of concubinage'. Byron later attested that Altamont was also a client of 'blue-eyed Caroline' Cameron, Byron's teenage mistress, a prostitute from a brothel operated by Mrs Durville, a notorious London bawd. Dining and drinking clubs, such as the exclusive True Blue and Beefsteak, each with mandatory costly member's uniform, provided further outlets for amusement for bored Cambridge undergraduates.

Loose morals associated with student life merely reflected a wider society blighted by scandalous behaviour, widespread male and female adultery, failed marriages, open marriages, multiple liaisons, a predominance of illegitimate children, numerous divorces, and salacious legal 'criminal conversation' actions among both royalty and aristocracy. The family-orientated and staid example of the ruling monarch, and the establishment in 1802 of the Society for the Suppression of Vice, had little effect. Fashionable society was led by the example of the monarch's sons, especially the 'prince of pleasure', the Prince of Wales, known in the news-sheets of the day as 'Prinny', who, with his younger brothers, was leader of the *haut ton*.

The history of royal and aristocratic hedonism was long established. From the time of Charles II in the seventeenth century, countless thousands of rakish libertines of status and means strutted and debauched their way through the demi-monde of celebrity sex and excess. From the depravities of male and female members of the infamous eighteenth-century Hell-Fire Club of Sir Francis Dashwood, to the Irish-born Earl Barrymore, known as 'Hellgate' (a brother, club-footed and equally depraved, was nicknamed 'Cripplegate', and another brother, 'Newgate', was a frequent inmate of the infamous prison, while their notoriously foul-mouthed sister was known as 'Billingsgate'), to the insatiable seducer, Eton-educated William Douglas, Duke of Queensbury, known as 'Old Q', the Rake of Piccadilly, whose wealth almost singlehandedly maintained London's thriving sex industry, the permissiveness of the upper classes was the subject of gossip, sermons and the famous lampoons of Gillray and Cruickshank. As an intimate of the royal circle and a friend of Byron, whose conduct and literary creations were to symbolise the indulgent and outrageous behaviour of the period, Altamont's participation in the world of bawds, brothels, courtesans, dancers, actors, cyprians, demireps and singers was, perhaps, inevitable. And in 1803 London provided an outlet to appease every known sexual appetite and deviation.

Commercial sex was a major industry, especially in London. Luxury brothels catering for royalty, aristocrats, politicians and wealthy businessmen were concentrated in the St James's area of the city. Operated by enterprising madams, they provided opulent surroundings, sumptuous food, drink and sex workers of all ages to cater for the predilections of their clients. A step above the ordinary 50,000 prostitutes who plied their trade on the streets of London was the courtesan, the cyprian, the 'High Impure', the captivating, cultivated and fashionable mistress. Maintained by a rich patron who endowed her with her own house and servants, an income and his protection, the courtesan's main duty was to please and charm and give him the exclusive privilege of her company and her sexual favours in a domestic environment.

Courtesans were the queens of the demi-monde and invitations to their parties, balls and entertainments were as eagerly sought after by princes, aristocrats, politicians, ambassadors, poets, dandies and rakes as those of the highest ranking aristocratic hostess of the grand monde. Presiding over this parallel social world, with its own etiquette and rules, were famous courtesans such as Julia Johnstone, Mary Ann Clarke, companion of the Duke of York, Amy and Fanny Dubouchet and their famous sister, Harriette Wilson. To be seen in the company of the divas of the demi-monde, to drive with them in an open carriage in Hyde Park, to promenade with them in the Vauxhall and Ranelagh gardens, to be received in their box at the opera, was considered both an honour and an achievement by prince, aristocrat, poet, politician or the Fellow Commoners of Oxford and Cambridge.

Harriette Wilson was the star of the courtesans. Dark, luminous eyes, framed by long eyelashes, her striking features were complemented by a large bosom, small waist and petite hands and feet. Independently minded, cultured, witty and outspoken, she became the lover and prized courtesan of some of the most famous men of the age, including Frederick Lamb, the supposed son of Lord Melbourne, Lord Ponsonby, the Marquis of Worcester, the Duke of Wellington and George Campbell, the decadent, hard-living Marquis of Lorne, son and heir of the influential Duke of Argyle. Altamont's initial attempt to engage with the formidable courtesan was smartly rebuffed. Introduced by his cousin Dominick Browne, whom Harriette unkindly described in her diary as 'a great big stupid Irishman',[18] Altamont was smitten. Harriette recorded in her infamous *Memoirs* the visit of the two Irishmen to her house in Mayfair. Both men 'sat talking on different subjects for about an hour and then drove off in His Lordship's curricle'. Altamont, however, invoked her ire by subsequently sending her an 'unsealed and unfolded' letter with his servant who, according to Harriette, was 'well-bred ... in a cocked hat and dashing livery [who] entered my room with many bows'. 'My Dear Miss Wilson,' the letter read, 'Will you be so condescending as to allow me to pass this evening, alone, with you, after Lady Lansdowne's party? Sligo.'[19] Miffed by the naive tone of the letter and at what she considered a breach of etiquette in sending her an unsealed letter, as she informed Altamont's servant: 'this letter could not be meant for me to whom His Lordship was only presented yesterday. Take it back, young man, and say, from me, that I request he will be careful how he misdirects his letters in future; an accident which, is no doubt, caused by his writing them after dinner.'[20] Despite her initial rebuff, Altamont was later admitted to the courtesan's circle and, for a short time, enjoyed her charms. Later in 1825 he was one of the many high-profile aristocrats and politicians cited by the courtesan for the purpose of blackmail.

The King's Theatre Haymarket, Drury Lane, and Covent Garden Opera House, were favourite haunts of Cantabrigians. And it was in the London theatres that the demi and grand mondes collided and where wives and mistresses met, albeit at a distance. From their theatre boxes (a season box at Covent Garden cost in the region of one thousand guineas), the most fashionable courtesans and the most fashionable and equally promiscuous society hostesses, their boxes often paid for by the same man, played out their off-stage dramas and through opera glasses spied on one another. The difference between each set of 'courtesans', according to Byron, being merely that the 'the last may enter Carlton House [the London home of the Prince of Wales] and any other house', while the former 'was limited to the opera and the bawd house'.[21] Described as being 'little less than a public brothel',[22] the Opera House offered many pleasures that Altamont and Byron gladly partook of, including, as Byron recorded, dining with 'seven whores, a Bawd and a Ballet Master' behind the scenes in the rooms of the famous Italian singer Angelica Catalani.

Altamont was also a patron of the regular theatre which flourished in London and where some of the greatest actors of the age – Edmund Kean, John Kemble and Sarah Siddons, 'the beau ideal of acting' – and Altamont's compatriot, the hard-drinking womaniser Richard Brinsley Sheridan, playwright, impresario, politician and confidant of the Prince Regent, ruled the stage. Another compatriot, the composer Thomas Moore, was at the pinnacle of his popularity with British high society. Altamont's love of theatre, from vaudeville to opera, formulated during his student years, continued throughout his life.

The Regency buck was both a dandy and a daredevil. Cut off by the war from the centre of fashion in Paris, England made do and created its own. The 'fashionista' of the day, George 'Beau' Brummell, supplanted the previous over-the-top peacock style of the eighteenth century with simple, elegant, tightly tailored coats, skintight breeches, fancy waistcoats, polished leather 'Hessian' boots and high, starched cravats. Fashion and style, as much as breeding, were considered distinguishing factors and it was imperative for an aspiring man-about-town to dress the part. The tie of one's cravat, the number of buttons on one's pantaloons, the cut of one's coat, had to conform to prevailing fashion dictates. Addiction to fashion, however, could not imply any deficiency in manliness. The streets of Regency London were dangerous and violent. Muggings, assaults, fights and duels, often provoked by the most trivial indiscretion, because of the absence of a police force, went largely unchecked. The threat of imminent French invasion upped the ante and young aristocrats were taught to use weapons to protect themselves.

Altamont became a pupil of the famous fencing master Henry Angelo. The library at Westport House contained a copy of his opus *Fencing and Boxing*. 'I was ... invited by Lord Altamont to dine with him at Jesus College, though harassed and fatigued, I could not refuse the honour,'[23] Angelo recorded in his memoirs. Altamont and Byron offered to mediate on Angelo's behalf with the college authorities to obtain the use of the town hall in Cambridge as a venue for his fencing classes, promising to 'bend the obstinacy of the upstart magistrate' who was, according to Byron, 'equally deficient in justice and common civility'.[24] In London, Angelo shared a gymnasium on Bond Street with the icon of pugilism 'Gentleman

Jackson'. There his students honed their skills with épée and sabre and sparred and boxed with some of the most famous pugilists of the day, including Tom Belcher and the Irish champion Dan Dougherty. It was the age of bare-knuckle prize-fighting. Deemed illegal by the authorities and confined to professional fighters, the contests were held in secret in remote locations, such as the Epsom Downs. They were organised and financed by wealthy society bucks known as 'The Fancy', who provided purses for the contestants. On attaining his majority, Altamont's involvement in the world of pugilism and prize-fighting was given freer rein and lured him into the underworld of gamblers, jockeys, hustlers and racing men.

Driving their carriages at a reckless speed through the streets of London, the modern-day equivalent of joy-riding, was another aristocratic 'pastime'. The Prince Regent was notorious for flying about the city in his phaeton. In the early years of the nineteenth century, thrill-seeking scions further pushed the boundaries of public safety by masquerading as drivers for hire. In their handsomely decorated coaches, aping the characteristic demeanour and dress of stagecoach drivers, their language laced with slang and oaths, frequenting coaching houses and gin shops, the Regency bucks vied to outdo each other as 'professional' drivers. If a member of the public mistook them for public transport and paid a fare to be taken to their destination, it added to their reputation.

Wagering and gambling infiltrated every social class in England but was most expansively pursued by the privileged classes, with more wealth and time to expend on their 'hobby'. In fashionable clubs such as Brook's, White's, Almack's and the infamous Crockford's, fortunes in land, property and money changed hands on the fall of the dice. Charles James Fox, leader of the Whig party, was said to have spent all night gambling and by five o'clock the next evening had lost £11,000 (equivalent to one million pounds today). The minimum bet at Brook's, one of Altamont's haunts, was £50 (£4,000 today), and it was quite common to win or lose

£10,000 at a single sitting. Gaming reached its zenith during the Regency period, with most of the aristocracy, as well as members of the government, addicted. At the time of his marriage to Princess Caroline of Brunswick, the Prince Regent had accumulated a staggering gambling debt of £800,000. In an effort to lure his heir from the gaming tables, the king had made clearing his son's debt conditional on his marriage. Altamont's Cambridge friend Scrope Davies became a professional gambler and for fifteen years maintained an indulgent lifestyle from his winnings. The 'rattle and dash of the box and dice and the glorious uncertainty', as Byron wrote, like a magnet drew Altamont and his friends to partake in games of hazard, faro, macao, piquet, casino and billiards. Horse racing, and the gambling that went with it, lured him into the clutches of bookies and hustlers at the race track. The races at Newmarket drew everybody from royalty and the *haut ton* to the working classes or 'the mob', as they were termed. Altamont, however, was eventually to become a true racing man and one of the leading lights of the Irish and English turf.

Hand-in-hand with indoor and outdoor pursuits, drinking was copiously indulged. Fifty thousand ale houses, gin shops, clubs and taverns catered for the drinking habits of the population of Georgian Britain. 'A three-bottle man was not an unusual guest at a fashionable table.'[25] Drink accompanied every meal – ale or claret at breakfast, hock for a hangover and sherry mid-morning, while dinner was served with champagne and wines, followed by brandy and port. Judging by the receipts among his papers, Altamont learned to imbibe with the best.

While much time was squandered in the demi-monde, the London season and salons of the *haut monde* were also open to the young aristocratic man-about-town. Despite the licentiousness of the time, marriage was still the desirable state for women of every class. For the daughters of the *haut ton*, marriage had to pay financial dividends and was planned with military precision. The matrimonial state was primarily a civil contract, albeit blessed by the church, to merge wealth and hereditary estates, love being an unnecessary and potential combustible danger to the marriage contract. For the mothers, matrons and chaperones, well practised in the art of snaring a husband of wealth and rank for their female charges, a young earl, such as Altamont, with prospects and royal connections, was a desirable catch. To compete with the sexual outlets on offer to philandering suitors in the demi-monde, the daughters of the *haut monde*, while retaining their obligatory virginity, adopted flirtatious habits and a seductive dress code to lure their men. Retaining their husbands' attention and affection after marriage was less important. Men with no fortune or prospects also preyed on the daughters of the wealthy, 'the golden dollies' whose fortune on marriage became the property of their husbands. During the season, the prospective brides were paraded at every opportunity at soiree, ball, dinner, theatre and promenade, their physical and financial attributes noted and evaluated.

As a youth of thirteen, Altamont's status in the marriage stakes attracted the attention of society matrons. In 1801, on a journey by canal boat with De Quincey, they shared the deck space with a party of chaperoned young ladies. News filtered below deck to 'Mama' that 'a young lord, and one of great expectation was on board'. Losing no time, 'Mama ... an awful personage ... and a leader of the *ton* in Dublin and Belfast,' as De Quincy recalled, came up on deck and, singling out his friend, tried to ingratiate herself with him, ignoring his lowly companion. 'Lord Westport, full of generosity in what regarded his own pretensions ... coloured with as much confusion as myself at her coarse insinuations.'[26] But like his later companion, Byron, whose mother was desperate for him to marry a woman of fortune, for many years Altamont resisted the temptations placed in his way to enter the marriage state. And when at twenty-eight he decided to marry, it was perhaps his experience of the negative aspects of the social marriage market that, to his credit, made love decide his choice of bride and which led to a loving relationship that lasted the course through many travails.

Altamont's participation in the debauchery and vice of the *haut ton* greatly troubled his father. Since the Union, Sligo found himself, reluctantly, having to spend more time in London. His arthritic condition had intensified and he walked with the greatest of difficulty. During his time in the House of Lords many momentous events occurred. In October 1805, the naval victory of his friend Admiral Nelson over the French fleet at Trafalgar saved England from invasion. The victory was countered that December by Napoleon's triumph at Austerlitz, which placed the whole of Western Europe at the feet of the French dictator. In May 1806, the 'Delicate Investigation' into the scandalous conduct of the Prince Regent's estranged wife, Princess Caroline, instituted by the Whig-led government, divided all shades of political opinion. Having little sympathy with the conduct of the Prince Regent, Sligo's compassion was for the much-maligned princess. The Catholic Question, which he had long supported, continued to fall foul of royal intransigence and weak leadership. The king dismissed the 'Ministry of All the Talents' from government when it attempted to bring forward a bill to open higher offices in the army and navy to Catholics. Sligo also witnessed the passing in March 1807 of the Abolition of the Slave Trade Act, which had implications for the economic viability of his Jamaican estates and which, unlikely as it may have then appeared, was also destined to turn his wayward son into one of the most determined champions of emancipation.

Parliamentary duties notwithstanding, management of his Irish estate continued to be Lord Sligo's main preoccupation. Taking advantage of improvements in agricultural trade in Ireland, he initiated additional improvements on his property, earning the praise of the lord lieutenant, the Duke of Bedford. On a tour of the province of Connaught in October 1806, the Duke stayed at Westport House, where he observed 'the extensive scale of improvement ... the costly works of general and local utility now carrying on there under your Lordship's auspices; the liberal encouragement given to every branch of industry throughout your large domain .... Happy would it be for Ireland were your Lordship's example more generally followed.'[27]

From both sides of his parentage Altamont's immediate relations were the epitome of restraint and discretion. Both his father and maternal grandfather, Admiral Howe, deplored the debauchery that plagued English high society. Gambling in particular was anathema to Lord Sligo, who feared for the fate of the family estates he had managed so assiduously during his lifetime. His disquiet became more marked as his health began to deteriorate. 'Worn down by sickness and sorrow' at his son's conduct, he penned a letter 'for my invaluable son to be opened by him after my decease'. Headed '*Matters of Recommendation to my Son in the Most Material Pursuits of his Life*', while admitting to be 'an indulgent father', he hoped that his advice might guide his future conduct.

> Marry as early in your life as you can. Find a woman that will make you happy, a pretty face alone will not do. Kindness, character, family and fortune are altogether the points most productive of happiness. Never go near the gambling table. If you ever touch a dice box or ever risk anything but a mere trifle on betting or games of dice, cards or horse racing, you fly in the face of the only absolute injunction laid upon you by your father .... Neither a borrower or [*sic*] a lender be, an economist if you wish to be happy.[28]

The Marquess ended his letter by urging his son against becoming an absentee from his Irish estate. He urged him to make friends with Denis Browne, 'my brother ... faithful friend and zealous assistant', and his brother's children, 'to return in friendship to them the attachment of my brother'. Despite the strained relationship that was to develop between Altamont and his formidable uncle, in this regard, he nevertheless tried his best to adhere to his father's wish.

Moved by his father's deteriorating health, Altamont resolved to devote time to his studies at Cambridge. Under George Caldwell's guidance, he was duly awarded a Master of Arts degree in 1808. His main interest lay in the classics, particularly Greek history and architecture. His life-size portrait in the long gallery of Westport House, painted by Sir William Beechey, shows him in his Cambridge robes with Jesus College in the background. Beechey's portrait of his mother, painted at the same time, was subsequently destroyed in a fire at Westport House.

On graduating from Cambridge, his father set procedures in train to secure Altamont a seat in parliament. Over three hundred and fifty seats in the House of Commons were controlled by the aristocracy, the remainder by wealthy commoners. 'Rotten boroughs' (boroughs with a handful of voters whose votes were controlled by the owner) were numerous, more were 'proprietary' boroughs in the giving of an aristocratic family, while some were for sale to the highest bidder. Few parliamentarians were advocates of democracy or universal suffrage. The mass of the common people had no say and therefore little interest in the parliamentary process. For aristocrats such as the Marquess of Sligo, with wealth and political and social contacts, the purchase of a seat in parliament, despite the fact that he was underage, was routine. The Marquess approached the Attorney General and future prime minister, Spencer Perceval. He located a Tory seat at Bletchingley, a three-seat borough in Surrey in the giving of wealthy industrialist William Kenrick, who in turn had purchased it from Sir Robert Clayton. The fall of the government in March 1808, however, foiled the arrangement.

As his health continued to deteriorate, the Marquess of Sligo's mind became focused on his legacy. His 'grand object', as he wrote to his lawyer, Thomas Metcalf, in London, was to leave his son 'so as to stand in property precisely as I do myself ... with seven or eight thousand a year & near fifty thousand of personal property at his entire disposal'.[29] In the autumn of 1808, to escape the winter weather, accompanied by Louisa and Altamont, the marquess sought the beneficial air of Lisbon. Portugal had been freed from the grip of Napoleon a few months previously when Sir Arthur Wellesley, the future Duke of Wellington, defeated the French at Vimeiro, north of Lisbon. Despite the change in climate during December, as Altamont informed Peter Browne, the Marquess was 'constantly delirious and very weak but the Physician entertains considerable hopes of his recovery'.[30] On 2 January 1809, however, following a severe stroke, he died at the relatively young age of fifty-three.

The return of his body in wartime was both a difficult and expensive undertaking but one from which his son was not to be deterred. Chartering a ship at his own expense, Altamont arranged to bring his father's remains, firstly to London and from there to his beloved Westport. 'Covered in crimson velvet, ornamented with gold ... with the crown and cushion bearing his rank' and followed by family mourning coaches, a large cortege accompanied the bier as far as Dunstable.[31] From there the body was brought to Holyhead and across the Irish Sea to Dublin, from where the funeral procession proceeded across Ireland to Westport. There it was met by thousands of the dead peer's tenants, who accompanied the body for burial in the Browne family tomb in the grounds of Westport House.

Some three months short of his majority, Howe Peter Browne, 4th Earl of Altamont, succeeded his father as the 2nd Marquess of Sligo.

Chapter 4

Pirate

I have got a most capital ship at last ... She has ten eighteen pound cannonades ... 500 Cartridges aboard besides
canisters of grape shot and 600 balls ... to make a defence
against almost any privateer.

Lord Sligo

The new Marquess of Sligo appeared to be one of the most
eligible bachelors in the United Kingdom of Great Britain and
Ireland, with five titles in the Irish and English peerages, 200,000
acre estates in the west of Ireland, plantations in Jamaica and an
income estimated at £30,000 per annum. His mother's share of
the Howe inheritance would, in time, also descend to him. The
privileges, patronage and contacts he enjoyed, both in Ireland and
in England, were as valuable as the land and wealth he inherited.
Sociable, urbane, unpretentious, exuding all the confidence and
self-assurance his aristocratic status endowed, he had matured into
a young man who could be said to be 'happy in his own skin'.
Of medium height, blue-eyed, fair-haired and tending, even in
his youth, towards corpulence, or of being just plain 'fat', as his
friend Byron attested, the sky appeared the limit for the impulsive,
adventure-seeking heir. While his father might well have advocated
that he settle down and marry, in 1809 marriage or settling down

was the last thing on his mind. On 4 March 1809, at a private levee at the Queen's Palace, 'upon his coming into his title and the Peerage', the 2nd Marquess of Sligo made his formal obsequies to King George III.[1]

Aristocratic wealth was tied up in land, property and securities; ready cash for day-to-day expenditure was a constant challenge. And the new marquess had not spared the cash. As he confessed to his 'darling mother … I certainly have been most acceptably extravagant this last year. But you may depend upon it I will be more cautious in future, at least I have such a lesson now as makes me rather sick of it.'[2] The world of the courtesan and the demi-monde was one laced with many perils, from indebtedness to blackmail. Sligo's extravagance started in Eton, where bills he had run up were still outstanding. Keeping up appearances in the fast lane of the Prince Regent's world of Carlton House, Newmarket, Holland House, Brighton and everywhere in between did not come cheap. Costly apparel, club and military uniforms, carriages emblazoned with his crest, servants in 'dashing livery', as well as his propensity for wagering, wenching and imbibing, involved serious financial outlay. Already committed to the turf, he had started to develop a horse-breeding and racing stable even before his father's death, had purchased the first of many racehorses, hired four grooms at £100 a year, a trainer at £100 and two jockeys at £50 each per annum.

As well as his personal outlay, his inheritance was encumbered with legacies, jointures and death duties, together with an outstanding sum of £10,000 owed to his relation Aylmer Bourke Lambert, in final payment for the purchase of the remainder of the Viscount Mayo estate. And in 1809 Lambert was clamouring to be paid. To retain political control in Mayo, whence his power, wealth and patronage emanated, large sums had also to be expended on election campaigns and on the practice of 'buying' the votes of eligible voters. The Westport estate was further charged with the maintenance of a large number of dependent retainers and their families. Consequently, the young heir found, like most of his fashionable friends, that his legacy fell short of his expenditure. On the death of his father, his estate was placed in trust with Denis Browne, Ross Mahon and Dominick Geoffrey Browne of Castlemacgarrett, while his mother was appointed his guardian.

His father's seat, as a representative Irish peer in the House of Lords, was Sligo's first priority. Following the fall of the 'Ministry of All the Talents', a Tory-led government was established. The elderly Duke of Portland became prime minister and his cabinet included many friends and political allies of Sligo's father, such as Spencer Perceval, George Canning, Arthur Wellesley, Lord Palmerston, Lord Liverpool and the secretary of state for war, Lord Castlereagh, whom Sligo had known since boyhood. Surrounded by family members, friends, supporters and political allies, on 13 March 1809 Sligo took his seat in the House of Lords on the government benches. Like many aspects of his life, his entry to parliament coincided with that of his friend Byron. Prior to his admittance to parliament, Byron took umbrage on being obliged to present proof of his grandfather's marriage. To register his displeasure, he chose to make his entrance unaccompanied and sat aloof, brooding and disdainful, affecting, as one contemporary noted, 'more aristocracy than befitted his years'.[3] While in theory a Whig, Byron could not 'say that my opinion is strongly in favour of either party', and instead resolved to 'stand aloof … [and] preserve my independence'.[4] Sligo and Byron agreed to be 'paired off' during the first sitting of parliament. While initially from opposing political sides, the college friends were at one, however, in their support for Catholic Emancipation, a decision that was to place Sligo at odds with his own party, as well as with the king. 'Should the Catholic Question come up,' he wrote to his mother in 1810, 'pray write to Lord Liverpool and say how sorry I am to vote against him but that in that one instance only

I must beg of him to give it in favour of the Catholics.'[5] As well as succeeding to his father's seat in the House of Lords, Sligo set about acquiring the honour he, like his father, prized above all others – the Ribbon of the Order of St Patrick.

In spring 1809 there was much for parliamentarians to ponder. The shadow of Napoleon hung over everything. Despite the threat he presented, the French dictator held a strange fascination for Sligo and his fashionable friends. Conqueror of the largest empire since the days of Rome, like a thunderbolt out of the heavens in some Greek saga, the lowly Corsican soldier, risen through the ranks, by strategic intelligence, personal charisma, arrogance and the aura of invincibility he evoked, mesmerised both friend and foe alike. It was fashionable among young liberal-minded aristocrats to sympathise with the revolutionary ideals of reform and emancipation and with the dissidence and radicalism that Napoleon's reign symbolised. In their personal lives, they too viewed themselves as rebels against narrow-minded, moralising authority. The Peninsular War was at its height and in January came news of the defeat of the British army under Sir John Moore at La Coruña, leaving Napoleon unopposed in Spain and his brother Joseph installed on the Spanish throne. The envy existing between Castlereagh and Canning, which eventually led to a duel, was also a topic of gossip and speculation among parliamentarians. The scandal involving the Duke of York, Commander-in-Chief of the army, accused of selling military commissions and promotions at the behest of his mistress, Mary Ann Clarke, also animated parliamentary and fashionable society.

Parliament rose for the summer recess, ending Sligo's first term as a legislator. On reaching his majority in June 1809, he finally came into his inheritance and returned to Ireland to formally take over his estate and accept the pledges of loyalty from his numerous tenants, friends and political associates. By now anglicised in outlook, appearance, accent and education, with a reputation for being an indulged, raffish playboy, to establish his authority over the extended Browne family, especially his influential uncle Denis Browne, was a formidable challenge. Since his father's illness and during his own minority, his uncle ruled supreme in Mayo. But Sligo's education and background also endowed him with a belief and confidence in his own abilities, albeit not always justified. His uncle's challenge to his authority in Mayo he met head on. 'There can only be one head of a family & and I will be that head of mine,' he stoutly declared to his agent, George Glendenning, on hearing that his uncle had countermanded an order he had given relating to the management of his estate.[6]

What the local Mayo tenantry made of their young landlord is open to conjecture. His family's status as 'good' landlords had not been adversely affected by the events of the 1798 Rebellion. The 1st Marquess was a progressive landlord and, after the Union, was one of the few who remained resident in Ireland. By the first decade of the new century Westport town and port was prosperous and the tenants on his estate seemed content with their lot. Westport House still remained open and accessible to all and continued to support a large and diverse number of retainers and hangers-on. Relationships between the shopkeepers in the town of Westport and Westport House were, however, at times frayed. As tenants, leaseholders and provisioners to their landlord, they were dependent on his goodwill, but issues over leases, overcharging of supplies to Westport House and emerging political differences were beginning to lessen the sense of dependence.

When the state of his finances, aggravated by the expense involved in the repatriation of his father's remains from Lisbon, became apparent, Sligo reluctantly accepted a programme of economic cutbacks, both in the running of his estate and in his own lifestyle. He promised to 'knock up' his recently established horse-breeding venture, with the exception of horses already registered to race, as well his prized brood mares. Plans were also put in train for the sale of the Lisduff estate in County Galway, inherited through his grandmother, Elizabeth Kelly, after the timber was first sold off, while his mother's estate at Porter's Lodge was also placed on the market. Owing to the great number of people living gratis off his estate, expenses at Westport House had risen, but his initial attempts to introduce economies there proved unsuccessful.

To relieve the financial pressure, in consultation with Glendenning and his uncle, Sligo resolved to live abroad. A series of trade embargoes, known as the Continental System, had been imposed by Napoleon, by which he hoped to bankrupt Britain by cutting off her trade with the Continent. In 1807 the British government retaliated by the imposition of trade tariffs which resulted in a surge in the cost of living. As well as financial necessity, other reasons motivated his move abroad. Foreign travel, the 'Grand Tour', was considered *de rigueur* to round off the education of young peers. Travel not only broadened the mind but enhanced and matured one's perceptions, judgement and experience. In Sligo's case, as an indulged only son, the chance to strike out on his own (albeit with a retinue of servants) was both a challenge and an adventure. Because of the ongoing war, much of Europe was out of bounds. Portugal, Malta, Sicily, Sardinia, Turkey, the Middle East and Greece, however, remained free of Napoleon's domination and drew wealthy British travellers in their droves.

Pressurised by even greater financial considerations, in 1809 Byron, with John Cam Hobhouse in tow, had already hit the trail. Part of Byron's motivation for travel, especially to eastern Europe, hid a more clandestine motive – to indulge his homosexual needs in a more accommodating ambience. 'In England the vices in fashion are whoring & drinking, in Turkey, Sodomy & smoking.'[7] Writing in code to his friends in England of his sexual experiences in Greece, Byron noted, 'we are surrounded by Hyacinths & other flowers of the most fragrant nature & I have some intention of culling a handsome Bouquet'.[8]

An additional reason prompted Sligo's decision to travel. Fired by the famous mineralogist, antiquarian and Cambridge lecturer Professor E.D. Clarke, he developed an interest in classical Greek civilisation. In 1799 Clarke had embarked on a tour of Europe and the Middle East and returned to Cambridge with a treasure trove of marbles, coins, sculptures – including the famous colossus of Ceres, the tomb of Alexander, a sarcophagus brought from Alexandria (now in the British Museum) and a bust of a woman with a basket on her head, thought to be from the Temple of Demeter at Eleusis – and many rare manuscripts, costumes, utensils, seeds, minerals and plants. Sligo's relationship with Dr Clarke deepened from their academic association into friendship. In 1806 he was chosen by the college authorities to present him with 'a piece of plate and a handsome letter, expressing their sense of his kindness and attention in his office' on the occasion of the professor's marriage.[9] Clarke's travels were also of interest to Lady Sligo. As the books in her library testify, Louisa had more than a passing knowledge of and interest in antiquities and made transcripts of many of Clarke's letters in advance of their publication in 1810. An inspirational and eloquent lecturer, Clarke's enthusiasm and knowledge whetted Sligo's appetite. His interest also reflected the frenzy for excavation and acquisition of ancient artefacts that, like some classical Klondike, had become an all-pervasive compulsion in wealthy British society.

While not an academic in the accepted sense, Sligo possessed more than a surface knowledge of the classics. He studied the works of Homer and Pausanias, the bible for treasure-seekers, and had read the letters and reminiscences of other modern-day travellers to Greece. His resolve to travel abroad and start 'digging' was moulded by a mindset that appears reprehensible today. The view of the establishment and of 'civilised' society in the early nineteenth century, however, was that ancient classical artefacts *needed* to be rescued. As Clarke's biographer, the Rev William Otter, noted, 'from the reach of Scythians or Tartars … to rescue from oblivion … those inestimable relics which are daily falling a sacrifice to time and to ignorant barbarians'.[10] It *behoved* the antiquarian dilettante, despite the often crude means employed in their removal, to provide 'asylum' for these unique relics in museums and universities and so 'assist the studies and inflame the ardour of youth who would have access to them'.[11] And there was some truth in that imperialistic attitude. On his travels, Clarke observed a magnificent Greek marble tomb being used by villagers in Crimea 'as the basin of their public conduit',[12] while Sligo later wrote of seeing the surviving ruins of the Pantheon in Athens being used as target practice by the occupying Turkish army. For some, however, there was a more mercenary motivation.

By the beginning of the nineteenth century the ancient Hellenic sites were infested with 'treasure-seekers' from many nations. At the end of the eighteenth century Louis Fauvel was despatched by the French Ambassador in Athens to collect antiquities to send back to Paris. News of the spectacular 'finds' made by Thomas Bruce, 7th Earl of Elgin, a Scottish peer and ambassador to the Ottoman Empire at Constantinople, among the sacred ruins of the Pantheon reached England and further spurred others to try their hand. The depredatory excursions of both Elgin and the 4th Earl of Aberdeen were subsequently satirised by Byron.

> Let Aberdeen and Elgin still pursue
> The shade of fame through regions of Virtu;
> Waste useless thousands of their Phidian freaks,
> Misshapen monuments and maim'd antiques:
> And make their grand saloons a general mart
> For all the mutilated blocks of art.

Professor Clarke, however, sought to differentiate between purloining abandoned and vulnerable classical artefacts for educational and preservation purposes and the deprecatory actions of Elgin and his agents, whom he accused of 'pulling down temples that have withstood the injuries of time and war and barbarism for ages, to adorn a miserable Scotch villa'.[13] Sligo's interest stemmed, not from thoughts of monetary gain or personal aggrandisement (many of his acquisitions lay, for decades after his death, forgotten in the basement of Westport House), but from a sense of adventure, challenge and fulfilment, as well as to possess something rare and beautiful and because, simply, it was the 'fashionable' thing to do.

By December 1809 preparations for his great adventure were in train. On 21 December at a royal levee, among those presented to the king was 'the Marquess of Sligo on his going abroad'.[14] While Greece was his destination, the route there, owing to the ongoing war, was less certain. Whatever doubts Lady Sligo may have entertained about her son's ability to reform his spendthrift ways, she did not flinch from supporting her 'beloved child'. During the course of his absence abroad, their voluminous correspondence reflects their mutual affection and respect and is replete with descriptions of his travels, humorous banter, gossip and exchanges of confidences and opinions on events, people, places and politics. While determined to be his own master, and sometimes ignoring her advice, Sligo trusted his mother implicitly. On the eve of his departure he transferred to her the trusteeship of his entire property. 'As to money matters I must leave all that to the Beast [Caldwell] and you: in full trust to your *honour* that you do not do anything for a convenience to me which might in the slightest degree inconvenience you.'[15] And he was not disappointed. For as well as funding his many expensive escapades, Lady Sligo oversaw the management of his estates, travelling from London to Westport on occasion to ensure that all was in order and that her son's orders were being implemented in his absence.

On 21 December 1809 Sligo set off from London for Falmouth, encountering the first of many mishaps, as he recorded in his journal:

'we had the ill-luck of finding the caravan containing all our baggage, tents etc overturned close to Hyde Park turnpike'.[16] His travelling companions included an English servant, Holworthy; his Irish servants, John and Patrick Walsh; as well as Barthold, an expert on Greek antiquities recommended by George Caldwell, who initially found favour with his twenty-two-year-old master. 'I am delighted with Barthold, he appears so quiet and unassuming and at the same time not addicted to fawning – has contradicted us several times in our conversations about Greece.'[17] After several unsuccessful attempts, Sligo eventually obtained passage on the *Elizabeth*, the same packet on which Byron and Hobhouse had earlier sailed for Lisbon. Contrary winds, followed by swells and calm, however, left him chomping at the bit at Falmouth for an entire month. 'I am sure I have been reduced to such a state of apathy by the continued disappointments I have had about the wind that I never so much as think of inquiring which way it blows.'[18] Desperate to start his journey, he rashly considered the possibility of asking Lord Wellesley to write to Napoleon Bonaparte for a passport to travel through France and Italy under the pretext of 'travelling for the purpose of Natural History ... it would be such a capital stroke to see France'.[19] By mid-January the wind had shifted and Sligo, armed with the sword of his grandfather, Admiral Howe, and with a final request to his mother to send on 'my leather pantaloons', finally sailed away on the first leg of his odyssey, inscribing on the front page of his journal *flebile principium melior fortuna sequatur* [*sic*] – better fortune follows a feeble beginning.

Sligo was the consummate traveller. From the moment he boarded the ship at Falmouth he was willing to jettison the indulgent pampering of his former lifestyle, adapt to the circumstances of his situation and accept what fortune and the elements threw in his way. From the cramped and noxious quarters of military frigates, transport barks, boats and feluccas, to rat-infested lodgings, threats from robbers and pirates, enduring extremes of heat and cold, dangers from human and natural sources, thirst and hunger, living for two days 'on bread and onions for we had no means of cooking',[20] illness, rough seas and 'provoking calms', he was prepared to endure, without complaint, what he accepted as being part and parcel of his grand adventure. While his destination was Greece, how and when he arrived there was less important: it was the journey there that mattered. Unlike his friend Byron, he was not predisposed by knowledge or burdened with any great intellectual reputation but viewed the countries and cultures he visited with a tourist's interest and enthusiasm. He employed a hands-on approach to the logistics of travel, from sourcing horses and lodgings to manning the tillers of the various vessels in which he sailed.

Interest in all things maritime permeated his correspondence. When writing at sea, his letters included the exact bearing of latitude and longitude and his language points to some degree of nautical knowledge. Ever conscious of the elements and their effects on the ships in which he sailed, he was familiar with the intricacies of sail, able to gauge distance in nautical miles and was knowledgeable about navigation and compass points. As a descendant on his paternal side of Ireland's sixteenth-century 'sea-queen' Grace O'Malley and of his more famous maternal grandfather, Admiral Howe, he felt at home on the sea, as he boasted to his mother: 'I always worked the ship myself & am become I assure you without flattery a very good sailor. You know I have it in my *blood* and cannot therefore be surprised at it.'[21]

From Lisbon, which he found bustling with British troops, his initial plan to travel overland, as Byron and Hobhouse had done, to Seville, Granada and Cadiz was sidelined by military developments. The French had overrun Spain and, despite Arthur Wellesley's victory at Talavera in July 1809, the British army was forced to retreat to Portugal. The alternative was to continue by sea to Gibraltar, where he landed on 3 February 1810. 'We have at last arrived in Gibraltar which is so like Clare Island in shape that I could almost fancy myself sailing out of Westport Bay,' Sligo remarked.[22] On the Rock, a swarming, multicultural enclave, he found all bustle and confusion in expectation of an imminent siege by the French army encamped within thirty miles. Spanish refugees thronged the narrow cobbled lanes of the British protectorate and every nook and cranny was occupied. Pitching camp at the Three Anchors, a basic pensione, Sligo was received by the British governor, Scottish-born Colonel Colin Campbell, who after showing him around the Rock, through the galleries and the batteries, invited him to dinner at his residence, a former monastery known as 'The Convent'.

While in Gibraltar, Sligo became involved in a clandestine military mission when, with a Colonel Roche, he volunteered to take dispatches from the British command on the Rock to the besieged Spanish commanders in Cadiz and 'to consult with them as to the propriety of admitting British troops into the Garrison'. On the way their felucca was almost swept onto the rocks 'by a most terrible wind' which forced them to return to Gibraltar. Setting off the next day, the volunteers eventually made their way across the salt marshes to Cadiz, a town, as Sligo noted, 'remarkably striking to a stranger, every house appears a palace and every building is white which gives an appearance of cleanliness'. Surrounded on all sides by the French army, Cadiz bristled with military fortifications and was protected by a twenty-thousand-strong Spanish army. Sligo met the commander of the Spanish forces, the Duke of Albuquerque, and noted the grim determination of the Spanish to resist the French, with 'friars, beggars, merchants and nobles all working at the new fortifications ... Spain is by no means yet conquered. Cadiz will hold out for ever,' he astutely predicted.[23] Their mission completed, Sligo and his companion made their way safely back to Gibraltar, to the approbation of the military authorities.

Gibraltar was the gateway for travel in the Mediterranean. Among the new arrivals, Sligo discovered a friend from his Eton and Cambridge days, Michael Bruce, son of Patrick Crauford Bruce, a wealthy Scottish businessman and landowner. While described as 'handsome enough to move any lady's heart', Bruce may also have had homosexual inclinations, as hinted by Hobhouse and Byron. With youthful exuberance, the college friends celebrated their reunion and proposed to travel together to Greece. Their plans, however, were destined to change on their introduction to one of the most radical women of the period, the formidable Lady Hester Stanhope.

The thirty-four-year-old grand-niece of Pitt the Elder, niece and confidante of the recently deceased prime minister William Pitt, she had quit England in February and landed in Gibraltar on the first stage of her travels, her direction and destination at the whim of both the war and her modest means. Described as 'the oddest mixture I ever saw of cleverness and folly', almost six-foot tall, handsome rather than beautiful, with shoulder-length cropped hair, clever, outspoken to a dangerous degree, happiest in male company and 'undaunted and proud as Lucifer',[24] her relationship to two of England's most prominent statesmen gave her an entrée wherever she travelled. The recent death of the love of her life, General John Moore, in the Peninsular War, followed by the death of Pitt and her brother Charles, induced her to seek release from the stultifying atmosphere of English society. Her unmarried status, as well as her modest allowance of £1,200 per annum (equivalent to some £65,000 today), further augmented her decision to live abroad. 'A poor gentlewoman is the worst thing in the world,' she adroitly recorded.[25] Accompanied by her brother James, an acquaintance of Sligo and Bruce, en route to join his regiment in Spain, her physician Charles Lewis Meryon and her companion-maid, Elizabeth Williams, her presence in Gibraltar was courted by the expatriate community, as well as by the governor, who invited her to stay at The Convent.

At a party to celebrate her birthday, Lady Hester was introduced to Sligo, who described her to his mother as 'attractive tho' past la première jeunesse'.[26] Lady Hester seemed taken with the young Irish peer. As well as being related through the marriage of William Augustus Pitt to his grand-aunt, Mary Howe, Sligo's charm, courtesy, good humour, stories of his racy past, his indifference to convention and their mutual acquaintances among the political and aristocratic milieu brought some relief from the tediousness of the company of her more stolid brother and physician. Over the course of their acquaintance, Sligo's innate kindness and generosity were appreciated by the older woman, who tried to protect her youthful admirer from his own and others' folly. 'Where have I a relation who has been as kind to me as he has been?' she later recorded.[27] While pleased by the attention of such a 'delightful woman' and impressed by her knowledge of politics, her eloquence, witty repartee and talent for mimicry, Sligo was initially wary of falling 'under the lash of her displeasure'. Her outspokenness amazed him. 'To hear a so near relation of Mr Pitt's say out so violently as she does against the present administration. I never heard such roastings as she has given several people, but as long as I keep out of her clutches I don't care how much she abuses anyone else.'[28] But he had no reason to fear falling into her clutches. It was not the young Irish peer who had taken her fancy but his companion, Michael Bruce, who seemed equally smitten. Their subsequent love affair was to become one of the scandals of the age.

Anxious to leave Gibraltar on the next leg of his journey, Sligo found passage by ship impossible to come by and determined instead to acquire his own vessel and crew. The *Griffin*, armed with fourteen guns and costing £2,000 to hire, was initially recommended but the deal fell through. With Lady Hester and Michael Bruce, he found passage instead on a ship bound for Minorca. Despite rumours that Sicily was about to be invaded by a French army commanded by Napoleon's brother-in-law Joachim

Murat, Sligo and Bruce decided to chance their luck there, while Lady Hester made for the safety of Malta.

In April in a brig 'just the same size as the Revenue cutter which was at Westport' and with the aid of 'most prosperous gales' they landed at Palermo after a voyage of three days. 'I don't think I have ever seen so beautiful a situation as that of Palermo,' Sligo enthused. 'The mountains round it form a most beautiful amphitheatre and the town of Montreal [Monreale] on the top of one of them is a most lovely object from the seaside.'[29] They were received by the British legation and entertained by Lord and Lady Amherst and Lord Ebrington, a mutual friend and also a client of the famous courtesan Harriette Wilson. Setting off by mule they visited La Favorita, the King of Sicily's hunting lodge, 'the most beautifully odd fantastic sort of building ... its outside appearance is that of a Chinese temple and the inside is fitted up more beautifully than anything conceived'.[30] The Capuchin convent of the 'BAKED Friars', where the bodies of dead friars were placed in an enormous oven and baked and afterwards placed 'standing up in niches in the clothes they wore alive', he viewed less enthusiastically.[31] From Mount Pellegrino, camping in the open countryside, he journeyed on towards Gigante to view Mount Etna. At the Temple of Concord he engaged an artist, Signore Bernardi, to paint a picture which he later forwarded to his mother. Impressed by the artist's ability, he promptly hired him full-time. While staying at the British mission he fell for the charms of Lady Maria Windson and 'only saved my heart by running away from Palermo'.[32] But getting away from Sicily proved more difficult. Their first attempt to sail from Gigante was thwarted by contrary winds. Taking charge of the ship, Sligo succeeded in navigating it safely back to port. When the weather settled, they embarked again in an open boat and, after two days, reached Malta.

The centre of Mediterranean commerce and hub for the English navy, Malta was a Mecca for English travellers. The governor,

General Hildebrand Oakes, provided Sligo with lodgings and he settled down to answer letters that were awaiting him from his mother and his estate agent in Ireland. Malta was the central postal sorting office for British expatriates in the Mediterranean. The delivery of mail was uncertain and slow, at the whim of sail, weather and the war. Those with influence, or like Sligo a member of the House of Lords, availed of the diplomatic postal service to send their personal correspondence, which was subsequently directed onwards to the Foreign Office in London for collection.

Sligo and Bruce found Lady Hester ensconced in a former hostel of the Knights of St John in Valetta, the home of the sister of her companion, Elizabeth Williams, who was married to the Commissary General. While still wary of Lady Hester's temper, her appetite for political intrigue drew Sligo. Both were fascinated with Napoleon, and Lady Hester hinted at a bizarre plot to cultivate the friendship of the French ambassador in Constantinople and thereby secure a passport to France, gain access to Napoleon and relate whatever information they gleaned to the British government. While Lady Hester did engage with the French ambassador later in Constantinople, it merely led to her alienation from the English diplomatic mission there. When Sligo eventually crossed his path, Napoleon was a prisoner on the island of Elba.

Behind the forbidding façade she presented in public, Sligo discovered a more caring side to Pitt's niece and, as he wrote, when 'she does bite her teeth melt generally'. The older woman was protective of the young Irish aristocrat, advising him to dismiss Holworthy, who had a reputation for dishonesty. While taken aback at her revelation, Sligo hesitated to dismiss his servant as 'I don't think the poor devil can afford to pay his passage home.'[33] His indulgence of those of inferior rank was in marked contrast to Michael Bruce, especially in his treatment of Charles Meryon. The doctor's initial opinion that Bruce was 'a most pleasing, clever young man' changed to that 'unpleasant fellow' in the face of

Bruce's openly contemptuous attitude and behaviour to someone he considered his social inferior. Meryon contrasted Bruce's manner towards him with the friendliness and equanimity shown by the Irish marquess, 'a true gentleman', and marvelled at how easily Sligo adapted to life without the trappings and luxuries to which he was accustomed.

However, Lady Hester's presence in Malta was to alter Michael Bruce's life, as well as his plans to accompany Sligo to Greece. Without the mantle of propriety afforded her by the presence of her brother, Lady Hester's unchaperoned state, as well as her outspokenness, raised eyebrows among the British enclave on the island. When a romantic liaison developed between herself and Bruce, it set the expatriate tongues wagging and letters flying back to England. To escape prying eyes and gossip, the lovers fled from Valletta to the governor's country residence in San Antonio. Unlike Sligo, Bruce had no personal means to fund his travel and relied on his wealthy father, whose plans for his son and heir did not foresee his attachment to such a radical, older, free-wheeling woman.

While his fellow-travellers embarked on their affair, Sligo had other things on his mind. Notification reached him that the king wished to confer him with the coveted Ribbon of the Order of St Patrick. The prime minister, Lord Liverpool, gave permission for the ribbon to be forwarded in the care of the governor of Malta, rather than oblige Sligo to return to London. As well as the customary enamel badge usually conferred on recipients, as a mark of his affection King George also made Sligo a present of a personal badge, 'an old-fashioned thing, made entirely of gold'.[34] Rather than await the ribbon's indeterminate arrival in Malta, Sligo decided to continue on his journey. Finding passage for himself and his entourage impossible to come by, he determined to find a ship of his own.

In May he dropped the bombshell in a letter, which must surely have aroused the greatest anxiety in his 'dearest mother'.

'I have got a most capital ship at last! ... She has ten eighteen pound cannonades ... 500 cartridges aboard besides canisters of grapeshot and 600 balls ... to make a defence against almost any privateer.'[35] The fact that her son had engaged John Llewellyn, an English sea captain, together with a crew of twenty-five, perhaps helped mollify Louisa's concern for his safety. That it cost £200 per month, with an option to purchase for £2,250 after six months, in addition to crew wages and supplies, made her doubt, however, his promise or indeed his ability to economise. The fact that the ship, the *Pylades*, as Sligo enthusiastically informed her, was a decommissioned British Navy sloop, or that it was the same ship that had conveyed Byron and Hobhouse from Athens to Smyrna, seemed inconsequential. Nonetheless Louisa agreed to make the necessary finance available. The hire of the *Pylades* was to have life-changing consequences for both mother and son that neither could ever have imagined.

Impatient to be on his way and blasé to the point of recklessness about the legal niceties, Sligo committed a crime that was to cost him dearly. The hub of the British navy, Valetta's narrow streets were thronged with thousands of sailors taking respite in the many taverns and brothels along the harbour. As grandson of Admiral Howe, Sligo was accorded special treatment by the British naval authorities on the island. The commanding officer, Admiral Martin, directed Captain Sprainger, commander of HMS *Montague*, to assist him in outfitting his newly acquired ship. Sprainger duly obliged, providing the services of Royal Navy riggers and carpenters and even supplying a gig, manned by a navy crew, to convey the young nobleman between ship and shore. Because of losses in action, disease and injury, as well as desertion, the British navy was seriously under strength. When Sligo sent two of his retainers, Mowbray and Walsh, to find additional crew in the taverns along the port, they returned with eight inebriated sailors who were, in effect, members of His Majesty's navy. Whether they had freely deserted or had been induced by his servants, or 'involved by the lies of traders' as Lady Hester Stanhope suspected,[36] Sligo did not trouble to find out. When two of his crew also went missing, Captain Sprainger, with due deference to his titled acquaintance, accepted Sligo's word that he did not harbour them on board the *Pylades*. Armed with a letter of marque, authorising him to pursue pirates who infested the seas between Sicily and Greece, the would-be privateer set sail 'under cover of darkness', as was later alleged.

Writing from his ship off Messina, with 'a gale of wind blowing right against us', blithely unconcerned and 'thinking it fine fun', Sligo encountered a 'serious tiff' with four pirate ships.[37] Becalmed between the islands of Milo and Candia, with his thermometer recording a temperature of 125 degrees, the only shade was under 'our fore and aft mainsail ... I am literally without anything on, but a straw hat 15 inches wide in the brim, a thin silk jacket, a waisted web shirt, a pair of trousers and a pair of slippers.'[38] With a silver-handled pistol stuck in his waistband, his hair grown long, his face adorned by a moustache, the once urbane Regency dandy had become as piratical as the quarry he pursued.

The issue of the missing navy men was not as lightly treated by the Royal Navy, and HMS *Active* was despatched from Malta to apprehend and search the *Pylades*. By now aware that his crew comprised navy deserters, Sligo still seemed unable or unwilling to comprehend the seriousness of the situation. When the *Pylades* was boarded by a Royal Navy search party, as if engaged in some elaborate game of hide-and-seek, he cheerfully assisted in the search of his ship, holding a lighted candle to enable the officer in charge to examine the nooks and crannies of the *Pylades*. 'I stowed them away so cleverly that ... they did not find one man ... and I complained most grievously that I should be suspected of having any such men on board. There was impudence for you.'[39] His not overly impressed mother, the daughter of an admiral, was more cognisant of the consequences of her son's reckless actions. Once the *Pylades* was safely out of sight, its unrepentant 'captain' released the deserters from under the floorboards of his cabin, 'dressed the ship, manned the yards and gave three cheers and a glass of grog apiece to each of the sailors to drink His Majesty's health'.[40]

Sligo volunteered to chase another flotilla of pirate vessels that had plundered the lands of a local ruler on Milo in exchange for permission to excavate for antiquities. As a further sweetener, Sligo gave him a 'grand feast ... combined with about two bottles of rum and two of wine which he drank'; together with 'a salute of thirteen guns and the sight of my silver handled pistol I have made him my friend to get me permission to clinch the thing'.[41]

In evidence given later against him (although, curiously, he makes no mention of the incident in his own correspondence) it was erroneously claimed that Sligo had abandoned nine of his crew, including some of the navy deserters, on Milo. The sailors, who had in fact deliberately ignored repeated signals to return to the ship, eventually made their way to the island of Scio.

Without seeming to realise the potential smouldering fuse he had ignited with the Royal Navy, Sligo, with a remaining crew of forty-five, raised anchor and set the *Pylades* on course for the Greek mainland and the next leg of his adventure.

Chapter 5

Treasure-Seeker

He had with him a Tartar, two superbly arrayed Albanians, equipped with silver-stocked pistols and silver-hilted yataghans, a Dragoman, an artist to sketch views and costumes, a Turkish cook and three English servants, two of them in livery.

Lady Hester Stanhope

By mid-June 1810 the *Pylades* lay anchored in the Piraeus. To the west lay the mountainous and deeply indented peninsula of the Peloponnese, linked to the mainland by the Isthmus of Corinth, while to the west lay the city of Athens. Like so many before him, the young Irish aristocrat viewed the fabled capital from a distance 'surrounded by beauty and grandeur ... as it was in the earliest ages of Greece. The Acropolis rose to view, looking as if intact and in its most perfect state, the temples and buildings seem entire ... Athens exceeds all that has ever been written or painted.'[1]

Since 1453 Greece had laboured under the oppressive rule of the Turkish Ottoman Empire, its people downtrodden, 'a middle race, between slaves and freemen,'[2] the remains of its heroic culture for sale to the highest bidder. Following the signing of the Treaty of the Dardanelles (1809) between Britain and Turkey, the Sublime

Porte of Selim III, Sultan of Turkey, was well disposed to his new ally. High-profile British visitors to Greece were lavishly entertained by local Turkish magnates. But the political situation in the region was complex and fluid. France still maintained a presence in the Ionian Islands and there was much intrigue and posturing among the various European powers for control of the ancient territories. The rise in Philhellenism and a growing interest in antiquities brought increasing numbers of tourists and collectors from Europe to view, and some to acquire, what remained of the ancient sites and monuments. Having little sympathy with the culture and history of Greece, the Turks were amenable, for a price, to permit the excavation and removal of monuments and manuscripts to be dispersed throughout Europe in an act of vandalism on a grand scale.

Overjoyed at having arrived at his destination and 'up to my eyes in delight at what I see and feel', Sligo was impatient to set foot on sacred ground.[3] His studies in classical history and archaeology at Cambridge, inspired by Professor Clarke's travels in Greece and the artefacts he had brought back to the college, as well as by the illustrations and descriptions he had read as a boy in the library at Westport House, were now a reality. 'I have been so romantic since I have been here that I begin almost to think that I am destined for a knight errant.'[4] Leaving his ship anchored in the Piraeus, he hurried overland to Athens, climbed the Acropolis and entered the Pantheon, the Mecca of his journey.

The sight that met his eyes was not the grand romantic vision of his imagination. Littered with the debris of centuries, he found the ancient monument despoiled by the passage of time, wars, plunder and pillage. While the Elgin excavations, which were still ongoing, had despoiled most of the ninety-two carved fifth-century sculptures on the Pantheon's frieze above its exterior colonnade, a range of bas-reliefs on the front of the temple and some other features remained. He found a mosque established within the confines of the temple, while the erstwhile custodians of the Acropolis, the Turkish army, passed the time by using the ancient monument as target practice. An anonymous inscription scrawled on one of the monuments on the Acropolis did not deter him from his quest:

Quod non fecurent Gothi
Hoc Fecurunt Scoti.
['What the Goths did not do here
The British did' – 'Scoti' was once the generic name given
by the Romans to the Celtic people of the British Isles and
Ireland]

Some monuments on the Acropolis, such as the Temple of Theseus, in use as a Greek Christian church, he found in a better state of preservation. In the temple he found the grave of the English antiquarian John Tweddle, who had died in 1799, ostensibly of a fever, but, as Sligo later heard in Athens, murder was suspected. He determined to mark the antiquarian's final resting place by erecting an inscribed headstone, which, with Byron's support, he later accomplished.

Sligo rented a house in Athens, with whitewashed interior, bare floors and unglazed windows with wooden shutters, simply and sparsely furnished. Once settled into his new quarters, he called on contacts given to him at Cambridge. 'Tell Clarke that Signora Theodora sends her love to him,' he advised Caldwell. He subsequently hired the signora's nephew, a young Greek named Petraki, who had accompanied Clarke on his travels through the Morea. Clarke's 'old lover Mrs Pickering erst Miss Abbott,' he later found, 'in a most miserable state of Poverty and … his old artist Picava laments extremely his absence from this country …. Old Logothekis … is still the gayest of the gay fleecing and cheating every Englishman that comes here.'[5] He made the acquaintance of Giovanni Lusieri, Lord Elgin's draughtsman, who, although 'most superabundantly civil' to him, nonetheless regarded him as a competitor in the antiquity market and became, as Sligo discerned, most anxious 'to get rid of me and studiously avoids taking me where I can get anything worth having'.[6]

He found Athens teeming with English visitors. A fellow student at Eton, John Fazakerley, had departed for Corinth and Trepolezza. Lord Plymouth, the Honourable Frederic North, Henry Gally Knight, antiquarian and poet, and 'a whole herd of English', including Byron and Hobhouse, who, as Sligo heard, had been 'kicking up the Devil's delight, doing nothing on earth but riding full gallop and firing pistols ... not scarcely been once to see the antiquities.' Byron and Hobhouse had departed from Athens for Constantinople but not before leaving more than a whiff of scandal behind them. 'In short you never heard of such a system of folly as they have been carrying on here.'[7]

Determined to start his excavations, Sligo immediately applied for the customary *firman* or permit from the Turkish authorities in Constantinople. His initial scrambles among the ruins of the Acropolis wreaked havoc on his wardrobe and he wrote home requesting the delivery of '2 dozen pr. of coloured silk stockings, 2 doz. pr. of white silk stocks', as well as 'a suit of Westport uniform', with which he hoped to impress local Turkish potentates. 'Never was anything done so exquisitely angelical,' he enthused when his mother instead sent him his more impressive 'Windsor uniform'.[8]

While awaiting the arrival of the *firman*, he set sail for the island of Patmos, some 158 nautical miles west of the Piraeus. Among the numerous manuscripts in Greek, Arabic, Coptic, Hebrew, Persian and Abyssinian which Professor Clarke had brought back from his travels, some of the rarest, including a Greek lexicon, estimated to be 1,386 years old, and the Patmos Plato, 'a monument of literature', remained on the island. It was Clarke's expressed wish to 'rescue' them, a wish his former pupil resolved to fulfil.

Associated with St John the Evangelist where, it was traditionally held, he had written the Book of Revelation, Patmos was dominated by the castellated monastery which sat perched like a crown atop a high mountain. Constructed in 1088, the heavily fortified structure was a repository for some of the world's most ancient codexes and manuscripts. And it was to this potential treasure trove that Sligo was drawn, to try to succeed where the professor had failed. Armed with Clarke's extensive notes, he gained access to the library but had as little success as the professor in locating the coveted manuscripts. He managed instead to obtain a catalogue of the library's contents which he hoped might be useful in his search for antiquities but was subsequently disappointed to discover that only one volume in the collection, by Diodonus Siculas, the Greek historian, related to classical subjects. Desperate to have it, he contemplated bribing one of the monks to steal it but had to admit defeat. He entrusted the Patmos catalogue to Barthold for safekeeping but the latter 'carried it off' when they acrimoniously parted company later.

By mid-July Sligo was back in Athens, having received permission to commence excavations at a number of sites, one of which was at the side of the Acropolis and another some 200 yards from the city walls on the road to Thebes. Employing a dozen labourers, he excavated in temperatures that at times soared to 130 degrees. He took the discomfort in his stride, shrugging off burns he sustained to his foot, the result of 'showing off', as he ruefully admitted to his mother, by engaging in 'phosphorous experiments'.[10] His health, he assured her, continued well and he had acclimatised both to the conditions and to the customs as he found them. With his hair fashionably curled, moustachioed and taken to smoking a long Turkish pipe, he was in his element. But the competition to secure a share of the ancient spoils was intense. While his excavations failed to yield anything of special significance, by mid-July he had unearthed some forty vases, lachrymators and coins.

Already the *Pylades* was proving an expensive disaster and he resolved 'to get rid of this accursed brig which is ruining me'.[11]

When rumours began to circulate in Athens, however, of a breakdown in the tentative alliance between Britain and Turkey, he stayed his hand. Barthold and Bernardi were at loggerheads over the latter's accusations that Barthold had defrauded his master of a substantial sum of money relating to the purchase of the ship, an accusation subsequently confirmed by the navy deserters.

Byron arrived back from his travels in Turkey, having parted from Hobhouse who had returned to England. He found the walls of his residence in Athens covered with student-like graffiti of 'all sorts of ribaldry' by Sligo who, as Byron related to Hobhouse, 'had added to your B.A. an A.S.S. and scrawled the compliments of Jackson, Deville, Miss Cameron'.[12] Byron had embarked on the first of his literary masterpieces, *Childe Harold's Pilgrimage*, a long, narrative, autobiographical poem detailing the experiences of a young traveller on a romantic quest. The poem was to establish him as the literary genius of his age. 'I awoke one morning and found myself famous,' he is said to have exclaimed on the subsequent publication of the first two cantos in 1812. What Sligo thought of the indictment written by his friend in *Childe Harold* about 'treasure seekers' like himself, he was, perhaps, too polite to say.

> Cold is the heart, fair Greece! that looks on thee,
> Nor feels as lovers o'er the dust they lov'd;
> Dull is the eye that will not weep to see
> Thy walls defac'd, thy mouldering shrines remov'd
> By British hands, which it hath best behov'd
> To guard those relics ne'er to be restor'd.
> Curst be the hour when their isle they rov'd,
> And once again thy hapless bosom gored,
> And snatch'd thy shrinking Gods to northern climes abhorr'd.

Byron did not tarry long in Athens, as Sligo informed his mother. 'Lord Byron ... arrived here yesterday and sets off tomorrow, so that I have not seen much of him, which I dare say is much to your satisfaction.'[13] The poet was accompanied by a prancing, volatile young Greek lover, Eustathius Georgiou. Their sexual antics, as well as their numerous public tiffs and reconciliations, were legion and an embarrassment to British residents in Athens.

Byron was fond of his Irish friend and more amused than critical of his treasure-seeking quest. 'Sligo has a brig with 50 men who won't work, 12 guns that refuse to go off, and sails that cut every wind but a contrary one, and then they are as willing as may be … He has ensuite a painter, a captain, a gentleman miss-interpreter (who boxes with the painter) besides sundry English varlets.'[14] More au fait with local customs and seeing his less experienced friend being frequently overcharged, Byron offered to act as his agent. 'You may safely trust *me* – I am no dilettante. Your connoisseurs are all thieves; but I care too little for these things ever to steal them.'[15] Byron, who declared he 'would not give three half-pence for all the antiquities in Greece', at one stage offered, as Sligo later related to Thomas Moore, 'to go and dig for him in the neighbourhood of Elis'.[16] But despite the cost he encountered, Sligo reckoned, as he informed his mother, that he could still 'live splendidly and carry out all my excavations with the greatest of ease for two thousand a year, including my companions, Artist and Servants wages,' less than Byron who, Sligo attested, 'has been travelling about with fifteen horses in his train and I don't know how many Albanians and Servants'.[17]

In July, to Byron's pretended irritation, being, as he wrote, 'woefully sick of travelling companions, after a year's experience of Mr Hobhouse',[18] Sligo accompanied him on a trip to the Morea. Leaving Barthold in charge of the *Pylades* and its unruly multinational crew with, as Byron recorded, 'the limner with a raggedy Turk by way of a Tartar, and the ship's carpenter in the capacity of linguist, with two servants (one of whom had the gripes) clothed both in *leather breeches* (the *Thermometer 125!!!*) followed over the hills and far away.'[19] The journey took longer than anticipated, as Sligo had his artist stop on numerous occasions to draw 'bellissimo sketches' of the countryside and the people they encountered (some of the sketches are extant in Westport House). Sligo and his un-acclimatised entourage suffered intensely from the heat, as Byron related to Hobhouse, 'a man of the Marchesa's kidney was not very easy in his seat, as for the *servants* they and their *leather breeches* were equally immovable at the end of the first stage.'[20]

Sligo's journal, however, shows an incisive awareness and appreciation of the rich heritage through which they travelled: 'along the Via Sacra by the monastery of Daphne to Eleusis, here we stopped and having eaten something I went to examine the ruins of the Temple of Ceres and was shown the place from which Dr. Clarke took the statue of Ceres.' In a single day they rode for nine hours, covering a distance of twenty-seven miles with 'the Thermo 98 in the shade'. In a steep mountain pass a group of horsemen suddenly appeared and blocked their path. 'When we first saw the soldiers we imagined them to be robbers and prepared ourselves for Battle and accordingly charged sword in hand but were stopped by a cry that they were soldiers not robbers.' Riding along the Isthmus through 'the most beautiful diversity of scenery that is possible to conceive', they debated what they had learned at Cambridge, 'that an army of Eteocles which marching to the siege of Thebes heard the waves on both sides roar but [they] could not,' as Sligo recorded, 'conceive the possibility of it being a fact.'[21]

At Corinth they parted company. Byron set out for Bostizza, while Sligo, with Bernardi and his servants in tow, remained for a time in Corinth, a town of scattered houses, a small bazaar and two communal public ovens, whereby the locals baked their bread and roasted their meat. It was also the seat of the Bey, the local Turkish ruler, who entertained his noble visitor in the citadel perched high on a craggy precipice above the town. On his return to Athens Sligo resumed his excavations. Disappointed at the quality of the relics he unearthed, and hearing of Fazakerley's success at Argos, as he informed his mother, 'about two hours after I closed my letter to you from Athens, I took it into my head to make a tour of Morea and according packed up a Portmanteau and put it on a horse with my bed on the other side and away I went'.[22]

Accompanied by a few servants and his artist, he again left Berthold, who protested that his master's latest 'lark to be perfectly unconnected with the original intention of my engagement', in charge of the *Pylades*.[23] With a wooden seat, covered by a *capote* or blanket for a saddle, a noose made of rope for a stirrup, a halter in place of a bridle and a piece of cord as a bit, armed to the teeth with swords and pistols, Sligo and his entourage set out again through the energy-sapping Greek landscape. Through vineyards and fields of maize, over high mountain passes, with fathomless abysses and magnificent views of the Gulf of Nauplia and the archipelago, they descended to a great plain and arrived before the walled city of Trepolizza, now Tripolitsa, capital of the Morea. Entering by one of its seven gates, Sligo found lodgings in a house built of sun-dried clay and immediately set out to explore the city. He visited the local bazaar and purchased a suit of Albanian national costume comprising a long white 'kilt', crimson-velvet gold-laced jacket and waistcoat and gold-worked cloak.

The Morea was ruled by Veli Pasha (son of the notorious Turkish despot Ali Pasha, governor of Albania) ostensibly on behalf of the Sultan in Constantinople. Sligo's arrival was conveyed to the palace, a large, gaudily painted wooden building, where it was mistakenly reported to Veli Pasha that he was 'the King's nephew ... on a secret mission of importance and secrecy that I should come at night secretly but I assured him of the contrary that it was merely a visit to show my respect to him.'[24] Anxious to curry favour with the British, the dictator insisted on entertaining Sligo, as he had previously entertained Byron. Interested in art, music and antiquities, Veli Pasha spoke Turkish, Albanian, Greek and Italian. Like his father, he had, according to Byron, made homosexual advances to him, 'throwing his arm around one's waist and squeezing one's hand in *public*'.[25]

Escorted by Veli Pasha's secretary, Banos, and, as Sligo recorded, by a

> ... long procession of people with bells suspended from long rods, two men with golden armour, all studded with precious stones ... his Vizier and a lot of Turks in fine dresses, with two most superb horses covered over with gold & silver harness for Me & the Painter to ride. Accordingly away we went in grand stile [*sic*] with a thousand Albanian soldiers besides Falstaff's ragged regiment and a whole herd of children.[26]

His beard reaching below his stomach, the Turkish dictator received Sligo in a chamber furnished sumptuously *à la turque*. Dismissing their entourage, the two men talked together for an hour, interspaced with smoking 'two pipes ... about ten or twelve foot long, each all studded with jewels'.[27] Veli Pasha presented him with a 'superb Gun brace of Pistols & Sword, belt etc in the Albanese fashion all covered in gold'.[28] Having received information that his guest had purchased a suit of Albanian costume in the bazaar, 'in came the principal clerk with a present for me of a complete suit of dress of the Albanese fashion and a beautiful horse which the Pasha begged me to accept'[29] as well as the services of two Albanian bodyguards for his protection and an invitation to a banquet Veli Pasha insisted on holding in his honour the following day.

The banquet took place in a traditional 'kiosque' or tent in the countryside, with guests sitting in a circle on fine rugs and cushions. Curious to ascertain his status vis-à-vis the British government, the wily dictator quizzed Sligo about his background. 'I told him I was not English but an Irish man, that I used to come over every year to the Divan [The Court of St James] etc.

etc.'[30] Whether or not the information gleaned reduced his guest's status and potential for leverage with the English authorities, Veli Pasha gave no indication. He and his father were well practised in the art of playing the English and French off one against the other. Having failed in his previous attempt to elicit weapons from the English, Veli Pasha had more luck with his Irish guest who, out of gratitude for his generosity, offered him two cannon from his ship. At first the Turk declined, then agreed, provided his guest accepted in exchange 'six columns of Verde antique and some other Trifles'.[31]

Dressed in his Albanian costume, Sligo arrived the following day for the feast. 'Eighty-seven dishes were brought on in succession of every one of which politeness obliged me to eat some till at last my nose burst out bleeding and I gave over about the 83rd!'[32] At the end of the feast 'incense was placed to burn which immediately destroyed all the smell of the dinner'.[33] Pipes and coffee with Turkish music, singing and dancing boys followed before Sligo managed to escape the Pasha's overpowering hospitality.

During Sligo's stay in Morea, one of his Greek servants stole his prized thermometer. On being confronted, he dashed it to the ground and broke it 'to Atoms .... Accordingly,' Sligo related, somewhat out of character, 'I gave him a tremendous beating, for which he was very thankful, for had I instead of that complained to the Pasha he would have bastinadoed which would have been very much worse than any beating I could give him.'[34] Sending orders to Barthold to 'bring the Brig from Athens to Corinth',[35] on its arrival he delivered the present of the cannon to Veli Pasha. The ship returned to Athens, while Sligo proceeded by land to Patrass, where he found Byron and Samuel Strane, the British Consul General in Morea, already ensconced.

The significance of the 'six columns of Verde antique and some other Trifles', initially given by Veli Pasha to Sligo, came to light many decades later when they were identified as being three parts of the columns which once flanked the doorway to the fabled Treasury of Atheus. There is no indication in Sligo's correspondence that he personally found or excavated the columns, or that he realised their significance. Known alternatively as the Tomb of Agamemnon or the Royal Treasury of Mycenae, the ancient monument was, in effect, a large *tholos* built between 1350 and 1250 BC as a burial chamber for a person of importance. Covered by earth and in a semi-ruinous state, the site was initially examined in 1780 by Louis Fauvel, the French consul in Athens, and subsequently by Lord Elgin's draughtsman, Lusieri. The doorway to the tomb was originally flanked by two green tapered marble columns, each sculpted in eight-foot-long solid blocks, richly decorated, with intricate spirals and zigzag patterns carved in relief over their entire surface. A 'relieving triangle' flanked by two smaller half-columns and masked by thin slabs of red and green marble with spiral decorations rested above the columns, reducing the weight of the dome on the lintel.

By the time of Sligo's visit in 1810, the entrance and exterior passage to the *tholos* were still choked with soil and debris and the two columns lay scattered in pieces around the site. Elgin purloined fragments of the columns, as well as some green marble ornamentation from the doorway. Veli Pasha insisted that his Irish guest should have what remained. Whether the Turk had already excavated and removed the three remaining pieces of the columns from the site prior to Sligo's visit is not certain, although 'the vague tradition of an excavation, not by Lord Sligo, but by Veli Pasha, lingered long on the spot'.[36] From Sligo's extant correspondence there is no indication that he actually undertook the excavation. 'I shall ... go back [to Tripolitsa] and get my horse and columns & off' is his sole comment.[37]

Sligo brought the two columns, which were in three pieces, with the rest of his treasure trove back to Westport House. In 1904, when his grandson, the son of the 5th Marquess of Sligo, an amateur archaeologist, 'took careful drawings and impressions of the columns and their distinctive patterns', their true origin came to light.[38] He subsequently travelled to Mycenae where he found the drawings to be analogous with traces of the broken bases still at the entrance of the tomb. His findings were confirmed by experts in the British Museum. In 1905 the 5th Marquess of Sligo donated all three pieces to the museum, on the proviso that 'some suitable record of their discovery ... be placed on them ... and that I incur no expense or responsibility in their removal from Westport House'.[39] The missing second part of one of the columns was later traced to the National Museum in Athens. Together with casts of this and other fragments, including some from the Elgin collection, the British Museum was able to restore the two columns, which were subsequently erected at the entrance to Room 11 where they are visible today. As examples of the early period of Greek art they are considered to be 'of the highest archaeological interest'.[40] The British Museum subsequently presented replica columns to Lord Sligo and these were erected on the south face of Westport House.

By now able to converse in Italian, which 'I speak as fluently as I do English, though of course very barbarously',[41] and some modern Greek, and setting his mind to learn Turkish and Arabic, with apparent ease and good humour Sligo absorbed and adapted to his surroundings. The absence of creature comforts, combined with the discomfort of travel, 'riding in the heat of 120 all day and frequently sleeping under a tree all night', he accepted with admirable stoicism.[42] On one journey he endured a stint of twenty-two hours in the saddle and on another he injured his leg when his horse stumbled on a steep mountain pass between Athens and Thebes. He apologised to his mother for his worse than usual 'scrawl' in a letter which he had to write on his knee, 'as I have not seen a table since I left Athens'.[43] He adopted local dress, which he found more suited to the climate and environment, and despite his servants succumbing to fevers and disease, he managed to escape relatively unscathed. A weakness for sugared coffee and honeyed pastries, however, made his weight spiral.

Despite the distance and difficulty in communication, he did not neglect the affairs of his properties in Ireland and Jamaica. From his mother and his estate agent, George Glendenning, he received regular reports and sent back his orders by return, involving himself in every aspect, down to the most trivial. His mother's wish for him to 'give up the Westport races … I could not think of for a moment, as Caesar said I have passed the Rubicon,' he cheerfully admitted. Despite his promise to end his horse-breeding and racing interests, he instructed Glendenning that during his absence 'the breeding of horses should go on with care as it is no actual expense and in the end a great profit & pleasure' and to retain his hunting hounds, 'as they are a trifling expence [*sic*] & of very great importance to my health and amusement in the exercise they give me'.[45] Determined that his absence should not be taken advantage of by his uncle, he reiterated, 'I will be master in my own family and if Mr Browne does not chuse [*sic*] to act in a subordinate capacity he may give up his seat and return into the country to use the words in the "Chevy Chase".'[46] During Sligo's absence, further differences arose between the estate and the shopkeepers of the town of Westport who had 'been so grossly cheating me' for supplies to Westport House, eliciting the response to '*interdict absolutely* my servants every [*sic*] buying a *single article* at any of their blackguard holes'.[47]

Keeping the *Pylades* afloat was proving untenable. One-third of the crew was laid low with a contagious disease, suspected of being the plague then widespread in Athens, while the rest, according to Byron 'were sadly addicted to liquor'.[48] The ship's doctor, whom Fauvel claimed to be 'like the Surgeon whom the Venetians fitted out against the Turks, with whom they were at war', ministered as best he could.[49] No longer able to maintain either ship or crew, and by now totally convinced of Barthold's dishonesty, Sligo determined to dismiss both back to Malta. 'An unruly crew to deal with, no provisions, no money, no possibility of meeting with the Marquis and no cash to be obtained for Bills,' Barthold subsequently complained to Sligo's lawyer in London when, on his return to England, he presented a bill for twenty-five pounds in salary arrears.[50] While suspecting Barthold of 'unfair dealing' in his financial affairs and by then finding him 'perfectly disgusting & disagreeable .... Behind my back speaking insultingly of me in terms too indelicate to be mentioned and that I did not pay him for his work,' their subsequent parting was to their mutual relief.[51] Sligo later arranged to pay Barthold's long-suffering wife the salary arrears claimed by her husband.

In mid-August Lady Hester Stanhope and Michael Bruce arrived at Patras from Zante on a British government transport ship. With his multicultural cavalcade of Tartars, 'superbly arrayed Albanians, dragomen, Turks, Italian, English and Irish', all 'armed to the teeth', Sligo travelled from Athens to escort his friends to Corinth, where he had lodgings prepared for them. Dripping with the humidity of high summer, rife with malaria from the nearby marshes, Corinth was anything but conducive to health. The journey from Zante had severely tested the constitution of Lady Hester and a three-day stop-over was deemed necessary. Sligo was delighted to see his friends, especially Lady Hester with whom he was becoming infatuated. 'It is really quite a delightful thing travelling with such a woman ... she is such a clever woman that no moment hangs heavy on our hands in her presence,' he confided to his mother.[52] Perhaps jealous of Bruce's relationship with her, he also claimed to be much more 'useful' to her than his friend, whom he accused (poking fun at his own impecunious behaviour) of being 'so little a man of business and *I* am so *completely* one that I do everything for her. I hire Servants for her, I act the part of interpreter in short without me she would be cheated abominably.'[53] That he was more smitten, perhaps, than he realised or felt inclined to reveal is hinted at by Michael Bruce in a naive attempt to solicit his father's approval for his relationship with his unconventional lover: 'My Lord Sligo is almost as fond of her as I am.'[54]

For her part, Lady Hester became equally fond of her Irish 'protector'. There was a lack of calculation about the twenty-two-year-old, overweight, genial and generous man, who was naturally thoughtful and kind, particularly in his conduct towards older women. In contrast to Bruce, and more especially Byron, he exuded an inherent innocence and a sense of joie de vivre. It was Lady Hester, contrary to his assertion, who tried to protect Sligo from his own expensive follies. 'She has undertaken (she says) to make me a smart man. God knows whether she will ever succeed for I am tired of her lectures and desired her to give them over which she has accordingly done.'[55] What Lady Sligo thought of her son's growing attachment to a woman closer in age to herself and with a reputation that had set English society talking, is not recorded.

The Bey of Corinth sent his harem, which included his wife and twelve concubines, to call on Lady Hester. When they arrived, covered from head to foot in the traditional *burka*, Sligo, Michael Bruce and Meryon were ensconced with Lady Hester. The Bey's interpreter insisted that the three men leave before he introduced the ladies of his master's harem. Judging it an opportunity not to be missed, Sligo and his two companions instead concealed themselves in a cupboard and from their secret vantage-point observed the meeting. Once alone with Lady Hester, the ladies of the harem began to discard various items of clothing to compare their bodies with that of the foreigner. To the delight and gratification of the hidden voyeurs, 'veil after veil was removed to expose beautiful jewelled wrists and ankles … long legs and naked feet … until finally a breast was laid bare'.[56] Responding to the look of horror on Lady Hester's face, muffled laughs emanated from her companions' hiding place, which provoked consternation among the ladies of the harem. Despite Lady Hester's attempt to calm them, they hastily re-robed themselves and fled in panic. What was a prank to the westerners was a matter of life and death should the Bey discover that his ladies had inadvertently exposed themselves to the gaze of other men.

With an escort of twenty-four riders, Sligo led his companions from Corinth across the isthmus and embarked for Athens on the *Pylades* from the little harbour of Kenkris. As they sailed into the Piraeus, Sligo recognised the scantily clad figure of Byron, a youth by his side, poised dramatically on top of the mole at Cape Colonna. Since his return to Athens, Byron had taken residence in a Capuchin monastery in the shadow of the Acropolis, home to a friar and six male pupils, and was living a life of lascivious excess. His sexual escapades with the students and, in particular, with Nicolas Giraud – or Nicolo, as the poet immortalised him – the nephew of Lusieri the painter, scandalised even the more worldly among the British expatriate community. Byron elicited Meryon's medical assistance to treat his lover for what was rumoured to be an anal rupture, the result of their robust sexual encounters. Even Sligo was appalled by the conduct of his friend and confided to his mother that Byron's 'character is completely done up, even the Pasha has been speaking about it, tho himself participates in *crimes* of the same *nature*. I have detected him [Byron] in many dirty meanness and lies in order to conceal his conduct.'[57] While Byron's sexual antics were notorious, where sexual gratification was concerned the rest of the British expatriates in Athens were not inactive, as the poet later confided to Hobhouse. 'I had a number of Greek and Turkish women, and I believe the rest [of the English] were equally lucky for we were all *clapped* [i.e. contracted gonorrhoea].'[58] From Sligo's extant correspondence there is no indication or admittance on his part that he was similarly affected. There is, however, a tradition among his descendants that some years after his death his son consigned a packet of Byron's more lurid letters relating to their time in Greece to the fire in Westport House. This was confirmed later in a letter written by Sligo's widow, who referred to 'Lord Sligo's old letters that were formerly in the large tin box in the middle of the Study, except those Lord Altamont [her son] burnt.'[59]

In Athens, acting like 'a true gentleman', as Meryon noted, Sligo offered to share lodgings with the doctor so that Lady Hester and Bruce might enjoy some privacy in the house he had found for them. The two properties were located side by side in the shadow of the Ottoman mosque. With only the most rudimentary furniture, the house allocated to Lady Hester and Bruce had the luxury of a bath and a small shady courtyard, where the party gathered daily for simple meals al fresco and where they entertained friends late into the night. In the stultifying atmosphere and heat, tensions among the group mounted. The strain of waiting for a response from Bruce's father and the implication for their future together began to tell on Lady Hester and her lover.

On Byron's visits the atmosphere became even more fractious, since his at once charismatic and disturbing presence provoked controversy and discord. His patronising moralising, his affectation, the cruelty that lay beneath the cloak of romanticism he espoused, cut no ice with Lady Hester. Sensitive about her age and looks, she keenly felt her inadequacy under Byron's disdainful scrutiny. 'He was a strange character,' she recorded. 'His generosity was for a motive, his avarice for a motive. One time he was mopish, and no one was to speak to him; another he was being jocular with everybody.' She dismissed both his poetry, as well as his much vaunted looks, as having 'a great deal of vice in them ... I saw nothing in him but a well-bred man, like many others.'[60] Byron was little match for the razor-sharp mind and political savvy of the older woman and found it difficult to accept that a female could be so intelligent, while Lady Hester's liberal lifestyle, her open affair with a younger man, threatened his own much-trumpeted permissiveness. With Meryon in awe of Byron's reputation and rank, and with Bruce developing a crush on him, Sligo had his hands full to maintain some sense of balance among the diverse circle. It was rumoured that he and Byron had quarrelled and had even fought a duel but, as Byron attested, 'there is not a word of truth in it from beginning to end'. However, Sligo was relieved when Byron decided to return to the Morea. In a final riposte, Byron confided to Hobhouse, 'Poor soul, he [Sligo] has all the indecision of your humble servant, without the relish for the ridiculous which makes my life supportable.'[61]

The party was also joined by the Whig MP John Fazakerley, John Galt, a future biographer of Byron, the diplomat Stratford Canning and other British expatriates. Sligo finally dismissed the *Pylades* crew and Barthold back to Malta and continued his excavations, unearthing some additional vases and 'a very beautiful white marble Pedestal with a very fine bas relief upon it' as well as some marble fragments.[62] Another Cambridge acquaintance, Charles Cockerell, part of a multinational team, which included Fauvel and Baron Haller von Hallerstein of Bavaria, was excavating nearby. They struck gold with a magnificent collection of eighteen marble sculptures originally from the Temple of Jupiter on the island of Aegina. Known as the 'Aegina Marbles' from the finest period of Greek art, they were described as treasures 'which a king or a nobleman should make a point of having'.[63] Sligo was the nobleman whom the team hoped to tempt but the purchase price, £6,000–£8,000, even he considered excessive. The marbles were subsequently purchased by the National Museum of Munich.

Combined with the oppressive heat and bickering company, ominous rumblings came across the sea from Malta, where the *Pylades* had docked. Sligo's 'scrape with the Navy concerning certain mariners of the King's ships', Byron informed Hobhouse, had been reactivated on the return of Barthold and his disgruntled crew.[64] Dismissive of such bothersome tidings, and to escape the heat and the squabbling, Sligo resolved to visit Mount Parnassus and Delphi, sanctuary of the fabled oracle. In mid-September, accompanied by Michael Bruce, he set off on horseback.

Located one hundred miles north-west of Athens, over rocky and mountainous terrain, dry and dusty after months of drought, they first visited Plataea, where in 479 BC a Persian army of 400,000 led by Mardonius was defeated by a Greek army of 100,000 led by Pausanias, King of Sparta. Across the plain from Thebes to Livadia 'so picturesque a thing I never saw ... the celebrated cave of Trophonius and the violent source of the River Hercyna.'[65] Onwards they rode through wild and desolate countryside and eventually reached Castri and the celebrated oracle of Apollo. 'I am now sitting on a large rock in the middle of the stream ... and I have just had a large draught of the water, so that I am quite astonished that this letter has not fallen into Rhyme,' Sligo wrote to Caldwell. 'There are at this moment exactly nine women washing here who from the odd coincidence [of number] I have named of course after the Muses, but as they were all old & ugly I must confess required a great stretch of imagination.'[66] The splendour of the ancient setting was, however, imprinted on his mind. On his return to Ireland, Sligo would rename one of the most beautiful and isolated valleys on his estate Delphi, in memory of his visit to the sacred site.

Returning to Athens, they found Byron returned from Patras where he had fallen ill. The poet had become extremely emaciated, a condition compounded by his self-imposed regime of starvation and, as Sligo later related to Thomas Moore, of 'taking a bath three times a week to thin himself, drink vinegar and water, eating only a little rice'.[67] Standing before a looking glass Byron exclaimed to his friend: 'How pale I look! I should like, I think, to die of consumption.' Why of consumption?' Sligo asked. 'Because then the women would say, poor Byron, how interesting he looks in dying.'[68] Sligo's reply to this self-indulgent utterance was unfortunately not recorded. Like many of Byron's friends, he made allowances for the excesses of the poet's conduct and behaviour. Whatever criticisms he may have written or voiced in private, in public he tended to stand by the tempestuous bard. When Byron petulantly fumed at the lack of hospitality he encountered from the Bey of Corinth, that 'circumcised dog', Sligo agreed to deliver his letter of complaint to Stratford Canning, the British consul at Constantinople. 'I have delivered your letter concerning Nouri Bey to Mr Canning and I have conjoined my testimony to that contained in your letter the effect of which will be a certain reprimand to the aforesaid Nouri Bey.'[69]

It was to his Irish friend Byron would later turn when a controversy threatened his reputation, celebrity status and freedom. By 1813 the success of the first two cantos of *Childe Harold*, published in 1812 on his return to England, made Byron into the superstar of his age. His subsequent publication, *The Giaour*, was a fragmentary tale of romantic chivalry where the hero, a Christian infidel (Giaour), avenges the murder of a harem slave-girl, Leila, who was tied in a sack to be drowned for infidelity by her Muslim master. After its publication, rumours regarding his homosexual activities in Greece and elsewhere were spread by his spurned lover, Lady Caroline Lamb. To protect his image as the romantic heterosexual hero, Byron needed someone to verify that the story of *The Giaour* was based on his own personal experience: that he, in effect, was the 'Giaour upon his jet black stead' who had an affair with a slave-girl and who had bravely rescued her from her fate. In a letter dated 31 August 1813, Sligo agreed to support his friend's claim, although, as he had to admit, he had not personally witnessed Byron's brave challenge on the 'barbarous Turkish ideas with regard to women.'[70] While Sligo tried his best to verify his beleaguered friend's version of events, his letter was punctuated by provisos, as well as by ten lines heavily deleted, most likely by Byron, who claimed that they were inconsequential. Thomas Moore, Byron's most fervent apologist, in conversation with Sligo some years later about the affair, was forced to admit that 'Lord Sligo did not seem very accurate in his memory of the transaction.'[71]

In early October, with Lady Hester and Bruce, Sligo travelled to Constantinople. Before leaving Athens, with the *Pylades* no longer at his disposal, he made arrangements for the transportation of his antiquities back to Ireland at a later date. His Grecian treasure trove included 'acquisitions' numbering 1,059 vases; almost a hundred – mainly fragmentary – marbles; sepulchral monuments, including a sarcophagus (*in situ* in Westport House); a marble bas-relief, the head of an athlete; 'two mutilated hands holding folds of drapery … of the very best period of Greek art' – the finest piece, according to one expert account; and 'a few terracottas and painted vases, among which … two signed by the artist Nikosthenes'; some coins and other items.[72] Among his personal items were listed 'a box of Havannhah [*sic*] cigars … Albanian Woman's dress … 2 umbrellas … heron's feathers … oil of roses … 6 Turkish rifles … 3 Turkish swords … bag of tobacco … Lord Howe's sword', as well as the broken thermometer.[73]

As his bills mounted, he was obliged to withdraw an additional thousand pounds but, as he assured his mother, 'not for one farthing more than is absolutely necessary'[74] to pay the final instalment for the hire of the *Pylades* (albeit no longer in use), as well as for various bills associated with his excavations and the cost of bringing his treasure home. He dispensed with the services of his artist who, as he rather belatedly admitted, was 'no great loss for he has always been in the habit of drawing figures and never put his hand to a landscape before he set out with me, which I did not altogether discover at first'.[75] With most of his wardrobe, personal effects and antiquities stored in Athens, with a vague assurance to his 'Dearest Mother' 'not to buy any foolishness at Constantinople, if I can possible avoid it', her 'affectionate son' set off on the next stage of his eventful but increasingly expensive odyssey.[76]

Chapter 6

A Good Man

Whenever Lord Sligo returns to England I hope you will be kind to him. Poor man he only gets out of one scrape to get into another. The longer I know that man, the higher I think of the qualities of his heart, and the more I regret that those of his head do not equal that *feeling* which will be his ruin.

Lady Hester Stanhope

On 16 October 1810 Sligo, Lady Hester, Bruce, Meryon and their entourages departed from Athens for Turkey. Byron declined an invitation to accompany them, which no doubt pleased Lady Hester, perhaps even Sligo. Byron's moody presence was divisive. Even Bruce's affection seemed to have shifted temporarily from Lady Hester to the poet, who intimated that Bruce had made a sexual advance towards him on the eve of their departure. 'Seriously, I can't think for the soul of me what possessed Bruce,' Byron wrote to Hobhouse, 'but the truth is, he is a little chivalrous & romantic.'[1] Sligo seemed, by now, to have fallen under the spell of the older woman, whom he expansively described to George Caldwell 'as the first woman in the world & I think very few men equal in her talent & strength & rectitude of judgement. Her, Bruce & your humble ser[vant] make quite an inseparable trio.'[2]

Sligo's travels in Greece and Albania had yielded much, not in antiquities, but in terms of his personal development. And it had been a sharp lesson, the more negative results of which were still to emerge. In a foreign environment, at times dangerous and unpredictable, without the advantage of more mature advice or direction, he had to contend with the circumstances with which he was confronted, make his own decisions, good or bad, and abide by the consequences. 'I assure you I have gained a great deal of knowledge of the world since I have been out.'[3] At times too trusting in those in his employ, he was still naively improvident in business matters, as he freely admitted to his agent George Glendenning: 'owing ... to my inexperience in Money Matters I have this year spent so much that I am sure it must have much inconvenienced my Mother and you to have answered my drafts'.[4] But ever eager and engaged, in terms of his personal development, his sojourn abroad was proving a rewarding, if costly, experience.

Despite the extremely hot temperature, the discomfort of travel, the unaccustomed diet and his own expanding girth, as he related to his mother, he had 'never been in my life in better health'.[5] He had inherited his father's rheumatic condition, and while it had plagued him in Ireland and England, it appeared to dissipate in the warmer climate. Adventurous by nature, he showed little fear for his personal safety, either by land or sea, and was able to account for himself in whatever danger he encountered. Unlike many travellers of the period, Sligo was non-judgemental of the people and cultures he encountered and was open to be amazed or appalled with equanimity. Socially, his pleasant and unpretentious nature, as well as his ability to laugh at his own mistakes, made him a welcome addition, even in such critical company as that of Byron and Lady Hester Stanhope.

His party set sail from the Piraeus in a cramped, rat-infested, lice-ridden polacca which was taking a cargo of wheat, part of a tribute from his Athenian subjects, to the Ottoman sultan in

Constantinople. The single cabin, reserved for Lady Hester, had first to be fumigated. A few days out, contrary winds forced them to anchor off Cape Sunium. Taking advantage of the delay, Sligo and his entourage went ashore to visit the ruins of the Temple of Minerva. On reaching Zea, an island in the Cyclades, they were again forced to wait until the wind turned southerly. A 'tremendous row', as Sligo related, ensued when the captain attempted to take on twenty-five additional passengers. 'The ship was loaded with grain so high that we had only three feet of height and about twelve foot square in the hold for Bruce & I, Lady H. and Doctor & 12 servants to sleep in.'[6] In the stand-off, the captain threatened violence but Sligo and his companions stood resolute and eventually the new passengers were forced to disembark. So foul were the conditions in the hold that Sligo took to sleeping on deck, secure in the presence of his Albanian guard, given him by Veli Pasha, who 'with great knife drawn & his pistol cocked'[7] insisted on sleeping by his side. A favourable wind propelled them towards the Dardanelles. Accompanied by a school of dolphins, they sailed past Tenedos and the Troad and from the deck saw the tombs of Antiochus, Achilles and Patroclus. With a fresh breeze, they sailed up the Hellespont, past Sestos and Abydos, whose high fortifications bristled with immense artillery that had discharged five-hundred-weight balls in 1807 during the British attack on Constantinople. In the Sea of Marmora they joined a flotilla waiting, some for as long as four months, for a southerly wind to take them towards Constantinople. A severe storm forced them to seek shelter in a small cove. Seasick, exhausted and totally disillusioned with the ability of the captain and crew to get them to Constantinople, they decided to disembark.

Leaving Lady Hester, Meryon and the servants lodged in a local monastery, Sligo and Bruce rode 'without getting off our horses except to change them once ... being a ride of 22 hours'[8] to Constantinople on a road infested with robbers and deserters from the Turkish army. On arrival, they acquired the necessary firman from the Turkish foreign minister, Reis Effendi, to allow them to take up residence in Constantinople. Armed with the essential documentation and with additional bodyguards for protection, they rode back along the coast, 'which I think,' as Sligo ruefully admitted, 'was no insignificant effort for so fat a man as I.'[9] On the advice of Effendi, they opted to travel by sea back to Constantinople in two open galleys 'as clean, as trim and as richly gilded as a nobleman's barge on the Thames'.[10] On 3 November at eleven o'clock in the morning they watched Constantinople rise from the shore of the Bosphorous. City of legend and history, of gilded seraglios, imperial mosques and minarets, markets and bazaars, hammans and fountains and 100,000 plastered wood-framed houses, it was crowned by the cupola of the impressive cathedral of Hagia Sophia.

Landing at Topkhana, the principal landing stairs for the suburb of Pera, in the pitch black of the night, they followed a porter with a single lantern who led them through foul, narrow streets and unpaved laneways heaped with rubbish. The area was notorious for packs of stray dogs who howled and snarled at them as they made their way towards their lodgings. So that Lady Hester and Bruce might enjoy some privacy, Sligo offered Meryon a room in his own lodgings which, coincidentally, had previously been occupied by Byron and Hobhouse. 'I find that I inhabit the same house that you did the Signora Onuphrio's,' he wrote to Byron, 'opposite some very pretty girls who are always at the window. I have a flirtation with one of them tho' I don't know her to speak to.'[11]

He found Constantinople dangerous, restrictive, 'infernally stupid' and very cold. 'I am obliged to sit sometimes a whole day with my legs wrapped up in a huge pelisse.'[12] At war with Russia, Turkey was also afflicted by much internal dissension. Within thirty miles of the capital a petty war raged between two provincial governors, regardless of Sultan Mahmud II, who had also to contend with the infamous janissaries, a turbulent armed militia. Foreigners were restricted to non-Muslim areas of the city across the Bosphorus, where the cost of living was prohibitively expensive.

> Constantinople is a very curious place to look at but the stupidest place to stay in .... In the first place the cold is excessive and in the next there is no society whatever here. Were it not for Lady Hester I should not stop a week but I dine there every day and that makes the evening pass pleasantly.[13]

Diplomatic missions from various countries, as well as wealthy merchants, were located in Pera, together with dynastic naturalised Europeans. This social class provided the indispensable 'dragomen' who acted as go-betweens and fixers for Europeans with the court and government of the Sultan. The centre of commerce and political intrigue, Pera comprised a cosmopolitan, multi-lingual and multi-religious society. Across the water in Stamboul (Stromboli), inhabited by the subjects of the Sultan, strict Muslim law and custom prevailed. From the high minarets, five times daily, the sonorous chant of muezzins called the faithful to prayer from bazaar, coffee house, market stall and hamam. The horror of public executions, with the decapitated heads of criminals exhibited in the palace gardens or handed around 'like a pineapple', as Lady Hester observed, whirling and howling dervishes, scavenging dogs, street entertainers and prostitutes, both male and female, existed alongside the splendour.

In the expatriate quarters, regardless of international wars and allegiances, the multicultural inhabitants mingled and socialised. Some familiar faces from Athens were already established, including Gally Knight, Fazakerley, James Morier, former Consul General in Albania, and Stratford Canning, British Consul at the Sublime

Porte of the Sultan. News of the war with France, as well as social gossip, was eagerly received and shared. 'Ferdinand the 7th (they say here) is going to be married to a sister in law of Bonaparte's .... England is going to the devil as fast as it can ... Lucien Bonaparte is gone to England ... the treaty for exchange of prisoners is broken off. I am afraid that their number will be much increased soon by the capture of Ld. Wellington,' Sligo informed Byron.[14]

The English minister Stratford Canning entertained them at his house. Hoping to obtain a passport to France, Lady Hester contrived to form a friendship with the French chargé d'affaires in Pera. This led to a bitter estrangement between her and the 'young, inexperienced, full of zeal, but full of prejudice' English minister.[15] Sligo, however, continued to enjoy Canning's hospitality, who obtained a firman for him to visit the Troad and Smyrna. The firman was, inadvertently, forwarded to Athens from where it was redirected by Byron.

In Constantinople Sligo found it more difficult to live within his allowance. 'Living is twice as dear here as in Greece .... Servants cannot I'm sure live on their board wages of one Guinea a week indeed I paid much more for them for a week until they should look about them a little.'[16] His promise to economise was also severely tested by the irresistible array of exotic merchandise on display in the local bazaars. 'It is a constant source of mortification to me to walk the streets for there are so many delightful things to buy that I am obliged every day before I go out to look at my account book and see the drafts I have drawn since I have been out.'[17] The area around his lodgings in Pera, however 'dreary and ugly', was also dangerous, with army deserters lying in wait for foreigners with robbery on their mind. Cooped up in his lodgings, he passed the time by 'reading or writing & smoking ... and feasting on luxuries ... eating nothing but wild boar, Roebuck, Bustard Pheasants and woodcocks' brought back from his occasional hunting forays with Meryon and Bruce in the surrounding countryside. 'The only thing

I miss … is butter.'[18] He acquired a white poodle for company and 'a wild dog which I discovered about 8 days after his birth on an uninhabited island'.[19]

By now his difficulty with the Royal Navy had developed into a full-scale investigation. Rumours of his possible indictment by the Admiralty reached the expatriate community in Greece. 'The Marquess of Sligo is in a great scrape about his kidnapping the seamen,' Byron informed Hobhouse. 'I, who know him, do not think him so culpable as the Navy are determined to make him. He is a good man.'[20] But the implications of the situation did not seem to fully register with Sligo and, as Lady Hester noted to Canning, 'it has been difficult to make him attach sufficient importance to it'.[21] His letter to Captain Sprainger from Constantinople, which was later produced in evidence against him, confirmed Lady Hester's observation. Redolent with the bravado of youth and privilege, because Captain Sprainger 'had treated him like a gentleman', Sligo acknowledged that during the voyage he had indeed discovered some navy deserters but that he had intended to send them ashore at the first opportunity and whatever expenses he might incur on their repatriation he would have 'put down to the score of humanity and glory in it'. As for the captain of the *Active* who had intercepted his ship off Messina, and who had lodged a formal complaint against him, Sligo rashly intimated that 'if the business was brought into court … he should do his best to defend himself; and if he did not succeed, he had an ample fortune and could pay the fines'.[22] His cavalier attitude, his status as a peer and his royal connections, however, left the Admiralty unimpressed.

By mid-December, restless and bored, Sligo considered travelling to Persia, crossing the desert in a caravan to Aleppo and Palmyra and from there through Syria into Egypt. But, following a severe snowstorm, the road via Trebizond to Persia became impassable and the alternative route via Baghdad, owing to the rebellion of a local pasha, was too dangerous. Fazakerley and Knight pressed him to go with them as far as Aleppo. A letter from Governor Oakes, informing Sligo of the arrival of a warrant for his investiture as a Knight of St Patrick, made him consider returning to Malta, as 'it might be thought contemptuous of the King's favour did I not go immediately to receive the investiture'.[23] An outbreak of fever in Carthagina with resultant quarantine restrictions in Malta forced him to cancel the trip.

When correspondence from his mother suddenly ceased, Sligo became worried about her welfare. His worries were compounded when Lady Hester received news from the Duchess of Richmond that Lady Sligo had to undertake a sudden journey to Westport. 'Left to rack my brain with the thought of what it can have been that could have taken her there: amusement I am sure could not be the cause, I can only attribute it to some unpleasant business going on which required her presence.' He resolved 'to take a ship and pack off immediately' to Athens, collect his belongings and return to Ireland.[24] On Lady Hester's advice that letters might already be in transit, reluctantly he agreed to wait. A letter from George Glendenning finally arrived with news about his estate and 'a most melancholy statement of my affairs'. A few days later he received 'three letters of my Dearest Mother', for which he was 'inexpressively delighted' and greatly relieved.[25]

The letters brought news of his estate, local and international events and much gossip. The reason for his mother's sudden departure to Westport was also revealed when, following a raid on the arms depot of the local militia, she went there to confer with the local authorities. In answer to her concerns about his health, he confessed, 'I was just (where the blot is in the other sheet) going to tell you that with respect to Rheumatism I had hoped that I had quite got rid of it but alas that illusion was done away at the instant' when a return attack necessitated him 'much against my will to put on a flannel waistcoat for the first time since I left England.' Affectionately, he ribbed her about her management of his affairs.

'I am very glad you have so much to do for me, I am sure it will do you a great deal of good & and keep your mind from brooding, I am, however, quite jealous of Westport for having you there when I am not there too.' About her concern regarding his proposed plan to visit the East Indies, which she understood from good authority was a very dangerous undertaking, he scoffed at the opinions of such '*Bullites* … how can they possibly know half so much about it as I do who am on the spot & have conversed with five hundred people who have made the same journey.' In any event he had given up the idea, not from any fear on his part, he assured her, but because of the inordinate time it would take to get there. He gave instructions about the hiring and firing of servants, planting 50,000 trees at Westport, new furniture he had purchased before his departure, including 'a new grate for the dining room'. Despite his mother's best efforts, his financial situation had deteriorated to an alarming extent. With bravado, he assured her that, on his return, he could settle his debts 'in a month by raising money in England tho' you *can't*'. But 'Mother Dearest' knew better and from her personal funds continued to meet her son's many drafts without reproach.[26]

In Constantinople, Sligo became acquainted with a down-at-heel diplomat, Count Wilhelm Moritz Ludolf, the Sicilian ambassador to the Porte. Of German origin, the ambassador was married to the daughter of a dragomen family in Istanbul. The ambassador, according to Sligo, had refused 'the most brilliant offers from Bonaparte'. Forfeiting his estates in Naples, because of his attachment to the English, he was 'rewarded by the Queen of Sicily for this unexampled conduct by not paying him one Farthing of his salary'. Consequently the ambassador found himself in such straitened circumstances in Constantinople that he was unable to pay even his 'washing bill'. Sligo and Bruce anonymously sent him fifty pounds 'in a way that will as little as possible hurt his delicacy.'[27] Sligo further promised to take the ambassador's son,

Joseph Constantine William John Ludolf, a former officer in the Austrian imperial guard, back to England and endeavour to obtain a commission for him in the German Legion.

His mother's safety assured and his investiture with the Order of St Patrick postponed because of the quarantine, Sligo felt free to continue his journey. When Lady Hester with 'her faithful squire Bruce'[28] decided to decamp from their expensive and dreary surroundings at Pera for a more spacious house in Therapia, a village ten miles along the Bosphorus with magnificent views of the Asiatic coastline, he accepted her invitation to join them. Lady Hester had been 'most alarmingly ill' from anxiety resulting from a letter she received from Crauford Bruce. Her response to his criticisms, that she 'never had or ever will have further claims upon your son than any woman he might have picked up on the streets',[29] hardly served to mollify her lover's father. The letter was followed by another from Hester's brother James, full of self-righteous indignation about her conduct and challenging her lover to a duel. The effect of the letters brought extra pressure on their relationship and the lovers agreed to live apart for a time. As Lady Hester confided to Sligo, she was under no illusion that her affair with Bruce was temporary. To ease the tension between them, Sligo invited Bruce to accompany him on a journey to Smyrna, Ephesus and the Troad.

On the first day into the journey Sligo's rheumatic condition flared into 'a pretty smart attack in the Muscles of the Abdomen'.[30] The pain was so severe that it made it impossible for him to sit on horseback. It was decided that Bruce would continue to Smyrna while Sligo returned to Therapia 'to be nursed by Lady Hester Stanhope who is so kind to me that you have no idea of it,' he informed his mother.[31] The Marchioness's reaction to the news that her son was sharing an intimate interlude with the woman who was the talk of every drawing room in England is open to conjecture. Whether their friendship developed into something more at this time is uncertain: that Sligo hoped it might but was rebuffed by

Lady Hester is, perhaps, more likely. With Lady Hester's nursing and Doctor Meryon's prescription of 'Turkish vapour baths',[32] Sligo recovered. Leaving one of his Albanians, 'a very reprobate fellow' given to 'firing off his pistols in the street', and his dog to guard Lady Hester, he followed Bruce to Smyrna.[33]

A 'must-see' on the grand tour, associated with Amazons, Alexander the Great and King Tantalus, Smyrna (Izmir) was rich in legend and archaeological remains. Considered by Christians as the site of one of the Seven Churches of the Revelation, it was also a place of worship for other religious denominations. By the ninth century the ancient city had developed into one of the foremost ports on the busy trade route between Anatolia and the Aegean. In the fifteenth century it became a strategic possession of the Ottoman Empire and continued under its control until the twentieth century when, after a brief occupation by the Greeks, it was virtually destroyed in the Greek–Turkish war and its mainly Greek Armenian population massacred.

Arriving in Symra, Sligo settled into life among the expatriate community, many of whom he knew from Athens and Constantinople. There was much to see and, according to his journal, he did not spare himself. Spending up to ten hours in the saddle by day, riding 'at full gallop' through the gently undulating landscape dotted with fig and almond trees, he climbed Mount Pagus with its ruined Acropolis and visited Ephesus, some forty miles to the north. He participated in the social outlets on offer in Smyrna, from horse racing, 'a masked ball which Ld P.th [Lord Plymouth] and I gave [and] was very fully attended', dinner parties and masquerades to gaming – although, in that regard, as he informed Byron, 'all the people being Turks and Turkesses we had very little fun'.[34] His plan to travel overland to Persia, via Tokat and Yerevan, a journey he reckoned to be of thirty-nine days' duration, followed by a nine-day trek to Tabriz and thence to Teheran and the court of the King of Persia, was destined to be abandoned.

By March 1811 news of the Regency crises in England filtered through to Smyrna. 'The King is dangerously ill,' Sligo related to Byron, 'and the Prince of Wales is appointed sole regent .... The Ministry are changed – Percival out, Lord Wellesley & Grenville in. We have lost six frigates at the Isle of France and a line of battleships in the North Sea, in short everything is going on as badly as possible.'[35] News that the Admiralty had issued legal proceedings against him also arrived. Blaming Sligo's misguided actions on 'the lies of traders', Lady Hester pleaded his case with Stratford Canning. 'I trust the naval men will hear reason, as I am sure he intended no disrespect to the service.'[36] When, out of the blue, the *Pylades* put into port in Smyrna from Malta, it appeared like a harbinger of impending doom. Bringing with it post from England, including two letters for Byron, one, as Sligo informed him, from 'your fair friend at Malta [i.e. Constance Spencer Smith with whom the poet had enjoyed a brief dalliance on his way to Athens in 1809] and the other from your servant Fletcher' who had preceded his master to England.[37] As well as Sligo's impending difficulties with the navy, the letters also brought word that Prince George Augustus had been appointed Regent. In the expectation of his more liberal stance on the issue of Catholic Emancipation, Sligo determined to hasten home to lend his support. 'You will see me shortly in Athens for I intend to go that way home,' he informed Byron, who was also on the point of returning home to try to save what remained of his inheritance.[38]

Taking his leave of Lady Hester and Michael Bruce, Sligo promised to intercede on their behalf with Bruce's father. 'It was with much regret that Lady Hester saw Lord Sligo depart,' Meryon attested. 'She always spoke of the qualities of his heart with commendation, and her friendship for him ever continued unaltered.'[39] Anxious for his welfare, she sought what was best for him and, while at times critical of his impulsiveness and irresponsibility, 'yet,' as she noted, 'he does not want sense in many things – far from it .... If he marries some pleasing, sensible girl, he may become a very respectable character. If not, he will surely be duped by some designing woman or other, and his character, as well as his fortune, will be gone in a few years.'[40] Sligo presented Lady Hester with a gold snuff box as a token of his affection. The gift was subsequently one of the few items that survived shipwreck off the coast of Rhodes when Lady Hester and Bruce were en route to Egypt. Years later she was forced to part with the snuff box, the only item of value she then possessed, to repay the Pasha of Damascus for some kindness received. Despite his promise to join her on her travels through the Middle East, Sligo was not to meet the object of his 'admiration, wonder and compassion' again.[41] They continued to correspond after the break-up of her relationship with Michael Bruce and during Lady Hester's subsequent nomadic wanderings throughout the Middle East.

Turning her back on England, Lady Hester would finally settle among the Druse community in a dilapidated monastery on Mount Lebanon, near the village of Joun where, immortalised as 'The Nun of Lebanon' in 1839, she died alone. Sligo kept her letters in Westport House. In 1846, after his death, being 'very yellow from having been smoked before they left Syria or the Holy Land', upon a request 'from a gentleman who is writing a book' Sligo's widow determined 'not to send [him] any that the late Lady Hester Stanhope would not wished to have published if she were still alive'.[42]

On 21 April 1811 Sligo, accompanied by his new friend Count Ludolf, sailed from Constantinople through the Sea of Marmora, past Gallipoli, where they encountered a violent squall 'and a sharp touch of an earthquake'. On 5 May they anchored in the Piraeus from where they went by horseback to visit Marathon and from there across the plain to see 'the tomb of the Persians'.[43] Returning to Athens, Sligo made a final visit to the Acropolis and bade farewell to his Greek friends. On 14 May he set sail for Argos, where 'we went ashore and carried off the three columns which lay on the beach'.[44] With Veli Pasha's gift safely stowed, he finally set sail for Malta.

Sligo linked up with Byron in Malta, at the Lazaretto, the quarantine hospital on Manoel Island in the Marsamxett Harbour. Established by the Knights Templar in the sixteenth century, the Lazaretto continued to function as a place of containment where passengers from countries where contagious disease was rampant underwent a period of quarantine. There they spent the time in various stages of boredom before being allowed ashore. Byron immortalised his detention in the lines:

> Adieu, thou damndest quarantine,
> That gave me fever and the spleen....

Suffering from a relapse of malarial fever which he had contacted in Greece, Byron was installed with his lover, Nicolo Giraud, in a house on the Strada Real in Valetta, while at the same time trying to disentangle himself from the persistent embrace of his former lover Constance Spencer Smith, whose letter Sligo had forwarded to him from Smyrna. Both men were returning to England to face personal difficulties. Byron's financial circumstances had deteriorated to such a degree that his ancestral home, Newstead Abbey, was threatened by bailiffs. Not knowing 'where to raise a shilling ... without a hope and almost without a desire ... embarrassed in my private affairs, indifferent to public, solitary without the wish to be social, a little enfeebled by a succession of fevers', it was a pale and depressed shadow of the former romantic hero who embarked from Malta.[45] Sligo, by contrast, although facing demons of his own, gave little indication regarding his impending trouble with the Admiralty or of his financial difficulties and served his time in the Lazaretto with forbearance.

Byron secured passage to England on a naval frigate which was returning from action against the French and Italian navies off the Dalmatian coast. For Sligo, by now a *persona non grata* with the

British naval authorities, passage was to prove more difficult to secure: 'No man of war will have anything to say to me now so that I must get home as well as I can.'[46] In a letter to Byron on the eve of his departure from Malta, Sligo wrote from his place of confinement 'to wish you a pleasant journey & to beg that you will inform all good people who may enquire after me that I am on my way home'.[47] He further requested him 'on your arrival in London to send to my rooms in Albany Buildings and say that I was to sail about a fortnight after you, and that they may prepare for me'.[48]

On his release from the Lazaretto, and despite his impending difficulties with the Admiralty, on 11 June, by special dispensation, Sligo was invested with the Ribbon of St Patrick by Governor Oakes. As he promised, he took the opportunity to intercede with the governor on behalf of Lady Hester and Michael Bruce. Oakes subsequently wrote to the couple to reassure them of his continued friendship and offered, in whatever way he could, to further their 'comfort and happiness'.[49] For the sake of propriety, the governor urged Lady Hester to accept Bruce's proposal of marriage, an offer, however, she chose to decline.

Sligo eventually secured a passage from Malta and, accompanied by Ludolf, arrived back in England in early August 1811 after an absence of almost eighteen months.

John Denis Browne, 1st Marquess of Sligo (*Westport House, Co. Mayo*)

Louisa Catherine Howe, 1st Marchioness of Sligo
(*Westport House, Co. Mayo*)

Elizabeth Kelly, daughter of Denis Kelly, Jamaica and Lisduff, Co. Galway (*Westport House, Co. Mayo*)

Howe Peter Browne, 4th Earl of Altamont (*Westport House*)

Hester Catherine de Burgh, 2nd Marchioness of Sligo
(*Westport House, Co. Mayo*)

Children of 2nd Marquess of Sligo (*Westport House, Co. Mayo*)

Westport Harbour, 1818 (*Westport House, Co. Mayo*)

Westport House, 1760 (*Westport House, Co. Mayo*)

The Cyprian's Ball
and *The Ton*

GEORGY'S DELIGHT.

George IV and Lady
Conyngham (*British Museum*)

Lord Byron

Roman Sarcophagus, First Century A.D. excavated in 1810 by 2nd Marquess of Sligo in Greece (*Westport House, Co. Mayo. Photo: author*)

Chapter 7

Jailbird

The country expects that you should receive such an admonition as may operate for a useful example and which may confirm that boasted principle of the English Constitution – that no rank, however high, no fortune, however ample, no regrets, however sincere, can prevent the due administration and enforcement of justice.

Sir William Scott

Resident in her house in London, Louisa was overjoyed at the return of her 'darling child'. As well as trailing a string of debts in his wake, the *Pylades* incident was beginning to take on a more sinister aspect than either mother or son could have anticipated. Despite his royal connections, status and relationship to one of England's most decorated naval heroes, the Admiralty determined to pursue the case against the Marquess of Sligo to its ultimate conclusion. The seriousness of the crime was beginning to excite London society. 'Lord Sligo has got into a very indiscreet scrape which is likely to be tried at the Old Bailey,' Lord Auckland predicted to Lord Grenville, leader of the Whig party.[1]

With the sanguinity of youth, Sligo blithely put his impending troubles on the shelf. It was a hot and humid summer in London. His friends were already dispersed: Byron's mother had died and the poet was at his estate in Nottinghamshire. The first literary result of his travels, *Childe Harold's Pilgrimage*, was being prepared for publication. John Cam Hobhouse, who had opted for a career in the military, had embarked with his regiment to Ireland. Charles Skinner Matthews had drowned in the Cam river at Cambridge, with much speculation whether it was suicide or a tragic accident. Parliament was in recess. The political situation in England was in a state of flux as the Prince Regent discovered that playing the king was far more onerous than he imagined. The Tory government, led by Spencer Perceval, wary of the Prince's Whig leanings, thwarted his efforts to establish a regency with unrestricted powers, while the Whigs were becoming increasingly disillusioned by the Prince's turncoat antics regarding Catholic Emancipation and reform.

The Prince's amorous frolics were surpassed only by those of his estranged wife, Caroline, Princess of Wales. Her husband's attempts to have their marriage dissolved resulted in the establishment of a Commission of Enquiry in 1806 to investigate alleged improprieties at the Princess's home in Blackheath. In the event, to the Regent's fury, the enquiry proved inconclusive. In June 1811 at Carlton House, already up to his portly neck in debt, the Prince Regent held an ostentatious celebration of his regency, costing £120,000, which further infuriated public opinion. The Regent sought solace in the arms of his latest mistress, Lady Hertford, and retreated to his pavilion at Brighton.

Accompanied by his mother, her niece Marianne Curzon and Count Ludolf, Sligo also retreated to his estate. After the free-wheeling, carefree months of travel, reconnecting with his responsibilities proved a difficult transition. His father had been a constant presence at Westport, a respected figurehead, his finger on every aspect of his extensive domain. His untried son was hardly known. The administration of a large estate, with thousands of tenants, tenants-at-will, leaseholders and mortgagees, spread over counties Mayo and Galway, together with the Jamaican estates, was an enormous undertaking, evident from the surviving deeds, conveyances, leases, judgements, rental and account ledgers, trusteeships, indentures, bonds, assignments, wills, codicils, probates, marriage settlements, family trusts and other documents.

Leaving such mundane tasks in the hands of his agent and uncle, Sligo passed the time sailing on Clew Bay, fishing the well-stocked rivers and lakes of his estate, hunting and shooting wild deer and game across stretches of moorland and bog. His cousin Marianne Curzon, an accomplished caricaturist, drew many humorous sketches of the family during this time. One at Aasleagh Lodge, dated September 1811, depicts an overweight Sligo feasting at a table, oblivious of flood waters which have invaded the room, while his companion, Ludolf, looks on in obvious discomfort. Overseeing his horse-breeding enterprise and racing on his new track at Ballyknock passed the autumn months. A member of the Irish Turf Club since 1809 (he was appointed senior steward in 1812), Sligo is recorded as being 'a noble addition of great importance for the history of breeding, racing and reputation of Irishmen on the English turf, as well as for the [Irish] Turf Club itself'.[2] A brief encounter with 'a fair lady of easy virtue at Westport' brought repercussions when, as he wrote, she thought 'it convenient to make me contribute to the maintenance of her child. It was the greatest piece of mischief I ever saw as she was one of the most abandoned sort and I never saw her but once in my life.'[3]

During the summer months he became embroiled in a family dispute that had been brewing during his absence abroad. The origins lay in an agreement concluded between Sligo's father and James Mahon, brother-in-law of Denis Browne (and also a cousin of the Marquess), an impoverished lawyer from Castlegar. In 1808, a few months before he died, to alleviate Mahon's financial difficulties, the Marquess had granted him the living of the Deanery of Dromore in County Tyrone, on condition that if the income came to £2,200 a year (then thought likely), Mahon would contribute a thousand guineas 'towards the support of the Parliamentary interest' and also pay £500 a year to the Marquess's brother, Denis Browne, to defray the 'heavy expense attending the education of his sons in England'.[4] During Sligo's absence abroad, Mahon and Denis Browne had come to blows over the terms of the agreement. Browne insisted that the money was to be paid every year, while Mahon contended that it was a once-off payment. Angered and embarrassed by the affair, unlike his father, Sligo had little taste for ecclesiastical jobbing. 'I assure you to alter the system. Jobbing is at an End with me … and I don't care if I lose the county by it,' he impetuously avowed.[5] To bring the unseemly family dispute to an end, he determined to personally reimburse his uncle. But the issue also smacked of his uncle's usurpation of his authority, something he had no intention of permitting. 'I assure you,' he informed his mother, 'I am not so weak or yielding a character as you imagine and that right or wrong no soul but yourself shall ever meddle with my affairs.' If his uncle refused to accept his authority and act 'in a subordinate capacity', then he should 'give up his seat & return into the country'.[6] Many such clashes were destined to occur before Sligo brought his influential uncle to heel.

In the spring of 1812 Sligo returned to London to attend parliament. Trusted by neither the Whigs nor the Tories, the Prince Regent struggled to form a government that would accommodate his objectives: to pursue the increasingly unpopular war in the Spanish Peninsula and to sideline the issue of Catholic Emancipation. The assassination in May of Prime Minister Spencer Perceval in the lobby of the House of Commons increased the political instability. Eventually a new government under Lord Liverpool was cobbled together with Irish-born Lord Castlereagh as Foreign Minister, leader of the House of Commons and, in effect, the real power in the cabinet.

The situation obtaining in Britain was daunting for the new government. As well as the ongoing war with France, food scarcities, inflated prices, lack of employment, the imposition of higher taxes and an upsurge in lawlessness plagued the country. Wellington's army endured terrible slaughter in the Spanish Peninsula and anti-war resentment seethed. Taking advantage of the weakened state of its former colonial master, America declared war in retaliation for Britain's trade embargo. A glimmer of hope appeared on the horizon when Napoleon moved the theatre of war northwards to rouse the supine might of Russia and removed thousands of French troops from Spain. The tide began to turn in Wellington's favour and by May he had taken Madrid.

In the English midlands weavers and knitters rioted when their livelihoods were threatened by mechanisation. An anti-mechanisation movement – Luddism – spread to the cotton industry in Lancashire and to the woollen industry in Yorkshire. A draconian Frame Work Bill, which made the destruction of the new 'wide-frame' machines a capital offence, came before parliament. In the House of Lords, on the crest of a wave of adulation following the publication of the two first cantos of *Childe Harold*, Byron used his maiden speech to oppose the bill. Having personally witnessed the riots in Nottingham, he gave full vent to his condemnation of the government's proposed legislation. While his impassioned words failed to stop the enactment of the bill, Sligo warmly congratulated him on his speech, which 'has set the whole town talking. I have just heard the highest eulogium on it which I assure you gave me the greatest pleasure,' as did the fact that Byron's second speech in the Lords was in support of Catholic Emancipation.[7]

Undeterred by his difficulty with the Admiralty, on his return to London Sligo reacquainted himself with the *bon ton*. On 16 April, for a bet of one thousand guineas, he accepted a challenge to determine the quickest route from London to Holyhead. Driving his own coach via Shrewsbury, and despite, as one newspaper reported, 'a considerable delay ... by the breaking down of his chaise', he completed the distance of 270 miles in a record time of

35 hours, 'expressing his confidence that he can perform the same journey in 32 hours'.[8] The carriage whips he used for the challenge are preserved in Westport House. The Prince Regent's 'Carlton House Set' was the apogee of society and Sligo was a favoured guest at the many sumptuous dinner parties, suppers and banquets presided over by the Prince Regent. He also enthusiastically participated in the debauchery that occurred within its walls, embarking on at least one affair with the wife of an acquaintance which, as he later confided to his mother, to relieve her 'from any apprehension of anything in that quarter', would not lead to any 'scrape' because both he and his paramour had agreed 'what line of conduct I should pursue with her'.[9]

Parallel to the world of aristocratic immorality, the demi-monde also flourished. Within its ranks, Sligo found what he hoped to be a more permanent relationship. Rosalie Pauline (Cherie) Pacquot was, ostensibly, a French ballerina but, as Byron more shrewdly observed, 'to my certain knowledge was actually educated from her birth for her profession' as a courtesan.[10] She was also known to some of Sligo's society friends, including Lord Lowther. But regardless of her past, Sligo fell head-over-heels for his 'Cherie' for whom, as he admitted, he 'was capable of making almost any sacrifice and in whom I was literally wrapped up initially'.[11] Their affair, which started in the summer of 1812, was short-lived but intense. Educated in the art of seduction and possessing a certain exoticism, to judge from her surviving letters, Pauline was also well-versed in emotional blackmail. Like most wealthy patrons, Sligo provided her (and her mother) with a house, at 40 Claridge Street, as well as paying her regular maintenance during the course of their relationship. However, as he later found out, he was not the only 'client' of his 'Cherie'. His former tutor in Cambridge, George Caldwell, subsequently found evidence of Pauline's unfaithfulness which, as Sligo admitted, 'turned me so completely sick that I could not eat one morsel all day'.[12] In July 1813 she gave birth to a son and claimed Sligo as the father. Byron, however, was of the opinion, as he informed Lady Melbourne, that 'malice says he [Sligo] divides the honours of paternity with the editor of the *Courier*'.[13] Despite doubts as to the child's paternity, he was christened William Henry Browne. Sligo continued to support mother and child long after the affair ended, with a substantial payment of £1,000 annually, payable in four instalments, provided Pauline continued to reside in England. Later disillusioned by Pauline's unfaithfulness, and in an attempt 'to have the whole thing off his mind', he amended the method of payment to one annual instalment.[14]

By December 1813 Pauline and her mother were back at the opera house in search of new clients. 'I went to my box at Convent [*sic*] Garden,' Byron related to Hobhouse, 'and my delicacy felt a little shocked at seeing Sligo's mistress … sitting with her mother … in a private box opposite.'[15] Observing that the female audience in the theatre was equally divided between professional courtesans and the 'intriquantes' of a higher social status, 'now, where lay the difference,' he mused, 'between her [Pauline] and Mama and Lady XX and daughter, except that the last may enter Carlton and any other house and the two first are limited to the opera and the bawd house.'[16] Somewhat cruelly Byron also wondered if Sligo's growing corpulence had led to the break-up: 'heaven knows what is to become of any [of us] … if our masculine ugliness is to be an obstacle.'[17] Sligo's mother attempted to get her son's mistress to 'relieve herself from the expense of having the child by sending it to me. I would give anything to get hold of it,' intending to place him with a suitable family as was customary. Sligo, however, loyally refused to 'consent to her [Pauline] being deprived of the person of her child …. I cannot so soon forget my feelings towards her as to give her that misery.'[18]

When Pauline later formed a new relationship, she unfairly accused Sligo of undermining her new liaison and 'taking away the only protection I had in the world. You will never see me nor hear anything more of me. You have betrayed the confidence I placed in your heart. I thought that at least I had a friend in you but I find you a most cruel, cruel enemy.'[19] Despite her unfaithfulness, Sligo found it difficult 'to forget my feelings towards her .... As long as I can keep out of her way ... I dread anything like falling in with her again.'[20] On learning that Pauline had reverted to her previous 'occupation' at the Opera House and to 'her appearing light-hearted and not regretting my departure, I can only say that that has been the most comfortable news'.[21]

His affair with Pauline Pacquot, however, left a lasting impression. Sligo named one of his horses, which he coincidentally purchased from his friend Lord Lowther, after his former mistress. Later in 1816, when he eventually found himself a 'suitable' wife, Sligo confided to 'his dearest Mother' how his intended bore 'the most extraordinary likeness to Pauline that I ever saw'.[22] His presumed son, William Henry Browne, died at four years of age in 1817 at 19 Rue de la Paix in Paris, where Pauline returned to live. The child's death certificate is preserved among Sligo's papers.

On Wednesday 16 December 1812, as London was en fête with news of the defeat of Napoleon's army and his inglorious retreat from Moscow, the public trial of the Marquess of Sligo opened at the Old Bailey. He was charged 'with unlawfully receiving on board his ship William Elden, a seaman in the King's service, and detaining, concealing and secreting him'. Further charges of 'enticing and persuading to desert the said seaman', with 'receiving the said Elden knowing him to have deserted' and a more serious charge of assault and false imprisonment of other seamen in the king's service, were also entered.[23] Because of his youth, status and family connections, as well as the nature of the crime, it was the trial of the decade. The courtroom was packed with many society celebrities, including the Duke of Clarence, brother of the Prince Regent, as well as members of the press eager to report the novelty of the public trial of a peer of the realm. Sligo's uncle Denis Browne, his cousin Lord Desart and Mayo neighbour Colonel Dillon accompanied his mother to the Old Bailey. Such was the importance of the case that Lord Ellenborough and Baron Thompson were appointed to assist the Admiralty judge, Sir William Scott, younger brother of the chancellor, Lord Eldon. The Attorney General prosecuted while counsel for the Marquess of Sligo was in the hands of the Dickensian-named firm of Dauncey, Dampier & Scarlett.

Sir William Scott charged the jury and the trial commenced at two o'clock in the afternoon. Sligo was not obliged to stand in the dock but was permitted to sit with his legal counsel. The seriousness of his situation, which he had so blithely erased over the preceding eighteen months, was further compromised by the letter he had rashly written to Captain Sprainger from Constantinople. The penal system obtaining in Britain was notoriously merciless and severe. Crimes such as arson, forgery and burglary were punishable by hanging, while transportation, branding, flogging and imprisonment were meted out for minor crimes. Treason was a capital offence and one on which His Majesty's case against Sligo bordered. Sir William Scott was known to be a strict judge and a determined defender of maritime law. Sligo's trial was sandwiched between two cases on which Sir William had pronounced the death sentence, unmoved by recommendations of mercy by the jury.

In his affidavit, Sligo admitted he had concealed the seamen from Captain Sprainger but that, on their initial arrival on board his ship, 'on his oath declared that he had no knowledge whatsoever at that time that any of the men had deserted'. He was 'deeply sensible of the error and folly of his conduct and had no other excuse to offer than his own rashness, indiscretion and mistaken feelings'.[24] The defending counsel informed the court that their client wished to plead guilty to part of the charges and not guilty to the rest. From the bench Lord Ellenborough ordered that the defendant must plead guilty or not guilty to all the charges or none and a guilty plea was thereby entered on the defendant's behalf.

The prosecution described the offences as being 'of the greatest magnitude'.[25] In his evidence, Captain Sprainger of HMS *Warrior*, who had helped Sligo fit out the *Pylades* in Malta, told how he became suspicious that two of his men were on board the defendant's ship and of the latter's subsequent denial 'on his honour'. He produced the letter received from the defendant from Constantinople which confirmed his suspicions and which also demonstrated the defendant's cavalier attitude to his crime. William Elden, a gunner's mate from HMS *Montague*, testified that while on shore leave in Malta he had fallen in with 'two persons in livery' in the employ of Lord Sligo.[26] They had plied him with drink and, on waking from his stupor, he found himself on board the *Pylades*, which by then was under sail. When the ship was searched, Lord Sligo compelled him to hide below deck and subsequently refused him permission to leave the ship at Messina. At Patmos, while on shore leave, he claimed the defendant had abandoned him and his mates, leaving them without money or clothes.

In defence, Mr Dauncey stated that it was not his intention to absolve the conduct of his client, who admitted having navy deserters on his ship and of not giving them up on discovering their true origin. He contested, however, that his client, 'a nobleman of high rank and grandson of Lord Howe who had carried to so high a pitch the glory of that Navy', had neither seduced nor knowingly received sailors from the Royal Navy aboard his ship at Malta and neither had he deserted them at Patmos.[27] On the contrary, 'every signal of departure had been given to these men; the flag was hoisted, two or three guns were fired and the vessel made tacks off and on during the greatest part of the night, to give them an opportunity of coming aboard, if they chose.'²⁸ When the defendant refused some of them passage at Scio, he did not, as was alleged, abandon them without the means of support: 'their clothes were handed to them and they received their wages, though they were entitled to none, having broken their contract'.²⁹ His client, the lawyer contended, was at the time 'a very young man, newly come from the seats of learning and education and was hardly of age'.³⁰ Furthermore, Dauncey contended, desertion for higher wages was rife in the navy and it was highly suspicious that the evidence against his client came from deserters who, although having been court-martialled for their crime, remained unpunished by the naval authorities. In his defence, John Llewellyn, captain of the *Pylades*, testified that he doubted if Lord Sligo knew *before* they sailed from Malta that there were deserters on board. Sligo's servant, Edward Needham, further testified that his master sent him to procure seamen for his ship and 'the men were employed by him without the privity of Lord Sligo, they representing themselves as not belonging to any ship of His Majesty'.³¹

The trial lasted until two o'clock in the morning. After a brief summing up by Lord Ellenborough, ominously blatantly favourable to the prosecution, the case was turned over to the jury. Without leaving the box, after a brief consultation the jury returned a guilty verdict on all counts, with the exception of the charge of false imprisonment. The following day the Marquess of Sligo stood in the dock to receive sentence. Making allowance neither for the youth nor status of the prisoner before him, it was his painful duty, Sir William Scott told the packed court, to affix the penalty which the country expected for violation of its laws and which supported the high principles of the English Constitution: 'that no rank, however high, no fortune, however ample, no regret, however sincere, could prevent the due administration and enforcement of justice'.³² With these words, he imposed a fine of £5,000 and sentenced the defendant to four months' imprisonment in Newgate. Without further ado, Sligo was led away by his gaolers and escorted to his place of confinement.

Amidst the consternation of his friends and supporters in the public gallery, the Marchioness of Sligo deliberated over the judge's words. While a prison sentence for a crime that smacked of treason was hardly a desirable start for her son, a peer of the realm, a legislator, and the grandson of her revered father, Sir William's eloquent admonition might better serve to shape her son's future conduct than any words she could muster. Impressed by the judge's remarks, she asked to be introduced and, from that initial acquaintance, a relationship that was to set society talking blossomed.

For Louisa's 'dearest child', however, incarceration in the most dreaded penal institution in the land must have held some element of apprehension. Behind the smoke-blackened, forbidding façade, Newgate was 'an emblem of hell itself': the constant clamour, the screaming and cursing of inmates, male and female, many driven to madness, others manacled to the walls of their cell for years on end, some half-starved, the all-pervading stench, the rats and lice, which spread dysentery and other diseases that killed more prisoners than the gallows. But the social inequality that existed outside its wall was replicated within. Laid out around a central courtyard, the prison was divided into two sections: a 'commons' area for destitute prisoners and a 'state' area which housed those able to afford the 'luxuries' which made prison life more tolerable. Concessions ranged from a private cell with the services of a cleaning woman, lighter or no manacles, food and drink, to the services of a prostitute – all could be obtained for a price.

Sligo took his punishment on the chin. His letters written during the term of his imprisonment make no reference to his situation. His ability to rent an apartment in the Keeper's House (the same apartment later occupied by his friend John Cam Hobhouse, who in 1819 was incarcerated for contempt of court) made confinement more tolerable. Surrounded by whatever furnishings, clothes, food and drink he could afford and the company of family and friends who chose to visit him, he put in his time. His friends, including Byron and Hobhouse, who came to call 'had dinner like a bawdy house banquet' in his cell.[33] But despite the relative comfort of his surroundings, he was still a prisoner and, like every inmate, had to forfeit his independence and privacy as well as conform to the prison regime, which included the opening of his letters.

Byron too was in the wars following the break-up of his romance with Lady Caroline Lamb. Distraught to insanity by her lover's rejection and by his new liaison with Lady Oxford, Lady Caroline threatened to make public his homosexual activities. Both Sligo and Byron needed to disappear from public view. On the advice of those protective of his future, in order to let the scandal of his trial and imprisonment abate, a loan of £2,500 together with a life assurance policy were raised to enable Sligo to go 'upon or into parts beyond the sea'.[34] A journey to Persia, which he had previously postponed in 1811, seemed a likely possibility. His travelling companion of choice was Byron, to whom, with a spurned and vengeful lover, as well as creditors threatening to ruin his new-won literary celebrity, the idea was also attractive. 'I am in the agonies of three different schemes,' the poet confided to Lady Melbourne. 'The first you know – the 2nd is Sligo's Persian plan – he wants me to wait till Septr. Set off & winter at Athens (our old headquarters) & then in the Spring to Constantinople (as of old) & Baghdad & Tahiran [Teheran]. This has charms too & recalls one's predilections for gadding.'[35]

Sligo spent his time in Newgate planning the trip and interviewing suitable staff, including a medical doctor and 'a Greek named Janier ... anxious to engage himself to any who is going abroad ... he is about 30, very active, a native of Smyrna (his family I knew there) speaks English, French, German, Spanish, Italian, Greek, Arabic & Turkish.'[36] With a Brummell-like attention to detail, Sligo and Byron deliberated over their wardrobe for the trip. Byron's preference for a 'gim crack coat' appeared to Sligo somewhat excessive. 'I mean ... to take out a plain one with a little gold lace round the button holes as that will suit much better .... I am going to have a regular South Mayo Militia uniform made at Davidson's and if you should on consideration prefer such a one I can give permission to you to wear it .... *Let me hope and entreat you,*' he added, in obvious reference to Byron's problems with Lady Caroline Lambe, 'that nothing may persuade you to remain at present or rather with *the present party*.'[37] Amassing a collection, as Byron noted, of 'large trunks – small clothes – & small arms for ourselves – snuff boxes & telescopes for the Mussulman gentry – & geegaws for such of the Pagan women as may be inclined to give us trinkets in exchange ... [they were] determined to go – God knows where – for he [Sligo] is bewildered and so am I.'[38]

On 6 April, on payment of the obligatory 'departure fee' to his gaoler, Sligo was released from Newgate. His intention was to go to Ireland and lie low until his planned departure for the Continent. But the most unlikely occurrence intervened to postpone the first part of his plan.

On his release, he was confronted not only by the news of his forthcoming paternity and the unfaithfulness of his mistress during his incarceration, but also with the unlikely prospect that his trial judge, Sir William Scott, as Byron sardonically related, was about to pass 'sentence of matrimony on his mother'.[39] In true Gilbert and Sullivan fashion, during the course of her son's detention an unlikely romance had blossomed between the judge and the Marchioness. Staid, parsimonious and stern, Sir William Scott (created Baron Stowell in 1821) was a judge of the High Court of the Admiralty, Vicar-General to the Archbishop of Canterbury and a member of the Select Committee appointed in December 1810 to determine the king's sanity. The sixty-eight-year-old widower owned a small estate near Reading and had two adult children, a son whom he intensely disliked and a daughter whom he adored.

The judge seemed an unlikely spouse for the forty-six-year-old Marchioness. That Sir William bore a resemblance to her father, perhaps, encouraged her initial interest. Of small stature and forbidding countenance, Sir William's status lay heavy on his shoulders. His views on marriage and on women, expounded in the divorce courts, might well have set alarm bells ringing for the wealthy, independently minded Marchioness:

> … notwithstanding the radical changes which, during the past 40 years, have been made in the law respecting the property rights of married women, the husband is still in many respects the ruler and his wife his subject. Her position is still one of obedience and, when she has no separate estate, it is also one of dependence.[40]

In view of the extent and complexity of the bride's fortune, the marriage settlement between Louisa and Sir William was both detailed and complex. Before her marriage, she transferred much of her English property to trustees out of reach of her future husband, a wise precaution in view of their tempestuous relationship.

On 10 April, regardless of all advice, Louisa and Sir William were married at St George's Chapel, Hanover Square and moved into Louisa's house on Grafton Street (later to a house at 16 Cleveland Row, purchased by the bride). The groom's brother, Lord Eldon, declined to attend the nuptials. It was reported that on the morning after the wedding he sent a messenger to Grafton Street to enquire after the newlyweds and was informed that 'Sir William Scott was as well as could be expected and that Lady Sligo was much the same.'[41] After less than a year's marriage, Lady Sligo realised that the stern and moralistic attributes she had admired about Sir William on the bench did not translate into a loving or suitable husband at home. 'You married me, I am ashamed to say it, partly from a sexual appetite (which you should have been ashamed of yourself, at your advanced age) but principally to gratify your pride in having a Marchioness for your wife.' He was also, she told him, 'a severe, harsh and unkind' father to his son and was totally ruled by his 'selfish and covetous' daughter.[42] While she may have made an unfortunate choice in her husband, there was little Louisa could do. Sir William's moralistic views on marriage and divorce, as well as the more practical advantages of marrying a wealthy and well-connected wife, prohibited any dissolution of their union.

At the receiving end of the judge's admonition from the bench and at odds with his opposition to Catholic Emancipation, it seemed that Sligo and his stepfather would have little in common. Initially, however, they got on passably well. Their shared antipathy towards the prime minister, Lord Liverpool, 'that white-livered rascal' as Sligo referred to him,[43] as well as their mutual interest in ancient history and archaeology, provided some common ground. Despite his mother's revelations about her new husband as being 'mean and low ... he is the lawyer not the gentleman',[44] initially Sligo tried his best to liaise between the warring couple.

In May 1813, notwithstanding his imprisonment, like his father Sligo was selected as a Representative Peer for Ireland. With final instructions to Byron to 'write me a letter to Westport Ireland, when you have made up your mind about going',[45] Sligo returned for the summer to the relative peace of his west of Ireland estate.

Chapter 8

Secret Agent

Lord Sligo, an Englishman [*sic*] of the highest distinction and very attached to the Emperor is entrusted to give you this letter and shall bring to the Emperor any letter you may give him for the Emperor.

Caroline Bonaparte

International events, however, overtook Sligo's plans to travel to Persia with Byron. Throughout the summer of 1813, following the failed invasion of Russia, the disastrous retreat from Moscow and defeat in the Spanish Peninsula, Napoleon sought to re-establish his hold on the German states. Initially he was successful, winning some hard-fought battles, culminating in a major victory in August at Dresden. A new anti-French force, the Sixth Coalition, engineered by Lord Castlereagh and financed by Britain, comprising Russia, Prussia, Austria, Spain, Portugal, Sweden and some of the German states, with an army almost one million strong, combined to oppose the emperor. Throughout that summer the tide of war fluctuated. In October the forces of the coalition launched a combined assault on Napoleon's army near Leipzig in Saxony.

The military campaign on the European mainland was a magnet for young men of means. Some of Sligo's college friends, such as John Cam Hobhouse and Douglas Kinnaird, grasped the opportunity to observe the military manoeuvres at first hand. Having freed himself from the entanglements of Lady Caroline Lambe, Byron pushed moral taboos to their limits by embarking on an incestuous liaison with his half-sister, Augusta Leigh. By July, he was contemplating fleeing to Sicily with his latest conquest and waiting there for Sligo, who, despite his recent contretemps with the Admiralty, was nonetheless confident of getting them passage to Malta on a Royal Navy ship. An outbreak of plague, which imposed quarantine on continental ports, including ships from England, forced a change of plan. 'Sligo is for the North,' Byron confided to Thomas Moore, 'a pleasant place, Petersburg, with one's ears and nose in a muff …. If the winter treated Bonaparte with so little ceremony what would it inflict on your solitary traveller. Give me a sun, I care not how hot.'[1]

Sligo decided instead to 'follow the war'. Accompanied by Count Ludolf and a college friend, Crackanthorpe, on 8 October they left London for Harwich. After enduring a rough crossing of the North Sea, they landed at Gothenburg in Sweden. A diary of his travels details his observations of the people, places and events encountered and the enormous logistical difficulties, physical danger and discomfort endured as he journeyed in winter through war-torn Europe. At Ystad in the south of Sweden, Sir Charles Stewart, brother of Lord Castlereagh, came to call with news of the victory of the Allies over Napoleon six days previously at Leipzig. In what became known as the Battle of the Nations, over a period of nine hours of intense fighting and bombardment the French were finally forced to retreat across the river Elster. Napoleon and the remnants of his army fled back to France. The slaughter at Leipzig was immense, with between 80,000 and 110,000 corpses strewn across the battlefield. Fascinated by Stewart's account, after 'getting him some breakfast and putting him on his journey having hired our coachman to take him up to Gottenberg [*sic*]', Sligo and his friends resolved to visit the battle site.[2]

From Bergen they proceeded along 'terrible roads' to Berlin. Duly impressed by the 'grandeur' of the city, they visited the Charlottenburg Palace and the Brandenburg Gate, bereft of its famous statue of Victory and her horses, which had been removed by Napoleon to Paris. From Spandau to Potsdam, to see the tomb of Frederick the Great and Voltaire's room with 'all the furniture left just as it was when he lived', they proceeded to the new Sans Souci Palace, built at the end of the Seven Years' War, 'the most magnificent thing that ever was seen'. There, among other treasures, 'we perceived what a taste Frederick the Great had for naked beauties, all his pictures are of women, quite naked'. They were shown around the palace 'by a man in whose arms Frederick died'. From Potsdam they travelled through Aachen 'over a road that had been much broken up by the cannon of the Crown Prince's army' and crossed the Elbe over a temporary bridge installed to facilitate the movement of troops. After some delay with axle trouble, they eventually arrived at Leipzig.[3]

As Sligo recorded:

About 3 English miles from the town, we began to find considerable traces of the action which had just taken place. The fields were all covered with the Caps, Knapsacks, shell and cartridge boxes of the poor killed Frenchmen. Every five yards in the ditch lay a body with a little earth over it but now a hand and now a foot remaining uncovered. These became more frequent as we approached the town.[4]

The bleak landscape littered with tens of thousands of unburied bodies and the carcasses of thousands of horses, many frozen solid in the winter ice, was a sobering sight.

Leaving Leipzig and its battlefield in the pouring rain, they journeyed on through Weimer, where their carriage got stuck in mud to the axle. At Gotha they found accommodation in an inn where Napoleon had stayed and 'went to bed in the same room where he had slept a fortnight before'. As they journeyed on through roads, some 'literally strewn with dead horses and men', with bridges destroyed by the fleeing French army, a scarcity of both horses and accommodation slowed their progress. At Frankfurt am Main they found the allied leaders assembled in the medieval town. 'One cannot walk along the street without knocking one's head against an Emperor or a king, there are here now two Emperors, three kings and eleven or twelve sovereign princes.' Sligo dined with Lord Aberdeen, a friend from his college days, and afterwards attended the theatre, which, despite the war, still flourished. The following day they journeyed to Hockheim, then under Russian command, and were escorted through the military lines right to the outposts 'within twenty yards of the enemy's sentries', as Sligo excitedly recorded. After spending two weeks at Frankfurt am Main, they continued their journey, stopping off at Darmstadt to attend the famous opera house. Onwards to Heidelberg and from there to Stuttgart, capital of the Duchy of Wurttemberg and 'one of the most beautiful and clean towns that I've had yet met with'.[5]

Stuttgart was also the home of Princess Charlotte, the Princess Royal, eldest daughter of King George III, whom Sligo knew from his boyhood days at Eton. News of his arrival was conveyed to the palace and he was commanded to attend the king and queen at a supper ball. Seated at the royal table, he renewed acquaintance with the princess. They chatted about England and his family, especially his grandfather and his aunt, Lady Mary Howe. At the ball the Princess Royal sent Count Benckendorff to where Sligo was seated, requesting that he dance with her. 'This was an honour too great to be refused and tho' not at all inclined to shake my fat sides I gladly laid by my sword and hat and set off with her.'[6] If her partner imagined himself too bulky to cut a dash on the dance floor, his matronly dancing partner had less misgivings about her girth, described as being of 'no shape – like snow'.[7] After the exertion of one dance, they agreed to sit out the rest of the evening in conversation, the princess 'speaking a great deal about Lord Wellington' who, as Sligo noted, 'seems here to be considered as the first Captain of the Age'.[8] The following day he and his companions were invited to a royal levee and afterwards to an intimate dinner party in the royal apartments, attended by the Grand Duke Constantine and Prince William of Cobourg.

As Napoleon continued to bluster from the safety of Paris, the Allied forces determined to cross the Rhine and march on the capital. Sligo and his companions found their way southwards, hampered by Austrian and Russian regiments all advancing towards France. The roads became quagmires in the sleet and snow while every inn and hostelry was packed to the rafters. Taking refuge in their carriage, they wrapped themselves in pelisses at night to keep the cold at bay. At a small village on the Rhine they found the bridge blocked by a large body of Swiss troops. Shortly afterwards a detachment of Austrians arrived with orders to force a passage through. With youthful bravado, Sligo and Crackanthorpe joined the Austrians to have, as Sligo gleefully recorded, 'the satisfaction to be the first English at any rate that had crossed the Rhine'.[9]

A visit to Konstantz on Christmas Day to view the famous falls and the sheer majesty of '120,000 cubic feet of water precipitating itself at once over this fall ... the effect of the spray ... even from the hill above Schaffhousen [*sic*] can be seen rising like a cloud of smoke and dispersing into the air' drew their admiration.[10] Having written their names in the 'album' supplied in the nearby visitors' pavilion, they travelled onwards, skirting Lake Constance, the heavily falling snow failing to dampen their enthusiasm or determination. Ascending into higher ground, Ludolf's finger and the foot of one of Sligo's servants became frozen, forcing them to seek refuge in Wengen. From there they travelled to Kempten, where Ludolf's mother resided and where they determined to spend the New Year.

Sligo's subsequent arrival in Munich caused a stir and he was summoned to the palace to meet the King of Bavaria. No admirer of the French, the king engaged his young visitor in a conversation 'containing', as he wrote, 'the most inveterate abuse' of the emperor. 'He went so far as to call him a damn little liar, a damned little Corsican Bandit, accursed scoundrel and many more equally expletive and elegant names!'[11] The king treated him and his companions with kindness and Sligo was impressed by his simple and unassuming manner. '*Si je puis le dire, Sire, que vous n'étiez parfait pour être roi* [If I may say so, Sire, you are the perfect king'),' Sligo told him. 'I cannot help recollecting that I was once a private man ... I began as Captain in the French Service ... and have risen gradually to my kingly rank,' his majesty, with admirable modesty, replied.[12] The king provided them with an escort to view the principal sights of the city, including the Bavarian mint with its innovative machinery for minting coins. A tour of the king's racing stud was followed by a New Year's dinner at the palace. There Sligo was introduced to many of the court ladies, most of whom, as he wrote, were 'like Mother Eve ... their nudity so completely disgusting'.[13]

Leaving the comfort and hospitality of the Royal Court of Bavaria, the party pressed on towards the Austrian frontier and on 8 January reached Vienna, where they remained for two months. Handsomely entertained, enveloped in a social whirl of dinners, balls and opera by the Viennese nobility, including the distinguished military strategist Prince Charles de Ligne, husband of Princess Maria of Liechtenstein; Josephine, Countess von Brunswick, Beethoven's 'immortal beloved', then unhappily married to the Baron von Stackelberg; the Polish-born Countess Rzewuska; Countess Esterhazy; and Countess Rosalie, the pace never slackened. In Vienna Sligo met Christine, a natural daughter of the Prince de Ligne, who was married to Maurice O'Donnell von Tyrconnell, from an old Irish émigré family, and also the Chevalier O'Hara, both happy to meet one of their compatriots. 'I can safely say,' Sligo concluded 'that nowhere in my life did I ever meet the same hearty welcome and polite attention with which I was honoured in Vienna.'[14]

The three companions then separated, Crackanthorpe to visit Hungary, while Ludolf remained in Vienna. Despite a heavy snowfall and contrary to advice, Sligo determined to return on his own to Munich. Staring out at four o'clock in the morning, despite appalling weather conditions, he reached Munich in four days, where he again enjoyed the hospitality of the king. From there he retraced his journey through Bavaria, Wurttemberg, into Baden-Baden, crossing, as he jubilantly recorded, four different German states in one day. His passport duly stamped, he finally passed over the border into France. Forced to make a detour around Belfort, then occupied by the French, he gave lifts in his carriage to Allied soldiers he encountered along the way, walking two leagues in the company of 'an intelligent peasant' who guided him through French occupied territory where, as he wrote, 'we expected to be fired at every moment'. On 22 March 1814 he reached Champagne, where he found every available horse requisitioned by the Russian forces in their haste to get to Paris. At Chaumont he fell in with his friend Lord Aberdeen, newly appointed ambassador to Austria and a representative at the Congress of Chatillon. During the night Chaumont was suddenly thrown into confusion at the unexpected approach of French columns. Unable to secure fresh horses, Sligo was forced to abandon his carriage and, with barely time to salvage 'a small portmanteau of trinkets, my writing box and a Turkish sword', fled with Aberdeen and the Russian count Andrey Razumovsky to the outskirts of Chaumont. On the advice of Aberdeen, Sligo decided to return to the safety of Basle where he remained for ten days.[15]

On 30 March 1814 allied forces descended on Paris from the heights at Montmartre and, after a fierce struggle, overcame Napoleon's old guard. A day later the Russian czar, accompanied by the King of Prussia, entered the city, to the acclaim of its mercurial citizens, while Napoleon fled to negotiate his future from the safety of Fontainebleau. The czar and king were joined by other Allied leaders, their entourages and armies. On hearing news of the Allies' entry to Paris, Sligo too set off at breakneck speed 'travelling day and night' and reached Paris on 11 April 'extremely hungry'. Scarcely taking time to have a 'warm bath and a fresh change of clothes', he immediately went 'to dine at Beauvilliers' and in the evening attended a performance at the Théâtre Française.[16]

Paris was *en fête*, the boulevards packed with uniformed officers of the victorious multinational armies. Bands played in the Tuileries and spectacular illuminations, grand balls and celebratory suppers were held in the salons of the French nobility, in anticipation of the arrival of the Bourbon king, Louis XVIII. Sligo linked up with John Cam Hobhouse who, accompanied by Henry Grattan, son of the Irish patriot, had arrived in Paris with despatches from the British Home Office for Lord Castlereagh. With other friends such as Lord Lowther, Francis MacKenzie Campbell and Douglas Kinnaird, and Ffrench, Gordon, Duff and O'Mara from Ireland, he sampled the delights of Paris – theatres, restaurants, gambling houses and the salons of the wealthy and aristocratic. With the cessation of twenty years of almost constant warfare, the city was once again open to British visitors who flocked across the English Channel. Starved of French culture, fashion and cuisine, with money to spend, they were warmly welcomed by the landlords, tradesmen and shopkeepers of Paris.

With the indifference of youth, Sligo socialised with such movers and shakers as Castlereagh, Talleyrand, Prince Metternich, Marshal Blucher, Marshal Ney, Count Pückler and the Duke Campochiaro. At a grand ball for the Russian Czar, given by Castlereagh's brother, Sir Charles Stewart, Wellington made a surprise appearance and was instantly acclaimed. On 3 May Sligo witnessed the entry into Paris of the uninspiring, overweight figure of King Louis XVIII, so badly affected by gout that he could barely put a foot on the ground. By the Treaty of Paris, Napoleon was permitted to leave France. Despite Castlereagh's reservations – he prophetically judged it to be a place too close to the French mainland – the emperor was allowed reside on the Island of Elba.

Towards the end of August, having recovered from an attack of measles, despite the uncertainty and difficulty, Sligo determined to continue his European journey. There was little to draw him home. The scandal of his indictment and imprisonment, coupled with the lower cost of living available on the Continent, where it was estimated a gentleman could live comfortably on £200 a year in comparison to £500 in London, propelled him on his way. The British parliament was also in its 'long recess', a period which lasted from July 1814 to February 1815. 'My intention is the Island of Elba,' he wrote. 'But whether I ever shall reach it or not is quite another thing.'[17] Following Napoleon's banishment, the island became a Mecca for British tourists, all anxious to catch a glimpse of the former dictator.

Accompanied by Grattan and fFrench, on 26 August he travelled from Paris through Fontainebleau onwards through the vineyards of Burgundy, through Auxerre and Avallon to Dijon. Up the steep ascent of Mont Jura, through Morez and by a secondary road surrounded by the peaks of Haute Savoie, they had 'a most beautiful panoramic view of Lake Geneva, Mont Blanc reared its lofty head right in front and below us lay the rich plain of Genoa .... No view that I ever saw except perhaps Constantinople could possibly equal it.'[18] At Geneva, meeting up with some acquaintances and suffering from a severe pain in his leg, he resolved to break his journey to see the famous glacier at Chamonix. Crossing the Alps on the road between Brigue and Milan, he marvelled at the engineering skills employed in its construction by Napoleon's army. 'I never had an idea of the obligations Europe has to that wretch [Napoleon] until I saw this road, it is so painful to humanity that he should have done anything so splendid.'[19]

Arriving in Milan on 25 September, he attended the opera at the Teatro alla Scala and visited the city's numerous art galleries and palaces. At the Library of Ambrosia, he viewed Ptolemy's famous fourth-century maps, noting in surprise that 'the first map in the book was that of Ireland and I soon found out the river of Westport called there by the name of "Librokpotlamos"!' From Milan, Piacenza, Parma, through the territory of the Duke of Modena to Bologna, he reached Florence, where he found many British acquaintances. He was invited to a 'conversazione' by the Countess of Albany, 'the widow of the last of the Stuart line,' and to dinner at the home of the Marchese of Montecatini. From Florence he travelled through the valley of the Arno; on 13 September he arrived at Pisa.[20]

Even in exile Napoleon continued to dazzle and excite, luring hundreds of British visitors to the little-known island of Elba in the hope of catching a glimpse of 'the world's wonder'. To some of Sligo's society friends, such as Lord and Lady Holland, the Duke of Bedford and Lord John Russell, Napoleon was a leader ill-fated and hard done by. Unwittingly or deliberately, his English visitors fed Napoleon news of political developments, shifting allegiances and the discord emanating from the Congress of Vienna, as well as disillusionment with the Bourbon king, especially within the ranks of the French army. Napoleon used them, in turn, to feed them misinformation, insisting that his only interest lay with his family, cows and mules.

Despite his family's experience of French incursion in 1798 in the West of Ireland, Sligo was as fascinated as his friends with the fallen emperor. Armed with a letter of introduction to the wife of Henri-Gatien Bertrand, Napoleon's marshal, he enjoyed a better prospect of gaining access to Napoleon than most visitors to Elba. Bertrand was married to Fanny Dillon, a half-Irish, half-Martinique Creole, descended from a landed family from the west of Ireland with whom Sligo's family were acquainted. Fanny's father, Count Arthur Dillon, was the last colonel of the Irish Brigade in the French army and had fought against the British in the American War of Independence. An ardent royalist, he was guillotined during the revolution when his daughter was nine years old. In 1808 Fanny married Bertrand and, as she subsequently complained to Sligo, had to make many sacrifices in her married life 'attending the Emperor', including exile on Elba.[21] Sligo was granted a travel permit to Elba by Napoleon's gaoler, Colonel Neil Campbell, whom he had previously met in Gibraltar.

By the Treaty of Fontainebleau (April 1814) Napoleon was granted sovereignty of the island of Elba and its population of some 110,000 citizens, together with a generous allowance for himself and his family, as well as the right to retain his imperial title. On 4 May 1814 he had arrived in the capital, Portoferraio, with a personal escort and household staff numbering almost one thousand. He was subsequently joined by his formidable mother, Madame Mère, his vivacious sister Pauline and, initially, by his mistress, Polish-born, Countess Marie Walewska, with whom he had a son. From his official residence, Palazzo dei Mulini, he conducted his court and maintained the strict protocol of his former glory, appointing Bertrand his Minister of the Interior.

Sligo crossed by felucca from Leghorn (Livorno) on 15 October 1814 to 'this miserable place, the wretched retreat of the man who but a short time ago thought Europe too small a scene for his plans'.[22] Marshal Bertrand invited him to dine at his home. The Bertrands had two young children, Napoleon, aged six, and Hortense, aged four. They were favourites of the emperor, who often played childish games with them. Bertrand's wife, Fanny, was unwell and received Sligo in her bedroom. In her late twenties, attractive, volatile and beloved of her husband, in English she complained to Sligo about her husband's frequent absences abroad, how the emperor had been deserted by his other marshals and of her personal dismay at their banishment to Elba. Dangerously outspoken, she also confided, as Sligo later reported in code to Lord Lowther, how 'Nap. will make another attempt whenever he has the opportunity' but, for the time being, he could do little, having, as she told Sligo, 'not a penny' to pay his troops.[23]

Bertrand brought his Irish guest on a tour of the island during which they encountered the 'Great Man', of whom Sligo wrote:

> He was in a little yellow low phaeton, drawn by four grey ponies with two postillions. He was dressed in a green uniform, very like the engraving I sent home of him, only fatter a good deal. He appeared in tolerably good spirits … saluted everyone of those who took off their hats to him.[24]

At Napoleon's cottage in St Martin, Bertrand later introduced Sligo to the emperor.

There was much speculation that Napoleon's subsequent escape from Elba was orchestrated by the British. Fanny Dillon's utterance to Sligo, as he later recounted to Hobhouse, '*avec de l'argent il pourrout bien faire quelque chose* [with money one can do anything]'[25] and later Napoleon's sister Caroline Murat's question to him, 'if it were true that the English had assisted the Emperor Napoleon in making his escape',[26] all add to the speculation. The Bourbon restoration was less successful than the Allies had hoped, and with Machiavellian figures such as Talleyrand, Metternich and Castlereagh busy redrawing the borders of Europe in Vienna, anything was possible. What part Sligo may or may not have played in such a scenario remains unclear. His friend Michael Bruce had become a confidant of Hortense de Beauharnais, the daughter of the former Empress Josephine, as well becoming invested in a romantic relationship with Aglaé Ney, wife of Marshal Ney. Bruce was rumoured to have accompanied Sligo to Elba, although Sligo does not mention him in his correspondence. Sligo's letters purporting to 'give a long account of Napoleon'[27] written to his mother from Elba at this time, which might well have thrown some light on his involvement in the murky circumstances surrounding Napoleon's subsequent escape, never arrived at their destination. As Sligo suspected, they were intercepted by the British authorities. Whether a participant in a more complex and wider conspiracy or merely involved by chance in the Machiavellian events relating to Napoleon's dramatic escape, remains unclear. Sligo's later association with members of Napoleon's family indicates that, whatever his motivation and the extent of his participation in these international intrigues, he would seem to have been out of his depth.

Leaving Elba, accompanied by Richard (Dickie) Prime, a fellow Cambridgian, Sligo returned, via Lucca, to Florence and walked into a controversy involving Princess Caroline, the estranged wife of the Prince Regent. By 1814 the royal marriage had descended into farce, providing every gossipmonger and caricaturist in Britain with an unending vein of the most salacious speculation. The antics of 'Prinny', the Prince Regent, 'a libertine and head over ears in disgrace', and 'the very large and coarse' 'Mrs Prinny', outspoken, bawdy and, as Sligo suspected, somewhat deranged, kept the British public both amused and appalled. The German-born princess countered the multiple adulteries, bigamy and cruelty of her husband by embarrassing him, their daughter, Princess Charlotte, and the British royal family at every opportunity. Adopted by the Whig Party merely as a tool by which to undermine the Prince Regent's alliance with the Tories, by August 1814 Caroline, to the relief of her husband and the disappointment of the Whigs, left England for her homeland, the Duchy of Brunswick.

Having exhausted the patience of her family she set out on a tour of Europe. News of her scandalous progress from Brunswick to Baden Baden, where she appeared with half a pumpkin on her head, and then to Geneva, where she arrived at a ball dressed or, as was reported, 'not dressed further than the waist' as Venus. In Genoa she paraded her expansive body in a child's pink and white outfit, her two large feet encased in long pink boots. Arriving in Milan, she became publicly attached to a married former quarter master in the Austrian army, Bartolomeo Pergami, whom she appointed her courier and lover. As news of her outrageous behaviour reached England, the Prince Regent determined to find hard evidence of his wife's adultery and to initiate divorce proceedings.

With the impulsiveness which had landed him in hot water in the past, Sligo offered to help the Prince Regent rid himself of his troublesome wife by engaging in a secret communication with the Prince through their mutual friend, Lord Lowther. The would-be sleuth instructed Lowther:

> Whenever I may have something secret to say to you on this business particularly, I will write with *lemon juice* in the intervals of the lines of my letter, by holding this close to the fire for a few moments the writing will come out plain enough. When I do so I will put a cross, X, so at the top of my letter and when you want to write to me anything secret do the same thing.[28]

As an intimate of the royal family, while critical of his opposition to Catholic Emancipation, on the question of his marital problems, Sligo's loyalty, at this juncture, lay with the Regent.

On his arrival at an inn in Florence, an immense crowd rushed excitedly towards Sligo's carriage, mistaking it for that of the Princess of Wales. When the princess eventually arrived, she was accompanied by a retinue which included her ladies-in-waiting, her fourteen-year-old 'adopted' son Billy Austin, whom she frequently hinted was her natural son, her chamberlains, or 'Jack Puddings' as Sligo described them, Sir William Gell and Keppel Craven, both 'dressed in the most extraordinary costume that can be imagined'.[29] Obliged out of protocol, as Sligo wrote, 'to present our cards in the evening we all went to be presented to her in full uniform'.[30] The princess insisted that Sligo attend her in her box at the theatre and he had little option but to agree, 'till some ladies coming in I of course … hopped off with all convenient speed'. Breaking every rule of diplomacy and etiquette, to further embarrass her estranged husband the princess publicly declared her admiration for Napoleon and went out of her way to show favouritism to members of the dictator's family.

> It was really abominable, there was the Princess, Borghese [Pauline Bonaparte's husband] and his Mistress, the Duchess de Lanti, Lady G. [E] Forbes and *Billy Austin* sitting in front of the Box, and all the English and most of the nobility of Florence standing behind her to pay their respects. Now really it was too bad to have that little bastard sitting in front while everyone else was standing up.

As Sligo related to Lowther, the princess insisted that he sit beside her but 'I did not like the company and so took the first opportunity of bolting.'[31]

Their paths, however, crossed again in Rome. To the outrage of Roman society, which had suffered much at the hands of Napoleon, the princess's constant companions were Napoleon's brothers Lucien and Louis Bonaparte and the banker Pietro Torlonia, whom Napoleon created Duca di Bracciano. When an English diplomat enquired about her lengthy audience with the Pope, the princess replied that he would see 'evident symptoms of it nine months later'.[32] Rumours abounded that she was pregnant and, as Sligo attested, 'from the immense protuberance of her *ventre,* if such things were possible I should guess that she were *pregnant* at this moment … but I hardly believe it to be true'.[33] From Rome the princess decamped to the Kingdom of Naples, ruled by Joachim Murat and his wife, Caroline Bonaparte, the emperor's sister. Resolving to keep her in his sights, accompanied by Dickie Prime, Sligo followed.

Naples became Sligo's favourite destination. 'I should like to stay here forever,' he enthused. 'There never was so delightful a climate, so beautifully situated a place or altogether one I should more like to live [in] if obliged to live away from home.'[34] He urged his mother to use her influence to have him appointed Minister to the Royal Court, which would, he blithely reasoned, 'be a great advantage to me and an introduction to public life'.[35] The Kingdom of Naples, once part of the old Kingdom of Sicily, from 1735 became aligned to the Bourbon kings. In 1805 King Ferdinand IV allied with the coalition against Napoleon. Following his victories at Austerlitz and at Campo Tenese, the emperor installed his brother Joseph as King of Naples before giving him the more influential throne of Spain. He subsequently bestowed the crown of Naples on his sister Caroline and her husband, Joachim Murat.

The new King of Naples was one of Europe's most unlikely monarchs. The son of an innkeeper, he enlisted in the French cavalry where his daring in battle brought him to the attention of Napoleon. Vain, ambitious and headstrong, he served in Egypt and commanded the French cavalry at the battle of Marengo. At Austerlitz, he displayed such courage during the battle that Napoleon created him Grand Duke of Berg and Cleves. He was general of the French army in the Peninsular War and had hopes of becoming King of Spain. Having to make do with the less illustrious throne of Naples, Murat, with the support of his ambitious wife Caroline, carved out his own niche, independent, as much as he dared, of his powerful brother-in-law. His first foray was to seize the British-controlled island of Capri.

The wily Austrian chancellor Metternich realised Murat's military capability and secretly offered to have his position as King of Naples copper-fastened by the Allies, as well as to obtain Britain's imprimatur on the deal. Dazzled by the opportunity it presented to extend his territory, establish a royal line and even achieve his ambition to become king of a unified Italy, without obtaining any guarantee from Metternich, Murat abandoned Napoleon and signed a treaty with the Austrians.

On his arrival in Naples, Sligo was warmly welcomed by the king and queen. Handsome, engaging, tall, powerfully built, his hair styled in ringlets and possessing a penchant for flamboyant military uniforms, Murat was, according to Sligo, 'a most capital sort of fellow' and his queen 'very pretty ... a most lovely woman and possessed of first rate talent'.[36] More able and ambitious than her husband, Caroline's ability to charm and cajole was matched only by her capacity to scheme and to use others to further her ambition. During her husband's absences in the service of her brother, to whom her loyalty took second place to her own ambitions, she ruled Naples with an iron hand. More benign a ruler than the deposed Bourbons, Murat introduced many reforms, including the abolition of feudalism in his kingdom. He curbed the control of French officials in his administration, making them adopt Neapolitan citizenship and, by indulging his passion for public entertainment, revelries and masquerades, became popular with his subjects. Despite his alienation from the British over his seizure of Capri, Murat was an ardent Anglophile. His household had English servants, his children English governesses, he rode English horses, drank English 'port wine' and he accorded parole to English prisoners-of-war in Naples.

The amphitheatre city, framed by its beautiful bay, with the islands of Capri, Ischia and Procida, under the smouldering funnel of Vesuvius, attracted many British visitors to avail of the city's temperate climate. 'Naples is now so full of English that there is no getting a place to put one's head into,' Sligo attested.[37] His royal hosts became enamoured with the well-connected Irish peer, who also had the advantage of an introduction from the Duke di Campochiaro, Murat's representative at the Congress of Vienna. Sligo's affability, his consideration of others, taking time to play whist with older, incapacitated visitors, saluting Lady Llandaff because 'she had been sitting all day alone and I had not seen anyone speak to her', endeared him to the expatriate community.[38] Picnic excursions into the beautiful countryside, treks to The Hermitage, an inn on the slopes of Mount Vesuvius, shooting wild duck and woodcock, fêtes and fireworks, 'each day the King's kindness to us is more marked than that of the preceding one,' Sligo informed his mother. 'I ride one of the King's horses almost every day and go to the theatre very frequently …. I am employed in making preparations for a grand ball which the English are going to give to the King and of which I am principal manager.'[39] He was given precedence at functions at the royal palaces of Caserta and Portici, being 'always placed at the Queen's side …. She made me stay and play Prison Bars with her and her Ladies and then I went in the open carriage with her and her daughters. I am called on to talk English to the daughters so that I see a great deal of them.'[40] 'Lord Sligo is a great man at the Neapolitan Court,' Hobhouse attested. 'The King gave him his picture … so Prime warned me I must never call him Murat before Sligo.'[41]

Hoping to advance his position with the British, Murat also bent Sligo's ear, praising the virtues of the English race and especially the Prince Regent. 'I wish the Prince Regent were to see him only I am sure he would like him,' Sligo enthused to Lord Lowther.[42] He sought to portray his host as a potentially useful ally to Britain against French and Austrian ambitions in Italy. 'I hope most sincerely that he [Murat] may finally be established here as if Ferdinand comes back three-fourths of the Neapolitan nobility will fly the country. The horrors committed by him on his former return here equal anything of Nero's.'[43]

Sligo's enthusiastic promotion of Murat was not appreciated by the British representatives at the Congress of Vienna, especially by Castlereagh, who was suspicious of Murat's designs. 'As you must have found from Lord Sligo it has been made a religion here with some to consider Murat as one of the great men of the time … as the best friend to England and the only sincere one,' he was informed by one of his secret agents in Italy.[44] Some of the British residents in Naples privately ridiculed Murat's pretensions. Lady Spencer

Stanhope recorded how her husband, 'the recipient of a letter from Lord Sligo inviting him to become a subscriber to a ball' to be held in honour of the king and queen, refused to take part 'in a measure which he considered that the Government would not approve, as England had not recognised the sovereignty of Murat'.[45]

As part of their charm offensive of the English, but unaware of the Prince Regent's designs against his wife, the Royal couple invited Princess Caroline to their kingdom. Murat rode as far as Capua to personally escort her to Naples. Queen Caroline organised numerous fêtes, suppers and pageants but, as Sligo observed, 'she [the princess] is so capricious a devil that she has made enemies of almost everyone here'.[46] The princess's scandalous behaviour, her outspokenness, her lack of decorum, her blatant discourtesy, made her hosts wonder if they had made both a political and social faux pas. Rumours abounded that she had seduced Murat, but which Sligo dismissed, bluntly informing Lowther that it was her 'courier Pergami who does the job for her'.[47]

As sleuth for the Prince Regent, Sligo determined 'to getting out all the confidence which the Princess reposed in the Queen'.[48] The Princess of Wales, however, was more than anxious to divulge information about her husband and her royal in-laws. Queen Caroline revealed to Sligo, who passed on the information to the Prince Regent, how the princess had referred to the Prince Regent as 'an ugly, disagreeable man, broader than he was long and only a fit companion for grooms and gamblers'. She also abused her mother-in-law, referred to the king as 'a good sort of creature but easily led by a little art' and gave vent to 'an indiscriminate abuse of all the Princesses, making very light of their characters and their manners'.[49] Everyone who heard her outbursts and observed her conduct concluded 'how lucky it is for the Prince that his wife has come out ... and justify him in the dispute'.[50]

More substantial evidence of the princess's suspected adultery Sligo found more difficult to come by. Having 'got hold of a prime channel for knowing all that passes within the Princess's establishment', he discovered that 'the *Courier's room is next to hers* .... She has made him her *Equerry* and he always rides by the side of her carriage when she drives out .... I have been enquiring whether he goes to the bawdy house and find that he never does now.' With a postscript, in which he implored Lowther, 'for God's sake, burn this letter when read and the contents remembered,' Sligo promised further evidence from a source he had planted within the princess's household.[51]

It was the princess, however, who made the next move. Despite her decision to abandon her Whig supporters, their leader, Henry Brougham, maintained discreet contact with her during her peregrinations around Europe. To lure her back to England, he informed her of the Prince Regent's plan to initiate divorce proceedings. At the prospect of being divorced from the future king of England, even Caroline had wit enough to realise the serious repercussions for her status and that of her daughter, Princess Charlotte. She had only agreed to live abroad, she told Sligo, provided she remained Princess of Wales. If, however, her husband initiated divorce proceedings against her, she would, although 'very unpleasant to herself but that *the interest of her daughter* required it ... come [to England] and appeal to the people of England to defend her'.[53] Sligo enquired as to the exact message she wished to convey to the Prince Regent. 'After a little *humming and hawing*,' she professed herself agreeable 'to make an arrangement with the P.R. and the Ministers' to remain in exile, provided the Prince Regent abandoned the proceedings.[54] Sligo duly forwarded her offer, via Lowther, to the Prince Regent and also reiterated his request to be appointed British Minister at Naples, so that 'I should be better able to attend to her [the princess] and watch what she was about, and he [the Prince Regent] might perhaps more depend upon me as to this affair, than whatever diplomat might be sent here.'[55] When, however, he attempted to get confirmation in writing from the princess to forward to the Prince Regent, he was met, as he wrote, 'with a great deal of shuffling' by her advisors who tried to 'humbug' him. Fearful of getting involved in another 'cursed scrape' if 'the damned personage should deny all this', he decided to back out of the business entirely.[56]

On 25 February 1815 Napoleon escaped from Elba and made landfall on the south coast of France. That he managed to leave the island with relative ease (his gaoler, Colonel Campbell, being conveniently absent from the island for the preceding ten days) gave rise to fresh rumours that his escape had been contrived by the British government to foment civil unrest in France. The entire episode was smothered in rumour, claim and counter-claim. As a favoured guest of Napoleon's sister and brother-in-law, Sligo's involvement is also open to conjecture.

It was also rumoured that, despite his cultivation of the British, Murat was in secret negotiations with Napoleon and was privy to his escape from Elba. Murat's position as king of Naples was becoming less secure. As Austria moved closer to Britain at the Congress of Vienna, so Murat's main supporter, Metternich, became more indifferent to his fate. Because of Murat's usurpation of his principality of Beneventum, Talleyrand, the wily French minister, had both a political and personal motivation to have Murat removed. Following Napoleon's escape, Talleyrand threatened to overrun Murat's kingdom if he moved his army into northern Italy. Deputations arrived daily in Naples from Rome and the northern Italian states, as Sligo informed Lowther, 'to urge him [Murat] to move forward and liberate them' from Austrian control.[57] Not knowing who or what to believe, against the advice of his representative in Vienna, his English friends and his wife, Murat assembled his army and prepared to fight for his kingdom.

Despite his intention, as Sligo informed his mother, to rent 'a little cottage on the waterside for the summer, as I think it most likely that I shall spend it here unless you send for me home',[58] events in Naples, as well as news of his mother's ill-health, determined his decision to leave. 'I don't atal [*sic*] like these headaches of which you complain. I am sure that the constant bleeding which you undergo must have not been healthy. Have they even given you digitalis[?] .... It has done me great good when I had the rheumatism.'[59] Louisa's increasingly acrimonious marriage was taking its toll on her health. 'My mother's ménage is going on infamously ill. I fear that the old couple after having committed the folly of being joined will commit the still greater one of separating afterwards,' Sligo informed Lowther.[60] Deciding that Naples was becoming too dangerous for the Princess of Wales, the Tory government sent a frigate to have her removed to the safety of Genoa, then under British protection.

Prior to Sligo's departure from Naples, Queen Caroline presented him with a framed portrait of herself, and two swords: one with a hilt inset with coral, the other 'a plain clumsy sabre taken in action by Murat'.[61] After her husband's death, to try to alleviate her then penurious circumstances, Queen Caroline asked Sligo to return the coral sword, a request with which he immediately complied. From King Murat he received an exquisite miniature ivory and gold-enamelled snuff box, inset with diamonds and bearing the king's portrait, which is now in the Napoleon Collection in Paris. The box bore the inscription '*Donné par JOACHIM – Roi de Naples – au Marquis de SLIGO à son depart de Naples, Mars 1815* [Given by Joachim – King of Naples – to the Marquis of Sligo on his depature from Naples, March 1815].'[62]

Suspicions that Murat and Queen Caroline were acting in consort with the newly returned emperor, who was preparing to march on Paris, seem, on the surface, vindicated by the letters Murat and his wife entrusted to Sligo on his departure from Naples. In one of the letters to the emperor's mother, Letizia Bonaparte, Queen Caroline described Sligo as 'very attached to the Emperor and shall bring to the Emperor any letter you may give him for the Emperor. You can do this with full confidence.'[63] In another letter to Napoleon, she referred to Sligo 'as an Englishman [*sic*] very distinguished and very attached to your Majesty'.[64] While a third letter from Elisa, Princess of Lucca and Piombino, Grand Duchess of Tuscany, the eldest sister of the emperor, written from her palace in Bologna, acknowledged receipt of a letter and a package brought by Lord Sligo from her sister in Naples and approving 'the discretion he showed by not coming personally to deliver it himself'. She also referred to the trust placed by her sister 'in the Marquis to deliver a letter for M. l'Empereur Napoleon and trusts him to deliver it himself or if this is impossible to return it to the Princess'.[65] The fact that the letter remained among Sligo's personal papers indicates that he considered a meeting with Napoleon was either not possible or, more likely, not advisable. The letters, however, give a tantalising glimpse into the clandestine role he played in the murky political situation then prevailing and in the uncertainties and intrigue which swirled around Napoleon and his family in the months following his escape from Elba.

At the beginning of April, Sligo arrived at the port of Ostend. There he encountered Hobhouse, who was on his way to Paris to witness the return of Napoleon. From evidence gleaned on his journey through Italy, Sligo was convinced that the emperor would not long survive. 'So strongly was I impressed with this idea that I made a bet of one hundred guineas that Lord Wellington would be in Paris before six months,' Sligo told his mother.[66]

It was a wager he was destined to win.

Chapter 9

A Racing Man

I am deeper than ever on the turf, having got several new and excellent horses such as will pretty well clip the wings of the lads at the Curragh.

Marquess of Sligo

On his return, Sligo walked into a domestic feud. He found his mother depressed, overweight and confined to bed. Louisa's alienation from her husband was compounded by a bitter aversion to his daughter, a person who, as Louisa informed Sir William, was 'hated and despised by all' and who bore 'a malignant spirit towards me ... from her dread of my influencing you to treat her unfortunate brother less harshly and cruelly ... whose affection for me has been an additional crime in your eyes and in your daughter's'. She further blamed her ill-health on 'the hopeless state of misery to which my unfortunate connection with you has reduced me'.[1] It was a situation that required delicate and sympathetic handling.

While totally loyal to and concerned for his mother's happiness, there is more than a hint of sympathy for his stepfather in Sligo's correspondence. Unlike his mother, he was not overly concerned with rank and status, preferring to accept people as he found them. An heiress in her own right, his mother was an indulged child of a 'beloved father' and the widow of a tolerant first husband who had allowed her extraordinary freedom. Accustomed, as she wrote, 'to such different society', she baulked at the restrictions enforced on her by someone she considered her social inferior. Her husband would not countenance divorce, not merely from financial considerations, but also because of the damage that would ensue to his political ambitions, especially those connected with the Church of England. Establishing that his stepfather had not been physically violent, Sligo endeavoured to ease the tension between them, hoping that 'all would terminate amicably ... that the good sense of both would get the better of their momentary anger'.[2] When Sir William agreed to discreetly absent himself more often from the marital home on Cleveland Row, the arrangement brought some respite.

By early June 1815 Sligo was back on his estate in Ireland. His finances continued in a perilous state and he determined 'to most certainly economize until out of debt but after that', as he ominously informed his mother, 'I shall hold myself at liberty to spend my time and money in the way most conducive to my happiness and pleasure.'[3] To show his intent, he embarked on an economy drive at Westport House. Despite his earlier attempts to rein in running costs and curtail the large numbers of surplus retainers who continued to live off the estate, he found the abuses had increased in his absence.

> I have at last laid the axe to the root of the expenditure of my fortune by clearing out the farmyard of every person who was in it. Such roguery and robbery as I found out could not be imagined .... I calculate that Peggy Burke costs me at least 80 pounds a year, with allowances and robbery besides.[4]

His household staff left a lot to be desired – as he humorously noted, 'My butler is only middling, my cook execrable, the footman good enough,' and he vowed to return the cook to London and 'get one from Paris'.[5] But the 'economy drive' became irrelevant in the face of the extensive building and refurbishment schemes on which he embarked.

By 1815 Westport House had evolved into one of the most impressive houses in the West of Ireland. Behind its Cassels's frontage, two spacious reception rooms occupied the entire space of the first floor level. An open area, which doubled as a drawing room, folded around an immense oak staircase to the north of the entrance hall, leading to family sleeping quarters on the upper floor and to the staff quarters in the attic rooms above, while the basement level accommodated numerous service and storage chambers. Against the dramatic backdrop of Croagh Patrick (the Reek) and island-strewn Clew Bay, with Clare Island like a sentinel on the distant horizon, the house overlooked a large lake into which the Carrowbeg River flowed. To the rear lay the busy port of Westport, flanked on one side by a row of impressive stone warehouses. To the front of the house a lawn stretched towards the main entrance, beyond which lay the town of Westport. The entire layout – bay, port, lake, house, demesne and town – was one seamless and compact entity that bespoke planning, commerce and control. The family owned many of the houses, as well as the land on which the port and town were built, and were in receipt of rents and ground rents from those who resided or who operated business there.

'Nature has done much for this pretty town of Westport,' William Makepeace Thackeray recorded, 'and after Nature, the traveller ought to be thankful to Lord Sligo, who has done a great deal too.'[6] Westport was 'a thriving little place; the streets paved and flagged the houses neatly built of stone and slated.'[7] It boasted a quarter mile of tree-lined malls along the embanked river, bordered on both sides by fine cut-stone houses, including the Dower House. The Octagon provided a spacious area for markets and fairs. The town also boasted a hotel, a theatre, linen hall, Courthouse, custom house, a Methodist chapel, a Church of Ireland church and the Catholic Chapel of St Mary's. A prosperous merchant middle class, both Catholic and Protestant, was involved in the commercial life of the town and port. Brewing, malting and later distilling, a tannery, salt works, water-driven flour and oat mills, built in 1808 by the 1st Marquess, as well as a linen industry and fishing grounds (herring and oyster), all contributed to the town's prosperity. A military barracks accommodated a regular army detachment and the South Mayo Militia. The commercial development of the town reflected its rising population, which increased from 1,000 in 1785 to almost 3,000 by 1815.

Shaped by the Regency period, the age that more than any other typified all that was elegant, tasteful and innovative, and augmented too by his experiences abroad, Sligo sought to put his own mark on his west of Ireland estate. The addition of a new 'north wing' to the old house was completed in 1816, followed by a new south wing and an extensive farmyard, incorporating rows of pony and mule sheds, pheasantries, laundries, sawmills and kilns for drying corn. Like his father, he encouraged and subsidised the local linen-manufacturing industry. In contrast to his grandfather and father, however, Sligo was no farmer. 'Though the farm buildings are the most superb and extensive establishment I have ever seen, replete with all kinds of machinery to give facility to the labours and promote the interests of husbandry,' one visitor noted, 'the farm no longer is the principal occupation of the proprietor.'[8] In the hauntingly beautiful Dubh Lough valley, Sligo constructed a single-storey Gothic sporting lodge, which he named Delphi Lodge in memory of his travels in Greece.

There is a sense in his correspondence at this period of his life that Sligo remained at Westport out of a sense of obligation, constantly awaiting the chance, or excuse, to leave. It is as if Westport was a duty to be borne rather than to be managed and enjoyed. His English education, his mother's family connections in England, the friendships he had made there, combined with the lack of outlets for his entertainment and sophisticated tastes, all contributed to make his ancestral home, as his father had predicted, appear a backwoods by comparison. His frustration in this period of his life was vented in a rare reprimand to his mother when she attempted to curb his horse-breeding and -racing pursuits. 'I have not the slightest idea of leaving the Curragh .... I will never give up what is almost my only country amusement. If you take that away from me I will leave the country altogether. Besides at 27 years old I must be able to judge what is the most agreeable occupation to myself.'[9]

News of Wellington's victory over Napoleon at Waterloo, on 18 June 1815, filtered through to Westport. 'You will be surprised when I tell you,' Sligo informed his mother 'that Bonaparte's abdication was not at all unsuspected by me. The fact was that I foretold that his power would melt away like a snowball if he was defeated in the first action.'[10] Later in the summer came news of Murat's defeat at Tolentino and his subsequent replacement as king of Naples. There is a tradition in the Browne family that Sligo hired a ship with the intention of returning to Italy to rescue his former friend. Francis Macirone, Murat's aide-de-camp, who had known Sligo in Naples, recorded that, while in hiding in Corsica after losing his throne, Murat specifically enquired about his 'good and honourable English [*sic*] friends', especially Lord Sligo, in the hope that he might come to his assistance. Murat's rash plan to recover his kingdom resulted in his capture, courtmartial and execution in October 1815. Daring to the last, he conducted his own execution, choosing six Neapolitan soldiers to fire the fatal shots. To commemorate his dead friend, whose name was by then ostracised in political and social circles, Sligo boldly named his two-year-old colt Murat 'after my unfortunate friend', adamant that 'it is I fancy the best horse in Ireland' and which he successfully raced at the Curragh.[11]

There was, however, a more personal reason which directed Sligo's path away from his ancestral home. As well as inheriting his estates, he had also inherited his father's rheumatic condition. After a mere ten days' residence in Westport the condition flared up and by mid-July 'he was seized with a fit of rheumaticism' and confined to bed.[12] The intense pain, as his cousin Robert Browne related to Louisa, which was 'not settled in any particular part but flies about his entire body',[13] was indicative of rheumatoid arthritis. His doctor ordered a strict diet, excluding meat and alcohol. 'You have no idea how svelte I am become with my fifteen days fasting,' Sligo joked.[14] Too eager to entertain his friends, including his cousin Lord Desart, he promptly suffered a relapse. 'I am happy to announce my perfect recovery,' he later reported, 'in as much as I am today [29 July] to begin eating meat and drinking wine … tomorrow I am to go out in the carriage, I shall not be able to ride for some time,'[15] and added, no doubt to his mother's consternation, 'I am told by the physicians that frequent intercourse with women is absolutely necessary for me since this disorder!'[16]

Sligo's indulgence in food and wine became more marked in adult life and was eventually to have a detrimental effect on his general well-being. From vintage wines to French delicacies, his preference did little to regulate his already expanding girth. In 1815, however, he was still agile enough to enjoy riding, hunting, fishing and sailing. At Finlough, a noted angling lake on his estate, on one night-time expedition he 'caught two salmon and 12 trout'.[17] He also indulged his racing passion at the July races in Westport and at Tuam, a noted venue on the racing calendar.

By mid-August he assumed his duties as colonel of the South Mayo Militia. There were two regiments quartered in Mayo, the North Mayo Militia in Ballina and the South Mayo Militia in Westport. The location of the militias reflected the status and political power of the local magnate, of which the Marquess of Sligo was the foremost in rank, estate, connections and influence.

The presence of a military barracks was an important commercial and employment outlet in the locality. Dashing in his splendid red uniform, Sligo paraded and drilled his regiment at Westport before being ordered to Tuam, where he was received 'to my great astonishment with bonfires and general illuminations. What could induce the good people to treat me to this, I have no idea, but I find that I am a great favourite in the town.'[18] His usual good nature did not deter him from imposing his authority on recalcitrant officers in his regiment. 'I have had a grand contest with an officer in the line and have defeated him and got a letter from the Commander of the Forces approving in the highest degree of my conduct.'[19]

Despite his mother's entreaties and the disapproval of his estate agent, George Glendenning, to whom he had also become financially indebted, the lure of horse racing and its even more calamitous attendant, gambling, burned as brightly as ever. Joseph Osborne, a fellow member of the Turf Club, recalled how he had seen Sligo wager a bet of £10,000. Racing tended to be the preserve of the gentry and attracted young bloods, such as the notorious Buck Whaley, who took an almost fatalistic view of gambling. Admitting to have dissipated 'a fortune of four hundred thousand pounds and contracted a debt to the amount of thirty thousand more', Whaley described himself as someone who 'was born with strong passions, a lively imagination and a spirit that could brook no restraint', a description that might well be applied to his fellow racing enthusiast, Sligo.[20] Gambling was an integral part of the racing scene. Patrons and owners, buoyed by usually unrealistic expectations of their horses, bet enormous sums on the outcome of races.

Sligo was registered as an owner in 1809. During his sojourns abroad, the arrival of the Irish and English racing almanacs were, as he admitted, 'the comforts of my life'.[21] For over thirty years he bred and raced many horses and owned progenitors of some of the best bloodlines in the world. At twenty-one he was elected a member of the Irish Turf Club, appointed a steward in 1812 and again from 1816 to 1818 and from 1840 to 1842. As soon as he had attained his majority, he started to build a breeding and racing establishment at Westport and at stables he leased from time to time on the Curragh of Kildare. In 1810 his filly Belleville, by Hyacinth, trained by Richard Nokes, was the leading two-year-old in Ireland.

In the early part of the nineteenth century, landed Connaught families such as Bowes Daly, Blake, Daly, Kelly, Moore, Gore and Kirwan dominated the racing and breeding scene in Ireland. Because of the perilous state of the Irish economy, which experienced a further setback on the ending of the Napoleonic war, Irish racing was not as developed as its English counterpart. Up to 1815 Irish racing had no corresponding classic races, such as the Derby or St Leger. It was largely unregulated and suffered from a dearth of quality bloodstock. But despite these impediments, there was a traditional affinity between the Irish people and horse racing, which encapsulated every class and creed, as evidenced by the existence of hundreds of racecourses throughout the country, many in obscure and remote locations. Race meetings attracted the ascendancy and the ordinary public alike, who flocked in their thousands, despite enactments from the clergy who tried to ban what they considered occasions of idleness and debauchery.

Between 1813 and 1842 Sligo was one of the small band of aristocratic patrons who, for the sheer love of racing, put their money, energy and influence into the establishment of what today has evolved into one of Ireland's most lucrative and prestigious industries. The Irish Turf Club arbitrated in disputes and regulated the racing rules, subscriptions and stakes, as well as the conditions, layout and upkeep of Irish racecourses. The Coffee House, a three-storey building erected with the subscriptions of racing patrons in the town of Kildare, became the headquarters of the Turf Club and the administrative and social centre for racing enthusiasts.

Three stewards were elected annually from among the Turf Club members.

The Ranger of the Curragh was appointed by the government to protect and preserve activities on the famous plain, including the supervision and running of the King's Plate, the first official race run on the Curragh. Sligo's cousin, Robert Browne, son of Dominick Browne of Kilskeagh and Ashford in County Mayo, held the position of Ranger for almost fifty years. By the early decades of the nineteenth century the Curragh incorporated a number of additional courses (including the Sligo Course) on which specific races sponsored by members of the Turf Club (Sligo sponsored the Sligo Stakes) were run. The stakes, one hundred guineas on average, compared favourably with the prizes on offer in England. In 1813, for a four-mile race, Sligo also donated a

> ... gold whip ... to be challenged for on Friday of the June meeting, to be run for on Friday of the following October meeting, each person at the time of challenging to deliver the name of his horse or mare, sealed up to the Keeper of the Match Book, and to subscribe his name to a paper to be hung up in the Coffee Room.[22]

By the mid-eighteenth century the Curragh was fringed by numerous training lodges where the more prominent breeders and trainers, including Sligo, who leased Curragh Lodge, kept their stables. The star of his string was Waxy Pope (also known as Waxy Sligo) son of the famous Derby winner Waxy (1790) by Pot-8-Os by Eclipse out of Maria by Herod. In 1807 Waxy was purchased by the Duke of Grafton, a leading light in both the horse-racing and demi-monde in England. Waxy was the leading sire in England in 1810, and four of his offspring, Waxy Pope, Whalebone, Blucher and Whisker, were each winners of the Epsom Derby. Sligo purchased Waxy Pope (b. 1806) out of Prunella by Highflyer for the 1,000 Guineas from Grafton and brought him to stand, initially at Westport. Waxy Pope was nine times leading sire in Ireland and produced winners such as The Dandy, Sligo, Mounteagle, Butterfly and Skylark, while his daughters also produced winners both in Ireland and England, including the famous Huntsman's Mare. Many of Sligo's other stallions, including Woodcock, Recordion, Oiseau, Navigator and Langer, also stood at Westport. Claiming one could 'never have too much Waxy blood',[23] over the years Sligo purchased additional Waxy progeny, including, for 3,000 guineas, the mare Wire, who in 1816 was champion money-winning horse in Ireland. She afterwards bred many classic winners, her bloodline spreading throughout the horse-breeding world. 'I mean to enter most deeply into the breeding system,' Sligo wrote, 'having now nine thorobred [*sic*] mares and about 45 other half-bred mares so that in three years I shall be pretty well in the horse line.'[24]

Sligo also purchased Economist, son of Whisker (by Waxy out of Penelope), as a yearling, winning seven races before retiring him to stud at Curragh Lodge. Economist in turn sired Harkaway, who went on to win eleven races in Ireland and the Goodwood Cup in England, and also Echidna who produced St Leger and Cesarewitch winners, including The Baron by Birdcatcher, sire of the famous Stockwell, three-times winner of the French Oaks. His chestnut colt, Langer (named after his grandfather's estate), won the Gascoigne Stakes at Doncaster and sired Elis, a St Leger winner in 1836. Skeleton (formerly Chanter), 'a magnificent grey thoroughbred stallion',[25] by Master Robert out of a mare by Sir Walter Raleigh, won five out of his six races at the Curragh and was subsequently sold by Sligo to his friend Lord Esterhazy for the substantial sum of 2,400 guineas. After his racing career ended, Skeleton was subsequently bought by Alexander Riley and sent to New South Wales. 'I know no stallion more likely to effect an essential improvement in the breed of horses,' Sligo later attested.[26] In 1831 he sold Fang, a half-brother to Skeleton, for 3,300 guineas, 'the highest price ever given for a two year old'.[27]

His brood mares included the famous Lady Staveley (1805) by Shuttle out of the dam Drone, winner of nine races, which he purchased for 525 guineas. She was dam of Starch, Stone and Stork, all champion winners in Ireland in the 1820s. In 1815 his two-year-old filly Lady Hester, by his stallion Cliffe out of Lady Sligo, won his own Sligo Stakes at the Curragh. 'Lady Sligo, your namesake,' as he informed his mother, did not fare as well and he sold her off. 'Don't you think me very unnatural to dispose of my respected mother in that sort of way?'[28] Sligo also owned Childe Harold, named after Byron's famous poem, as well as Dean Swift, Prendergast and Canteen, who came second in the 1824 St Leger, and Cant, Vat, Fang and another colt, Bran, a runner-up in the 1834 St Leger.

He developed his great-grandfather's old racecourse at Ballyknock on what is now part of Westport's championship golf course. In the fifty-acre natural amphitheatre he laid out a racecourse complete with winning post and a stone observation tower, the latter still visible today. There he trained and tested his young horses before bringing them to courses such as the Curragh, Newmarket, Ascot and York. He had three stable blocks situated near the course, one of which, Ballyknock House, was the residence of his trainer, Richard Nokes. Westport Races, which he inaugurated in 1810, were held annually on 23 July. He commissioned Dublin-born artist John Doyle, later a famous political cartoonist and grandfather of Sir Arthur Conan Doyle, to paint six equestrian portraits entitled *The Life of a Racehorse*. Some portraits of his horses are still extant at Westport House. From 1822 to 1825 Sligo was the leading champion owner in Ireland, winning seventeen top races in 1822, valued at £2,045, and seventeen in 1825 to the value of £1,700. It was estimated that in his racing career he won 22,000 guineas in wagers and prize money, twenty-seven King's Plates, three Lord Lieutenant plates, seven Gold Cups, the Waxy Cup (now at Westport House), two Gold Whips, one Royal Whip, his own Sligo Whip, The Peel Cup (twice) and the Silver Cup. What he lost, however, was not recorded.

By the end of October 1815 Sligo moved with his regiment back to Westport. Discontent among Irish rural tenants and small-holders, fuelled by a decline in agricultural prices and a rapidly rising population, manifested itself in armed revolt. As he neared Loughrea, his regiment was deployed against one such revolt and he was forced to fire over the heads of the angry crowd. While it went against his nature to confront people driven by sheer desperation, as his orders stipulated 'there was no reason why the general officer should not give military aid he may have at his command to preserve the peace'.[29] An invitation to the home of the Earl of Clanricarde, at nearby Portumna Castle, introduced him to 'the ever famed Lady Catherine de Burgh',[30] an encounter that was to end his free-wheeling bachelor lifestyle.

On his return to Westport, letters from his mother begged him to intervene once more with her husband. Taking in a race meeting at the Curragh, where his horse Murat was victorious, accompanied by his cousin Robert Browne, he set off for London. With her customary impulsiveness, Louisa had 'adopted' Sligo's friend Count Ludolf, who had become her confidant and go-between with her husband. There is some evidence to suggest that Ludolf also benefited financially from his association with the Marchioness and that she gave him money to re-establish himself on his return to Constantinople. In one draft of her will, made after her marriage to Sir William, her initial intent was to bequeath the sum of '£30,000 to the absolute use of my adopted son, Joseph Constantine William John Count Ludolf.'[31] Wiser counsel obviously prevailed and the sum was subsequently reduced to £2,000.

Having done his best to ease the continuing tension between his mother and Sir William, Sligo made a return visit to Paris and by November was installed in the Hôtel des Princes on Rue Richelieu. After the Hundred Days' reign of Napoleon and his subsequent surrender and exile, King Louis XVIII had returned to Paris. His arrival, 'in the baggage train of the foreigners', particularly the British, was deeply resented by Parisians. The second Treaty of Paris, concluded in November, exacted a heavy price on France. Territory on her northern and eastern boundaries, seized by Napoleon with much loss of French blood, fell into the hands of the victorious Allies. A war indemnity of 700 million francs and the upkeep of an army of occupation at an annual cost of 150 million francs were imposed on the French people. While Napoleon may have been defeated at Waterloo, his huge army was still practically intact and resentful of the puppet status of the king with their former enemies. But for the moment the mercurial citizens of Paris cheered Louis along the boulevards as they had Napoleon a few months previously.

Sligo found the atmosphere in Paris much changed from his previous visit. 'Everyone is discontented. There is great confusion which I think will *eclate* before very long.'[32] Almost one million Allied troops were dispersed throughout the city. Violent clashes occurred daily on the streets, particularly with Prussian soldiers who, with difficulty, were restrained from pillaging the city. Brawls, rampages, duels, murders and general mayhem erupted on the boulevards, along the banks of the Seine and in the Tuileries. Supporters of Napoleon were in hiding, in exile or had simply changed sides. Those who remained added to the seething sense of discontent and grievance directed against the Bourbon regime. 'Affairs are going on here as badly as possible. If our troops left Paris the Bourbons would not remain 2 days on the throne, their tyranny is not to be equalled,' Sligo astutely observed.[33] Only the Duke of Orleans appeared to find favour with the people, he noted; 'every class of people look to him and every party would be satisfied with his appointment [as King]'.[34] The Bourbons' English masters fared as badly. 'Lord Wellington is detested by all classes and nations, French and English …. Lord Castlereagh … has great influence here.'[35] English tourists, who on the capitulation of Napoleon and on the reinstatement of the king, flocked to the capital, experienced open antagonism on the streets. The intensity of the anti-British feeling was further exacerbated when it became known that the treasures accumulated by Napoleon on his predatory expeditions into Egypt, Italy and Spain, and housed mainly in the Louvre, were, on the orders of Wellington, to be repatriated.

Sligo's friendship with Joachim Murat came to the attention of Élie Decazes, the new Minister for Police. Previously a follower of Napoleon, Decazes was transformed into a confirmed royalist. In autumn 1815 Murat's former aide-de-camp, Francis Macirone, was apprehended by the secret police and interrogated in the dreaded Conciergerie, before being confined at liberty in Paris. Sligo made contact with Macirone and other adherents of Murat he had known in Naples and who were lying low in Paris. 'I have seen them,' he related to Caldwell, 'but from the activity of the police here which is more outrageous now than in the time of Robespierre, I did not see all of them.'[36] Decazes and his assistant, Menares, were aware of Sligo's presence in Paris and, in view of his past association with Napoleon's family, and especially with Murat, tried to elicit information about him from Macirone. 'By the by do you know Sir Robert Wilson and Lord Sligo, what are they doing here? Are they not of the opposition?'[37] While suspicious, not even Decazes had the temerity to apprehend a British aristocrat, especially one with influential connections.

Even in Paris, there was no escaping Sligo's mounting debts. His estate agent Glendenning, as a miffed Sligo informed his mother, urged him

… to awake from my lethargy respecting my expenses. He must be dreaming, for he himself allowed repeatedly to me

at Westport that he could not imagine anyway to save more
than I did ... One thing strikes me as very extraordinary
I am supposed to have a large fortune with all that I am
not to have the enjoyment of a thousand ... I went away
from home for near 2 years in order to pay debts and when
I come back I find none paid. Why in God's truth it is
enough to disgust a man.

Vowing not 'to tease myself anymore about it', the unrepentant
spendthrift resolved to avoid involving 'no person anymore into
scrapes respecting money matters'.[38] Like so many of his well-
intentioned resolutions, it was honoured more in the breach than
in the observance.

An invitation to attend the Prince Regent at Brighton further
delayed his return to Westport. If Sligo's personal finances were a
cause of concern, the Regent's were truly staggering, amounting
to £350,000 in 1815. The prince determined to increase his
indebtedness further by embarking on a major reconstruction
programme at Carlton House and also at his home in Brighton,
one of the most extravagant and exotic buildings ever constructed
in England. Brighton was the prince's refuge where he pursued
his pleasures away from the prying eyes of his many critics.
Originally a modest marine pavilion, an elaborate scheme for its
transformation, complete with onion-shaped domes, conical roofs,
minarets, Saracenic arches, its interior resplendently decorated
in Indian–Chinese style, then much in vogue, had commenced.
Taking eight years to complete, the Royal Pavilion eventually cost
(the British taxpayer) £155,000.

Sligo's presence among the Regent's fashionable party at
Brighton received extensive coverage in the newspapers with the
resultant 'ridiculous effect', as he wrote, 'of receiving no less than
ten letters from people I do not know at all, beginning "seeing
by the papers that your Lordship was at Brighton with the Prince

Regent and knowing your exalted character for benevolence".'[39] His association with the Prince Regent was also the subject of caricaturists and satirists. George Cruickshank's portrayal of *The Court at Brighton à la Chinese* depicted an obese Prince Regent surrounded by his friends, all dressed in Chinese costume, among whom is Sligo wearing a mandarin's costume with a star and the ribbon of St Patrick with the words 'A SLY GO'.

It was in the unlikely surroundings of the Brighton 'pleasure dome', however, that Sligo first heard sentiments espoused by one of the Prince Regent's guests, William Wilberforce, about the growing movement for the abolition of slavery in the British West Indies. The contentious issue and its implications for plantation owners such as Sligo were later to become a turning point in his life that, in 1815, seemed unimaginable.

Chapter 10

The Good Husband

I am really so happy. I do not very well know whether I am laughing or crying … May God bless them both. I can only say that if he makes as good a husband to Lady Catherine as he has been an exemplary son to me, she will be the happiest woman breathing.

Marchioness of Sligo

The ending of the Napoleonic war that had devastated Europe, redrawn state boundaries, caused the deaths of millions and seen hereditary crowns and thrones revolve, as if in some crazy game of roulette, brought in its wake not merely great change but also great hardship. The fall of Napoleon and his banishment to St Helena, while removing the threat of further military upheaval, also ushered in a period of economic, political and social instability in Britain. A fall in demand for British manufactured goods, combined with the return of thousands of soldiers from the war, added to the existing unemployment minefield. The passing of the infamous Corn Laws, designed to protect the price of corn at the expense of the urban poor, resulted in serious rioting in London and attacks on the houses of members of parliament. Luddite violence flared again in Nottinghamshire, while demands by the middle classes for parliamentary reform and an end to aristocratic political privilege became more vociferous

The ending of the war brought fundamental change also to social attitudes and behaviour. The wild excesses of the wealthy and aristocratic were less tolerated. The figurehead who most epitomised the period of self-indulgent excess, the Prince Regent, was attacked by a mob as he returned to Carlton House after the state opening of parliament. The days of the demi-monde and unbridled excess were drawing to a close. Courtesans like Harriette Wilson were finding it difficult to entrap aristocratic protectors and eventually resorted to blackmail. Harriette's threat, 'I certainly do not feel disposed to strive for the glory of keeping the secrets of those who never did anything with the view, nor with the intention, of contributing to my future comfort,'[1] would later have embarrassing repercussions for many of her former high-society clients, including the Marquess of Sligo. The evangelical movement no longer confined its efforts to the abolition of slavery in the British colonies. It also targeted home-grown social ills, such as the proliferation of beggars and alcoholics on British streets, the physical and sexual abuse of children in the teeming urban slums and the vast numbers of prostitutes working in the sex industry. While dismissed as mere 'cant' by Byron, the new moralising movement, and the many societies and institutions it spawned, began to seep through the consciousness of society and make even the aristocracy consider the moral implications of their behaviour, in public at least.

Former participants in the demi-monde began to adopt a more conformist lifestyle. Even Byron, the 'systematic poet of seduction, adultery and incest',[2] in January 1815 entered the state of matrimony, if only for a short period. Accusations of an incestuous relationship with his half-sister Augusta Leigh, combined with his past indiscretions in Greece and given the homophobic atmosphere in Britain, led to his enforced exile from England in April 1816. Hobhouse contemplated a career as a radical politician, while the fashionista to the Regency bucks, Beau Brummell, fled to the Continent to escape his creditors, to be followed a few years later by an equally bankrupt Scrope Davies. The days of riotous living and debauchery were fast becoming passé.

Now in his twenty-eighth year, Sligo's life of carefree abandon was also drawing to a close. By October 1815 he too was actively contemplating the prospect of marriage, urged on by his uncle Denis Browne. Marriage, especially to an Irishwoman, his uncle reasoned, might restrain his nephew's proclivity for living abroad, curtail his spending habits and even augment his volatile financial situation with a handsome dowry. And for once nephew and uncle were in agreement. Sligo expressed his aversion to his mother's preference of 'forming an English connection' and agreed instead to consider a suitable candidate that 'my uncle has laid out for me'.[3] That someone was 'the ever famed' Lady Hester Catherine de Burgh, whom he had previously met in Portumna Castle. She was the eldest daughter of John Thomas de Burgh, 13th Earl of Clanricarde, descendant of the great Norman de Burgo family of Connaught. Her father owned an estate of 56,000 acres in County Galway and another in Hampshire in England. The earl died in 1808 while his eldest son and heir, Ulick, was still a minor and the Clanricarde estate was ably administered on his behalf by the earl's widow, Elizabeth, the second daughter of Sir Thomas Burke, a Catholic landowner from Marble Hill, County Galway. Lady Clanricarde's sister Ellen was married in England to George Smith, the eldest son of Viscount Strangford. Sligo's relations, the Mahons of Castlegar, were also connected with the Clanricarde family, for whom they served as land agents.

Sligo had first glimpsed his future wife riding in a carriage with her mother through the town of Loughrea. He was struck, as he informed his mother, by her 'most extraordinary likeness to Pauline that I ever saw. I should certainly have imagined it was her had I seen Lady Catherine driving thro the streets of London.'[4] He assured his mother that Catherine would not, as Louisa feared, be shackled with 'a set of beggarly Catholic relations' but on the contrary that 'in case any of her brothers have any accidents she could be one of the first heiresses in Ireland'.[5] In 1800 the Earl of Clanricarde obtained letters patent to permit his eldest daughter to become his successor, with the title of 'countess', in the event of lack of male heirs. (On the death of the last Earl of Clanricarde without issue in 1916, the title passed to Catherine's grandson, the 6th Marquess of Sligo.)

Given his experience of the demi-monde in London, and with the prevalence of extra-marital affairs in society, Sligo was content that in Lady Hester Catherine de Burgh he had, at last, found himself an ideal partner. 'I looked a good deal into her character and manners and thought that they were such as would suit me exactly.'[6] On his return from Paris in early January 1816, he set about wooing and winning his intended's affections.

From her portrait Catherine de Burgh appears to have walked out of a Jane Austen novel. Striking, with auburn-hair, eyes of marine blue that evinced a steady look of someone capable and steadfast, she proved an excellent partner for Sligo. A loyal and loving wife, wise and level-headed, she was an ideal counterbalance to her more impulsive husband. Reared in a mixed religious household – her mother still adhered to the Catholic religion – much of her early life, together with her younger sister Emily and brother Ulick, was spent in the family estate in Hampshire. Financial and social considerations notwithstanding, Sligo's choice of bride had the added advantage of physical attraction that deepened into a genuine loving bond that remained constant throughout his lifetime. While indisputably the head of his household, he shared and consulted his wife about his political and business undertakings. Ever solicitous of her well-being, comfort and safety, he valued her opinion and, as his son later recorded, 'he was devoted to her and could never bear her out of his sight'.[7]

Despite his initial self-centred assertion that her 'character and manners' suited him exactly, Sligo became smitten by his young bride-to-be. 'Here I am as happy as a Prince,' he wrote to Caldwell from Portumna Castle. 'I assure you I am more in love every day. Nothing is more charming and free from affectation than the conduct of Lady Catherine.'[8] From the start there was an endearing humorous dimension to their relationship. Sligo retained a schoolboy's predilection for inventing nicknames for those closest to him. Caldwell became known as 'old Beast' or 'Beastie', while his mother was designated 'Mrs Dowager' or more usually 'Mink' in his correspondence. His appellation for his bride-to-be was 'the Chatte' while hers for him was 'Poux'. Despite his racy past, Sligo became the epitome of a faithful and loving husband and a good, if somewhat stern, father to the fourteen children which, from 1816, he and Catherine, with almost constant regularity, produced.

The Dowager Marchioness of Sligo's delight and relief that her son had, at last, found himself a suitable mate was palpable:

> I am hardly in my senses with delight at my beloved child's marriage …. I have written to Lady Clanricarde but for God's sake read them before they see them and if they are like the letters of a madwoman, do not give them but put them into the fire.[9]

To Catherine she wrote of her impending 'delight with which I shall meet a being so dear to Him as yourself'.[10] Impatient to make the acquaintance of her prospective daughter-in-law, even though, as she admitted, 'I shall be fairly dubbed "dowager" … I can put up with tolerable patience with that addition to my name but the thing that provokes me is people already talking about the *Young* Marchioness!'[11] To Lady Clanricarde, Louisa promised to be a 'second mother' to her daughter.[12] Her husband, Sir William Scott, more sanguine than his wife regarding the past foibles, amorous and otherwise, of his stepson, urged Sligo to ensure, that the union 'may never be interrupted by uneasiness arising from any quarter'.[13]

As with most events in his life, Sligo sought to conclude the marriage formalities as quickly as possible. Over the winter months he seldom strayed from Portumna Castle, taking part in local seasonal hunts, balls and parties. A friend made him a present of a grey hunter named Goliath 'on which I trust', he joked to Caldwell, 'I shall cut no mean figure in my red hunting coat'.[14] To celebrate their engagement, he showered Catherine with presents of 'trinkets … such as chains, crosses, earrings, etc' as well as a 'handsome watch, chain and seals' with her cipher 'HCS'. Ordering a new carriage, he further instructed Caldwell to ensure that 'they quarter her arms rightly on the panels' and informed him how Catherine 'said last night that her greatest happiness would be to gain your good opinion, a wish,' he jocosely added, 'I *cursed* her for having.'[15] Following the official announcement of the engagement, he made a quick dash to London 'to bring over the Chatte's diamond', as well as to pay off some pressing debts. Lady Clanricarde promised to do her best to see 'that the thing should take place as soon as her [Catherine's] guardian had inspected the papers'.[16]

Impatiently, Sligo made plans for a low-key wedding celebration and honeymoon. 'We will go down to Portumna,' he advised Caldwell, 'where the ugly Dean [Peter Browne] will meet us and do his job. After that we will go to Westport. My own idea is and in which C[atherine] most fully agrees in it to go and join you in June in Paris and go on with you.' He promised to consult 'his maps' as to the best route through Belgium, France, across the Alps into Italy, provided, 'we can scrape up money enough and join you'.[17] Westport House, so long without a family, was prepared for the arrival of the new chatelaine. Sligo fretted that the household staff, left so long to their own devices, would not measure up. To his great delight, he found a 'treasure' in a new cook, whom he asserted, his steward 'John Mealy says saves more than his wages in meat'.[18]

The legal requirements surrounding the marriage, however, dragged on. Impatiently he chafed at what he perceived to be the unnecessary paperwork between Catherine's lawyer and guardian, Appleyard, at Lincoln's Inn in London, 'full of quirks and quibbles', and his own lawyer, Livesay, in Dublin. He urged Thomas Metcalf, his mother's lawyer in London, to intervene to 'speed things up'.[19] Eventually, on 4 March, the details of the marriage settlement were concluded to the satisfaction of both parties: £10,000 and a further £20,000 for the benefit of children of the marriage, excluding his eldest male heir, were levied against the Sligo estate.

On the same day he signed the marriage settlement, the 'Most Noble Howe Peter, Marquis of Sligo and Lady Hester Catherine de Burgh' were married by special licence of the Archbishop of Armagh, by Sligo's step-uncle, Peter Browne, in the Parish Church of St Mary in Dublin. Fearing, as he wrote to Caldwell, 'the times are so doubtful that no certain plans can be formed', the newlyweds first stayed at the lodge of his racing colleague Bowes Daly on the Curragh to take in a race meeting, before journeying on to Westport. On arrival, they were greeted with the customary bonfires in the town, addresses of welcome from the Westport House tenants and visitations from the extended Browne family and neighbours, all anxious to view and welcome the new Marchioness.

Barely sixteen years old, Catherine adapted quickly to her new role as wife and chatelaine. She took a keen interest in her husband's renovation plans at Westport House and was responsible for the layout and design of new pleasure gardens, which she planted with many rare species of trees and shrubs. Some of the grounds planted were recorded as being originally 'made out of bog from which turf had been regularly cut up to that time, cut for the use of the house and the farm'.[20] An avid gardener, she was knowledgeable about and interested in new species of flowers and plants, instructing the gardeners in the technicalities of propagation, grafting and planting. An accomplished hostess, she entertained many notable visitors, including several Irish viceroys and statesmen, as well as the famous writer Maria Edgeworth, at Westport House.

While the young Marchioness of Sligo settled into married life, the troubled marriage of the Dowager Marchioness finally reached an impasse. In her fiftieth year, overweight and overwrought, by early 1816 she was again writing 'to my dear, my affectionate son' about her 'unfortunate state', news of which would reach him, she dramatically told him, 'when I am no more'.[21] To circumvent the conditions of her marriage settlement, by which Sir William enjoyed right of residence in her house at Porter's Lodge during his lifetime, Louisa set out to make it as uncomfortable as possible for him by leaving all the furniture to her son 'so that I might leave you as much hold over him [Sir William] as I possibly can'.[22] In a further letter, she made an

> ... earnest request to you, my child, to remove all the furniture that you may have left at Porter's Lodge or in any house in town in which Sir William Scott may live or which he may hold by my marriage settlement, all which furniture books plate linen, etc I have left to you and if Mrs Townsend Sir William's daughter sleeps *one night* in any of them, as I am determined she shall not be mistress of any of my houses after my death, tho she often attempted it in my life.[23]

Sligo again took on the role of mediator. 'For God's sake don't meddle between Sir William and his law, it will do him no good and only make you and he quarrel.'[24] Despite his mother's admission that she did not 'pretend that I am never wrong for I know I often lose my temper when driven', there was to be no reconciliation. Despite or because of her marital difficulties, she decamped to Paris in May, from where she issued another broadside in her battle of wits with her husband, instructing her lawyer to countermand her husband's attempt to replace trustees she had appointed with his own. 'Half dead from the weather' Sligo and his new bride followed the Dowager Marchioness to Paris for their postponed honeymoon.

From the start, the two women closest to him became firm friends. Catherine's letters to her mother-in-law, 'Dearest Mink', are affectionate and playfully precocious. 'Adieu, horrid Mink, I wish you were here that I might teaze [*sic*] you to death.' She poked fun at Louisa's increasing girth, advising her that if 'Poux was only to show you to his enemies they would run away in a fright at the sight of your Minkship.'[25] Relieved that her son had at last settled down, Louisa reciprocated her young daughter-in-law's affection. They corresponded regularly, the Dowager Marchioness purchasing material, accessories and '2 pairs of stays, not for Poux's kitten but for Lady C de Burgh [Catherine's mother]' and sourcing suitable household staff in London for Westport House.[26] Already pregnant with the first of her many children, Catherine was introduced to society in post-war Paris and was dazzled both by the city and by its sophisticated ambience.

As well as introducing his new bride to the delights of Paris, Sligo had another duty to fulfil. The treasures purloined by the vanquished Emperor of France from various countries during his turbulent reign were, in turn, being acquired by its victors. The Prince Regent had his eye on some of the loot and requested Sligo to purchase, on his behalf, a number of marble statues amounting to the sum of £200 sterling. In an addendum to his letter, notifying the prince's secretary about the proposed shipment of the statues to Carlton House, Sligo also requested to 'present my humble duty to the Regent & tell him I had no news to send him and did not therefore write', intimating that he was still engaged in gathering information on the Prince's behalf regarding the Princess of Wales.[27]

On his return to Westport, Sligo became embroiled in a long-simmering feud between his uncle and Sir Neal O'Donel about the non-payment by O'Donel of head rent owing to the Westport Estate and of a personal loan to Denis Browne. By autumn 1816 the feud had descended into a bitter war of words between Browne and O'Donel, who accused the latter 'of being drunk every morning

... even obliged to have a whiskey before he left his bed and ... in the constant habit of beating his wife'.[28] During Sligo's absence in Greece and Turkey, his mother had tried to patch up the dispute. It was her opinion that Denis Browne 'had ill used Sir Neal' but, as she informed her son, despite 'the violent abuse he threw out against Denis', O'Donel had assured her that 'I love your son.'[29] Truculent and heavy-handed, Denis Browne, as the power-broker in his nephew's absence, endeared himself to few in Mayo.

The O'Donels of Newport were lineally descended from Niall Garbh O'Donnell, cousin of the famous sixteenth-century Gaelic confederate leader Red Hugh O'Donnell, chieftain of Tir Conaill (Donegal). Transplanted from their ancestral lands during the Cromwellan confiscations in the mid-eighteenth century, a branch of the family settled in Newport. By virtue of an illicit but profitable smuggling business, their fortunes prospered. Converting to the Established Church, in 1780 Neal O'Donel was subsequently conferred with a baronetcy. With land an obligatory accessory for ennoblement, in 1785 he outbid the Earl of Altamont for the Newport-Pratt estate of some 70,000 acres in the barony of Burrishoole, on which he built himself a fine new mansion. The estate was originally owned by John Medlycott of Dublin who in 1774 sold his interest to the first Earl of Altamont for £16,000, but retained a lease for lives in perpetuity in the estate on the payment of £980 in annual head rent. Medlycott sold his lease interest to Sir Neal O'Donel, who consequently became liable for payment of the head rent to the Marquess of Sligo.

The personal animosity that existed between Sir Neal and Denis Browne further complicated the situation. As well as defaulting on his debt, O'Donel had incurred Browne's hostility for turning a blind eye to the activities of rebels on his estate during the 1798 rebellion. O'Donel's opposition to the Union in 1800 also put him at odds with his more powerful neighbour in Westport House, as did his family's inclination for smuggling. Initially, perhaps by virtue of his lengthy absences abroad, his less antagonistic nature, his uneasy relationship with his uncle, as well as his more pragmatic approach to the management of his estate, Sligo remained aloof from the dispute. Despite the arrears in head rent (which by 1828 amounted to the substantial sum of £6,000), Sligo was more tolerant of O'Donal, knowing he faced crippling death duties following the deaths of five members of his family, some who were killed in duels. Unlike his nephew, however, Denis Browne was unwilling to allow another landowning dynasty to steal a march on his family. To take the heat out of the long-standing feud, Sligo reached a temporary settlement with O'Donel. Hostilities between his uncle and O'Donel, however, continued to simmer below the surface to eventually explode and dilute the political prominence enjoyed by the Marquess of Sligo in Mayo.

Neither the dispute with O'Donel, his uncle's obduracy nor the worsening economic situation in Ireland, however, could curtail Sligo's joy at the birth of his first child, Louisa Catherine, born at Westport House in December 1816. In keeping with his predilection for nicknames, Louisa was referred to in family correspondence as 'Kitten'. Sligo took his responsibility as a parent seriously and happily did his share of babysitting: 'Kitten has caught a bad cold and I am sitting in the great white armchair writing on the green table in its room.'[30] An outlay from his estate for his daughter's dowry of £10,000 ensured her future eligibility in the marriage stakes. Over the Christmas period the happy parents were joined by an equally ecstatic Dowager Marchioness from London to see her namesake, her 'darling Louisa'. The minutiae of her granddaughter's progress over the succeeding months were eagerly received by the doting grandmother. 'The Kitten has grown prodigiously since Mink saw her,' Catherine reported. 'I am afraid she will soon be nearly as large as a kitten. She is teething and has a little rash.'[31] By March Catherine was again pregnant and, according to her delighted husband, 'was greatly annoyed at the idea of having two wet nurses at the same time in the house ... and says she will fit up the gallery as a nursery which is the largest room in the house. Hurra!'[32]

With the trepidation of a young first-time mother, Catherine reluctantly consented to leave Louisa and accompany her husband and her mother to Dublin. The viceroy, Lord Whitworth, was on the point of departure from Ireland. A staunch opponent of Catholic Emancipation, he was married to the wealthy and formidable Lady Dorset, a friend of the Dowager Marchioness of Sligo, who had stayed at the Viceregal Lodge on her return journey from Westport. Sir Robert Peel, Chief Secretary of Ireland, a friend of both Sligo's parents, entertained him at Dublin Castle, making him appreciative, as he informed his mother, of 'the attention I have met with from everyone here ... the Lord Lieutenant in particular'.[33] Sligo and his young bride were also welcomed at the Viceregal Court where they attended a concert. 'There are balls and parties in Dublin every night,' Catherine wrote to her mother-in-law. 'Maman goes to a great many of them. I hear that quadrilles have put all other dances out of fashion.'[34] Given her pregnancy, Catherine's time in the capital was spent on less energetic activities, including sitting for her portrait.

Arriving back in Westport via the Curragh, where Sligo's horses won 'five races which has put me in very good spirits',[35] they found that their English butler had handed in his notice, pleading 'the dampness of Westport'.[36] With so young a bride, the management of the domestic arrangements at Westport House required an experienced hand. 'For God's sake send over a housekeeper as soon as possible, as I do not know what to do without one,' Sligo appealed to his mother.[37] All was dust, noise and upheaval, with the ongoing building and remodelling programme and the arrival of library shelving and furniture from the English cabinet-makers Gillows, including two immense, richly carved mahogany sideboards, complete with eagles, the Browne family crest. Sligo also commissioned James A. O'Connor, then unknown and virtually destitute landscape artist, to paint seventeen landscapes of Westport House and its environs, as well as of Catherine's home in Portumna.

Following her return from Ireland, much to her son's relief, the Dowager Marchioness enjoyed an interlude of relative tranquillity with her husband, who had written to her in conciliatory terms during her stay at Westport. 'I am very happy to hear that Sir William and you are going on so well and I hope it will continue.'[38] As well as becoming reconciled with his wife, the judge intimated that it might be appropriate if he was also reunited with his wife's furniture, which she had sent to Westport for safe-keeping. To prevent further dissension between the warring pair, Sligo immediately concurred: 'I am happy to tell you that the 2 ships are at last arrived .... Please God I will have 12 carts sending off your furniture and another [ship] belonging to this port called *The Lady Sligo* which I am about chartering so that I trust Sir William will not have long to grumble.'[39]

The 'truce' with Sir William, however, did not last long. By early summer Louisa, accompanied by her niece Marianne Curzon, embarked on an extended tour of Europe. On 20 August 1817, in her fiftieth year, Louisa died suddenly in Amsterdam. The death of his mother, who had been such a constant in his life, was a deeply emotional wrench for Sligo. Their relationship, especially since the death of his father, had been deep and affectionate. He trusted her implicitly and valued her opinion in relation to his business affairs and, unusually for a son, she became his confidante in the personal affairs of his life. Unwavering and loyal in the face of his many scrapes, failures and shortcomings, she was both mother and friend, a financial and emotional support in all his endeavours. With the exception of minor bequests to Marianne Curzon, her nephew Richard Penn Curzon, her personal staff and 'an annuity of £300 ... to George Caldwell of Jesus College, Cambridge',[40] Louisa left her son a substantial estate in land, property, investments, jewellery and plate, in addition to the £60,000 already expended on subventing his travel and debts. His inheritance helped him purchase, for £23,000, the Lehinch estate in Kilmaine on the Mayo–Galway border. According to her wishes, Louisa was buried, not with her first husband in Westport, but with her father, Admiral Howe, in the village church in Shenley.

Her widower continued to reside for a time at his wife's house at 11 Grafton Street and at Porter's Lodge, which was later sold. Elevated in the peerage in 1821 as Lord Stowell, Sir William eventually retired to his estate in Berkshire, where he lived until his death in 1836 in his ninetieth year. Despite his stepfather's fractious relationship with his mother, Sligo maintained contact with his stepfather and also with his daughter, Louisa's adversary, who, on the death of her first husband, married Sligo's friend Henry Addington, Viscount Sidmouth.

In 1818 the British prime minister, Lord Liverpool, called a general election. Electioneering in Britain was dishonest, fractious and disorderly but it paled in intensity to the process in Ireland. Issues such as Catholic Emancipation, the enforced payment of tithes and the appalling condition of the great proportion of the population brought passions to the fore. There were two ways to stand for election: to be nominated and financially backed by a wealthy (usually aristocratic) proprietor or by purchasing one of the many 'rotten' boroughs openly for sale, some for as much as £20,000 (almost £500,000 today), to the highest bidder, regardless of the purchaser's qualifications, local knowledge or nationality. As in England, elections in Ireland were mainly dictated by the landowning class, with some twenty-seven of the thirty-three boroughs in Ireland controlled by landed proprietors. The small number of electors entitled to vote, mainly leaseholders of land worth more than forty shillings per annum, ensured that the majority, whether voluntarily or through intimidation, voted according to the dictate of their landlord.

In Ireland selection for election was confined to Protestants. A candidate was nominated by a local magnate, who spared no expense to bring his freeholders to the polling station. In the far-flung estates along the west coast, electors were transported and maintained in local towns, at the expense of the landlord, for the duration of the election process. Pitched battles between supporters of opposing candidates, riots, duels to the death over election issues, bribery and kidnapping of the freeholders of rivals to prevent them from casting their votes, fuelled by the liberal distribution of alcohol, ensured that Irish elections were fraught and, for the landlord, expensive affairs.

Mayo returned two MPs to parliament. Since the early 1700s, when the Browne family had first involved themselves in parliamentary politics, through the continual absenteeism of their local rivals, the earls of Lucan in Castlebar and the viscounts Dillon in the barony of Costello, as well as by virtue of their status as the accepted protectors and representatives of their disenfranchised Catholic neighbours, the family controlled the political representation of the county. Sligo's uncle, Denis Browne, represented Mayo in parliament for thirty-six years. For the 1818 election he persuaded his nephew to support his son James in Mayo while he stood for a vacant seat in County Kilkenny.

While effective and industrious as a political representative, Denis Browne evoked mixed feelings among his peers. On his retirement from politics in Mayo, when his supporters attempted to commemorate his contribution to the county's affairs 'almost unexampled for the promotion of its welfare'[41] by having his portrait hung in the County Hall in Castlebar, it was strongly opposed. 'We will not enter into the merits or demerits of the Parliamentary conduct of the Right Honourable Gentleman, yet we feel it necessary, upon mature consideration, to enter our protest against the admission of the portrait of any private individual into the public hall of the County.'[42]

Denis Browne, perhaps more than most Irish MPs, merited having his portrait hung in the County Hall. His long service in parliament and, in the absence of his nephew, in local government in Mayo endowed him with an intimate knowledge of the problems that bedevilled the country, both at national and local level. From the inequity of the nefarious tithe tax, to the problems posed by a rising population then approaching seven million, or, as he noted, 'about two hundred and forty persons per square mile – including bog land and water,'[43] his attack on the deplorable state of Church lands under the control of the Church of Ireland, to his outspoken aversion to the 'evil' of the absentee landlord (which, for a time, included his nephew), his views were both radical and relevant. During his nephew's absences abroad he kept the Browne flag flying at election time, which involved adroit organisation, not a little danger and a substantial financial outlay. Much depended on a successful outcome, since from it flowed 'the patronage of the county' which, in turn, was judiciously shared among family and political allies who, in turn, distributed their favours to their tenants and thus, as one commentator noted, 'this fertile spring of corruption flows in a strong current'.[44] While such blatant nepotism might, in hindsight, be decried, it was preferable to the alternative – the return of a nominal member who was not only non-resident in the area but had no 'greater knowledge of its real situation than they have of Tibet or Abyssinia'.[45] Like a parliamentary representative today, a local voice in parliament ensured that the county got its share from the public purse to fund local commercial and infrastructural development. And in this regard, during his long career, Denis Browne made sure that County Mayo received its share. Despite his earlier reservations, his nephew also came to realise the significance of government patronage. 'This patronage is very necessary for me for the purposes of keeping up my influence in the County and has always been used for that purpose.'[46] For the election of 1818, however, in Mayo there was little threat to the political status quo. A pact with the absentee landlord Viscount Dillon ensured the return of James Browne as MP for the county, while Denis Browne was returned for Kilkenny.

On 27 May 1819, Sligo was formally installed as a Knight of St Patrick in St Patrick's Cathedral in Dublin, the 'youngest person who ever received the order of knighthood', for which, as he acknowledged, 'I principally owed to my being one of the representatives of the Howe family.'[47] His esquires for the occasion were his wife's uncle, Sir John Burke, and his cousins James and Robert Browne. He celebrated the occasion with his extended family, which included a second daughter, Elizabeth, born in December 1818. In 1819 he was also elected as a life member of the Royal Dublin Society and a Senior Grand Warden of the Masonic Order in Ireland.

On 31 January 1820, his son and heir George John, Earl of Altamont, was born and named in honour of his godfather, King George IV. The king often entertained his godchildren, entering goodnaturedly in their games and presenting them with gifts. At seven years of age Altamont was invited by the king to a party in Brighton Pavilion. 'As he danced with his partner around the room he bumped into another young guest who admonished him loudly saying "I say, Altamont, you might look where you are going." The king, overhearing his name, took him by the hand saying, "God damn your eyes, my boy, you must be Sligo's son."' Later in Westport House at a family dinner, to the consternation of his parents and grandmother, on being taken to task by his sister Elizabeth, Altamont rebuked her with the words, 'God damn your eyes, Elizabeth, how you do pull a chap up.' A shocked Lady Clanricarde asked her grandson who had taught him such impolite language. 'The King, my godfather,' Altamont replied.[48]

The new king acceded to the throne on 29 January 1820. Florid and hideously overweight, his dyed blond hair crimped and curled, his face powdered and rouged, his swollen fingers encrusted with rings, his current mistress was Marchioness Conyngham, the lady of Sligo's boyhood adventure with De Quincey. Wife of the Irish peer Marquess Conyngham from Slane Castle and mother of five adult children, she had replaced the equally mature Lady Hertford in the Prince's affections. His long wait for the throne being realised, true to form, George set plans in motion for an extravagant coronation. A summons to the coronation at Westminster Abbey, planned for 1 August 1820, commanded the Marquess of Sligo 'to make your personal attendance on Us … furnished and appointed as to your Rank and Quality'.[49] But one obstacle to the great event remained: the monarch's estranged wife. If George was to become king, then Caroline, the wife he detested, would become queen. The coronation was subsequently postponed until the king obtained his long-desired divorce.

Despite the protestations of the prime minister, Lord Liverpool, the Duke of Wellington, whom he brusquely ordered to 'hold his tongue', and the foreign secretary, George Canning, who subsequently resigned, the king determined 'to deprive her Majesty Caroline, Amelia, Elizabeth of the title, prerogative, rights, privileges and exemption of Queen Consort of this Realm' and to have their marriage dissolved on the grounds of her adultery.[50] A bill to that effect was introduced in parliament. On the advice of her supporters, the queen returned to England. While salacious gossip about her unseemly conduct in Europe abounded, the king, desperate for hard evidence, recalled the Marquess of Sligo's investigations on his behalf in Italy and summoned him as a witness against the queen for her alleged adultery with Pergami. Since the evidence against the queen rested mainly on the testimony of foreigners and people of inferior rank, the testimony of a marquess of the realm became vital to the king's case.

The proposed trial of the queen threatened political meltdown in England. Ordinary citizens vehemently objected to the hypocrisy of their licentious monarch pursuing a charge of adultery against his spouse. The radicalisation of the disenfranchised middle and lower classes had grown alarmingly. In August 1819 sixty thousand men, women and children who had gathered near Manchester to demand parliamentary and social reform were attacked by the army, resulting in eleven deaths and countless injuries. Public reaction to the 'Peterloo Massacre' was further exacerbated by the publication of a letter signifying the king's satisfaction at the outcome. The queen's cause now became a rallying point and a propaganda tool for the proponents of political and social reform. Many of Sligo's friends, such as John Cam Hobhouse, supported the queen. Mobs congregated outside Carlton House and hurled abuse at the king, whom they likened to Nero. Tory ministers were shouted at and jostled in the streets. Castlereagh's London house was attacked by a stone-throwing mob. Hero of the Napoleonic wars, the Duke of Wellington, was accosted by road-menders in Grosvenor Place who compelled him to utter the words 'God Save the Queen', to which Wellington was said to have replied: 'Well, Gentlemen, since you will have it so, God Save the Queen, and may all your wives be like her.'[51] There were riots everywhere and it was feared the unrest had infiltrated the army. Regardless of the public outcry, the king would not be deterred and on 17 August 1820 the queen was summoned for trial in the House of Lords.

The prospect of appearing as principal witness against the lawful queen of England placed Sligo in an extraordinary dilemma. His personal friendship and close family ties with the king, godfather to his son, as well as his sleuthing in Italy on his monarch's behalf, obligated his appearance as a supporting witness. But the magnitude of what was envisaged and its likely repercussions made everyone, regardless of political persuasion or personal affiliation, step back from the brink. While convinced of the queen's guilt, many of Sligo's fellow peers were against the drastic measure propounded by the king. Despite being summoned to attend her trial, many members of the House of Lords chose to incur their sovereign's ire, as well as the fine imposed for their non-attendance, and remained closeted in their country estates. Even leaders of the reforming Whig party, such as Lord Holland and Lord Grey, feared the trial would bring social and political chaos in its wake.

With the distance of the Irish Sea and the breadth of Ireland between him and the king, with honesty bordering on naivety, Sligo wrote to George IV from Westport to explain his non-attendance. Having been informed 'that His Majesty had expressed yourself to be deeply afflicted at my ingratitude towards you, after having received so many kindnesses at your hands', he blamed his own public trial in 1812 and his subsequent imprisonment in Newgate. It was, he reasoned

> ... absolutely necessary for me to carefully avoid ... attacks which ill-minded, disappointed persons or a licentious press never fail to make .... Your Majesty must be aware that the circumstances of my being principal witness against the Queen was almost universally believed ... utter ruin of character would follow ... had my name appeared in a small minority .... The very probability or possibility of this was more than I had the courage to face.

Hoping that 'Your Majesty will extend to me your usual consideration and forgiveness for what perhaps may be deemed to be an act of cowardice' but, as he boldly added, 'any man may be called on to risk his life but character is too high a stake lightly to be ventured.'[52] Sligo's decision was, however, vindicated. The trial, which proceeded without him, resulted in a stalemate between the warring couple and was eventually abandoned. Denied access to her husband's rearranged coronation at Westminster Abbey on 19 July 1821, natural causes finally granted the king his wish. Three weeks after her public humiliation, Queen Caroline died on 7 August 1821.

By then the king had embarked on a state visit to Ireland where, despite his opposition to the cause of Catholic Emancipation, he was nonetheless received with adulation by a vast concourse of people, including Daniel O'Connell. The servile welcome by his disenfranchised Catholic subjects brought a savage riposte from Byron in his poem 'The Irish Avatar':

> Shout, drink, feast, and flatter! Oh Erin! how low
>   Wert thou sunk by Misfortune and Tyranny, till
> Thy welcome of Tyrants hath plunged thee below
>   The depth of thy deep in a deeper gulf still!

An extended period of appalling weather, coupled with the refurbishment work ongoing at Westport House, as well as to absent himself during the king's state visit to Ireland, induced Sligo to go abroad. By the end of May 1821, with Catherine and his young family, which by then included another son, Howe, born 31 January 1821, he arrived in Paris in early June. His entourage included children's nurses, servants, coachmen and Miss O'Connor, Catherine's companion, referred to as 'Miss O'C' in the diary Sligo kept of their travels. The journey was a major logistical undertaking, between weather conditions, two sea crossings, rough roads, intimidating frontier guards, poor food and miserable lodgings, and all with four infant children in tow.

Acompanied by 'Lady Sligo and Miss O'C', Sligo attended almost every popular theatre in Paris, from the Feydeau, the Vaudeville, le théâtre du Gymnase-Dramatique, le théâtre des Variétés, le théâtre du Panorama-Dramatique to the Italian Opera for a performance of *Romeo and Juliet* which 'I thought very stupid.'[53] Promenades on the fashionable boulevards, visits to the Louvre, Jardin des Plantes, les Invalides, the Panthéon and Père Lachaise, walking in the Palais-Royal, St Germain, Jardin des Tuileries, the Champs-Elysées and farther afield to Versailles and Saint-Cloud occupied their time. They attended the famous fair at Auteuil, where, as Sligo recorded, they 'bought toys for the children', the Fête de Vincennes, public illuminations, which he found 'very contemptible', and various public military displays. They were received and entertained by English and Irish friends and acquaintances, including Lord and Lady Charlemont and Lady Emily Stewart, wife of Lord Castlereagh, and in turn entertained visitors, many from the west of Ireland, including George Glendenning, 'the Dalys, Moores, Frenches, Lindseys and Mr & Mrs Burke',[54] in their rented house on Rue de Provence. To avoid the effects of the hot summer temperatures, the children and their nurses were sent to Saint-Cloud. Miss O'Connor, having 'taken very ill', was attended by Lady Sligo, while Sligo's own health also gave cause for concern. He kept in touch with matters relating to his estate in Ireland through the weekly reports he received from his land steward, George Hildebrand, which detailed estate activities from 'putting in hay to farmyard ... drawing timber out of woods' to 'shipping grain to Liverpool'.[55]

In mid-September the family left Paris for Fontainebleau and travelled onwards through Briacé and across the hills of the Tarace, before descending 'by Napoleon's new road' to Lyons, where a 'large packet of letters' from Ireland awaited. Following along the border between the kingdoms of Savoy and France, they ascended 'Mount Cenis by six parallels' in two and a half hours. Onwards to Turin, crossing the field on which the famous battle of Marengo was fought, they descended by a 'most tremendous road' through a fertile valley. They spent three days sightseeing in 'the splendid town of Genoa', taking a boat journey 'to see the view of the town from the sea and indulging in the traditional evening "passegiata"'. Sligo busied himself to get his carriages 'embarked in the felucca for Lerici', the party following overland in hired carriages. Crossing mountainous terrain to Lecco, Portofino and Rapallo, they eventually reached Sestri. There in the Albergho di Londra, where 'mosquitoes, bugs and fleas competed for our blood and bit Lord Altamont so furiously as to close up one eye and nearly close the other', they rested. Then on towards Bracca, where they found the narrow, dangerous road under repair and the adult passengers were forced to walk behind the carriages, while the two eldest children were 'put into two baskets on each side of a mule'.[56]

The dangers adhering to nineteenth-century travel almost turned to disaster when, after ascending a steep incline, the mules pulling the carriages suddenly started 'to gallop down the hill which is several miles long totally unfenced and hairpin over precipices the whole way'. No sooner was that disaster averted when later, on the road to Spezia, the party experienced what Sligo described as 'the most tremendous drive that in my life I ever went'. Torrential rain and landslides had swept away the main road and they were forced to take an alternative route which hung precariously above a sixty-foot drop to a raging torrent beneath. In the darkness, rain and wind, the adults were again forced to follow on foot behind the carriages. The road was so narrow that for part of the journey one wheel of the carriage was but a few inches from the edge. 'Anything to equal the horror of that night,' Sligo recorded in his diary, 'I never witnessed in my life, the feeling of expectation every moment of hearing the other carriages containing my children upsetting, the consequences of which must have been the inevitable destruction of all of them.'[57] At Lagana they transferred to their own carriages which had arrived by sea and, without further mishap, travelled on through Lucca, Pisa, Livorno and, following along the course of the Arno, reached Florence on 21 October. Such was the 'extraordinary cheapness' of the cost of living in Florence, they resolved to winter there after first travelling south to see the splendours of the Eternal City.

After a few days' rest in Florence, the entourage duly set off south, through Siena and onwards 'over hills of the bleakest and most barren description', lodging in a 'most miserable cow barrack which is called an inn' skirting the edge of the beautiful Lago di Bolsena, through Montefiacone to Viterbo. On 30 October they reached Rome, where 'we found our most expensive but comfortable house ready for us'. The following day the party set out for St Peter's, 'lucky to have come there on the Eve of All Saints and heard the divine music of the soprano voices'. Throughout December, they spent the time sightseeing, visiting the ancient ruins, churches, galleries and museums, returning to St Peter's on numerous occasions. Catherine and Miss O'C climbed to the top of the famous cupola of Michelangelo; a reoccurrence of his rheumatic condition prevented a disappointed Sligo from accompanying them. The party attended a mass celebrated by the Pope at the Church of San Carlo in Caiso at which they had 'a full and leisure view of this well-meaning old man ... at least as much as his draperies would allow us to see'. Finding Rome 'tiresome and expensive', they decided to return to Florence. Other than the pole of their landau breaking near Viterbo, to which 'after a great deal of trouble ... by means of an iron clip and several strong sticks' a temporary repair was made, they reached their destination without further mishap.[58]

In February 1822 their youngest son, thirteen-month-old Howe, died suddenly in Florence. While naturally devastated at the loss of their child, with the stoicism and emotional restraint common among the aristocracy, there is no mention of the baby's death among his parents' extant correspondence. Infant mortality in the nineteenth century was rife, even within families of the upper classes. Baby Howe Browne was buried in the Old English Cemetery at Livorno. The birth of a third daughter, Catherine, in

April helped relieve the sadness of Howe's premature death. By 6 April the family were re-established in Paris on the appropriately named Rue Byron, where they were joined by Catherine's mother, Lady Clanricarde.

Sligo's extended absence from Westport House was becoming a cause for concern in Mayo, placing at risk his family's identity, influence and standing in the county. The ageing Denis Browne valiantly attempted to fill the gap left by his nephew by keeping local rivals at bay, eliciting grants from central government for a new road network, ensuring maximum funding from state coffers for improvement schemes and grants for the promotion of the fishing industry, as well as '£800 without interest to poor fishermen to repair their boats.' Taking up residence in Westport House, he assumed personal responsibility for the administration of his nephew's estate. 'Your old uncle is grown young again in all these schemes and projects.'[59] Browne's taciturn nature, however, tended to alienate rather than forge loyalty. Tenants preferred to deal directly with their landlord, whom they trusted more than an agent or middleman. George Glendenning, Sligo's agent, for example, was accused of pocketing 'the yearly the sum of £15,000 clear profit out of the tithes of the Union of Westport' during his master's absence.[60]

Sligo's continued absence from Westport House was being taken advantage of by those who, as his uncle bluntly told him, 'want to uproot us that they may take the place we have got'.[61] Sligo's cousin Peter Browne also pleaded with him to return and oppose those 'pitted against you … who like the devil follow the system of kicking from under the feet the ladder by which they have ascended to their eminence. I am convinced that you are at present used as an engine against yourself.' Urging him to rely on those 'who are tied to you by natural as well as by the objectives of self-interest,' his cousin further cautioned 'that outside of the Browne circle, we can trust no one an inch from it.'[62] The sentiments expressed by his uncle and cousin epitomised the basic realities of nineteenth-century power politics in rural Ireland, where an estate without a resident landlord was open to exploitation by rivals. To Sligo, however, such bickering and backbiting were repugnant. His education and preference was in the wider world outside of the claustrophobic confines of local politics. The emerging power of the Earls of Lucan (Bingham) in Castlebar and their acolytes, however, as Denis Browne realised, threatened the long-standing prominence of his family.

His fears were confirmed when the prime minister, Lord Liverpool, conferred the position of Vice Admiral of Mayo on Lord Clancarty. Unable to disguise his anger, Denis Browne placed the blame squarely on his nephew and on 'the infamous character of your friends and of you. You had three times the property of Lord Clancarty in Connaught and thirty times the influence ... as well as your superior rank.' Rather than waste his time abroad on friends of no great advantage, 'it is my bounden duty to tell you that if you had acted in any way as your Father had done you would now be in line for a Duke's patent in Ireland and no one could have been put over you in anything.'[63] Despite Browne's subsequent intervention with the government on his nephew's behalf, the post remained with Clancarty, Lord Castlereagh indicating that he could not 'with any propriety interfere ... and, as a private friend, ask Lord Clancarty ... to divest himself of the appointment'.[64] Denis Browne upped the pressure on his nephew. 'Come to your home and live there. Your mind will find better employment than in France.' The welfare of his young family, in light of the death of his infant son, 'injured by the climatic weather', should make him ask how 'you can reconcile yourself by keeping them there .... You should send them home. Your children while young will imbibe that attachment to Westport that made your father and his brother.'[65] Sligo hotly denied his uncle's assertions and took him to task for casting aspersions on his character and that of his friends. Realising that he may have overstepped the mark, his uncle apologised, claiming to 'have been drunk or mad when I so expressed myself'.[66]

Finally, in late November 1823, in the face of a natural disaster and a threat to his power from an unexpected quarter, Sligo finally acquiesced to his uncle's advice to 'come home and play Lord Sligo'.[67]

Chapter 11

The Poor Man's Friend

The Poor People ... see a dawning of the light of freedom just twinkling in their eyes and this dawn, which I heartily thank God for, will soon spring into open mid-day sunshine .... I would not have on my conscience the sin of checking this improvement by any heartless act of mine.

Marquess of Sligo

Forewarned by his uncle that 'the state of distress of Ireland is beyond description ... the whole of the population is now supported by charity. We shall none of us, I fear, get any rents or at best very little,' Paris must have appeared another world to what confronted Sligo on his return to Mayo in November 1823.[1] The nefarious socio-economic conditions that had been allowed to develop in rural Ireland for hundreds of years were moving slowly on an inexorable course that would result in starvation, death and economic ruin for all classes, from landless labourer to landlord, as the former strove to stay alive and the latter strove to remain solvent.

There were many forces that contributed to the crisis. As in England, a decline in agricultural prices resulted in a switch from tillage to grazing which required fewer labourers, leaving more and more of the population without the means to support themselves and their families. In Scotland this was manifested in the notorious 'clearances' or wholesale removal of native crofters who, like their Irish counterparts, were victims of an inequitable land system that had evolved over centuries. This was aggravated in Ireland by the almost complete absence of alternative employment outlets. A rapidly rising population and the 'curse' of subdivision resulted in more people dependent on less land. In Sligo's home province of Connaught, as much as 64 per cent of agricultural holdings were less than five acres. On this meagre allotment, a family, often an extended family, had to eke out a living, pay rent, county cess and church tithes, as well as feed and clothe themselves.

The countryside was also inundated with a class of wandering paupers, the 'conacre' men, who hired a few roods annually from a larger farmer or tenant, usually at an exorbitant rent, to grow potatoes and keep starvation at bay. Landlord, land agent and middleman, large farmer, shopkeeper and merchant, all depended for their survival on those least able to pay. The payload for this chain of existence, the potato crop, on which the fortunes of the few and survival of most depended, had failed for two consecutive years. Nature further conspired to exacerbate the perilous situation when extreme weather conditions produced poor quality grain harvests, which was aggravated by a depressed market. For the vast majority, the potato failure brought untold hardship and distress. For landlords, it brought a loss in rental income on which most depended to maintain their estates and households, pay their bills, provide medical and employment assistance for their tenants (in the case of the Marquess of Sligo) and live commensurate with their status.

From 1821 to 1824 desperation, disenfranchisement and hunger boiled over into a campaign of agrarian terror as a series of outrages, murder, rape and arson were perpetrated against individual landlords, tithe proctors, agents and their families. Across Munster groups of hungry and repressed tenants and labourers wreaked their vengeance on Protestant landlord and large farmer. Loosely banded into a secret society, under the command of the fictitious 'Captain Rock', the Rockites, as they became known, were a foretaste of what might happen if the impoverished and disenfranchised millions banded together in a countrywide armed rebellion.

The task which confronted the Marquess of Sligo on his return was daunting. His tenants numbered over ten thousand and the boundaries of his far-flung estate encompassed some of the most remote and poor quality land in the country. Even the viability of the linen industry which, in the past, had employed many hundreds of men, women and children on his estate was being undermined by a more efficient mechanised textile industry in Britain. The grain he received from his tenants in lieu of rent, because of the depressed market, found a poor price in Liverpool, while the inability of many of his tenants to pay any rent, either in money or in kind, added to his personal indebtedness. But whatever shortcomings he may have displayed in the course of his lifetime, unlike many of his class Sligo was not immune to human deprivation and injustice, especially regarding those dependent on him. And as De Quincy and others had noted of him as a young man, he had a good heart and was not given to the aloofness normally associated with nineteenth-century status and wealth which, in the West of Ireland, mattered. While criticism of his class and the system it represented was to become more vocal, one newspaper, not given to praising the Irish landlord oligarchy, noted of Sligo that 'his charity is unbounded ... his money is now and has been for some time the main source by which the destitute in the several parishes surrounding Westport have been kept alive, his bounty extended to all who require relief without enquiring from whence they come.'[2]

The blame for the appalling situation, in truth, could not be laid at the door of any one class or any single generation. Over many centuries, for weal or woe, tenants inherited a dependency on their landlord who, if not an absentee or an ogre, reciprocated that responsibility in a paternalistic relationship more akin to the days of Gaelic chieftains and feudal magnates. Such benign autocracy, however, emanating as it did from centuries of state-sponsored disenfranchisement and political, economic, educational and religious disadvantage, served only to maintain the majority in thraldom. When nature conspired to ruin the fragile economy on which everyone depended, it threatened their very existence. To alter the engrained mindset would take a natural disaster on an enormous scale and a political and agrarian revolution. For the moment all that stood between the tenant and disaster was whatever exertions his landlord was willing to expend on his behalf out of his own pocket and what he could extract from the tightly drawn purse strings of the government in Dublin and London. In both regards Sligo was not found wanting.

Being, as he often admitted, averse to public speaking, Sligo chose instead to engage on a one-to-one basis. To hear at first hand the problems that beset his tenants, he arranged to receive 'any of my numerous tenantry that may choose to speak to me on their own affairs every Thursday morning at 8 o'clock' at Westport House. From this face-to-face dialogue some quite extraordinary opinions and resolutions emerged. One concern, his tenants informed him, was the practice whereby, in addition to the payment of rent, they were also liable for other charges incurred in the administration and the registration of their leases, amounting to nearly half a year's rent. This, Sligo agreed, was 'most injurious to the poor people to pay'. While his tenants agreed to 'cheerfully pay' for stamps, paper and printing, he offered to cover all other administrative and registry fees, whereby 'the tenants are relieved from a load that would materially injure them'. The new arrangement was not well received by George Glendenning, who cautioned his master about 'the population not valuing what they get for nothing'. Sligo stood firm. Reminding Glendenning that 'in

England and Scotland this system was utterly done away', he did not wish, he told him, 'to have on my conscience the sin of checking this improvement .... I am, in truth, in hope of a new era in the state of Ireland is now approaching and it will be a high satisfaction to me to have it to say that I have contributed to it.'[3]

To tide his tenants over the worst, through his shipping agents in Glasgow and Liverpool, he purchased '700 Hogsheads of American seed', as well as a consignment of flaxseed from Riga, to be shipped directly to Westport, where 'I deliver it in the month of March or April to my tenants who never pay me till December following.'[4] In autumn he purchased the grain they harvested for cash or in lieu of rent 'at prices far above what they would bring in the market, upon a calculation that leaves a fair profit to the growers'.[5] He also made arrangements to increase the export of kelp and salted fish to provide them with additional income. 'To forward the cotton business to which I am so devoted', he imported yarn from Glasgow 'for the use of my cotton factory in Westport' and initiated the production of corduroy and other fabrics to replace the faltering trade in linen. 'I have a good number of looms now at work here, producing calico, gingham, checks and C [corduroy] for which the home market is more than adequate.'[6] A book of samples of the various cloths and patterns produced at his factory is on view in Westport House. Anxious to develop his fledgling textile business, he planned to 'carry it out on a much more extended scale. My object is,' he enthusiastically wrote to one English manufacturer from whom he sought technical assistance, 'to benefit this Country by introducing such manufactures into it as will give employment to the people ... I am anxious that unless I do it to show the way nobody will follow.'[7] He had a personal interest in the technicalities of the manufacturing process and corresponded with factory owners in industrial centres in England about 'cutting and finishing, warps, wefts, double twists and dyes'.[8]

Illness from malnourishment during the hungry years of the 1820s forced some of Sligo's tenants to seek relief in the fever hospital and dispensary established and maintained at his expense in Westport. When the South Mayo Militia, of which he was colonel, advertised for a new regimental doctor, Sligo let the prospective appointee know 'in a private manner' that he would expect him also to provide medical services at the hospital and to 'the more indignant of my tenantry gratis. I trust you will come down here,' he urged him, 'with as little delay as possible as fever is very prevalent and I am anxious to have medical advice for my poor people in my hospital.'[9] Following the near shipwreck in March 1823 of the cargo vessel *Endeavour*, which ran aground on a sandbank in Clew Bay, he donated lamp oil, varnish and coal for the lighthouses on Clare Island and Inishgort to protect shipping using the port. To provide additional employment, he revitalised interest in mining, signing a lease for twenty-one years to the Hibernian Mining Company to mine in the Sheffrey Mountains for a royalty of 'the 12th part of profits'.[10] His efforts to establish a bank in Westport to promote trade and manufacturing in the town bore fruit when, in autumn 1825, a branch of the Bank of Ireland was opened, with Alexander and George Glendenning as joint agents. A branch of the National Bank, founded by Daniel O'Connell, also became established in the town.

The population of Westport continued to grow and, by the mid-1820s, numbered over four thousand. The town comprised four hundred houses and some fifty-three licensed premises and was the commercial hub for the extensive hinterland, with four annual fairs and a weekly market. From its port, agricultural produce, grain, wool, spirits, linen and flax made up the bulk of exports. Sligo robustly opposed any attempt to curtail the commercial interests of the town. In January 1825 he successfully intervened to prevent the government transferring, from Westport to Connemara, the lucrative business of victualling the revenue cutters who patrolled the coastline intercepting contraband and smugglers. 'This will take out expenditure of near six thousand pounds a year altogether out of the town .... The loss of that expenditure, including the residence of forty families who are resident in this town in consequence of the vessels coming in here to victual, is a serious inconvenience to Westport.'[11] In March 1826 he forwarded a memorial to the government on behalf of the merchants of Westport to 'retain the privilege of bonding goods ... as a sensible advantage to us in promoting our trade'.[12] Through his intervention, the route of the daily mail coach, linking Westport with Dublin, was retained.

As chairman of the Mayo magistrates, and later as the first Lord Lieutenant of County Mayo, Sligo's efforts to eliminate the inequality that bedevilled the legal system brought him the appellation of 'the poor man's friend', as well as the animosity of some of his fellow landlords and magistrates. The justice system that prevailed in Ireland, as in England, in the early nineteenth century centred on the rights of property. In Ireland there was rank suspicion and disregard for the law among the majority Roman Catholic population. Statutory justice of a limited kind, through ad hoc assizes and quarter session courts, was controlled by magistrates, usually the local landlord or his nominee, and was further complicated by a language barrier which often required the services of an interpreter. Consequently civil justice for tenants and labourers, depending as it did on the whim of their landlord, could be intimidatory, as well as an expensive process, and tended to be shunned by the majority as a method of settling disputes. The Petty Session courts established in 1823 attempted to regularise the practices relating to the processing and administration of the courts. It was to prove a slow and acrimonious transition, however, and the system of justice continued to be inefficiently and ineffectively administered. Local magistrates sought to retain exclusive control within their own districts and resisted any encroachment in 'their' courts by outside attorneys or stipendiary magistrates. As late as 1832 the entire system still lacked cohesion. As Lord Lieutenant of Mayo, on numerous occasions Sligo was forced to seek clarification and guidance from the government on basic legal procedures regarding the nature of cases to be heard in different courts and the appropriate sentences applicable for various crimes.

As early as 1824 he wrote to the Lord Chancellor 'of the corrupt, partial and infamous system that has been carried on by Magistrates' in Mayo, which he considered 'a disgrace to my country'.[13] He invoked the ire of local magistrates, some of whom were his political allies, over the suspension of William Carr, a magistrate he had appointed from outside the county who, as Sligo wrote, 'has set up the example of an honest magistrate which is a mortal offence to some persons whose plans are thereby thwarted'.[14] He was particularly scathing about the administration of justice in the district of Newport. 'The Country people try by all means in their power to remove their causes from the sessions there under the idea that cases are decided, not by their merit, but according to party feeling.'[15] He lambasted magistrates 'in that neighbourhood whose tyrannies to the Poor, until checked by Carr, were really quite infamous'.[16] When the Lord Chancellor, 'that petulant old fool', denied him 'the common courtesy due one gentleman to another' of a reply, Sligo took his complaint over the chancellor's head to the Viceroy.[17]

As chairman of the Mayo magistrates, Sligo strove to make the legal system more accessible to ordinary people and personally intervened in cases of worst legal practice. In January 1832 one such case made headlines in Ireland and England and became a subject of debate in the British parliament. In a period of appalling hunger and destitution, turf was collected in the Newport area for the poor, under the supervision of a local Church of Ireland rector. When an impoverished tenant, William Murphy, attempted to take some fuel to heat his cabin, he was refused by the rector on the pretext that the turf was for the poor. 'Then the poor ought to get it,' Murphy was reported to have answered. For his impudence he was tried, found guilty and consigned by the local magistrates to the public stocks with a note pinned to his back denoting his 'crime'. The magistrates sent a policeman to Murphy's cabin to demand six shillings in compensation from his wife and twelve-year-old son for 'taking a basket of turf'.[18] Murphy appealed his sentence directly to Lord Sligo.

Despite objections from the magistrates, who protested that his involvement was 'derogatory to their station and office', Sligo convened a public trial of the three magistrates involved. Without the benefit of legal representation, but under Lord Sligo's protection, Murphy conducted his own defence. When laughter and sneers emanated from the magistrates and their supporters at the lack of legalese of 'the humble complainant', Sligo intervened 'indignantly reminding them that they enjoyed the advantage of education which the poor man had not .... It was his duty to protect the poor man and we would protect him.'[19] Murphy was subsequently exonerated and presented his thanks in person at Westport House, declaring that under Lord Sligo's jurisdiction 'now the poor have some chance of getting justice'.[20] Despite his best efforts, however, during his later absence, much to his annoyance, Sligo found that many of the malpractices he had eradicated in the local justice system 'the moment I turn my back ... was in an instant upset'.[21]

His intervention in the cause of justice also extended to the Court of Admiralty and to the conduct of Admiralty officials on the island of Inishbofin. Originally part of the Clanricarde estate, in 1824 Sligo exchanged lands in Galway with his brother-in-law in lieu of others on the island. A delegation of islanders came to meet him 'in the greatest distress ... complaining in the most indignant terms of the conduct of the Court of Admiralty,' Sligo informed Henry Goulburn, Chief Secretary of Ireland. Two years previously, 'at great personal risk and trouble', the islanders had salvaged a cargo of timber from a stricken vessel. Officers of the Admiralty subsequently seized the cargo and refused to pay the islanders the usual salvage money. Referring to the Admiralty Courts as 'Augean Stables which require cleaning ten times more', Sligo demanded that the islanders be reimbursed.[22] He also intervened with the government on behalf of labourers who had not been paid their wages by the state engineer, Alexander Nimmo, whom he accused of 'maladministration' in the building of local roads and piers. Because of Nimmo's withholding of money due to them and 'with their store of old potatoes just out', the people were compelled to start digging the new crop at 'a great loss' and a threat to their survival over the winter.[23]

Sligo's interest in the education of his tenants brought him into conflict with both Catholic and Protestant vested interests. On a personal level he had an aversion to and suspicion of religious extremes, both Catholic and Protestant, and considered religion, as he informed the Protestant rector of Westport, 'the bane of the country'.[24] Having donated money to the establishment of Catholic schools at Louisburgh, Leckanvy and Aughagower, in 1826 he proposed to establish in Westport 'a Grand Coalition school wherein children of all classes without any religious distinction might be educated together'.[25] His plans were, as he noted, 'knocked up' by the opposition of local Catholic interests, directed, he suspected, by the Catholic Archbishop of Tuam, Dr Oliver Kelly. Later, when a Protestant clergyman sought his financial support for the establishment of a Protestant school in Westport, while most anxious, as Sligo told him, to promote education, he considered such a step to be 'injurious to the cause' of inclusive education and that it would only add to the 'irritation which now exists between the two religions'.[26] His 'irritation' deepened with the rise of the Hibernian Bible Societies and their promotion of a more strident Protestantism, which, in his opinion, 'far from being a benefit to the Protestant religion they [the Bible

Societies] have been directly the reverse'.[27] The activities of the Bible Societies and other evangelical groups in Mayo, who, taking advantage of the poverty and desperation of the people, sought to lure Catholic children to Protestant mission schools through the distribution of food and clothing brought, as Sligo predicted, a hostile reaction from the Catholic authorities leading to a further polarisation between the two dominant religions. Despite rebuffs from vested religious interests, he continued to support 'the cause of education in general'[28] and donated £40 towards the purchase of the land and £50 towards the building of the Westport Free School. In 1842 he donated a site to the Sisters of Mercy for a new school for girls in the town.

Sligo's financial affairs continued to deteriorate. The fall-off in his rental income was exacerbated by payment of various family trusts and marriage settlements provided for by the wills of his grandfather and father. His father's illegitimate daughter, Elizabeth Mathews, on the death of her husband, was pressing for additional support threatening, if it was not forthcoming, 'to give up that feeling of delicacy which has hitherto restrained me'.[29] To maintain the standards expected of him as premier landlord in the locality, maintain his house and estate, pay staff, subsidise local industries, be a benefactor to the educational and medical well-being of his tenants, contribute to various charitable and philanthropic organisations, subvent electoral and parliamentary expenses, promote the careers of numerous family members and retainers, combined with emergency expenditure to combat the potato failure, all involved a substantial financial outlay.

There were other, less expected, demands on his finances. In February 1824 Harriette Wilson, former doyenne of the clandestine underworld of Regency London, set a time bomb ticking among the *ton*. The former habitués of the demi-monde, by then a veritable who's who of British society, had presumed their days of youthful debauchery long forgotten. In her middle years Harriette's looks and attributes had diminished and, abandoned by her illustrious and wealthy patrons, she was in need of an alternative income. With William Henry Rochfort, a shady adventurer of Irish descent, seven years her junior, whom she was said to have married, Harriette embarked on an exercise in blackmail on a spectacular scale.

On 6 January 1825, to the consternation of her former clientele and the salacious anticipation of the British public, armed with a collection of compromising correspondence, she gave public notice in the newspapers of the impending publication of the first instalment of her memoirs. The king and his current mistress, Lady Conyngham, with whom Harriette had once shared the same lover, Lord Ponsonby, every high-ranking aristocrat of note, prime ministers, ambassadors, politicians and other notables would, she promised, feature. However, she generously offered each named participant the opportunity to 'buy out' of her memoirs – at a price. The manner and attendant publicity was guaranteed to make the memoirs a bestseller, as well as exact the maximum 'hush' money from those not willing to have their former behaviour made public or, even worse, ridiculed by the courtesan's scornful pen. Advance notice of the Marquess of Sligo's impending appearance in parts IV, V and VI of the memoirs was heralded alongside other former clients such as the dukes of Argyle, Beaufort, Leinster and Wellington, the marquesses of Anglesey, Bath, Headfort and Worcester and politicians such as George Canning, the British Foreign Secretary.

Sligo's relationship and letters to Harriette were part of an intemperate youth. By now a devoted husband and family man, against a rapidly changing political climate in Ireland in which the struggle for Catholic Emancipation had intensified and with an election pending, revelations of his debauched past had to be avoided. While never a constant in the courtesan's life, memory of their brief interlude had been reawakened by her more recent dalliance with his brother-in-law, Ulick de Burgh. With 'a fondness for low company' while a student at Oxford, de Burgh had fallen for the charms of the mature courtesan and had followed her to Paris before being ordered home to Galway by his mother. Some of the courtesan's clients, such as the Earl of Clanricarde and the Duke of Wellington, refused to pay up. Wellington was said to have sent the famous riposte 'publish and be damned' to the potential blackmailer and suffered the consequences of not only having their relationship made public but also of being lampooned as 'the rat catcher'. Sligo received but passing mention in the infamous memoirs having paid, as he later ruefully admitted to Lord Strangford, 'the man who made me buy my letters so dearly from him in London'.[30]

A more willing financial outlay was his subscription towards the erection of a memorial to his friend Byron, who died in 1824. After a sojourn in Italy, the poet returned to Greece in 1823, the land of their youthful escapades. Motivated by a desire for glory, even 'honourable death' in the more noble cause of Greek freedom, Byron received a hero's welcome. On 19 April 1824 at his headquarters on the coastal town of Missolonghi, at the age of thirty-six years, he died before striking a blow for the freedom of his adopted country. His body was returned for burial to England. Refused a resting place among his peers by the Dean of Westminster, who urged Byron's executors 'to carry away the body & and say as little about it as possible',[31] the poet was buried in the family vault in Hucknall, Nottinghamshire. The poet's memoirs, with their explicit revelations about his sexual exploits and erotic adventures, were consigned to the flames by a group of his closest friends, including John Cam Hobhouse and Thomas Moore. While Byron was refused a place of rest in Westminster Abbey, in 1826 his friends, including Sligo, donated £1,000 towards a suitable memorial to the greatest, if most notorious, poet of their age.

A further drain on Sligo's finances was a consequence of the fraudulent management, over a protracted period, of his Jamaican estates. Despite his extensive correspondence with his agents and attorneys, he suffered the fate of most West Indian absentee proprietors of being overcharged and defrauded. The building of the farmyard complex at Westport House also proved more expensive than anticipated, as did the work on the interior of Westport House. The work by architect Benjamin Wyatt, who became known in the family as 'the destroyer', having undone much of his father's superior artistry within the house, and would have done more but for the intervention of Lady Sligo, had also to be curtailed. To defray his increasing indebtedness, Sligo reduced his racing interests and sold the Lisduff estate in Galway, inherited from his maternal grandmother, Elizabeth Kelly. In 1831 he also sold his remaining Galway estate, Rahmore, and was forced to raise an additional mortgage against his newly acquired Lehinch estate in Kilmaine.

The year 1826 got off to the worst possible start. A severe winter brought on bouts of colic and gout which confined Sligo to bed under doctor's orders. A fire in the newly built south wing of Westport House in January resulted in extensive damage 'to the account of two or three thousand pounds'.[32] Caused by overheating flues installed to warm the interior by hot air, it also destroyed the magnificent library, designed in 1821 by Gillows of Lancaster and which contained 10,000 volumes, some of which were saved from the conflagration. Other valuable pictures, rare books, manuscripts and documents belonging to Admiral Howe and his family, transferred to Westport House after the sale of Porter's Lodge, also perished. The admiral's family bible and sea chest were saved. Sligo immediately commissioned designs for the restoration of the library and other rooms affected by the fire, as well as having the original central courtyard covered with lead worked from his mines in the Sheffrey mountains. In a strange quirk of fate Portumna Castle, Lady Sligo's family home, was also damaged by fire that same year.

The greatest threat to his pocket, however, stemmed from the 1826 parliamentary elections. In 1823 Daniel O'Connell established the Catholic Association and the cause of Catholic Emancipation entered a more aggressive stage. By involving ordinary people and the Catholic clergy, the association set in train a mass agitation for emancipation never seen before. Funded by 'the Catholic Rent', a subscription of one penny a month collected from tenants and labourers after Sunday mass in every parish church throughout the country, it provided the means to further the cause of emancipation and, for the first time, gave Catholic labourers and tenants a stake in the struggle. The rent also provided a subvention fund in the event of evictions. The association expanded into every parish throughout Ireland to become, as one Church of Ireland bishop attested, 'a complete union of the Roman Catholic body ... in truth, an Irish revolution'.[33] With the formation of the association came a hardening of attitudes, borne from decades of frustration, and the emergence of an undercurrent of militancy and invectiveness, often preached from church pulpits which, for the landed classes, evoked fears of mass rebellion.

For traditional promoters of emancipation, such as the Marquess of Sligo, the emergence of the Catholic Association and the intervention of Catholic priests in what they perceived as their role as protectors of their disenfranchised Catholic neighbours and tenants was as much a rebuff as it was a shock. Sligo's tenants joined the ranks of the local Catholic Association and their penny rent swelled its coffers. Public speeches by the leaders of the association, including O'Connell, became more strident and filtered down through the ranks. Information of an 'inflammatory sermon' preached by Peter Ward, a priest in the village of Aughagower and educated in the Irish college at Salamanca, was brought to Sligo's attention. Ward's speech was reported as 'being almost seditious'.[34] While not wishing to be alarmist, as Sligo informed the Chief Secretary to Ireland, Henry Goulburn, large bodies of men were parading and congregating in the local district and 'that previous and during the rebellion of 1798 there was now so much more agitation in the minds of the Common people'.[35] The proselytising efforts of the Bible Societies and the intransigence of the Orange Order, he maintained, added to the state of general unrest. He requested additional arms and supplies for the South Mayo Militia which, as he noted, 'only consists of 40 men ... [and] at present they have not a single cartridge'.[36]

Following the king's speech to parliament in February 1825, in which the Catholic Association was declared 'irreconcilable with the Constitution', a bill for its suppression was presented by William Plunkett in the House of Commons. Ironically one of the foremost champions of emancipation by constitutional means, and hated as such by the king, Plunkett considered O'Connell's outspokenness and the element of sedition being promoted by the association as damaging to the Catholic cause. Many other supporters of emancipation, including George Canning, also voted in favour of the bill. For Sligo and his family, it was an agonising decision. Aware that coercion was also an option being contemplated by the government to curtail the association, this, at all costs, Sligo wanted to avoid. Reluctantly, both his uncle Denis Browne and his cousin James Browne cast their votes in favour of the bill, which was duly passed by 278 votes to 123 in the Commons. In his speech during the debate, however, Denis Browne expressed the view, shared by his nephew, that 'the only permanent foundation for the prosperity of Ireland was a total relinquishment of all civil distinctions founded upon religious differences'.[37]

The bill to outlaw the association had little effect. O'Connell merely remodelled its constitution, changed its name to the 'New' Catholic Association and the 'new' Catholic rent continued to be collected as before. Another bill was immediately prepared by supporters of emancipation, including Plunkett, O'Connell and Sligo. The bill was presented by Sir Francis Burdett on 23 March in the House of Commons and was duly passed in April. After an emotional intervention by the king's brother, the Duke of York, however, it was defeated in the Lords, to the dismay of Sligo and to the anger and grim determination of Catholics in Ireland. As Denis Browne bluntly told the House of Commons:

> for a long period he had advised the Roman Catholics in his neighbourhood to place their trust in the wisdom of Parliament. For some time they had done so; but at length when the proposition … was rejected, they asked him how it was possible they could have a chance, when that measure failed …. He was unable to give them an answer, and they then joined the Catholic Association.[38]

The defeat of the Emancipation Bill had an impact on the 1826 general election and changed the direction of local politics. A previous Relief Act in 1793 conferred the franchise on tenants known as 'forty-shilling freeholders'. Living in unremitting poverty, frequently in rent arrears, dependent on the forbearance of their landlord, at election time they were 'driven like cattle to the polls to vote for their landlord's nominee'.[39] The forty-shilling freeholders, through the exhortations of local priests, were now mobilised and prevailed upon to cast their votes for the nominee who publicly advocated emancipation. The election also saw the traditional role of the liberal landlord class as leaders of the Catholic majority challenged, for the first time, by a new and powerful opposition – the Catholic clergy.

In Mayo the emergence of this new and determined opposition to the political status quo threatened the traditional ties of dependency that existed between the Marquess of Sligo and his tenants. His frustration and sense of betrayal were palpable. 'Those very Catholics who had been our principal friends became our determined enemies and instigated by the Clergy held public meetings for this avowed purpose of opposing and injuring us,' despite, as he wrote, that 'my family have for fifty years enjoyed the representation of the county of Mayo and did for the whole of that period uniformly support the Catholic cause.'[40] His frustration changed to incredulity when it emerged that local Catholic support had shifted to the son of Lord Lucan, landlord of an extensive estate in Castlebar. A confirmed absentee, Lucan was resident on his property in Surrey while his Castlebar estate of some 60,000 acres was administered in his absence by his agent, Charles O'Malley, and later by his son St Clair O'Malley. The emergence of Lord Lucan's son, George Bingham (later of Light Brigade notoriety), proud, arrogant and easily riled, into the political fray caused incredulity among the Browne family, especially when, to elicit the votes of the forty-shilling freeholders, Bingham belatedly espoused the cause of Catholic Emancipation.

An additional problem emerged to hamper the Browne election campaign. Government patronage, the vital honey-pot, had all but dried up in Mayo – ironically because of Sligo's promotion of the Catholic cause. A contested election campaign, moreover, was an expensive undertaking and was also the source of public disorder. To avoid a contest, Sligo tried to engage, albeit unsuccessfully, with Lord Lucan to arrange an alternative parliamentary seat outside Mayo for his son, 'at joint expense of the present members ... I think it would stop a most desperately expensive and I feel unnecessary conflict in this County.'[41]

During the campaign, another development emerged which further jeopardised the Browne vote. From church pulpits within his own estate, members of the Catholic clergy, as Sligo complained to his Catholic cousin Louisa Moore, 'have openly and violently opposed me' in preference to the Binghams, 'whom they themselves well know to have always been their enemies and who now are their friends for political purposes only and by whom they will be thrown off as encumbrances in a few weeks after the election is over with'.[42] Some of the clergy within his own estate 'refused to give absolution to any of my tenants who do not produce their leases in order that they may be examined to find out any flaws therein that will do away with their votes'. He accused the Catholic clergy of 'changing their sacred character as Ministers into that of Election Agents, a charge not much to their credit, in my opinion'.[43]

Sligo also had to contend with a virulent anti-Browne campaign in the local papers, instigated by Bingham's supporters, which Sligo counteracted by employing the services of the editor of the *Daily Mail* newspaper. His previous support for the magistrate William Carr also alienated powerful interests within the judiciary, especially Lord Lucan's agent and local magistrate, Charles O'Malley. The ageing but indefatigable Denis Browne also become a liability to Browne interests and, as his nephew acknowledged, had 'so many enemies who from his violent brusque manner have such just causes of complaint'.[44]

It was his uncle's long-running dispute with the O'Donel family of Newport House, however, that put the cat among the proverbial pigeons. Despite the ongoing issue of the non-payment of head rents, the O'Donels traditionally supported the parliamentary nominee of the Marquess of Sligo, delivering their freeholders to cast their votes on his behalf. In October 1825 Sir Neal O'Donel withdrew support from James Browne and pledged the votes of his freeholders to Bingham. A noticeable shift in the support of the Catholic minor gentry followed as, exhorted by the priests, their freeholders revolted, leaving them, as well as some liberal Protestant landlords, vulnerable to intimidation and physical violence and, consequently, less willing to support the Brownes.

In desperation, Sligo wrote personally to his erstwhile political allies to stem the flow of support for Bingham. Reminding John Knox, a landlord in Killala who wavered in the direction of his opponent, that his nominee, James Browne

> ... has better claims on the County with a family consistently resident in it than Lord Bingham whose family has never for a series of years been near the place and whose only

connection with the County has been his draining it of near £25,000 without ever exposing himself to any of the dangers which have threatened it, or without contributing even a mite to alleviate the distress of his people during these times of difficulty and starvation.[45]

To those for whom he had secured government patronage in the past, he 'urged on my own part some little claim for my own exertions in your favour'.[46] Referring to the rumours and 'false and treacherous system of tale-bearing and invention', he decried the activities of 'a certain set of persons in this County whose object it is for their own purpose to create confusion ... to put between gentlemen who would otherwise stick together.'[47] He protested to the government in Dublin about the appointment of William Brabourne as High Sheriff of Mayo, 'a man who has been a most decided enemy of my family ... and a near relative of Lord Bingham ... and of his secret conclave of advisors'.[48]

During 1825 and the early months of 1826 the contest hotted up as the Bingham and Browne factions traded blows in public and insults in the newspapers. James Browne avoided being implicated in a duel only by being forewarned that 'he was about to be struck by Lord Bingham' after the assizes in Castlebar.[49] A campaign of slander and misinformation was conducted by both sides. Sligo used the office of some friendly provincial papers to counteract the insinuations and accusations of the rival Bingham faction, but, as he insisted, unlike his opponents, 'without any criticism of Personalities'.[50]

The work of registering the votes of freeholders went on apace. As his former Catholic supporters wavered, to fill the vacuum Sligo sought the support of their Protestant counterparts. To secure the votes of the freeholders on the Palmer estate in north Mayo, a target of both sides, required delicate handling. The absentee owner, Mrs Palmer, whom Sligo described as 'a violent Orangewoman'[51] but mollified by the attack of the Catholic clergy on the Brownes, pledged support to James Browne. Despite the opposition of the Catholic clergy, Sligo remained firm in his support for emancipation, as he informed Daniel O'Connell, who, in January 1826, sent him an 'honourable invitation' to attend a pro-emancipation dinner in Dublin. Because of his attendance in the House of Lords, Sligo was unable to accept but, as he noted to O'Connell, 'I trust that my declining it will not be construed into the slightest diminution of my good will to the Cause.'[52]

In January 1826 Sligo's family numbered six children under the age of ten years. As the election campaign intensified, together with Catherine, they were 'all laid up with the measles'.[53] In January also the marriage of his brother-in-law, Ulick de Burgh, 14th Earl of Clanricarde, to Harriet, only daughter of the British foreign secretary, George Canning, was of significance for both the Clanricarde and Sligo families. A brilliant orator and charismatic personality, despised by the king for his pro-Catholic Emancipation stance, Canning was heralded as a future leader of the Tory party. Sligo assisted his mother-in-law, Lady Clanricarde, with the legal arrangements regarding the marriage settlement and accompanied her to Dublin to welcome Canning and his daughter to Ireland.

As the premier peer in County Galway, like his brother-in-law, Clanricarde was a liberal in politics and a supporter of Catholic Emancipation. Like Sligo, he too had indulged in a youth of dissipation and excess, leaving the management of his estate in Ireland in the hands of his mother. A noted horseman, he raised the profile of steeplechasing as a sport and was one of the first 'gentlemen' riders to compete at the Curragh. A good orator, he made many speeches in the Lords, mainly on matters relating to Ireland. His connection to the influential Canning family later helped his appointment as envoy at the Court of St Petersburg and as Postmaster General and Lord Privy Seal.

By June the three candidates for Mayo, James Browne, Dominick Browne and George Bingham, were running neck and neck, with

Sligo's nominee considered the most vulnerable of the three. As the election drew near, however, rumours circulated that O'Donel was wavering in his support for Bingham. 'I don't think they will be able to keep Sir Neal O'Donel till the Election and if he kicks, the game is up,' Sligo noted.[54] The positive reception accorded to James and Denis Browne in Bingham's home town of Castlebar further denoted a change in attitude. 'They were cheered by the mob ... with the cry "up the Brownes".'[55] It was the decision of Dominick Browne, however, who, claiming financial difficulties, withdrew from the contest that settled the outcome. On 24 June James Browne and Lord Bingham were duly returned as MPs for Mayo. As the result was announced, the courthouse in Castlebar was overrun by Bingham supporters who chaired their candidate from the building with cries of 'Lord Bingham for ever' and 'Down with the Brownes'. Rioting between the two factions broke out in the town. As James Browne and his party made their way from Castlebar to Westport, they were waylaid by a pro-Bingham mob with, it was alleged, the connivance of Sheriff Brabourne, who withdrew the police to barracks. Browne's carriage was attacked with bludgeons, branches of trees and stones and he barely escaped with his life. Two of his supporters were killed and many injured, including Colonel Jackson, a pro-Browne landlord, who sustained a broken rib. An official investigation into the incident later deemed that both parties were equally culpable and the case was not pursued.

The outcome of the 1826 election had implications for the Marquess of Sligo that reached beyond local politics. The contested election cost him the enormous sum of £20,000, which further adversely affected his financial situation. His Jamaican estates had also become heavily indebted to his shipping agents, Gibbs, Bright and Co., in Bristol. With his 'income eaten up' and smarting from the rebuff from those he presumed were his friends and supporters, he resolved never again to spend his own money on an election and to 'restrict myself from all unnecessary expenditure'.[56] This included financial assistance to his extended family and friends, voluntary contributions to various charities and rent reductions to tenants, as well as financial assistance to local schools, including payment of teachers' salaries, a decision he later reversed. In his thirty-eighth year, his health was also causing concern and 'in consideration of the tender age of my children' he resolved to put their welfare foremost.[57]

The intensity and extent of the enmity directed against Sligo during the election affected him greatly, especially 'the ingratitude of the inhabitants of my own town towards me'. As he noted, on the occasion of a 'grand dinner to Eneas MacDonnell here at the Free School ... no one but little Con Jordan ever thought of proposing my health ... and indeed was told that he would be turned out of the room.'[58] Barrister, editor, lobbyist and novelist Eneas MacDonnell, the son of Charles MacDonnell, a merchant in Westport, was the Parliamentary Agent for the Catholic Association in London. While Sligo's support for emancipation remained unaffected by the actions of the Catholic Association in Mayo, and by his nature he did not tend to bear grudges, in the immediate aftermath of the election his sense of rejection was palpable. 'The loss of friends is more grievous than even it could be considered ... I must confess that I am disappointed at it.'[59] It was the actions of the Catholic clergy within his estate, however, which cut him the deepest. 'I am so disgusted with the conduct of the Priests that I have determined on coming to live in England for some time and they will feel the loss of me.'[60] He also directed his 'disgust and anger' at 'the Government and especially the Duke of Wellington' for refusing his requests for patronage at such a critical time.[61]

Nationally as well as locally, however, as he recognised, power was moving from the landlord class to the Catholic clergy, while a new spirit of dissension and agitation permeated the Irish tenantry.

The priesthood here say openly that they have only now learned their power and that they will in future make more use of it. The people say that they have only just learned their rights and that they are resolved to obtain them at the price of their blood. That they will have to fight and they are prepared for it. I never saw such a change in the minds of any body of people as has been effected within the last few months in this Country.[62]

As he prophetically told his agent Glendenning, 'the time is gone for crying over the power of the priests. They have proved their power ... they are masters of the proprietors of Ireland, nay more, they are the masters of the Government of Great Britain.'[63]

A dispute with his uncle over the latter's 'violent language and manner' towards some of 'the principal gentlemen of the county'[64] during the election campaign led to an angry exchange of correspondence and to their eventual estrangement. The partial break-up of his horse-racing establishment continued with the sale of his most famous stallion, Waxy Pope, then standing at Munster Yard in York. Following the birth of another son, John Thomas, at Westport House, Sligo resolved to move himself and his family to London. Being nearer the centre of political power would, he wrote, 'enable me the better to carry my points ... not being known to the official people is a great injury to me'.[65] Being resident in London also enabled him to fulfil, as he informed George Canning, the numerous 'applications [for patronage] arising out of recent events in Mayo'.[66]

With Catherine, their young family, attendants and retainers, he departed from Westport House in November 1826, leaving the running of his estate in the less compassionate hands of his agent, George Glendenning.

Chapter 12

Emancipator

Much blood will I fear flow before we get rid of the bad consequences of their having long refused the Catholic Question to the country and of their granting at last to intimidation what they refused to Justice.

Marquess of Sligo

The family took up residence at 2 Mansfield Street, a large mansion in the heart of Marylebone, adjacent to Regent's Park, which Sligo leased from Sir Robert Pole. Built for the Duke of Portland in 1770 by the famous architect Robert Adam and known as 'Duchess Palace', its interior was resplendent with the artistry of Adams's elaborate and intricate plasterwork, delicately carved marble chimneypieces, a grand staircase of Portland stone and richly ornate reception rooms, including a ballroom. Catherine's brother Ulick and his new wife, Harriet, resided nearby in St James's Square.

Following the arduous journey from Westport, Sligo was confined to bed and unable to 'drive down to the House to take my seat' until the end of November.[1] The activities of the Catholic Association and local clergy in the election in Mayo did not deter his commitment to emancipation. In February 1827 he presented pro-emancipation petitions in parliament on behalf of various

towns, including Westport, in Mayo. He again made his support of
the Tory government conditional on the progress of emancipation.
'I have felt myself compelled to declare an unequivocal hostility
to all Governments till something is done for Ireland .... I have
always been attached to the principles of this Government and am
still, excepting on the Catholic Question. Were that question once
passed I would support them with as much warmth as ever.'[2]

In the aftermath of the election, retribution against the forty-
shilling freeholders for voting against their landlord's nominee was
widespread and resulted in evictions and intimidation. O'Connell
immediately instituted a new Catholic Rent to assist the affected
tenants. In January 1827 the Catholic Association convened for
two weeks and O'Connell used the occasion to berate the prime
minister, Lord Liverpool, the Duke of Wellington and Sir Robert
Peel for their continued antagonism to emancipation. His attack
on George Canning, a pro-emancipation supporter, referring to
him as one of the 'disguised enemies', drew condemnation even
from within the Association.[3] By 1827, while most members of
parliament were supportive in theory, in practice it continued to
be emancipation *festina lente*. The virulent opposition of the king
and his brothers, grandees in the Tory party and in the House of
Lords, and the antagonism of the Anglican Church and the Orange
Order, all combined to obstruct progress. In his London home
Sligo entertained and discussed tactics with pro-emancipation
supporters such as Lord Plunkett, the Marquess of Anglesey and
his friend from college days, John Cam Hobhouse.

On 15 February 1827, Lord Liverpool, the long-serving
Tory prime minister and opponent of emancipation and reform,
suffered a stroke and resigned. Appointing a successor became
a tussle of conscience for the king, torn between the ultra-Tory
Wellington and the charismatic liberal-Tory 'Catholic' Canning,
whose popularity among both liberal Tories and Whigs, made
him indispensable to the formation of any government. Caught

between the devil of Canning's pro-emancipation stance and the necessity to form a government, the king finally selected Canning on condition he did not press the Catholic question. Despite his relationship to the new prime minister, Sligo resolved to continue to withhold his support from the new government until the Catholic question was addressed. Following Canning's elevation, Sligo was inundated with requests from neighbours, friends and relations in Ireland seeking his help to secure positions in the new administration. To escape such calls and in view of the stalemate over the Catholic question, as well as experiencing a bout of poor health, making him 'aware of the probable duration of my life',[4] he rented his London home and moved with his family to Paris.

Arriving in the French capital in July 1827, they found the atmosphere tense and unpredictable. After the re-establishment of the Bourbon monarchy under Charles X in 1824, and his ecstatic reception by Parisians, because of the king's association with the Church, press censorship introduced by his Ultra-royalist government, headed by the Comte de Villèle, as well as the decommissioning of the National Guard, relations between the monarchy, the royalist government and the city continued to deteriorate. 'There is a deep discontented feeling prevalent, excited by the power of the Jesuits and the Bigotry which prevails to such an extent about the Court,' Sligo observed.[5] In August the funeral of the left-wing politician and revolutionary Jacques-Antoine Manuel, as Sligo recorded, was 'a scene of the most anxious nature', despite the 'great efforts … made by the Government to prevent its being known'.[6] The event led to much rioting on the boulevards. Sligo made the acquaintance of the Vicômte de Peyronnet, the Minister for Justice, who later in 1830, together with other government ministers, was tried and found guilty of treason and sentenced to imprisonment and forfeiture of rank, title and wealth. In 1878, Sligo's son and heir, George, 3rd Marquess of Sligo, would later marry Isabelle de Peyronnet, the Vicômte's daughter.

Eighteen-twenties' Parisian society was fluid and ever-changing as the *noblesse d'empire* and the remnants of the *noblesse d'ancien régime*, together with the 'self-ennobled', the aspiring bourgeoisie, the political liberals, Ultra-royalists and constitutionalists, all mingled in the parliament *chambres* and in the celebrated society salons. Presided over by influential hostesses, such as Madame Récamier and Madame de Montcalm, the salons attracted most of the *haut ton*. Many of the *ancien régime* had 'recovered' their ancestral city mansions, and their salons functioned as private extensions of the parliamentary *chambres*. There the movers and shakers of the political, social, intellectual and cultural, as well as the scandalous, life of the city, met to exchange views, debate politics, devise strategies, play whist and exchange gossip. 'Politics invade everything,' the Duchesse de Broglie complained. 'No one has time any more to read, to please or even to make love.'[7] Bilingual, sociable and connected Sligo was at ease in the cultured and elegant society of Paris between the empires.

Following the Revolution there was much intermingling between the British and French nobility. Many of the latter had sought refuge in Britain during the rule of Napoleon. Paris continued to be a magnet for British aristocracy as a splendid and inexpensive pied-à-terre. One-third of Sligo's colleagues from the House of Lords were resident in the city at any one time. Gentlemen's clubs, modelled on those in London, were popular meeting places. Sligo became a member of one of the most famous, Cercle de l'Union, situated on the corner of the Rue de Gramont and the fashionable Boulevard des Italiens. Founded by the English-reared Duc de Guiche, it fostered links between the French and British elites, as well as with politicians from all parties. Tickets to debates in the Chamber of Peers, situated in the Palais du Luxembourg, and for the more volatile Chamber of Deputies in the Palais Bourbon, were as sought after as tickets to the Paris opera and provided an additional stimulating and sociable outlet. Both visitor and citizen alike were shaped by the reforming nationalism, new thinking and freedom of expression that permeated Parisian society from the salon to the café. The conflicts between royalism, socialism and capitalism, the cultural, educational, scientific and educational advancements of which Paris was the epicentre, offered a new vision for the future. For the aristocratic order it was an exhilarating, as well as a threatening, development.

Sligo's rented house on the Rue du Provence became the rendezvous for his and Lady Sligo's extended family and for friends and neighbours from home. The visit of Catherine's sister Emily and her new husband, the Earl of Howth, and Sligo's cousin John Browne almost ended in tragedy. As the capital of pleasure, Paris afforded an outlet for the British *haut ton* to indulge in social excesses that were less tolerated at home. Duels continued as a way of settling disputes and were often provoked for unscrupulous reasons. Captain George Christie, son of Sir Archibald Christie of Chatham, who, according to Sligo, was an 'unblushing liar ... so black a scoundrel, I never met with in all my life... and his saying it was a fine day would make me directly take up my umbrella',[8] provoked a duel between Lord Howth and John Browne so that, as Christie later maintained, Howth might 'attempt to draw Lord Sligo of £6,000' to prevent death or injury to either of his relations.[9] As Sligo related to Lord Strangford, 'when he [Christie] was beat out of the story',[10] on being made aware of Christie's deviousness and that Browne had no case to answer, Howth pulled back from the brink and apologised. Christie was later imprisoned in the King's Bench Prison in London.

Paris was also on the cusp of a musical and literary renaissance and was the medical and educational capital of Europe. French was the language of choice for international politics and diplomacy. British families came to the city so that their children might become bilingual and absorb French culture. Sligo employed a French governess and his children were bilingual from an early age. The arrival of another daughter, Harriet, in February, swelled the family numbers to seven.

Swirling beneath the ambience of refinement and pleasure, however, on the reintroduction of censorship in November and Villèle's attempt, by nominating seventy-six new peers, to engineer a royalist majority in the Upper House, the relationship between the king, the government and the citizens of Paris deteriorated further. In November 1827 serious rioting resulted in over thirty casualties and many injuries. Theatres and clubs were empty as people feared to venture into the streets or public places. 'It is openly here attributed to the Government who wish thereby to separate the Ultra-Royalists from the Constitutionalists. I think Villèle must go out .... Indeed I was assured yesterday that he had tendered his resignation which was refused,' Sligo noted.[11] On 17 November the French parliament was suddenly dissolved and elections called.

> Decazes and Talleyrand have just arrived in Paris. The latter and Chateaubriand are said to have been a good deal together ... The report last night was that the Duchesse d'Angoulême (the wife of the Dauphin) had written to Villèle to say that it was necessary he should be sacrificed ... I don't believe it, though I hear that Villèle has realised a million of francs stock jobbing and that he wants to retire.[12]

In the ensuing election the liberal opposition triumphed and the Villèle ministry resigned in January.

By then Sligo had returned to London to face an equally disturbed political situation. George Canning had died suddenly in August 1827. During his short premiership, little was achieved in the cause of Catholic Emancipation. A government consisting of 'liberal' Tories and Whigs under Lord Goderich, an associate of Canning and a personal friend of Sligo, was chosen to succeed him, on the understanding that the 'King's conscientious feelings should not be disturbed upon the painful question'.[13] Unable to control the disparate groups within his fragile administration, in January 1828 Goderich promptly offered his resignation. Reluctantly the king had to accede to the reality that no government could be formed without the iron will of the 'Iron Duke'. Wellington became prime minister with Robert Peel appointed Home Secretary. In light of both men's past opposition to emancipation, Sligo chose 'not to join the Government' but to continue to be his own man in the House of Lords.[14]

Sligo's uneasy relationship with the Duke of Wellington was further exasperated on the latter's appointment as prime minister. In early March Sligo was elected chairman of the new West Indian Proprietors Association. The association was formed to protect the viability of colonial properties from legislation passed in 1823 which had adversely affected the price of sugar and its derivatives. With the value of Jamaican property in freefall, Sligo had unsuccessfully tried to find a buyer for his heavily indebted estates. Leading a delegation from the association at a meeting with Wellington and Peel, Sligo outlined the association's concerns, which Wellington agreed to consider. Following the meeting, Wellington wrote personally to Sligo outlining draft proposals towards safeguarding the interests of the West Indian proprietors. Presuming the letter to be of a 'semi-official character', rather than 'a private communication from one gentleman to another', Sligo considered himself 'fully justified in communicating the contents to a few of those persons in the Association'.[15] Wellington subsequently accused Sligo of a breach of confidentiality. Sligo robustly rebutted the accusation and informed the prime minister that the accusation would preclude him from forwarding additional information which 'I should have supposed you would have been glad to have obtained from persons so well acquainted as they are with the state of the colonies'. The tone of the prime minister's letter, as Sligo further stated, 'was made to me in a manner which would render it very unpleasant for me to communicate any further with His Grace on this subject.'[16] Wellington's ire, however, stemmed from other considerations than a presumed breach of confidence. Sligo's public and sustained opposition to his government's stance on Catholic Emancipation also fuelled his antagonism.

For Wellington, maintaining religious division in Ireland was a way of keeping Ireland within the Union. 'Abolish the distinction & make all Irishmen alike,' he warned, 'and they will all have Irish feelings, which tend towards Independence and Separation.'[17] Such state-sponsored discrimination was anathema to Sligo. His own roots were Catholic and, despite his family's conversion, they had supported, as he attested, 'from time immemorial without a single exception … that question which involves in it the real peace and prosperity of Ireland'.[18] His almost pathological aversion to public speaking (which, perhaps, accounts for the sheer volume of his written correspondence) prevented him from making his views in public, but it did not prevent him and his nominee, James Browne, 'from working hard on people to this effect in both Houses of Parliament who think as I do'.[19]

In June the struggle for Catholic Emancipation was finally brought to a head when Daniel O'Connell offered himself as a candidate in a by-election in County Clare. While a Roman Catholic could not sit in parliament, there was nothing, as O'Connell deduced, preventing one from offering himself for election. His resultant overwhelming victory finally convinced Wellington that a solution to the issue could no longer be avoided. As the parliamentary session drew to a close, the pro-emancipation campaign intensified. Behind the scenes Sligo conferred with other supporters in the Lords and Commons. In July, in the House of Lords, his brother-in-law, Clanricarde, with his approval, 'made a furious attack on both the Duke of Wellington and Lord Dudley' for their delaying tactics.[20]

As the possibility of emancipation moved centre stage, efforts were initiated in Mayo to heal the rift between Sligo and the Catholic clergy. Dr Oliver Kelly, the Archbishop of Tuam, wrote to thank him for his support and for his contribution towards the building of a new Catholic cathedral in Tuam. 'It was painful for me to be on bad terms with those of whom I am naturally the friend and whom from circumstances peculiar to my property it is my duty as well as my inclination to cherish and protect,' Sligo replied.[21] Sligo did not agree with the privileged position enjoyed by the established Church of Ireland or with the involvement of clergy in politics. 'There ought to be a law to prevent Clergymen of all persuasions from voting or being at all present or interesting themselves about elections.'[22]

Following the summer recess, he returned with his family to Paris. On 14 August 1828, the long and controversial life of his uncle Denis Browne came to an end. As a magistrate, chairman of the Grand Jury and MP for thirty-five years, his life of public service was devoted to retaining the power of his rank, the prestige of his family name, protecting the political status quo and developing the industrial, agricultural, commercial and infrastructural interests of his locality. His experiences during the 1798 Rebellion undoubtedly coloured his attitude and actions in relation to public order, and throughout his lifetime he continued to be 'a terror to all who proved themselves inimical to public safety and to private tranquillity'.[23] His imperious and abrasive manner tended to alienate many, including his nephew. Devoted to advancing his family interests to the end, his last letter to his nephew enshrined that motivation: 'I should die happy if I could leave you in power and influence as was your Father.'[24] His last intervention with the government was to elicit for Sligo the post of Custos Rotulorum. Despite their fraught relationship, Sligo appreciated his uncle's loyalty, service and affection, retaining his last letter, on which he wrote, 'my uncle's last letter to me written the day before he was taken ill'.[25] Despite their differences, after his uncle's death Sligo stood by his family, considering it, as he wrote, 'my most sacred duty under the will of my uncle who was always ready to make any personal sacrifice for my advantage'.[26]

In his later life Denis Browne had undergone a radical transformation. In 1822, at his own expense, he published a pamphlet entitled *A Letter on the Present State of Ireland*. With knowledge born out of mature deliberation and from forty years' experience, he presented remedies for what he considered to be six of the most pressing problems besetting Ireland. Addressing 'this extraordinary anomaly' whereby Catholics were obliged by law to financially support the Church of another denomination, he urged the removal of such inequalities and that 'a fair and moderate stipend be allotted' to the Catholic clergy. Much of the growing social unrest in Ireland, he contended, stemmed from the 'evil of the tithe system' and he urged its substitution by a 'Land Tax for Tithes'. On the deplorable state of 'Church land', which he attributed to short-term leases and renewals taxed on the basis of productivity, which, in turn, affected the amount of rent payable by hard-pressed tenants, he urged the introduction of longer leases and that renewal fines be converted into 'augmentation of rent', thereby benefiting both Church and tenant.

He was unequivocal in his condemnation of absentee landlords. 'They consume the produce of the soil ... never return to enrich it or fertilize it,' and 'the protecting eye of the landed gentlemen of the country, the natural protectors of the lower classes, does not watch over their wants or difficulties,' and who 'being consigned to agents and bailiffs and middlemen ... are neglected, impoverished, become miserable and are rebels'.[27] Contributory factors to absenteeism, he maintained, were tax avoidance and the lower cost of living available on the Continent and he recommended that the assessed tax on landowners be substituted by a property tax, as well as by a reduction in excisable duty on some products deemed peculiar to the needs of the landlord class, so that they were less likely to be lured abroad. Browne was the first to propose an Irish banking system, which he deemed critical to the development of Irish manufacturing and commercial activity. To alleviate Ireland's rapidly increasing and unsustainable population, then approaching seven million, he advocated a system of assisted passage to the colonies, a government-funded scheme for the reclamation and improvement of waste and fallow land and the development of the fishing industry to provide a source of both employment and low-cost food for the poor. He personally provided capital to some of his own tenants at a low interest rate, to enable them to purchase boats and fishing tackle to supplement their income and, as he attested, 'never lost one shilling of the money so advanced'.[28] The depiction of Denis Browne in historical record as a cruel, reactionary and rapacious landlord is balanced by an obverse view which shows an informed, intelligent and experienced public representative, au fait with the stark political, social and religious reality of the west of Ireland in the nineteenth century and who, contrary to perceived opinion, did not accumulate any great wealth during the course of his public life.

The government's offer of the office of Custos Rotulorum placed Sligo in a dilemma. Having publicly declared his 'unequivocal hostility' to the Tory government until they agreed to emancipation, 'if the office was construed as a mark of favour from the Government, I could not accept of it after such a declaration'.[29] Acceptance of the office might also serve, he feared, 'to injure the Catholic cause'. On being assured by his friends, including those in the Catholic Association, that, on the contrary, it would serve to promote the cause, he wrote personally to the Lord Chancellor, his pro-emancipation colleague Lord Plunkett, 'I am happy to accept from you any mark of approbation.'[30]

His family of seven children, four girls and three surviving boys, ranging in ages from eleven to baby Harriet, aged one year, were a close-knit family group. Sligo and his wife ensured that their children were well educated and reared without pretension.

> Altamont has arrived here, looking remarkable well indeed. He has dexterously left behind all his school books so that I have no opportunity to examine him at all. I find however that he has lost considerable ground in his French .... Our French Governess says he has lost all knowledge of his verbs since he has been away.[31]

When a relation bemoaned the fact that, on having to eschew her carriage out of financial necessity, her son would have 'to travel in a public vehicle', Sligo dismissed her concerns, remarking that 'it was by public vehicle alone that all my children travel *everywhere* – from here [Westport] to Dublin, from Liverpool to London and back again and I never knew one of them the worse for it.'[32] For an indulged only child, he was, as one of his sons later recalled, a somewhat strict father and not averse to administering punishment, both physical and verbal. One such punishment, his son recalled, 'took the form of being made to walk up and down Portland Place with a footman behind him, instead of going to play with other children in Park Crescent'.[33]

By autumn 1828 the emancipation question was again in the melting pot. Wellington's softening attitude was obstructed by the king who, incited by his brother the Duke of Cumberland, had become more intransigent. Convinced that emancipation was necessary to prevent civil war in Ireland, Wellington set out to break the impasse. By February 1829 Sligo was hopeful that 'the question will be carried by a vast majority in the House of Commons and a respectable one in the House of Lords'.[34] From various towns in Mayo he was presented with resolutions demanding liberty of conscience and the removal of penal obstacles against 'His Majesty's Roman Catholic Subjects'. Indicating his pleasure at being 'entrusted with any task that was so grateful to my feelings', he duly presented the resolutions in parliament.[35]

As he predicted, the vote for emancipation was finally passed on 10 April 1829 with an overwhelming majority in the Commons, but by a mere thirty votes in the Lords. Sitting among his ermine-and-crimson-berobed peers, in the splendour of the Upper House, Sligo anxiously awaited the outcome. Faced by the royal dukes, brothers of the king, intimates of his maternal family, many of whom he had known since boyhood, now stony-faced in their intransigence, he listened as his fellow countryman the Duke of Wellington, a green sash slashing his waistcoat, delivered one of the most eloquent speeches ever heard in parliament. Then the hushed expectation as the vote was taken, the 'ayes' and 'nays' counted and the relief and satisfaction that the long-held aspiration of his family, which had ebbed and flowed in the face of rebellion, famine and political upheaval, was at last achieved.

On 13 April 1829 George IV reluctantly signed the Roman Catholic Relief Act. While the act removed most of the remaining restrictions on Catholics in Ireland and in Britain, it was achieved at the expense of the forty-shilling freeholders. The freehold qualification for voting was raised to ten pounds' valuation, thus disenfranchising those whose actions in the last election facilitated victory. In the general election that followed, O'Connell was re-elected unopposed and, as the first Catholic, took his seat in the Commons, duly dubbed 'The Liberator'.

In Mayo, news of the imminent return of the Marquess of Sligo to Westport was warmly reported in the local papers. It was also hoped 'that the Noble Marquess will hence spend a larger portion of his time at Westport House than he has lately done'.[36] Preparations in the town of Westport 'to entertain him to a grand dinner' and in the countryside 'by bonfires ... that would have hailed the long-wished return of the Noble Marquess'[37] were abandoned on the expressed wish of the recipient, anxious for a more low-key welcome owing to the imminent birth of another daughter, Emily Charlotte (born at Westport House on 14 July), as well as his personal aversion to such public demonstrations. In June, on his arrival for a race meeting at the Curragh, 'the inhabitants of the town of Kildare, anxious to testify their affection to the Noble Marquess ... proceeded in great numbers to the extremities of the town for the purpose of drawing his carriage which with great difficulty his Lordship prevented them from doing'.[38] His support for the Catholic question and the euphoria that emancipation wrought on his community was palpable. 'I have made friends with all those who were most opposed to me last election,' he cheerfully recorded.[39] As he prophesied, however, the reluctance shown by successive British governments to accede to emancipation in the past, embittered rather than pacified Irish Catholics.

Many who had deserted him at the election once more sought his intervention with the government for patronage for themselves and their families. Because of his continued opposition to the government, augmented by his personal antipathy towards the Duke of Wellington regarding the West Indies incident, 'wherein I have felt more bitterly hurt than in any other that ever occurred to me', induced him 'to discontinue the acquaintance with the Duke', whom he found to be 'cold in his manner'.[40] Consequently, as he told one petitioner, being 'in direct and explicit opposition to the Government ... [I] therefore cannot apply to them for any compliment.'[41]

Many members of the extended Browne and de Burgh families visited Westport during the summer months. Altamont attended his first race meeting at the Curragh, and in August Sligo's horse Economist won the Knavesmire handicap at York. When personal and financial problems threatened to overwhelm the political career of his first cousin, John Browne, Sligo managed, with some difficulty, to keep his cousin's creditors, for a time, at bay. However, as he himself admitted, 'he [Browne] never thinks of anything for more than half an hour together ... and possesses every fine quality but Prudence and Common Sense ... and is easily led ... I would as soon that he should go out of Parliament tomorrow as remain in it.'[42] Over the summer at Westport House Sligo entertained political allies such as Sir John Byng, Lord Francis Leveson-Gower and the Percy family, seeking their support in parliament for the protection of Irish exports, which, as he warned, 'some enactments must take place this year and a modification of the free trade system or we should not be able to grow at all'.[43] If the government did not address Ireland's economic woes, as Sligo realised, behind emancipation lurked the more contentious issues of reform, tithes and, most divisive of all, repeal of the Union.

On 26 June 1830, King George IV died, his passing, as Sligo observed, 'nobody seemed to regret'.[44] The sixty-eight-year-old figurehead of an age of indulgence, dissipation and excess had become irresponsible with the duties of monarchy and out of touch with his subjects. On the other hand, both as regent and as king, he was generous and loyal to friends, a patron and supporter of artists, writers and actors, while his abhorrence of the more savage dictates of the English criminal code led him, on numerous occasions, to intervene against the severity of legal punishments meted out to the humblest of his subjects. He also interested himself in the animal anti-cruelty campaign instigated by his friend Richard Martin MP, from Ballynahinch, County Galway, founder of the Royal Society for the Prevention of Cruelty to Animals (RSPCA), whom he nicknamed 'Humanity Dick'. Still 'attached' to the last in a long line of mistresses, as Sligo noted with tongue in cheek, 'all the world rejoice at Lady Congnyham getting the turn act',[45] the king, nevertheless, ordered that he was to be buried with a picture of the love of his life, Mrs Fitzherbert. Despite Sligo's refusal to give evidence at the trial of Queen Caroline, his relationship with the king had remained cordial, while his son Altamont retained a special place in the king's affection.

The Duke of Clarence, once a navy cadet under Sligo's grandfather Admiral Howe, succeeded as King William IV. Sligo and Catherine attended the coronation, held on 8 September 1831 at Westminster Abbey, a 'short and cheap' affair in comparison to the lavishness of the coronation of his brother. At the ceremony they made their formal obsequies to the new king and queen, as their titles of ennoblement required. Sligo's cousin Earl Howe was chamberlain to the household of the new queen, Adelaide, while Catherine's brother, the Marquess of Clanricarde, acted as captain of the Yeomen of the Guard at the coronation ceremony.

The accession heralded, not only a new royal dynasty, but also an era epitomised by a clamour for change and reform, as middle England revolted against rotten boroughs, electoral corruption and the aristocratic monopoly of the franchise and demanded parliamentary and electoral change. Cities like Manchester and Liverpool, with hundreds of thousands of citizens, had no parliamentary representative, while places such as Looe in Cornwall, comprising a handful of villagers, returned two. Violent disturbance also swept through the English countryside as starving agricultural labourers smashed the machines and pulled down enclosures that had replaced their labour and which threatened their existence. Such demands and outrages sent shockwaves through the old order. Reform, if not acceded to, could as easily metamorphose into rebellion, as evidenced by the bourgeoisie revolution in Paris, which resulted in the ousting of the Bourbon king Charles X and his government.

The movement for reform spread to Ireland where, with its millions of subsistence agricultural tenants and labourers, the possibility of rebellion constantly hovered. The benefits of emancipation, especially following the disenfranchisement of the forty-shilling freeholders, delivered little improvement to the lives of the landless majority. Rents, rates and tithes still had to be paid and life went on as abjectly as before. The state of the majority population in the west of Ireland was appalling, as the newly established *Telegraph and Connaught Ranger* newspaper in Castlebar reported in January 1830.

> Their miseries are now increased to a pitch at which even credulity pauses – famine goads them on – they see their wives and children perishing of hunger before their eyes – they call upon their landlords for assistance and we blush to say that there are among the pampered sons of fortune, men who are deaf to the calls of humanity.[46]

During the month of January 1830, augmented by a harsh winter, people grew more desperate and turned once more to secret societies. Demands for rent reductions and the abolition of levies were accompanied by intimidation and physical violence against people, livestock and property. Sligo wrote:

> I am sorry to say that this country is in a most alarming state .... There are large bodies of men who patrol the country at night, swearing in people to pay no rents. I have received information that I am to be visited by 10,000 of my tenantry who are coming to seek a half year's abatement in their rent .... I will take no precautions and will meet them on my own .... We shall have a famine here this Spring and then distress will be added to disaffection.[47]

Thousands of hungry tenants from estates in the Newport area threatened to march on the town of Westport and burn it to the ground. A detachment of militia, led by Sir Samuel O'Malley, faced down six thousand tenants. Following the killing of one militiaman, a stand-off ensued and a massacre was only averted by the intervention of a local magistrate who, with the help of the local Catholic curate, persuaded the people to disperse.

As famine conditions worsened, Sligo ordered an emergency shipment of 500 tons of potatoes from Scotland and distributed meal at a reduced rate among his tenants and 'exerted himself to the utmost to employ those on the outposts of his estate ... making boreens ... leading to country villages and also introduced a bounty for burning lime'.[48] Convening a meeting of landlords and merchants in Westport, he solicited their opinions and suggestions 'on the great evil Ireland had to complain of, namely an entire absence of employment among the labouring classes'.[49] He was again critical of Nimmo, the state engineer, for failing to employ the poor in public works and for starting the few public works available 'too late in the season to be of service' and accused him of continuing 'to owe the poor people various sums of money'.[50] He requested the government to provide immediate additional works 'for the purpose of affording employment to the labouring poor of the town and neighbourhood'.[51] His efforts were appreciated locally and also recognised by Daniel O'Connell. In one of his first speeches in the House of Commons, the Liberator attested:

> I do not think, Sir, the landlords of Ireland ever did their duty towards their tenants. If they always did what Lord Sligo is doing now, the country would not be reduced into a vast lazar house. But I also say that if every landlord in Ireland were now following the example of the Noble Marquess, still the evil is beyond their reach. It has overgrown individual grasp or effect.[52]

O'Connell's latter assertion was one with which 'the noble Marquess' concurred.

Wellington's intransigence to parliamentary reform, which he viewed as a preface to revolution, brought down his government in November 1830 which was replaced by a reforming Whig government. Led by Lord Grey, it included many of Sligo's political allies and friends, such as Brougham, Goderich, Melbourne and Palmerston. In Ireland, hopes were raised by the reappointment to the Irish administration of pro-reformers such as the Marquess of Anglesey as lord lieutenant and Lord Plunket as chancellor of the exchequer of Ireland, albeit with the hardliner Edward G. Stanley as chief secretary. For the first time Sligo felt able to support a government 'now that my friends are in power'.[53]

On 1 March 1831 Lord John Russell introduced a Reform Bill in the House of Commons. The bill consisted of two parts: the first for electoral reform to outlaw pocket and rotten boroughs and to provide representation for the new industrial cities of the north and of greater London; the second granted voting rights to £10 freeholders or leaseholders, thereby confining the right to vote to the more prosperous middle class. Although passed by the Commons by a single vote, for almost two years, despite widespread national agitation, monster meetings, rioting, intimidation and threats of assassination, it continued to fall foul of the combined opposition of the House of Lords, the Church of England, Wellington and the king. Reform by its very nature meant a dilution in the traditional power of the aristocratic and landowning order and was viewed as such by many of Sligo's fellow peers in the House of Lords. While supportive of the reforming aims of the new government, Sligo's comment to Lord Strangford, 'I assure you that tho a reformer I am not quite so mad a one, as you may think',[54] had more to do with the emergence of a more divisive issue in Ireland, to which the issue of reform became attached.

Following the success of his emancipation campaign, Daniel O'Connell's star was in the ascendant, not only in Ireland but in the British parliament, where his vote was essential to the reforming Whig Party. In early 1830 he founded the Society for the Repeal of the Union 'to restore the Irish Parliament with the full assent of Protestants and Presbyterians as well as Catholics ... an Irish Parliament, British connection, one King, two legislatures'.[55] Repeal was to dominate politics in Ireland for the next decade as well as to divide opinion. For landowners, an independent parliament in Dublin revived memories of revolution and foreign invasion. It found little support among the Catholic mercantile middle class or from the Catholic hierarchy, more interested in local government reform, tithes and law enforcement, issues where success seemed feasible rather than the more utopian notion of repeal. Sligo also drew the line where repeal was concerned. 'For my own part I shall not feel one moment's hesitation in giving up the return of the County sooner than allow any person returned through my influence voting for the Repeal of the Union.'[56]

He too favoured practical reform. 'We have lost ... our woollen trade, our linen trade, our cattle are now so depreciated in value as hardly to be worth rearing, all that we have remaining as articles of commerce is our grain and for provision our potatoes.'[57] Sligo urged the government to provide employment schemes for the poor which, because of the sheer scale of hunger and need, he now judged was beyond the power of any one individual to deliver. He warned of the great 'disaffection in this neighbourhood ... the result of despair occasioned by extreme misery'[58] and which, if not addressed, would be taken advantage of by demagogues. 'Men ... whom I have seen submitting without a murmur to misgovernment and oppression for years past, now talk openly about reform and repeal. Whether it is owing to the speeches of O'Connell or to some secret agency all business seems neglected here & nothing but politics are thought of.'[59] As he confided to his friend the new viceroy, Lord Anglesey, if the government did not act to alleviate hardship, 'one thing you may rest assured of that no member will be elected for any county in Ireland who will not be called upon to pledge himself on the question [of repeal] and that I feel few will feel themselves strong enough to refuse'.[60] Anglesey agreed with his assessment. 'No one can expect a whole population to lie down and starve patiently.' If alternative employment outlets, improved land tenure and fair rents 'to enable them to sustain themselves and their families' were not forthcoming, he warned the British Government, they would have to bring in 'a legislative Provision to sustain the poor'.[61] As both Sligo and Anglesey realised, however, if the people resorted to acts of violence, the government might as easily resort to coercion. This they sought to avoid at all costs.

During 1831, as the Reform Bill continued its tortuous path through parliament, Sligo's predictions proved correct. 'The Country is in a state of all but rebellion because anything it wants in bad feeling is made up by starvation and distress of the most horrible nature.' He journeyed to Dublin to personally intervene with the Viceroy 'to get public works commenced to try and relieve the poor or troops to keep them quiet'.[62] Murders, assaults, riots and intimidation were fuelled, he told the government, 'by violent demagogues everywhere exciting the people to madness and they visiting us occasionally in *little parties* of about 3,000 or 4,000, declaring what they would do *if* we don't surrender Rents, Taxes, Tythes and Grand Jury Cesses .... Would that O'Connell be hanged.'[63]

Combined with a ruinous land policy, a decline in agricultural prices, as well as agitation for repeal, the situation was further exasperated by a dramatic increase in the population of Mayo from 293,112 in 1821 to 376,956 in 1831. As Sligo recorded, 'all the gentry of Mayo are beggars,' their estates 'mortgaged or engaged for one million and a half of money', with tenants as much as three years in rent arrears.[64] 'I have not yet received one half & am £5,000 short of what I have ever been before the first of January.'[65] As the parliamentary term commenced, he handed over his vote in the House of Lords, rented his London house and determined to remain at home to try and manage the situation as best he could. 'Poor Ireland seems to be fated to be the scene of ever varying agitation,' Lord Goderich, the colonial secretary, responded to Sligo's request for assistance. 'You at least ... have done your duty. I wish everyone who had it in his power to do the same would profit by your example.'[66] While conscious that his vote was necessary to support the Reform Bill through the House of Lords, 'I left it to Lord Anglesey to say whether I should be more useful to the Government here or in London & and he told me to stay here.'[67]

Describing himself as 'a poor reformer in a distant land' against an increasing state of lawlessness, Sligo pulled out the political stops in his disposal to do what he could. With England convulsed by the reform controversy and by internal disorder and distress, the culpability of Irish landlords in the eyes of the British government, coupled with, as one of his associates informed him, the 'dissatisfaction that prevails amongst those who contributed most loyally to the subscription in 1822',[68] made it difficult to extricate any relief. In what surely must be one of the most moving and profound letters in his vast correspondence, Sligo interceded directly with the prime minister, Lord Grey. In words that were both critical and intemperate of the government, he painted a picture of the situation prevailing in the west of Ireland.

> Were your Lordship a spectator of the state of the People, I am confident that you would at once break thro all systems of economy and non-interference however strongly they have been impressed in your mind. Whatever may be the opinion held as to the conduct of the Irish landlords ... I would say that the People ought not to be allowed to die of want. Save them & then make any enactment you please to prevent a reoccurrence of the sort.[69]

Despite their terrible circumstances, the people continued 'most patient and quiet' but, he warned, in the prevailing political unrest, 'a line of conduct which would cost the Government much more men and money to allay' would erupt if something was not done to alleviate their terrible situation. Calling for a renewed programme of public works without 'one day's delay' he urged the prime minister 'in the name of economy ... as well as Humanity ... for a timely liberality on the part of the Government'.[70]

Following his meeting with the merchants and landholders in Westport, while they were resolved, as he told the government, 'to go to the utmost extent of their means ... to alleviate the misery they cannot conceal from themselves', their efforts should not release the government from their duty to provide public works.[71] The government responded by sending two additional emergency shipments, each with 150 tons of potatoes, to Westport. Through Sligo's efforts, an Irish Distress Committee was established in London. A corresponding committee, which he chaired, was formed in Mayo and included the Catholic and Protestant archbishops of Tuam; Dr John McHale, the Catholic Bishop of Killala; Charles O'Malley, the Lucan estate agent; and Arthur Gore Knox, a landlord in north Mayo, who ' all cordially unite in the cause of Charity'.[72] Funded by the London committee, ships brought additional food supplies to Westport for distribution to the worst-affected areas and also placed '£1,000 pounds at the disposal of the Mayo Committee ... to the purchase of oatmeal in Mayo.'[73] Together with his brother-in-law Clanricarde and their wives, Sligo attended the Royal Irish Fundraising Ball at the Drury Lane Theatre in London, 'superbly decorated and brilliantly illuminated for the occasion'.[74] The king and queen and members of the royal family attended, as well as the dukes of Norfolk, Argyle, Richmond, Devonshire and Wellington, at which an additional sum of £1,675 towards the relief effort was raised. Sligo's intercession with the prime minister also bore results when Grey sent 'another vessel from Liverpool to Westport with potatoes and meal ... and a supply of oatmeal from Deptford'.[75]

Not everyone on the ground in Mayo pulled their weight. Other than Sligo and Edward Garvey of Murrisk, few landlords subscribed to the Westport Relief Committee. In April the committee was forced to send a deputation to intervene with local landlords, including Sir Samuel O'Malley, whose tenants, especially those on Clare Island, were reported to be in a state of extreme distress. In the area around Castlebar it was reported that 'a large portion of the tenantry and the cottiers of Lord Lucan, Sir William Brabazon and the cottiers on a farm of Major O'Malley, were literally starving and that these landlords had left them destitute and that the only assistance they received to sustain life was from the funds of the Westport Committee'.[76] Reports of the lack of humanity shown by the notorious 'middlemen' and land agents, as well as the better-off Catholic farmers, flooded into the committee. Their conduct was contrasted with 'the unbounded charity of the Marquess of Sligo ... his money is now ... the main source by which the destitute in the several parishes surrounding Westport have been kept alive ... without enquiring whence they come'.[77]

Sligo's action in the face of the disaster that gripped his world was of a landlord who was prepared to take responsibility for the welfare of his tenants. Despite the superiority, imperviousness and laissez-faire attitude usually associated with his class, it is clear from his correspondence at this time that he was deeply affected by the suffering around him and tried to alleviate it as best he could. From his youth he displayed an admirable and generous humanity towards others less fortunate and, while protective of his status as an aristocrat and landlord, tried to do the right thing. Judging from her correspondence, Lady Sligo shared her husband's sense of responsibility and humanity and showed herself both capable and innovative. As she displayed in the rearing of her own large family, she had a practical, down-to-earth, no-nonsense approach to the management of the disaster.

To further highlight the appalling situation in his home county, Sligo invited the lord lieutenant, the Marquess of Anglesey, to Westport to see at first hand the extent of the hardship. A hero of Waterloo, where he lost a leg in action, Anglesey's liberal views on Ireland often brought him into conflict with more conservative elements in his party. 'The mischief of Ireland is not in the People. It lies with the Absentees and with the demoralized gentry. The lower orders are, for the most part, vilely oppressed and wickedly misled and imposed upon by the Priests and ground down by excessive exactions.'[78]

On 9 April 1831, in a carriage 'drawn by four beautiful greys ... most magnificently caparisoned with all the wealthy and higher orders of the citizens on horseback, decorated with ribbons of Anglesey Blue',[79] followed by the carriages of local dignitaries, including the Catholic Archbishop of Tuam, the Marquess of Sligo met his guest on the borders of his estate at Delphi Lodge, where the lord lieutenant spent the night. As cannon shot intermingled with the acclamation of the people assembled in their thousands along the route, Sligo escorted his guest, who was dressed 'in a plain suit with the ribbon of the Order of the Garter and the Cross and Order of St Patrick',[80] along the scenic coast road. Entering the town of Westport through a laurel arch, they were cheered by the citizens who thronged the streets. The party entered Westport House demesne where thousands of estate tenants and workers waited. Addressing the multitude from the steps of Westport House, the lord lieutenant offered his personal (if revolutionary) suggestions on how the famine-like conditions might be relieved: sufficient land, sufficient remunerative employment and a compulsory measure of relief for the peasantry. On being presented with an address from 'the Gentry, Clergy and Freeholders' of Westport and another from the inhabitants of Newport, the lord lieutenant withdrew inside.

Intending to stand godfather at the christening of the latest addition to the Sligo family, Henry Ulick, born 14 March 1831, on Anglesey's being suddenly summoned back to Dublin, 'they decided to have the christening at once ... in the dining room'. The child was duly baptised 'out of a racing cup that had been won by Miss Stavely', Sligo's prize-winning mare.[81] Next morning, following a meeting with local representatives, Sligo escorted his guest as far as Mountbellew, County Galway. Through Sligo's intervention, a substantial sum of money was allocated by the government for a new scheme of public works in Mayo and west Galway.

Lord Sligo's efforts to alleviate the worst effects of the famine received due praise in Britain, as well as across the political and religious divide in Ireland. The fundamental problems, however, economic and social, remained unresolved. As the future archbishop of Tuam, John McHale, prophesied, the funds raised by well-intentioned people such as Lord Sligo were 'but temporary checks which will not prevent the reoccurrence of the evil. It is a reproach to any Government that a hardy and industrious people should be thrown so often into the humiliating attitude of mendicants for food'.[82]

In the 1831 election Joseph MacDonnell of Carnacon, County Mayo nominated by the Catholic clergy, entered the political fray. Opposing him were the sitting MPs, Dominick Browne, who had replaced George Bingham in a by-election, and Sligo's cousin John Browne, who had replaced his less than satisfactory brother James, whose attitude, as Sligo admitted, 'was not sufficiently liberal for me'.[83] While both the clergy and the *Telegraph and Connaught Ranger* newspaper threw its support behind John Browne, solely on the basis 'that Lord Sligo ... the poor man's friend ... is eminently entitled to public support',[84] the paper reserved its most virulent criticism for Dominick Browne, whom it accused of reneging on previous election promises. Behind MacDonnell's candidature, however, lay the contentious issue of repeal. Both Brownes were elected, due to the Marquess of Sligo's personal popularity, the 'Protestant Parsons alone', as he noted, under the orders of Archbishop French, 'have refused their support ... because I subscribed to a Catholic Cathedral in Tuam'.[85] Sligo was under no illusion, however, about the change in political attitudes. 'No person will be returned for Mayo but a demagogue and a repealer,' he told an acquaintance; 'neither of which suits my Book, as our sporting term is.'[86]

In September 1831 lord lieutenants for each county in Ireland were appointed by the government: the Marquess of Sligo was appointed lord lieutenant for County Mayo. The post encompassed a wide range of responsibilities, from maintaining the peace, gathering intelligence, regulating the local magistracy, commissioners of the peace, the judicial system, tithe proctors, prison and asylum authorities, the constabulary and the militia, to the apprehension of smugglers and poteen-makers. To judge from Sligo's extensive correspondence, he adopted a hands-on approach to his new office, involving himself in hundreds of individual cases, as well as corresponding with government officials and ministers in the government. The post not only encompassed an immense administrative workload but also submerged him in a seething stew of local disputes, rivalries and jealousies.

Remote areas, such as the barony of Erris, he found, 'in a shocking state ... a place of refuge for all the ruffians in the County'.[87] Local landlords in the barony, notably the Binghams, 'by the hatred of their rule ... and their oppressions',[88] contributed to the violent disorder. Throughout Mayo, members of secret societies went 'night-walking', swearing in recruits and intimidating those who refused the oath. On his appointment, he was also inundated with applications for posts as magistrates, peace commissioners, prison warders and water bailiffs from political supporters and opponents alike. To one such applicant he made his position clear: 'that I will not then or ever give the most remote pledge as to what may possibly and probably be my conduct in any matter wherein this office is concerned'.[89] His resolve, however, on which local political supremacy depended, proved more difficult to implement.

Approaching his duty humanely, disciplining local magistrates whose legal judgments he found suspect and interceding in individual cases where he found the law inequitable or biased, Sligo's objective was to 'promote the due administration of justice within the county'.[90] His attempt to reform the local magistracy, of which he had long been critical, brought him into conflict with many incumbent magistrates, particularly when he attempted to appoint more objective members to the bench from outside the county. He objected to members of the Church of Ireland acting as magistrates considering, as he informed the Protestant Archbishop of Tuam, that 'it would be much better that they should not be in a position to come in collision with the people'.[91] Appalled by the conditions he found on a visit to the county goal in Castlebar, he set improvements in train regarding the medical care of prisoners. 'Out of compassion for his horrible state of illness and debility and pain', he obtained a pardon for one of its more desperate inmates.[92]

Sligo's appointment, however, coincided with a period of intense political and social agitation. Exhorted by secret societies such as Ribbonmen and Rockites and by individual members of the Catholic clergy, it was the long-simmering issue of tithes that, more than any other, served to inflame passions as well as drive the wider issue of repeal. Despite the granting of emancipation in 1829, the obligation on Catholics to pay for the upkeep of the Church of Ireland (as well as payment of dues to their own clergy) continued. Tithes were the first charge on income, taking precedence over landlord's rent or county cess. Failure to pay was met by seizure of crops, livestock and household utensils by the tithe owner, leaser or their agent. An entire business had developed around the collection of tithes with lay leasers, valuers and collectors, known as 'proctors', all employed in the practice. The tithe tax from which there was no return, either materially or spiritually, for the majority of payees was aggravated by the slump in agricultural prices in the 1820s. In 1823, in an effort to remedy some of the worst practices, a Tithe Composition Act was passed whereby tithes, hitherto payable as a portion of agricultural yields, were permitted to be paid in money. The act also allowed for tithes to be levied and paid by an entire parish instead of by individual tenants. A further act also provided for the inclusion of pasture land, thereby sweeping larger graziers into the tithe net.

While initially in favour of the proposed changes, when Sligo discovered that his tenants would also be liable for arrears and, as he informed the parish priest of Kilgeever, 'would have to pay up two years tythes at once and the next Spring pay the first half year's Composition gale, this would press heavy on them',[93] he urged them to await the outcome of a survey of the system initiated by the government. His stance found little favour with his agent. As a leaser of tithe property and in receipt of substantial tithe revenue, Glendenning called his master to task. Despite their long-standing association, Sligo refused to countenance his agent's sense of grievance or condone 'the enormities which are committed by your operative Tythe Proctors', about which, as Sligo unequivocally informed him, he had received numerous complaints. Neither was he prepared, he told Glendenning, to subscribe to

> ... the common failing amongst us all to shut our eyes on the manner the business is done. Better to bend gracefully to the storm than to be overthrown by its violence. My conscience whispers in my ear that I am the natural protector of all the poor and helpless around me and that I have too long neglected this duty and that if I were to sacrifice them to your pecuniary interests, I should be guilty of a most wicked breach of trust.[94]

While the question was debated in parliament, on the ground the anti-tithe campaign intensified. Attempts to recover arrears from defaulters by the seizure of goods and chattels led to increased public disorder. Claims of overcharging, violent enforcement and the seizure of goods by some clergymen and their proctors was, as Sligo concluded, 'enough to justify any feeling of dissatisfaction among the people'.[95] He was particularly scathing of individual Church of Ireland clergymen: 'I know no Clergyman the collection of whose tythes is more oppressive than the Rev. Mr Stoney.'[96] Despite his personal aversion, however, as lord lieutenant he was obligated to protect proctors and process-servers at tithe seizure auctions where emotions often spilled over into violence. Beneath the campaign for the abolition of tithes, which was to continue until 1838, lurked the issue of repeal. As election time approached, as a confirmed opponent of repeal, Sligo was to feel the full backlash of its proponents.

The attack was spearheaded by Frederick Cavendish, editor of the *Telegraph and Connaught Ranger* (later renamed the *Connaught Telegraph*). Born in Derby in 1777, and following a career in the civil service, on his marriage to Agnes MacDonnell from Castlebar, Cavendish came to live in the town where, in 1828, he established the newspaper. A fervent supporter of repeal, he set out to undermine the political status quo in Mayo. He attributed Ireland's many social injustices to the Union: 'An English Parliament never knew, never will know, how to legislate for the advantage of Ireland.'[97] To supporters of the Union, such as the Marquess of Sligo, his attacks were to become personal and unrelenting.

Determined to undermine the image, reputation and standing Sligo enjoyed within the county as a fair and benevolent landlord, Cavendish, in a series of articles under the pen name Philodemus, questioned Sligo's reputation as a model landlord, the political influence he exerted within the county and even the veracity of his endeavours on behalf of the poor. 'Turn your attention to lighten the burden of your oppressed tenantry – ease them of your grinding, your devouring rack-rents. Instead of wasting your income in bribery at elections ... expend it generously and wisely in aiding works of charity and national utility.' He further urged Sligo 'to prove your patriotism by voting for Ireland's interests. Make atonement ... for your Father in voting away and selling the national independence of his country by becoming *yourself* an advocate for the repeal of that disastrous and accursed measure.' He was particularly scathing of Sligo's 'gripping and ambitious' agent George Glendenning, whose 'pernicious and inhuman counsel' he urged Sligo to ignore.[98]

The Reform Act, of which Sligo voted in favour, was passed in the British parliament in March 1832. It provided few concessions to Ireland, granting only five additional parliamentary seats, no disenfranchisement and no major transfer of electoral power. In the first election held after its passage, the issue of reform merged with that of repeal to become the main election issue for the *Telegraph*:

> If you find impartial justice denied to you ... ought you not demand a law enabling you to have pure and honest magistrates appointed by yourself. If Tithes and Church rates have galled, insulted and plundered you .... If Grand Jury Laws have enabled the corrupt and dishonest to impose intolerable burdens .... If the Union has brought us national ruin and degradation ... ruined your trade and manufactures, deprived you of employment and created absenteeism ... Vote Repeal.[99]

In November, the newly formed Mayo County Independent Club, which included landlords such as Sir William Brabazon, publicly declared itself pro-repeal.

In Autumn 1832 electioneering got underway in a contest that was to become a watershed, not only in the context of Mayo politics but also for the supremacy of the Browne family in their traditional role as political representatives of the county. Sligo's nominees were his cousin John Browne and Dominick Browne, while Sir William Brabazon, a landlord from the Barony of Gallen, emerged as the pro-repeal candidate. Formally one of his supporters, Sligo received news of Brabazon's defection with equanimity, hoping, as he wrote, that 'it will make no difference to our private relations and friendship'. In regard to the question of repeal, however, he placed Brabazon on notice that should his 'political views ... be of such a nature as to compel me with my peculiar sentiments on some subjects', he would relinquish his declared 'neutrality ... to politically and publicly oppose any such individual'.[100] Formidable opposition to the two Browne candidates, both of whom declared themselves opposed to repeal, emanated from the Repeal Movement and from individual Catholic priests. As the contest hotted up, many of Sligo's freeholders were intimidated, physically attacked, boycotted and censured from the pulpit. 'I have to say with regret that the conduct ... was not such as might be considered suitable to a Christian Minister,' Sligo complained to the Catholic Archbishop of Tuam.[101] As the registering of freeholders commenced, the *Telegraph*'s Philodemus, addressing 'The Freeholders and people of Westport and the Barony of Murrisk' on Sligo's estate, demanded their votes for the repeal candidate in preference to John Browne, 'of moderate talents ... the boastful and arrogant betrayer of your interests ... he whose insolent abuse was poured on O'Connell and the agitators' and who was merely 'a seat warmer for young Lord Altamont (who I wish was of age when we might expect better things)'.[102] Once acknowledged as 'the friend of the poor', Cavendish depicted the Marquess of Sligo as 'rapacious and unjust, having fleeced and flayed you until nothing has been left', whose Irish tenants were worse off than his Jamaican slaves, and he urged them to 'rend asunder Browne Chains in which you have been bound this half century'.[103]

In November, at the height of the election frenzy, Sligo fell ill. While by now used to the cut and thrust of local electioneering, the intensity of the campaign perpetrated against him caught him off guard. That the people, exhorted by the Catholic clergy, should promote Brabazon, who had done so little to alleviate their suffering during the recent famine and on whose estate, as he wrote, 'the rates charged to tenants were enormous ... and enough to justify any feeling of dissatisfaction' but who, having jumped on the repeal bandwagon, was being hailed as their champion, was beyond his comprehension.[104] His duty as lord lieutenant to maintain law and order within the county, as well as his reluctance to use government patronage as a means of eliciting political support or, as he wrote, 'if the support of individuals is only to be obtained by this kind of repayment, I must ... retire from contesting what is now but an honour and means of doing good for the County in general but by no means to any individual' all served to alienate him further from his traditional supporters.[105]

During the election the state of disorder throughout Mayo was aggravated by an outbreak of cholera in Westport, which spread rapidly and resulted in many deaths. 'To make every preparation to avert the frightful ravages of the pestilence', at his own expense Sligo engaged a doctor who had experience of the disease in England and brought him to Westport.[106] To prevent the contagion from spreading, he donated a paddock near the hospital for the burial of cholera victims. From constantly 'attending more than most people to the business of the County', his own health subsequently suffered, and rumours of his death were widespread.[107] 'We had you dead and buried here last week,' a relieved Eneas MacDonnell wrote to Sligo from London.[108]

As well as being divisive and bitter, the December election was also closely contested. By the slimmest of margins the two Browne candidates were elected, 'indebted for their return as representatives of this county', the *Telegraph* implacably claimed, 'to the corrupt influence and power of the Marquess of Sligo'.[109] While elections tended to be fraught and violent, Sligo considered that the editor of the *Telegraph*, 'that vile paper … the greatest promoter of every evil project … the greatest engine for bringing into disrepute all the Authorities of the Country', had overstepped the mark.[110]

In November 1833 he instituted libel proceedings against the editor in the Court of Common Pleas in Dublin for 'the injury and stain which the defendant has cast … on his character'.[111] In a packed courtroom the Honourable Frederick Cavendish was found guilty and fined the sum of £200, with two sureties of £250 pounds and one month's imprisonment. The case was widely covered in Irish and English newspapers. Collections were held throughout the country to pay the editor's fines, while Sligo donated his damages to charity. Undeterred, on his release Cavendish continued his vendetta, denouncing the Mayo gentry as 'cringing, servile adherents of a man for whose smiles and claret they sold their tenants and their country'.[112]

After the election, a state of public order turmoil persisted, particularly in the Barony of Gallen. In 1833, in his capacity as lord lieutenant, Sligo's attempts to enforce law and order in the barony became a cause célèbre and the subject of debate in the House of Lords. As early as September 1832 the chief constable of Mayo made an official request for additional troops to curb the state of lawlessness and the activities of secret societies in Gallen. The situation was aggravated by the actions of tithe proctors who were subjected to obstruction and physical violence. The military detachment Sligo despatched was confronted by a violent protest which resulted in a number of fatalities. To calm the situation, he despatched an additional detachment of police to be quartered 'between Swinford and Foxford ... to patrol for a short time'.[113] The situation, which he claimed was 'entirely attributable to the inflammatory speeches of the electoral agents of Sir William Brabazon, combined with the utter incapability of the magistrates there',[114] grew more violent and by mid-November the chief constable reported that the barony 'was in a state approaching of open Rebellion'.[115] Convening a meeting of the Mayo magistracy, attended by eighty magistrates, on the evidence produced Sligo subsequently signed a proclamation placing the Barony of Gallen under the Peace Preservation Act of 1814.

While the presence of additional troops on the ground succeeded in curbing the activities of the secret societies and restored peace in the barony, it evoked a furious backlash from individual Catholic clergy and from pro-repealers, including Daniel O'Connell. Irish, English and Scottish papers accused Sligo of introducing 'a system of tyranny ... worthy of the Bey of Algiers'.[116] Lord Teynham, a relation of Sir William Brabazon, during a debate on the introduction of a Coercion Bill for Ireland, brought the Gallen issue to the floor of the House of Lords.

He accused the Marquess of Sligo of proclaiming the barony for reasons of political rivalry and without 'any application to the resident magistrates ... or without any application from the managing proprietors'.[117] In his defence, declaring himself to 'have been assailed by calumnies of the basest kind, at once unfounded and cruel and which were the work of agitators whose trade was to disturb the country', Sligo vehemently denied acting from any personal animosity towards Sir William Brabazon.[118] He presented evidence of murder, assault, rape, intimidation and rioting he had received from the military authorities on the ground in Gallen. The disorders had intensified during the election campaign when 'no man could reach the hustings unless he came to vote for the candidates who supported the repeal of the Union, or unless he was protected by the police or the military'.[119] Moreover, Sligo informed the House, the proclamation of Gallen was made on the recommendation of eighty magistrates and 'two-thirds of the actual proprietors of land in the barony'.[120] Following a lengthy debate Lord Teynham was forced to admit 'that the noble Marquess had given such a satisfactory explanation that he could no longer doubt that the affidavits he had received were erroneous' and he withdrew the motion.[121]

Despite the passing of the Coercion Act, which empowered lord lieutenants to proclaim districts, as well as suspend habeus corpus, by the summer of 1833 Sligo was able to recommend a reduction in the number of soldiers required to keep the peace in Gallen and, as was acknowledged and appreciated locally, 'without having recourse to the more oppressive enactments of the Coercion bill'.[122] But the animosity of individual members of the Catholic clergy, the pro-repeal clubs and 'the most violent resolutions against me and mine Cavendish's paper vomited forth, accusations of broad unblushing falsehoods', while bruising, made him resolve nevertheless 'to go on conscientiously in the path I know to be correct and face the consequences. I dare say it will be necessary for me to bow to the storm, if so I will, but when the storm is over the sunshine will come again ... and people who will see my conduct will feel I have no object in it but my Country's good.'[123] The issue of tithes was partly appeased by the payment of £1 million by the government to tithe owners for outstanding arrears and by the suspension of police or military involvement in their collection, strategies of which Sligo had long been in favour.

Sligo remained in London during the summer months to attend parliament. In March, accompanied by Lady Sligo, together with the dukes of Wellington, Richmond and Argyle, Lord Melbourne and Catherine's brother, the Earl of Clanricarde, they were guests at a gala dinner given by King William in St James's Palace. 'At homes' in the Belgravia mansions of society hostesses, such as the Marchioness of Lansdowne, brought Sligo into contact with many British statesmen and some of his Paris acquaintances, such as the influential Princess Lieven (wife of the Russian ambassador to Britain) and Prince Talleyrand. In May the king entertained the knights of the orders of St Patrick and the Thistle to a state dinner in the banqueting hall at St James's Palace. At his house on Mansfield Street, Sligo also entertained family, friends and political allies. 'I dined at Lord Sligo's,' John Cam Hobhouse recorded. 'I sat next to Lady Clanricarde and was trying to find out the resemblance between her and Canning.'[124] In April Hobhouse was appointed chief secretary of Ireland to replace the more conservative Stanley, whose departure from Ireland was 'greeted with many dry eyes'.[125] A liberal and radical, Hobhouse's appointment was welcomed by O'Connell but was of short duration and he was replaced by another liberal, E.J. Littleton.

In mid-June the return of the Marquess of Sligo to Westport was reported to have 'diffused universal joy among all classes of his attached tenantry'.[126] The warm summer weather, with its prospect of an abundant harvest, augured well. Taking up the administration of his estate, together with the duties associated with his official offices, left him little time for relaxation. His antipathy to repeal remained and, as his correspondence shows, he opposed the appointment of pro-repeal candidates to local offices in the county. In his capacity as lord lieutenant, he resorted to transportation as a punishment for convicted 'Ribbonmen'. A regular punishment for common crime in Britain, in Ireland it was mainly used as a means of curbing the activities of secret societies. Personally Sligo was not immune to the grim realities of the punishement for those convicted. In one such case in which, as he admitted, 'I was the cause of his transportation', he interceded with the Lord Lieutenant of Ireland to pardon a convicted individual because his wife was too ill to join him in Australia.[127]

Surrounded by his young family, which numbered four sons and five daughters, all under seventeen years, life in the congested living quarters at Westport House was both noisy and time-consuming. Accompanied by a tutor, William Hudson, and Miss Midgely, the governess, sailing on Clew Bay, visits to Clare Island, indulging in the latest craze of 'sea bathing', carriage rides through the scenic areas of their father's estate, interspaced with visits to and from relatives, occupied the children's summer months, while Sligo ensured that school lessons were also part of their daily routine. A stickler for good manners, he expected a similar standard from them, especially in their relationships with household staff and retainers. An illicit amorous approach by his cousin George Browne, home on leave from Jamaica, to Miss Midgley, in which his sons Altamont and James (Jem) and his daughters Louisa and Elizabeth became inveigled, led to their chastisement and to the sacking of their tutor. Family troubles also intruded, including the ongoing indebtedness of his cousin James Browne, and of Dominck Browne of Castlemacgarrett, against whom, together with other creditors, Sligo reluctantly was forced to initiate legal proceedings. His general ill-health, which in the summer of 1833 included an attack of influenza and conjunctivitis, in addition to frequent bouts of gout and rheumatism, were aggravated by his ever-increasing workload. By early autumn rumours began to circulate that the Marquess of Sligo and his family intended to leave Ireland for Italy. While an absence abroad was by then under consideration, Italy was not their intended destination.

In 1833 an act for the emancipation of slaves in the British colonies was passed in parliament. In August 1833 Edward Stanley, the colonial secretary, advised Sligo that the incumbent governor general of Jamaica, Lord Mulgrave, was 'anxious to be relieved on account of his health'.[128] The prospect of a posting abroad was opportune. Sligo's disillusionment with the political situation in Ireland, his continuing poor health, his mounting indebtedness and, as he admitted, 'for the sake of clearing off encumbrances and saving money for his children … of getting rid of what my folly had in former times incurred', induced him to accept the government's offer to become Governor General of Jamaica.[129]

The decision was to have major repercussions on his personal outlook and fortune as much as it was to have on the history of Jamaica.

Chapter 13

The Governor

To me it appears quite impossible to deny, that much abuse
of the intentions of the Abolition Act has taken place, and
that every species of evasion within the letter of the law –
certainly beyond its spirit – has prevailed.

Lord Sligo

For many decades the Jamaican estates inherited through Sligo's
paternal grandmother, Elizabeth Kelly, helped sustain Westport
House through the bi-annual sale of sugar and rum. Barrels of
sugar, puncheons of rum and coffee and spices from the plantations
enhanced his diet, while hardwoods from the Jamaican forests
glowed in the doors and furnishings of Westport House. In 1833
it appeared inconceivable that the great-grandson of 'Jamaica
Kelly' was about to set out on a course that would render virtually
worthless his Jamaican estates and help dismantle the system of
slavery on which the prosperity of Jamaica, as much as his own,
depended.

In 1834 Jamaica was about to enter a new and critical period
in its troubled history. The horrors of the slavery system were
brought to the attention of the British public by white missionaries
and abolitionists. Driven more, as one commentator noted, by
'sentiments of sympathy and social justice for passive victims

rather than by notions of equality', their efforts to end slavery were nonetheless fought tooth-and-nail by powerful vested interests, especially by the owners of plantations (many of whom were members of the British establishment) as well as by commercial interests.[1] In the years following the abolition of the slave trade in 1807, many factors contributed to the demise of 'King Sugar'. The price of West Indian sugar no longer enjoyed differential rates in Britain, and many plantations fell into economic decline. The white-dominated Jamaican Assembly was effectively bankrupt. A slave revolt in December 1831 on the island resulted in much damage to property and heightened the alienation and fear that existed between the white and black population. When the Jamaican planters refused further concessions to their black workforce, the anti-slavery movement demanded full and immediate emancipation. This resulted in the passing of the Abolition of Slavery Act on 31 August 1833, which was to take effect on 1 August 1834. Twenty million pounds (over £800 million today), said to have been 'squeezed from the bones of those who worked as white slaves' in British mills, factories and mines, was paid in compensation to slave-owners in the British colonies.[2] Over £6 million was paid to proprietors in Jamaica, of which the Marquess of Sligo was in receipt of the sum of £5,526 in lieu of the 586 slaves then working on his estates.

The 1833 Abolition Act, however, did not grant full freedom to the enslaved. While all slave children under six years were immediately freed, an 'apprenticeship' system was put in place whereby adult slaves were compelled to remain in their owners' employment (i.e. apprenticed) for up to six years before being set fully free. In return for forty and a half hours' weekly unpaid work, the 'apprentice' was entitled to free food, lodging, clothing and medical assistance from his former master. Described as 'slavery under another name' by the emancipation movement, reviled by the plantocracy and initially misunderstood as freedom by the former slaves, the act served only to embitter relations between former slave and owner, offering the prospect of future freedom to the enslaved and the prospect of financial ruin to their masters. Given the potentially explosive situation where, on the one hand, slave-owners strove to retain control over those on whom they depended for their economic survival (even threatening to secede from the British Empire and join the United States of America where slavery still flourished) and, on the other, where slaves demanded total emancipation, a seamless transfer of power from one governor to the next was deemed vital. Strict secrecy, therefore, surrounded Lord Sligo's appointment as governor general.

The governorship of Jamaica, second in precedence to the viceroyalty of India, was, despite its many difficulties, a prestigious appointment. Previous incumbents included the Earl of Balcarres, the Duke of Manchester, the Earl of Belmore and the Earl of Mulgrave. Despite his best endeavours, news of the Marquess of Sligo's appointment became public knowledge in Ireland, with the inevitable consequence, as he informed the colonial secretary, 'I have had at least 100 applications within the last week to make people's fortunes in Jamaica.'[3] From his relations and friends he was inundated with requests soliciting positions in his administration. 'I have not the patronage of a single place in Jamaica ... but one appointment of £2,100 a year but, hard to say,' he bluntly informed one of his cousins, 'there is not one of my own family capable of it.'[4] Sligo also hoped that Jamaica's semi-tropical ambience might help relieve the chronic arthritic condition with which he was almost constantly afflicted. A salary of £8,000, given the fall-off in rental income from his estate in Ireland, was a further consideration.

From the start he was adamant that his wife and nine children, ranging in age from seventeen-year-old Louisa to two-year-old Henry Ulick – and, as he confidently predicted, 'there may be others' – would accompany him to Jamaica. Initially the Colonial Office balked at the idea but the governor-elect refused to be separated from his family. 'My children are numerous, I grant you, but surely no person would work to divide them from me ... to seek to deprive me of the happiness of my family accompanying me.'[5] What his wife and children thought about relocating thousands of miles across the ocean, far from family and friends, to a colony riven by dissension and brutality, about which stories of slave revolts, disease, earthquakes and hurricanes were widespread, is another matter.

Throughout her married life Catherine proved a loyal and stoic consort and confidante of her husband, although, as he freely admitted, to his cost, he did not always take her advice. Their closeness as a family unit was commented upon in Ireland and in Jamaica. Both parents maintained a short rein on their large brood. Sligo held realistic hopes that his heir, George, then at Eton, 'a very clever boy without being a prodigy ... will, I trust, pass through Cambridge with distinction'.[6] After much deliberation it was agreed that George would remain at Eton to complete his studies before joining the rest of the family in Jamaica. For Sligo, his children's future security was paramount, to the detriment of the wider Browne family, who traditionally looked to him for their material advancement. By 1833 his assets were confined, as he bluntly told one of his cousins, 'in land and instead of [having] ready cash I owe some'.[7] A further reason for accepting the governorship of Jamaica stemmed from reports he had received about the gross mismanagement of his Jamaican estates and the mistreatment of 'his negroes'.

In 1833 there were some 760 sugar plantations in Jamaica, averaging 900 acres, with an average slave workforce of 223 slaves per plantation. Many of the largest estates had as many as 1,000 slaves. There were some 1,000 cattle-breeding and grazing farms, known as 'pens', and a few hundred smaller plantations producing cotton, coffee and pimento. Sligo's largest estate, Kelly's, was situated in the old parish of St Dorothy, beside Old Harbour;

another plantation, Cocoa Walk, lay inland in hilly terrain in the north-west of the parish. By 1833 Kelly's had 138 acres under cane, 118 acres in pasture, some under crops, mainly pimento and coffee, with the rest given to wood and waste. Cocoa Walk had 261 acres in cane with some pasture; the rest comprised mountain and woodland.

Each Jamaican plantation was, in effect, a self-contained commercial entity with a hierarchical structure. By 1833 some 54 per cent of the enslaved in Jamaica lived and worked on properties owned by absentees, their day-to-day supervision in the hands of paid employees. While absenteeism played a negative role economically and socially in Ireland, in Jamaica it was compounded by 'all the evils of a community resting on slavery'.[8] At the top of the plantation hierarchical chain was the attorney, usually a lawyer or merchant, who acted on behalf of the absentee proprietor. Paid on a commission basis, usually 6 per cent of gross profits, the arrangement encouraged the attorney to extract the maximum production from the land and from the slaves, to the detriment of both. The attorney managed a number of properties but had little input in their day-to-day management which, as Sligo discovered to his cost, 'made laziness and dishonesty unnecessarily easy'.[9] At the heart of the slavery system was the white overseer (busha) who lived on the estate and made the daily decisions regarding crops and labour. On a salary of between £120 and £150 per annum, plus subsistence, pressurised by the difficulties associated with sugar production, the expectations of the owner, living in close proximity to a system that brutalised him as well as the enslaved he controlled, the busha could do little to change the environment in which he operated and so he resorted to whatever means were necessary to extract the maximum labour from the slaves to produce the maximum crop. The life of the eponymous bookkeeper, usually white and single, on a salary of a mere £50 per year, was at times intolerable. Described as 'a sort of voluntary slave', from dawn to dusk he supervised the work of the slaves in the cane fields and in the furnace-like atmosphere of the boiling house. Shunned by white society, the bookkeeper was left much to his own devices and accepted the prevailing standards of the slave-based society, adopting its attitudes, privileges and morals, becoming as callous and dissipated as the rest of his white counterparts. The estate artisans – cooper, mason, carpenter – were usually white, sometimes free coloured or free black. The driver, promoted from within the ranks of his fellow slaves, supervised the gangs of field slaves and meted out punishments with the dreaded cart whip. Domestics, black females and males, were engaged in housework, while, at the bottom of the scale, were the majority, male and female, field and mill labourers.

The sugar estate was usually situated in a rich alluvial plain or valley convenient to the sea. The owner's 'Great House', two storeys high, spacious and high-ceilinged, often with a large covered veranda, dominated the landscape. Because of absenteeism, many of the estate great houses, such as Kelly's, fell into disrepair. Close to the great house were the houses of the white busha, bookkeeper and artisans; and beyond lay the sugar works with mill house, boiling house, cooling house, trash house, curing house, distillery and the workshops of the coopers, carpenters, masons and blacksmiths. At a further distance lay the slave village, which comprised one-roomed cabins made of wood, wattle and mud. Racially, economically, socially and culturally apart, but interdependent with the white plantocracy, a parallel society flourished with its own rules, family groupings, religion, language, music and customs. While numbered as part of the 'property' of the proprietor, over time the enslaved population, unlike the more transient white management, accumulated a specialised knowledge of the sugar-making process on which the viability of the estate depended and which, in the struggle for emancipation, was to provide them with a measure of leverage. The enslaved had access to a designated patch of ground, usually at a distance from their habitation, on which they cultivated crops for their own consumption or to sell in local markets. Many became thrifty and used the money they accumulated to purchase their freedom.

As early as 1809 Sligo's estates were indebted to the tune of £2,000, which, as he informed a fellow absentee proprietor, Lord Henry Holland, had increased to '£10,000 when I reached Jamaica'.[10] Like his father and grandfather, he had never visited his property. 'One of the things I most regret in my past life,' he had informed his Jamaican attorney, 'is that amidst my various peregrinations I have never visited Jamaica.'[11] His estates were managed by a succession of Jamaican-based attorneys. As the properties had fallen further into debt, he attempted to involve himself more in their management. 'I beg also to know,' he wrote to one attorney, 'if there is a house belonging to me [at Cocoa Walk] … and whether it was worthwhile to keep it on cultivation or to waste it and transfer all the slaves to Kelly's.'[12] On the death of one attorney in 1825, Sligo discovered that there had been gross mismanagement of his estates, including blatant robbery and embezzlement, false returns of sugar and rum, overcharging for provisions and services and double-jobbing his negroes to work on other estates. With income from his estates not covering even a basic outlay on wages, provisions, agency fees, medical and other necessities he provided for the negro workforce, as well as the increasing charges and commissions charged by his shipping agents, in 1825 he determined on a change of management.

On being informed by William Clarke, a native of Mayo who had gone out to Jamaica to take charge of his own estate, of the extent of the problem on Kelly's and Cocoa Walk and of the maltreatment of his negro workforce, Sligo resolved to employ someone 'belonging to myself on whom I have dependence and who will feel an interest in my welfare'.[13] In September 1826 he persuaded his cousin George Browne, a constable of police in Killarney, to become manager of his estates. A brother of Robert Browne, the Ranger of the Curragh, Browne had been 'rather intemperate lately ... in his Protestant feelings and all his neighbours being Catholic', especially in Killarney, 'a regular O'Connell county', and Sligo was anxious 'to get him away as soon as possible' before he did further damage.[14] Not totally assured of his cousin's managerial ability, he also sent out two bookkeepers to assist him. One subsequently suffered a mental breakdown on the island and was forced to return. George Browne arrived in Jamaica at the end of 1826 and confirmed his cousin's worst fears regarding the condition of his estates and of the slave workforce.

For centuries slavery was one of the economic cornerstones of empires and countries. First introduced by the Spanish in the West Indies in the sixteenth century, trafficking in slaves from the coast of West Africa became a lucrative business for every seagoing European nation. In 1660 the trade became regularised by the establishment of the Royal Africa Company (RAC) with a monopoly to supply African slaves to the plantations in colonies in the British West Indies. Sugar and its derivatives became the new gold and slavery the bedrock on which fortunes were made. The RAC was superseded in 1750 by the Company of Merchants, which opened the slave trade to individuals. From the mid-seventeenth century until the abolition of the slave trade in 1807, some 900,000 people of African origin were taken as slaves to the island of Jamaica.

Jamaican slaves originated mainly from West and Central Africa. Snatched from their tribes and sold into slavery by fellow Africans, they were forced-marched hundreds of miles from the interior to the dungeons of slave-holding forts dotted along the west coast, before being herded onto slave ships. The triangular trade voyage originated from English ports, with cargoes of manufactured goods to purchase slaves in West Africa, across the Atlantic on the infamous 'middle passage' to sell their human cargo in the West Indies and to return with loads of sugar, rum, coffee, hardwoods and spices to England. The putrid and suffocating conditions the slaves endured in the holds of the slave ships were matched only by what awaited them on arrival. Manacled and man-handled, the black human cargo was put on public view. Tribes and families were separated as each slave was individually auctioned to the highest bidder. Fifty pounds was the average price for an able-bodied male, while females were valued both as slaves and as the producers of future slaves. 'I have purchased for Cocoa Walk sixteen fine young negroes with which our people seem highly delighted,' his attorney informed the 1st Marquess of Sligo in 1802.[15] Once sold, the slaves became the absolute property of their white owners and were 'stripped of every right ... outcasts from the common privileges of humanity, deprived of the essential attributes of man, without a legal claim to the produce of their own labour or even the possession of their wives or children'.[16] Whipped, burned, manacled and chained, branded by hot irons, the punishments inflicted on the enslaved by their white masters varied in type and severity. Black slaves were considered no more than beasts of burden and were listed as such on estate documents. Condemned to toil long hours planting and cutting in the cane fields and in the boiling houses, the working day of both male and female field slaves was regulated by the nefarious cart whip and the common-held belief that 'a stripe on the back was a furrow in the field'.

Persecution and racism in Ireland did not deter Irish Catholic emigrants from participating in the lucrative trade. After the Jacobean war, many French-based Irish émigrés fleeing racial persecution at home built their fortunes on the back of slavery. Irishman Antoine Walsh, domiciled in Nantes, founded the slave-trading company 'Compagnie d'Angola' which provided slave labour for the French West Indies. On the establishment of the Company of Merchants in England, with Irish ports prohibited by the British government from directly participating in the lucrative slave trade, Irish emigrants established themselves in Bristol and Liverpool as slave-ship owners and captains, merchants, provisioners, agents and importers. Salted and pickled commodities for the slave colonies in the West Indies were the mainstay of Irish cities, such as Limerick and Cork. In Jamaica, Irish place-names such as Irish Town, Lynchvale, Leinster and Sackville roads and Killarney and Kinsale avenues, estates such as Clonmel, Kildare, Athenry, Kelly's, Belfast, Midleton, Ulster Spring and Bangor Ridge abounded. Sligo's fellow county-man (no relation) Dr Patrick Browne, from Crossboyne, County Mayo, physician, mathematician, astronomer and botanist, gained much acclaim for his map of Jamaica published in 1755 and for his seminal work *The Civil and Natural History of Jamaica*, a copy of which was in the library at Westport House.

Despite the rigours of the voyage, the debilitating climate and disease, Catholics from the west of Ireland emigrated to Jamaica and other islands in the Caribbean to make their fortune. Many became plantation owners and some, like Sligo's paternal grandfather, Denis Kelly, were also prominent in the legislative, legal and administrative offices in Jamaica. Over the decades they were joined by a constant flow of relatives and neighbours to work as attorneys, bookkeepers and overseers. Most never returned, succumbing to the climate or disease, or married the daughters or widows of plantation owners. Some of the daughters of this wealthy plantation class, such as Sligo's grandmother Elizabeth Kelly, returned to Ireland and married into the Irish aristocracy.

Nineteenth-century white society in Europe and America considered black people inferior, even subhuman. Academics in the fields of science and anthropology propounded the theory that, both physically and mentally, black-skinned people were inferior to white. Thomas Carlyle, the nineteenth-century political philosopher, urged that the 'primitives' must be kept enslaved for 'their own good'. From a commercial perspective, as a form of cheap labour on which the prosperity of individuals, companies and countries depended, slavery was deemed to be essential.

Prohibited from marrying their fellow slaves, black women were sexually exploited by their white masters in a society where, even by the standards of the day, immorality was widespread, every sexual inclination was indulged in and sexually transmitted disease was rampant. The son of one such liaison between a planter and his black 'house women' testified that 'among his own slaves my father was a perfect parish bull; and his pleasure was the greater, because at the same time he had increased his profits [i.e. made an enslaved woman pregnant]'.[17] Thomas Thistlewood, an eighteenth-century plantation manager and owner, recorded that he had 'engaged in 3,832 acts of sexual intercourse with 138 women in his thirty-seven years in Jamaica'.[18] White men sent to administer estates in Jamaica established liaisons with black or brown slaves who became their 'housekeepers' and who considered it 'more genteel to be the paramour of a white man than to marry ... with their own kind ... agreeing with the native proverb that marriage "had teet' an' bite hot".'[19] The wives of the plantocracy were not only aware of their husbands' sexual activities but were complicit in the belief that there was neither 'sin nor shame in cohabiting with his slave'.[20] The formation of a sexual relationship with a white man provided an opportunity for a female slave to better ensure her protection, elevate her social status and sometimes, if her white consort was generous, lead to financial security, even freedom, for herself and her offspring.

Slaves were denied access to education, their African language and customs derided and forbidden. To counteract the high incidence of suicide among the black slave population, legislation was enacted by the Jamaican House of Assembly which condemned the body of a black suicide victim to be hung up in chains in a public place until it was devoured by birds and wild beasts. While some owners were more humane than others, slavery, by its very nature, demeaned and brutalised slave and master alike. Jamaica, in particular, was notorious for the savage treatment endured by its slave population. 'No country exceeds them in a barbarous treatment of Slaves, or in the cruel Methods they put them to death.'[21] Together with sexual indulgence, gambling and alcohol were other currencies that mattered in white Jamaican society. 'Men eat like cormorants and drink like porpoises,' Lady Nugent, the wife of one governor general, observed of white Jamaicans.[22]

White slave masters, however, were the product of their backgrounds and of the harsh ethos that permeated eighteenth- and nineteenth-century western society. The predisposition of white society to the absolute rights of hierarchical authority, combined with the religious confirmation of white superiority, contributed to society's justification of slavery. Most white proprietors of Jamaican plantations and the industry that fed off slavery – slave traders, agents, attorneys, overseers, bookkeepers and merchants – originated from England, Scotland and Ireland. They came from societies where the working class, be they Irish farm tenants or English industrial labourers, enjoyed little return for their toil and little protection from the law which was exclusively on the side of the property owner. Grinding poverty and starvation, in both countryside and city, was their lot. Women and children worked long hours in British factories and mines. The Factory Act of 1833 merely prohibited the employment of children *under age nine*. An English farm labourer could be sentenced to transportation for life for poaching a rabbit; an Irish tenant could be evicted from his mud cabin at the whim of his landlord; public flogging was a regular punishment in the British navy. Treadmills were frequently used both as an exercise and as punishment in British and Irish gaols. (During his tenure as lord lieutenant of Mayo, Sligo requisitioned a replacement treadmill for the county gaol, as he later did for the notorious 'houses of correction' in Jamaica, considering it a more humane method of punishment than the much-feared and widely used cart whip or cat-o-nine-tails.) The dreaded workhouses, established throughout Britain and Ireland, the last refuge of the hungry and the destitute, were explicitly conceived as 'places of hardship, coarse fare, degradation and humility ... administered with strictness, with severity ... as repulsive as is consistent with humanity'.[23] In Ireland the mass of the population were victims of racist legislation, hunger and deprivation. Two-thirds of the population existed on an economic knife-edge. 'I only wish the poor Irish were half as well off,' Lady Maria Nugent, who had also lived in Ireland, observed of the conditions pertaining to the Jamaican slaves.[24]

The mentality and outlook of white slave-owning society was thus predisposed to and further reinforced by a pervasive and, given that the slave population outnumbered their white masters by nine to one, a realistic fear of annihilation. 'Jamaica was a society at war. Slaves had to be kept cowed through arbitrary, tyrannical and brutal actions supported at all times by the full weight of state authority .... Only in this way could white fears be assuaged.'[25] As in Ireland, where there were many benign landlords, not every Jamaican planter was a tyrant. But the very ethos of life in Jamaica, in which both oppressor and victim were separate and yet inseparable, was distorted, abnormal and ill-defined. With nothing to prohibit them, unconstrained by any moral or legal consideration, other than whatever dispensation they may choose to personally grant, with the laws of the land made by and geared to their exclusive needs by a government which represented only their interests, the minority white master-race held sway over their fellow black countrymen.

As a colonial proprietor, Sligo's attitude to slavery might well be expected to reflect that of his peers. Since entering his inheritance, he had purchased slaves to work his estates, even as late as 1828, when he debated paying '£1,000 sterling worth of negroes to make up the necessary gang for Kelly's.'[26] His knowledge of the slave society, on whose labour the viability of his property depended, was confined to reports from those who managed his estates and who merely enumerated and alluded to his slaves with the same detachment as they did his livestock. But even from his detached position, the sentiments expressed in his correspondence showed an unusual concern for the welfare of the slaves who worked his estates. 'I am very anxious to ensure to the Slaves a humane system of treatment which I hear they have not been used to,' he informed one of his Jamaican agents in January 1826. On learning 'that my Negroes are wretchedly clothed and worse fed', he ordered the exact size and age of each slave be forwarded to him, so that 'I will have their clothes ready-made in England.'[27] To amend the widespread immorality existing between the white overseers and black slave women reported in Cocoa Walk, he demanded to know 'if any care or trouble has ever been taken either to educate or instil principals of Religion into any of my Negroes', if they were all 'prostitutes that is if they are ready to admit the embrace of any man ... or have they any ideas of Chastity like an English or Irish woman'.[28] On learning that 'the Negroes on Cocoa Walk are in a most deplorable state of disease from venereal disorder', he ordered that a building on each of his estates be turned into a hospital 'with both male and female wards' to care for them.[29] Doubting the veracity of his agents and overseers, he ordered, with well-intentioned naivety, that a 'letterbox' be made available on both his estates whereby the slaves 'might get someone to write to me their grievances. Tell the slaves that I know nothing of their grievances and that if at anytime they write to me at Westport, Ireland, I will do my best to relieve them'.[30] Against the prevailing ethos of the planter class, his attitude was rare.

Combined with the economic downturn and society's growing aversion to slavery, the writing was on the wall for Jamaica's slave-based economy. However, as the Jamaican plantocracy complained, the slavery system had been established by the same

'Mother Country' who now wished to have it dismantled, leaving the plantocracy to bear the brunt both commercially and morally. 'Year after year, encroachments had been made on our rights. We have been calumniated and held up in the Mother Country as monsters in human shape.'[31] Such criticisms, they maintained, emanated from people with little understanding of a system of labour not dissimilar to that which regulated the labouring classes in Britain. To save their properties from ruin, in March 1828 the Association of West Indian Proprietors, of which Lord Sligo was appointed chairman, was formed.

In the years prior to his appointment as governor, like his fellow proprietors Sligo realised that emancipation would further encumber his heavily mortgaged estates. 'I have hardly since I obtained possession made anything of these properties.'[32] In 1829 he tried unsuccessfully to sell his estates. On his appointment in 1832 as a member of the House of Lords Committee, however, his attitude to emancipation changed. On hearing evidence regarding the treatment of slaves in the West Indies, his disillusionment with the slavery system changed to that of abhorrence. 'I entered that room a colonial advocate; I left it a decided abolitionist.'[33] Initially, like many advocates of abolition, he was of the opinion that freedom was best granted on a gradual basis in order 'to prepare the minds of the Negroes for freedom'.[34] In light of his experience in Jamaica, however, that opinion was to alter.

Into this cauldron of despondency, fear and brutality, Sligo was entrusted with the daunting and unenviable task of implementing the provisions of the Abolition Act and to establish the apprenticeship system. 'I feel that in accepting of this office, I have undertaken a most painful and difficult task,' he wrote to his predecessor in office, Lord Mulgrave.[35] A political ingénue, the reason behind his appointment to such a sensitive post, at such a difficult time, is open to speculation. His support for Catholic Emancipation, as well as his gregarious and unaffected personality, was, perhaps, deemed suitable to smooth the diplomatic and political pitfalls that lay ahead; or, perhaps, the task was of such an impossible nature that, in the event of failure, he would carry the blame. 'Faced with the high task of governing men ... excited by unreasonable hopes, shaken by unreasonable fear, sullen, bitter or hopelessly foolish,' and, to dilute the powerful opposition to emancipation that awaited him in Jamaica, even the advantage of patronage was not at his disposal.[36]

That it was also a dangerous posting was not lost on Sligo. 'I am going on an arduous voyage and undertaking a desperately difficult task,' he told his step-uncle, Peter Browne. 'But if I have the good luck to do well & succeed I shall proportionately gain credit .... It may please God that we should not meet again but do think wherever I am nothing can alter [my] affection.'[37]

The journey to the West Indies was physically arduous, at the whim of the elements, while the death toll among Europeans on the island was inordinately high. As well as his ongoing rheumatic condition, corpulent by nature, now in his middle years, he had become seriously overweight. To judge by his accounts with food and wine merchants in Ireland, Britain and France, an indulgent diet was, in part, accountable for his weight gain, perhaps also for the bouts of gout with which he was regularly afflicted. In anticipation of his move to Jamaica, he ordered '500 bottles or the content of about 2 Hgds [hogsheads] of Lafitte ... 24 dozen bottles of the remaining champagne ... and a hogshead of White Hermitage' from his supplier in the Place Vendôme in Paris, together with a case of Hoch, 72 bottles of 'vin de Grave of the first quality Carbonnières 1822 ... a half quarter cask of fine Malmsey and a quarter cask of very old rich Agoa de Mel.'[38] In addition, he also purchased the remainder of Lord Mulgrave's cellar in Jamaica. An order for five cases of confectionery, 24 bottles of French mustard 'without garlic', boxes of sardines, olives, anchovies and 'Pâté de Strasbourg' guaranteed that,

The Court at Brighton *à la Chinese !!*
(© *Trustees of the British Museum*)

Lady Hester Stanhope

Portrait of Caroline Murat, Grande-Duchesse Of Clèves and of Berg
(Caroline Bonaparte) by Vigée Le Brun Elizabeth Louise

Gift Box from Joachim Murat, King of Naples to 2nd Marquess of
Sligo (Foundation Napoleon, Paris)

Kelly's Estate, Jamaica (*National Gallery of Jamaica. Photo: Kent Reid*)

Cocoa Walks Estate, Jamaica (*National Gallery of Jamaica.*
Photo: Kent Reid)

Highgate, Jamaica, (*National Gallery of Jamaica. Photo: Kent Reid*)

Sligoville, Jamaica (*Jamaica: Its Past and Present State:* J.M. Phillippo)

Emancipation Day, Spanish Town, 1 August 1834 (*Jamaica: Its Past and Present State:* J.M. Phillippo)

Treadwheel (*Jamaica: Its Past and Present State:* J.M. Phillippo)

11th Marquess of Sligo, Sligoville, 1996. (*Photo: author*)

Lord and Lady Sligo and author Anne Chambers lay wreaths on the
family graves of the Rev. James Phillippo, Jamaica 1996. (*Photo: author*)

where his weight was concerned, there was little likelihood of improvement.[39]

From the first public announcement in September 1833 of his impending appointment to the time of his departure in March 1834, initially, as he hoped, 'in the interest of my Family ... as early in the year as possible so as to get as much seasoning as maybe', he immersed himself in the practical arrangements relating to his posting.[40] 'Not knowing anything which has passed either on the island or between the Colonial Office,' he requested to see 'the despatches or notes of what has occurred since the new Bill has passed ... and to read carefully over them ... in any spare room in the Colonial Office ... and make myself master of them'.[41] He also conferred with fellow Irishman Lord Belmore, former governor of Jamaica, and with the Earl of Mulgrave. Prior to embarking at Portsmouth, he met with another Irish-born former governor, Major General Sir John Keane, hero of the Peninsular War, then on his way to command the British army in India. Keane's advice on how best to deal with the Jamaican House of Assembly – 'always to give them a blow first and then to be as conciliatory afterwards as possible' – Sligo had good reason to remember.[42]

He resisted attempts by the Foreign Office to retain the services of his predecessor's private secretary. 'I can assure you ... unless I am allowed to take out with me a man I have confidence in, all hopes of comfort & success in the arduous task now before me will vanish.'[43] In the event he appointed Colonel C.J. Doyle as his private secretary but, following Doyle's decision to return to England, he was replaced by W.G. Nunes, a resident of Jamaica. To transfer his unusually large family and entourage to Jamaica also proved problematic. Together with Catherine, his four daughters and three sons, his private secretary, a governess, two secretarial assistants, two nursemaids, 'Hanna the Butler and Byrne the Cook', his entourage was augmented by additional domestic staff hired in London. During the winter months his letters flew across the

Atlantic on almost every packet with orders to his cousin George Browne to prepare for his arrival. 'Look sharp about a Country house which will be in a cool position ... near to Spanish Town ... up the Mountains where I can detach my children in order to be in a somewhat cooler climate,' but he cautioned him, 'not to engage for any until I arrive.' He ordered Browne to make use of the produce from his own estates and have 'beef and mutton ... fattened to save butcher bills', together with whatever other household articles, such as candles, butter, meats and groceries, Lord Mulgrave intended to leave behind.[44] Advised that horses brought from Europe to Jamaica did not acclimatise well, he resolved to purchase those of his predecessor. 'I mean to bring over my own phaeton and to buy a sociable or open barouche with a hood or awning over it to keep out the sun.'[45]

Before he embarked, Sligo was summoned to an audience with King William IV at Brighton, who formally invested him with his new office. The king had a special interest in Jamaica, being 'the only King of England to have visited the Colony' while serving in the Royal Navy.[46] King William took a personal interest in the progress of the apprenticeship system in Jamaica and, during his tenure as governor, Sligo often communicated directly with him regarding its progress and the difficulties he encountered. During his audience at Brighton, the king also appointed him a member of his Privy Council.

The British naval ship HMS *Blonde*, en route to Rio de Janeiro, was hired to convey the new governor to Jamaica. A forty-six-gun, fully rigged frigate, it was captained by Francis Mason, a cousin of Lord Byron. Aware of the difficulties posed in accommodating such a large entourage and, as he wrote, of 'how utterly subversive such a cargo must be of the comforts of the Captain and crew', with his usual consideration Sligo assured Captain Mason that 'if you are so kind as to consent to take charge of us, it shall not be my fault if everything is not done on my part & that of my family to render it as little inconvenient as possible and to show how sensible we are of your kindness'.[47] Expressing his gratitude to the captain for making his cabin available to Lady Sligo, then six months pregnant, and his younger children, for the duration of the voyage, for himself he asked to be accommodated in whatever way was least disruptive to ship and crew. On 14 February 1834 all was in readiness and the governor-elect embarked at Portsmouth for the 4,000-mile voyage across the Atlantic.

Depending on the vagaries of the elements, the voyage to Jamaica could take between four and six weeks and was a veritable endurance test. Cramped quarters, little comfort or privacy, basic food and sanitation, sleep deprivation from the creaking of the timbers, the rattling of the shrouds, the shouts of the crew and seasickness were compounded by the dangers from storms, swells, shipwreck and piracy. From their extensive travels in Europe, Sligo and his family were well seasoned to the hardship and vagaries of nineteenth-century sea travel. For the younger children, the voyage was more an adventure, the nooks and crannies of the ship an exciting playground, interspersed with school lessons and card games.

In the Bay of Biscay they encountered a severe storm. Lady Sligo became 'very sick and the doctor was afraid of her being prematurely confined'.[48] Captain Mason confided to Sligo that if his wife's condition did not improve, he would have no alternative but 'to have her landed' in Lisbon. In the event, Catherine recovered sufficiently to continue the journey. On 7 March the *Blonde* made landfall on the island of Madeira to take on fresh provisions. Sailing past the Azores and crossing the Tropic of Cancer, the rise in temperature, the bright azure of the sea, the incredible clarity and lustre of the night sky, coupled with the sighting of such rarities as flying fish and whales, were harbingers of the exotic nature of their final destination. On 27 March they sighted Barbados and touched Martinique before the outline of Antigua, the first of the Leeward Islands, came into view.

At daybreak on 4 April 1834 from the deck of the *Blonde*, with both relief and delight, Sligo and his family watched Jamaica's imposing mauve-tinted mountains, their tops enveloped in clouds, their sides adorned with forests and shrubs, the rolling verdant hills and the shoreline, washed by white-foamed breakers, fringed with mangrove, cocoa nut and palm trees hove into view. Escorted by a flotilla of smaller vessels, they dropped anchor in the harbour of Port Royal. A former haven of buccaneers and pirates, in 1692 the city port had been partly swallowed up by an earthquake.

As protocol dictated, the governor-elect remained on board while news of his arrival was sped to the incumbent governor in Spanish Town, the political and administrative capital of the island.

The following morning, under a salute from the gun battery from Fort Charles, the new governor was escorted ashore at Port Henderson and into a political and social maelstrom that was to more than mirror what he had left behind in Ireland.

Chapter 14

The Big Buckra

I do not like thee Marquis S
The reason why I will confess
Because your Ex'lency delights
In acts that most annoy the whites
At least My Lord it is well known
You give a preference to the brown
The plain truth here I must express
You're Buxton's tool, Lord Marquis S
'Tis hardly needful to expose it
For ev'rybody living knows it
Therefore Most Noble Marquis S
Each day I like you less and less

Kingston Chronicle

The island of Jamaica has wooed natives, conquerors and visitors from the time of Christopher Columbus. Encapsulated in a landmass of just 4,411 square miles, 146 miles long and 51 miles wide, Jamaica has a remarkably diverse and beautiful semi-tropical landscape, with high mountain ranges, tumbling hills, deep ravines, mountain forests, wide, lush plains, luxuriant undergrowth and innumerable rivers, caves, cliffs, cascades, waterfalls and hot springs, all canopied by an azure sky, perfumed by exotic fragrances of pimento, orchid and tamarind, caressed by tropical breezes and washed by the warm, blue waters of the Caribbean. As the Marquess and Marchioness of Sligo and their young family disembarked, they were overwhelmed by the vibrancy and diffusion of sounds, sights, colours and smells that seemed to proclaim they had landed in a veritable paradise. But, as they were soon to discover, it was a paradise in which more than one serpent existed.

The new governor was welcomed with a guard of honour at Port Henderson. Responding to the cheers of the huge concourse of people gathered on the wharf, Sligo was escorted by a detachment of the local militia along a dusty track towards Spanish Town. His eyes feasted on the exotic vegetation through which he passed: pasturelands covered in guinea grass; trees bearing papaya, avocado pear, mango, guava, lime, lemon, orange, fig, melon, pineapple and breadfruit; the dark green-leaved pimento, with its all-invasive spicy fragrance; cocoa and tamarind trees; rows of tall palms, bamboo, silk-cotton and logwood. Flowering plants and shrubs, over three thousand varieties, some he had only previously seen confined in hot-houses, in Jamaica grew wild in profusion, their intense colours dazzling the eye. Hummingbirds, parrots and parakeets flitted among the branches, while the John Crow turkey buzzard lazily scoured the countryside from on high. He passed by the enclosed fields where tall sugar canes, the source of wealth and misery, stood line after line, attended by an army of black slaves, wielding hoe and bill. They stopped their work to wave at the new governor who, as they understood, was bringing them their freedom.

Spanish Town, or St Jago de la Vega, the name given by its Spanish founders (and the name Sligo invariably referred to it as in his official despatches and personal correspondence) in the seventeenth century, was where the battle for ownership of Jamaica between Spain and Britain had started and, in 1834, where the battle between slavery and freedom was about to begin. Situated on the banks of the River Cobre, with a population numbering 10,000, its overall appearance was dilapidated and run-down. Its crowning feature was a gracious square laid out in Spanish style, with a railed garden in the centre. Around it were the official offices of state, including the House of Assembly and King's House, the official residence of the governor general, a large red-brick, two-storey building, built in the Georgian style, with an impressive portico. At the northern end of the square stood the arsenal and guard house, as well as a somewhat incongruous Grecian-style temple with a semi-circular colonnade, commemorating the victory at the Battle of the Saintes in 1782 of the British admiral Lord Rodney over the French.

Arriving at King's House, Sligo was greeted by members of the House of Assembly who 'were received by the Marquis with the greatest politeness and condescension'.[1] Later, at a ceremony at the courthouse attended by the lieutenant governor, Sir Amos Norcott, the president of the Legislative Council and other state officials, Sligo was formally sworn in as governor general. That evening at King's House, together with 'his lovely and amiable family', he held his first levee attended by local worthies.[2] The following day his predecessor, Lord Mulgrave, took his leave, his relief at leaving Jamaica short-lived when, on his return home, he found himself entrusted with the equally contentious post as viceroy of Ireland.

After the state formalities, Sligo and his family took stock of their new home. King's House comprised many spacious rooms, including a grand ballroom known as 'The Egyptian Hall' used for formal engagements and which also accommodated sittings of the Court of Chancery. Another smaller gallery accommodated suppers and musical soirées, usually presided over by the governor's spouse. During her husband's tenure in office, Lady Sligo hosted few such social events but her Jamaican memorabilia contain invitation cards to her weekly 'At Home'. The Jamaican newspaper *The Gleaner* carried a notice to the effect that from September 'the

Marchioness of Sligo will receive Visitors on Tuesdays and Fridays, between the hours of *Twelve and Two* o'clock' at King's House.

The new governor's reluctance to socialise with white planter society was evident from the start. 'Lord Sligo is almost a stranger to the inhabitants [white]; he is seldom seen anywhere.'[3] His reasons were both personal and political. White Jamaican society was notorious for indolence and sexual promiscuity, something to which he was reluctant to expose his family. 'The society I met here in point of education and refinement are as you may guess not that attractive,' he confided to Lord Holland.[4] Instead his wife and daughters busied themselves with 'good works', mainly among the black and coloured community. One of Jamaica's most revered Baptist missionaries, Rev. James Phillippo, subsequently testified how the family, by their example, had 'exerted an especially beneficial influence in elevating the tone and character among the upper classes'.[5] Personally, Sligo found little among planter society to engage him, 'nearly all of them men without education, a liberal feeling and very few of them with any principle'.[6] When it became clear that the policies he aimed to pursue were at odds with their interests, the planters' criticism of the new governor became more vocal and personal. His appearance, weight, his nationality and youthful indiscretions, even his 'miserable Connemara made white jacket', became the subject of ridicule in the pro-planter press. And when he granted his 'sambo and mulatto friends' access to King's House, the criticism became more virulent. 'Our Emerald Isle is on the eve of being governed by a dynasty of Brownes ... but not a tribe of hungry relatives ... for Browne by cognomen is not Browne by complexion.'[7]

Through generations of inter-breeding between white plantation owners, overseers, bookkeepers and attorneys with black slaves, Jamaican society was multi-layered and complex. Over the generations, liaisons between white and black had produced subtle distinctions in colour, status and class, with definitions such as mulatto, sambo, quadroon, mustee and musteffino abounding. Some white men manumitted their black and brown offspring, both male and female, often endowing them with money, education and land. Some former slaves subsequently become owners of slaves, over whom, as Sligo observed, 'they were much more tyrannical ... than the whites'.[8] By 1834 'free coloureds' and 'free blacks' numbered some 40,000 and, while still regarded as 'inferior' by white society, they became wealthy and influential. Mainly town-dwellers, they challenged white dominance in trade, commerce, education and politics and were also prominent in the struggle for emancipation. Sligo later infuriated white planter society by employing one of their number, Richard Hill, as his secretary, with whom 'no gentleman in the West Indies was he in social life on terms of more intimate friendship'.[9] In 1829 two free coloured men, Edward Jordan and Robert Osborn, established *The Watchman* newspaper, which was at the forefront in the emancipation struggle.

The Jamaican Legislature consisted of the House of Assembly, which comprised forty-five white members, and a Legislative Council, a body appointed by the ruling governor. By 1834, however, the all-powerful assembly had wrested the legislative initiative from the council and, through its control of local authority boards, from public accounts to public works, in effect, usurped its power. The governor was the representative of the Imperial Parliament through whom, in theory, all orders and bills from the British parliament were transmitted to the assembly. As well as commander-in-chief of the island's military forces, vice-admiral and chancellor, the governor was also the chief executive of the Legislative Council. From earliest times, conflict existed between the British-appointed governor and the House of Assembly. In 1834 the main issue of contention centred full-square on slavery. Sligo's predecessor had endured the enmity of the assembly when he attempted to introduce measures for the better treatment of slaves. When the assembly refused to accede to his endeavours, to their intense anger, through the Act of Emancipation, it was imposed over their heads by the British parliament. Despite the cordial reception he received from the assembly members, Sligo was in no doubt about the difficulties that lay ahead: 'My reception has exceeded anything I could have anticipated. I cannot however expect this to last and I doubt not that before many months are over I shall meet with the usual fate of my predecessors, that of unpopularity.'[10]

The assembly's powerbase rested in local vestries situated in twenty-two parishes throughout the island. Headed by a custos, usually a chief magistrate, and consisting of ten members elected annually from among the white freeholders of the parish, two of whom were also elected to the assembly, the vestries constituted a powerful legislative and administrative block to any unfriendly governor and 'they certainly looked on Sligo as unfriendly'.[11] Another weapon in the assembly's arsenal, one that was to cause Sligo particular grief, was the island's agent, Jamaica's representative in London. In reality the agent represented the views of the planters and through him they sought to bypass the resident governor and gain direct access to the British government. During Sligo's term of office the Jamaican agent in London was William Burge, 'that arch impostor', who, together with the Speaker of the assembly, was to become his bête noir.

To implement the provisions of the Emancipation Act and the apprenticeship system, thirty-three Special Stipendiary Magistrates were allocated to Jamaica. Sligo succeeded in having their number increased to sixty. Mainly former British navy and army men, they were recruited in England in the expectation that they would prove more objective than the local Jamaican magistracy in implementing the rules and conditions of apprenticeship. From a meagre annual salary of £300, the Specials, or 'Stipes' as they were known locally, had to provide their own transport, accommodation and sustenance and work under conditions that, at times, as Sligo admitted, were beyond the bounds of human endurance. The salary allocated to a special magistrate, as he also attested, 'cannot nearly support him. In fact five of those appointed, have, since their arrival, told me that if they had the means of returning home they would do so at once.'[12] He successfully applied to have their salaries increased to £450 per annum. The workload of the Specials was both physically and mentally exhausting. Travelling by horseback an average 120 miles weekly with, as Sligo acknowledged, 'a courage and perseverance unequalled … in all directions defying the sun and the rain and disease', during the first two years of apprenticeship, some twenty Specials fell victim to the climate, to disease and to drink.[13]

Under the Emancipation Act, the former slaves, while technically free, were nonetheless bound or 'apprenticed' to their former owners; field workers (praedials) until August 1840 and non-praedials until 1838. Those with means could buy themselves out of apprenticeship during that period or could be manumitted by their owner. If the slave refused to work for his former master or if, on the other hand, the master forced the slave to work outside his allotted time or refused to pay him in lieu of extra time worked, it was deemed to be a transgression of the conditions of apprenticeship.

The task of adjudicating on each individual transgression fell to the Specials, who found themselves trapped between two incompatible forces that made the implementation of their orders both difficult and dangerous. Because of their meagre means and the extreme discomfort under which they worked, their impartiality was often compromised. Sligo's instructions to them 'to keep out of all parties and not let private friendships induce him to compromise his public duty' were often disregarded.[14] The house of the white planter, attorney or overseer was invariably the only hospitality and respite available to the itinerant magistrate on his travels throughout the island. Some found it difficult to resist the temptation and were often seduced by their hosts from reporting incidents of unfair or cruel treatment of apprentices. Because regardless of the will of the new governor or of the British government, the white plantocracy in Jamaica, accustomed, as Sligo noted, 'to the most despotic exercise of absolute power over their dependants', found it intolerable that through the intervention of a 'foreign' magistrate they could be 'deprived of the power of inflicting punishment on the apprentices'.[15]

The plantocracy sought retention of their long-held right to punish apprentices via the intervention of local justices, most of whom were without education or experience of the law. 'It is the constitution of our Courts that gentlemen of the Colony should be judges therein. I believe it to be a wise provision of our forefathers and a great protection to our liberties and property,' was the opinion of Richard Barrett, the Speaker of the House of Assembly.[16] Specials who tried to do their duty impartially invariably fell foul of the planter, often enduring physical violence and social exclusion in the process, while the 'buckra magistrates', those who looked the other way, were cosseted and rewarded.

The Specials became Sligo's eyes and ears. 'The weekly reports of 60 special magistrates traversing the country in all directions afforded me the means of acquiring a more perfect knowledge of the slavery system ... and equal opportunities of being made acquainted with the evasions of the laws practised by both sides.'[17] As his voluminous correspondence with them testifies, Sligo maintained a tight rein on their activities and the workload he demanded of them was exhaustive: to visit every slave-owning establishment in their area twice every month; to forward him weekly and monthly reports of their findings, detailing incidences of the number of apprentices on each estate, the names of the proprietor, attorney and overseer, details of the complaints received, their judgment on each individual case and on the punishment inflicted on any apprentice found guilty within their jurisdiction. The execution of each punishment had to be personally supervised by a Special, who had also to ensure that there was no unlawful confinement or concealment of apprentices by their masters. As well as weekly and monthly reports, the Special had also to keep a diary showing the miles he travelled, expenses incurred and number of properties inspected. In the month of May 1835, for example, the Specials travelled some 14,196 miles and visited 3,440 properties on the island. 'I do not scruple to say that an apprentice has no chance of justice against his master unless at the hands of a Special Magistrate,' was Sligo's implacable opinion, which was as implacably resented by the plantocracy determined to retain the right to be master, judge and jury over their black workforce.[18]

Among the Specials were a number of Irishmen, including Dr Richard Madden, a native of Dublin and one of the first Catholics, after the granting of Catholic Emancipation, appointed to the British service. Accompanied by his wife, Harriet, he abandoned a successful medical career in Mayfair in London to become a Special Magistrate in St Andrew's Parish. Uncompromising in his support for emancipation, a man who 'wouldn't agree with an angel from heaven', as Sligo humorously noted, he valued his fellow-compatriot's company and advice.[19] They had first met in Naples, where Madden was the resident doctor to the British expatriate community during the reign of Joachim Murat.

Including his handwritten instructions to each Special Magistrate, his written observations on the thousands of individual cases referred to him (one of his extant letter books contains over three thousand such cases), his extensive correspondence with the Jamaican Legislature, the Colonial Office, various British government ministers, friends and interested parties in the anti-slavery movement, as well as his personal correspondence, Sligo's Jamaican correspondence was prodigious. His working day as governor began at five in the morning and often lasted into the small hours of the night. During the course of his governorship, the weekly packet never sailed to England without a consignment of his official and private letters. This propensity for letter-writing was much ridiculed by his Jamaican critics. 'That the Marquess of Sligo is a politician, we deny, but that he is an indefatigable scribbler, we admit, and we ask, to what purpose? Is it to show he can work or is it from a desire for posthumous fame?'[20] His practice of making a handwritten copy of almost every letter, both official and private, ensured that his wife and children, his main copyists, were seldom idle. It is of interest (and a relief to this author, given Lord Sligo's atrocious handwriting) that both Catherine and her daughters frequently acted as his secretaries, copying his correspondence into numerous letter books. During their time in Jamaica, his children also cut and pasted into large ledgers extracts about their father, mainly antagonistic and often denigrating, from local newspapers.

The chief justice of Jamaica, Sir Joshua Rowe, occupied the position once held by Sligo's great-grandfather Denis Kelly. A native of Cornwall, he was the youngest chief justice in the island's history. A protégé of Henry Brougham, an ardent abolitionist, his appointment had so riled the Jamaican Assembly that they refused to pay his salary. While some differences were later to arise between them, Sligo valued Rowe's personal company as well as his support. Irish-born Dowell O'Reilly, appointed Attorney General in 1831 – 'that bold and humane officer', as Sligo wrote of him, 'who has never hesitated a moment, no matter at what professional loss, to stand forward as the protector of the oppressed'[21] – became his close personal friend and confidant.

On 10 April, Sligo made his first official visit as governor to Kingston, a city of some 40,000 inhabitants and the commercial capital of Jamaica. He was greeted with full military ceremonial and held a levee at the lieutenant governor-general's residence, which was situated on a slope of the Linguanea Mountains. Across the harbour from Port Royal, it owed its existence to the earthquake that had virtually destroyed the original 'pirate city'. Sprawling, brawling, crowded and chaotic, Kingston was laid out in streets of long straight lines, which intersected each other at right angles and which were described as being 'narrow, dirty, unpaved and infested with domestic animals'.[22]

From Kingston, Sligo travelled to his own estate in nearby St Dorothy's, one of only two visits which, owing to his official commitments, he was able to make during his term of office. Situated on a rich alluvial plain, Kelly's produced sugar, powered by a modern steam engine which Sligo had installed to facilitate the crushing of cane. As he drove up the avenue, under the luxuriant branches of the tamarind trees, to Kelly's great house and past the sugar works, thoughts of his great-grandfather and his 'Creole' grandmother, Elizabeth, whose portrait hung in Westport House and from whom he had inherited his Jamaican property, perhaps crossed his mind. Some of the black workers who came to meet him were descendants of those who both had known and worked for his great-grandfather and would have known 'Miss Elizabeth'. Under the management of his cousin George Browne, production on both estates had increased and expenses and charges had diminished. In November 1833 Browne fell into ill-health but had promised to await his cousin's arrival on the island. 'Having nearly lost the usage of one side', however, he returned to Ireland before Sligo's arrival.[23]

At Kelly's Sligo saw at first hand the gruelling and labour-intensive methods involved in the production of sugar. The productive life of the cane stalk was three years, one-third of the land being replaced by 'ratoons' or new shoots each year. The cane was harvested usually twice yearly. The land was first ploughed and harrowed before the toilsome work of digging and manuring the cane holes and planting (usually by young boys) the ratoons into four-foot-square grids commenced. In a ten-to-twelve-hour day a field slave was expected to dig between sixty and eighty cane holes. During the growing season the canes were weeded regularly, thinned and banked. Crop time on most estates started in spring, when the canes were cut by hand by the strongest male and female slaves then tied and transported by oxen cart to the estate mill house. They were then fed into iron rollers to extract the juice. The cane residue, known as 'trash', was transported to the trash house to provide fuel for the boiling house. The juice flowed through a series of cold receivers to separate the impurities before finally passing into the great copper 'clarifiers' in the boiling house. In an atmosphere of suffocating heat, day and night, it was boiled and then simmered, any impurities constantly skimmed with long iron ladles into a gutter that carried it to the distillery for rum-making. The final simmering stage of the process required great skill, for any divergence in the temperature would adversely affect the quality of the sugar. The transparent juice was then ladled into a gutter and conveyed to the cooler, where it was turned until it crystallised. Once cooled, the sugar was carried in pails to the curing house, emptied into hogsheads and allowed to stand for two days. Plugs were then pulled from the hogsheads to allow the residual molasses to drain away to be later distilled into rum. After three weeks the sugar was ready for shipment, every sealed and stamped hogshead (weighing 800–1,500 pounds) loaded on board ship before 1 August to avoid double insurance rates. Every step in the lengthy process required much labour and great physical exertion, augmented by the need for speed and diligence. Sugar's main derivative, rum, made from a mixture of molasses, water and the scum left over from the sugar, was fermented in wooden casks and distilled.

At Kelly's, Sligo addressed his 120-strong workforce about the forthcoming Emancipation Day and of their responsibilities as apprentices. He initiated a payment system on his estate whereby, during the course of their apprenticeship, the apprentices were paid in metal tokens of threepence, sixpence and one shilling denominations, each with a central hole to string for safe-keeping. Each Friday the tokens were redeemable for money for work done over and above regular apprenticeship hours. Some of these tokens were preserved at Westport House for over 160 years. In 1996, Sligo's great-great-grandson, the 11th Marquess of Sligo, presented a selection of the tokens to the National Museum of Jamaica. Sligo also inspected the slave accommodation at Kelly's and his recently established hospital or 'hot-house'. Despite being unable to visit his estates more than twice, his presence on the island improved both the output and running costs and, together with the compensation he received under the terms of the Abolition Act, for the first time, he found his Jamaican inheritance was 'clear and a couple of thousands in my pocket'.[24]

After visiting Cocoa Walk, Sligo proceeded into the interior of the island towards the foothills of the majestic Blue Mountains. Travelling along roads which narrowed in places to mere pathways, over precipices, hanging precariously above rushing rivers, through deep and gloomy ravines, skirting hardwood forests of prime mahogany, cedar, black and green ebony, along lush low-lying vales, interspaced with clusters of bamboo cane and towering cocoa palms, through a countryside dotted with sugar estates and pens, he was joined by Lord Seaford, one of the most extensive proprietors on the island. Together they travelled by steamer around the island to Montego Bay to visit Seaford's Montpelier estate in the parish of Westmoreland.

Seaford's family had been plantation owners since the seventeenth century and had accumulated a vast acreage, a workforce of over one thousand slaves and enormous wealth. A supporter of George Canning, and part of the liberal Whig set of Lord Holland, whose plantations lay close by, Sligo and Seaford were well acquainted. Albeit a supporter of the apprenticeship system, Seaford's primary concern was the viability of his estates. The recent slave rebellion had brought him to Jamaica to inspect the destruction wrought on his property. To prevent further disturbances, he donated an eight-acre site for the erection of an army barracks. Their friendship did not deter Sligo, however, from investigating incidences 'of the grossest misconduct and maltreatment' of apprentices by Seaford's overseer which, as Sligo confided to Holland, if 'he [Seaford] did not know of them, he ought and he should have selected under people who were not capable of such conduct'.[25]

After a brief stay at Montpelier, Sligo moved on to Sweet River, one of Lord Holland's estates, managed by Thomas MacNeill. There he addressed the black workforce of whom, as he reported to Holland, 'I have not seen a more respectable set of Negroes since I have been on the island and ... Mr. MacNeill seems an excellent character for acting and good management'.[26] In the course of his journey he also visited the territory of the Maroons, a community composed of former black rebels and runaway slaves. In 1739, after a series of rebellions against the British, the Maroons were granted freedom and 1,500 acres of land between Trelawny Town and the impenetrable Cockpits, a limestone plateau pitted with cone-like vegetation-covered hills, where they continued to live independent of the government in Spanish Town.

A casual perusal of the Jamaican press provided the new governor general with a graphic sense of the violent and despotic society he had come to govern. On 23 May 1834 the trial of an overseer charged with flogging a slave with 'a cat with eight tails ... ten lashes on one shoulder and ten on the other and then confined in the stocks for upwards of a week' because he failed to report the death of a steer, was one of many such reports carried in the local papers. The local magistrate decreed the overseer's conduct 'free from all blame' and condemned the complainant to a further 'thirty-nine lashes on his back'.[27] To institute change in a society which considered such behaviour both normal and legal was a formidable undertaking. 'Persons who have been used to the diplomacy of the lash,' Sligo observed to Thomas Spring Rice at the Colonial Office, 'were seldom acquainted with the best method of influencing the human mind by persuasion.'[28]

As the date for the formal abolition of slavery drew near, Sligo endeavoured to manage the expectations of the majority black population and the fears of the minority plantocracy. A deep-set and understandable trepidation was widespread among the white population in expectation of another rebellion. To prevent such an occurrence, Sligo deployed troops throughout the island and also issued pardons to runaway slaves to encourage them to return to their plantations. While a revolt by the slaves was predicted by the whites, it was Sligo's opinion that whatever trouble might erupt was more likely to be occasioned 'by the impudence of the overseers who are unwilling to give up the power they have wielded so improperly hitherto'.[29]

Sligo's first public pronouncement in April as governor was made to the black population. His 'Address to the Negro Population throughout the Island of Jamaica', copies of which he had posted in public places, addressed people who for generations were deprived, not merely of their freedom, but also of the right to think and act on their own initiative, uneducated, illiterate, speaking a patois both unintelligible and derided and most without money or means. He had, he informed them, been sent by the king

> ... to take care of you and to protect your rights: but he [the king] has also ordered me to see justice done to your owners and to punish those who do wrong .... You will on the 1st of August be no longer slaves, but from that day you will be apprenticed to your former owners to fit you all for freedom?

In simple terms, he explained the conditions of their future employment:

> There are 168 hours in each week, out of which you will have to give to your master only forty and a half hours and have one hundred and twenty seven and a half at your own disposal. Your master must give you clothes, provision grounds and medical attendance if you are sick. Bear in mind that everyone is obliged to work. Some work with

their hands, others their heads .... Your lot is to work with your hands .... If you follow my advice ... nothing can prevent you from being your own master ... at the end of four or six years .... Neither your master, your overseer, your bookkeeper, your driver, not any other person can strike you, or put you into the stocks, nor can you be punished at all except by the order of a Special Magistrate.

He intended, he told them, to establish

... a social system absolved forever from the reproach of Slavery which will stimulate the class for whom this great boon is secured. Take my advice for I am your friend – be sober, honest and work well ... for should you behave ill and refuse to work because you are no longer slaves you will assuredly render yourselves liable to punishment.[30]

As Emancipation Day drew nearer, the anger of the slaves became directed against the new governor: 'Gobernor Mulgrave gave us free, but Gobernor Sligo keep we slaves because him hab slaves of him own.'[31] To eliminate the possibility of either accidental or deliberate misinterpretation, Sligo arranged for the conditions of apprenticeship to be read aloud by the Special Magistrates directly to the slaves on every plantation throughout the island. In this the magistrates were assisted by missionaries, mainly Baptist preachers, who laboured among the plantation slaves. His efforts proved successful and most slaves consequently became reconciled to the terms of their apprenticeship and the threatened revolt was thereby averted. 'Would to God that kings and rulers ... would take a lesson from the Governor of Jamaica and address themselves to the understandings and the hearts of their people.' His preparations 'for the momentous day of emancipation ... were crowned with the most brilliant success ... and by his beneficial arrangements the horrors of intestine revolution have been happily avoided'.[32]

On the first week of June, Sligo convened an extraordinary session of the Jamaican Legislature, the Assembly and the Legislative Council and came face-to-face with white proprietors, managers, attorneys and overseers for whom apprenticeship meant the loss of power over their black labour force and jeopardised the future viability of their properties. While the Act of Emancipation was forced upon them by the British government, its implementation was another matter. During the passage of the Abolition Act in the Assembly, they had forced through provisions to retain the right of physical punishment, including flogging, and ensured that the notorious workhouses or 'houses of correction' remained under the control of the local magistracy.

From the tenor of his speech to the Assembly and from his earlier proclamation to the black population, it became clear to members of the Assembly that, while their new governor might well be a proprietor in his own right, he shared little else in common with them. One of his most determined opponents was the Speaker of the House, Richard Barrett, master of Barrett Hall and Custos of the parish of St James. Related to the English poet Elizabeth Barrett Browning, while promoting himself as a humane master to his enslaved workforce, he was an implacable opponent of emancipation. From the start Sligo fell foul of the 'personal and petty jealousies of the Speaker', who threatened, as he wrote, 'to make Jamaica too hot to hold me'.[33]

In Jamaica the outward signs of slavery were everywhere evident. At five o'clock in the morning the estate bell rang the start of the working day, during which time the field slave's every movement was monitored, his labour enforced under threat of the cart whip, until eight o'clock when the bell sounded the end of the working day and he returned to his home. Evidence of cruelty abounded. Flogging of both male and female slaves, as punishment for the most innocuous transgressions, was enshrined in law. The conditions enforced in the houses of correction were brutal. Even

Sligo's earlier well-intentioned effort to replace the cart whip, which he detested, by the installation of the treadmill as a more 'salutary mode of punishment' was abused. The large cylinder, with a series of wooden steps on which the prisoner was forced to walk, in the hands of the planters, became an instrument of torture. Prisoners were strapped by the wrists and forced 'to dance' by the lash of the cart whip, often losing their balance to be battered by the revolving steps. The slave-gangs on the streets of Spanish Town and Kingston, both male and female, chained by neck and ankle, were everywhere evident.

'The law is entirely on the side of the planter,' Sligo observed. 'Every offence, every neglect, every breach of the law is recognised as a crime and punishable as such.'[34] Among his Jamaican memorabilia in Westport House is a branding iron, one of the most evocative and abhorrent symbols of the inhuman system he observed and was determined to end. The physical abuses inflicted on the slaves affected him emotionally and he was unable to conceal his repugnance in public. As he had done in Ireland, he took a personal interest in the grievances of individual apprentices, much to the scorn and indignation of their masters. 'It was his custom (unprecedented in the West Indies) to give a patient hearing to the poorest Negro who might carry his grievance to Government House ... and despatch an order to the Special Magistrate of the district ... desiring him to enquire into the case.'[35]

Sligo's foreboding about his relationship with the Assembly and the fact that they had 'quarrelled with every Governor from the Duke of Manchester down to your humble servant' were soon confirmed. 'I never saw so contemptible a publick [*sic*] body ... such a set of Children, if large size, or men who acted like them in the face of publick opinion and publick principle without the least remorse but to meet their own private interests.'[36] When the Assembly refused to pass a Police Bill and stonewalled the introduction of the Emancipation Act, the governor put down a marker. Initially using

British government compensation as leverage, he secured passage of the Police Bill, only to have it returned from the Assembly 'in such a shape that transferred all the power of directing it from me to the Assembly'.[37] By then, as he found out to his annoyance, the compensation to the planters had been paid in full by the government. The Assembly 'members do not scruple to say with a sarcastic grin on their countenances: "What can England do now. We are paid. What fools you are to do this, till you had your measures completed and permanently passed."'[38] To confront their blatant obstruction he instead prorogued the Assembly and, on its recall, the Police Bill was passed without protest.

Buoyed by the victory, he next tackled the Court of Chancery, which he found inefficiently run and corrupt, with widespread overcharging for services and legal fees. Estates in Chancery were administered by resident attorneys and managed by overseers and bookkeepers who made fortunes for themselves by robbing their absentee owners, as well as permitting abuses of all kinds on the enslaved. Sligo's diligence, however, drew further condemnation from the plantocracy, especially from Richard Barrett, who in the past had benefited personally from such practices.

Abolition Day on 1 August 1834 was commemorated by the *Jamaica Despatch*, a pro-plantocracy newspaper, with a large black border on its front page. It forecast the demise of prosperity and predicted turmoil and revolt. Contrary to such forebodings, however, as Sligo noted, the event 'was celebrated and made memorable by the most extraordinary, nay almost universal, attendance of the Negroes at the different places of worship'.[39] Slavery was at an end and apprenticeship to full freedom had commenced and, as such, it was celebrated and welcomed by most of the black population. No longer mere property, 'the former slaves were now to labour, not at the caprice of an absolute owner, enforced by the whip ... but by settled rules'.[40] From under the portico of King's House, with Catherine and his children by his side, flanked by his staff and Baptist missionaries, Sligo looked out on the historic scene on King's Square. With bands, flags and banners, in an air of joyous expectancy, a huge concourse of black men, women and children converged to hear the governor pronounce the words of their deliverance.

Planters who were prepared to grant the new system a chance gave celebratory dinners for their new apprentices: 'steers were killed by the proprietors and given to the Negroes, besides their usual holiday allowances of sugar, rum and salted fish'.[41] With the exception of some minor disturbances, the widespread turmoil predicted failed to materialise 'due to the judicious arrangements put in place by the Governor through the offices of the Special Magistrates which made the Negroes think of the first of August with the same indifference as they would the arrival of any other day'.[42] The predicted wide-scale abandonment of estates by former slaves also failed to materialise, except in one parish, where, on the assumption, as Sligo related to the king, 'that King William had given them free and they would take it', apprentices refused to work.[43] With the assistance of a military detachment and with the help of the Specials and missionaries, the apprentices were persuaded to resume work. Where planters agreed to pay the apprentices for work over and above the forty and a half hours required under apprenticeship, this was accepted on 758 estates. On 376 estates wages were neither offered nor refused, and in only 126 estates did the apprentices refuse to work outside the required hours, with the result, as Sligo reported to the Colonial Office, that 'the transition from slavery to apprenticeship had been effected in the most satisfactory manner'.[44] To replace a political and social system, even one as repugnant and flawed as slavery, would, as Sligo realised, take time to accomplish. Apprenticeship was the first step in the process and he determined to do his utmost to make the transition successful. 'My heart and soul are wrapped up in the success of this great measure.'[45]

On 1 August 1834, from the steps of King's House, as he proclaimed the words of freedom to the former slaves gathered before him, his heart was full of hope and optimism. He could not have foreseen the forces being marshalled against him, both within and without Jamaica, or how his personal belief in the apprenticeship system was destined to undergo fundamental change.

Chapter 15

The Great Leviathan

Those who are acquainted with the West Indies will be aware that the black and coloured population are viewed by the white inhabitants as little more than semi-human, for the most part as a kind of intermediate race, possessing indeed the form of man, but none of his finer attributes.

Marquess of Sligo

While Sligo immersed himself in the responsibilities of his office, his family were coming to terms with life in their semi-tropical surroundings. For all of them, as for every newcomer to Jamaica, it took time to become 'seasoned' to the conditions of their environment. The high summer heat and humidity of Spanish Town was stifling and most of their time was spent confined indoors or to whatever shade was available in the environs of King's House. For Sligo's daughters, their social outlets were limited to attending official functions which, owing to their father's aversion to such events, were rare. Their integration was further limited by his intense dislike of white planter society. A few months following their arrival in Jamaica, he transferred his family from King's House to Highgate, a house purchased from his predecessor, Lord Mulgrave. Accessed along a rough track, through primeval forest, accessible only by foot for the final rocky stage, Highgate was isolated and remote. Described as 'hanging between heaven and earth', it commanded spectacular views over Kingston and Port Royal harbour. Situated some 2,000 feet above sea level, it was fanned by cool mountain breezes. Given her advanced state of pregnancy, for Catherine it was a welcome release from the oppressive heat of Spanish Town.

Sligo and his wife utilised the three acres of ground adjoining the property to cultivate plants, such as sarsaparilla, so that it 'might be turned into a profitable production in this island' as well as specimen gum and milk trees, which they imported from Colombia.[1] In an effort to establish a white labouring class, German-born immigrant families were brought to Jamaica as indentured workers. Many died from disease and neglect shortly after their arrival. Moved by their plight, Sligo provided work for some of their number at Highgate, paying them a weekly wage of eighteen shillings and fourpence, plus accommodation, together with a garden on which to grow their provisions. 'They are quite content and happy,' he wrote. 'I doubt not that if properly treated they will heretofore be of great service to the island.'[2]

Sligo considered education an essential tool to promote self-respect and confidence among the black population and to incentivise them to acquire skills to compete outside the confines of the plantation. 'As I know you have turned your mind to the education of the poor Negroes,' he informed Rev. James Phillippo, 'I should feel much obliged if you would communicate to me any plan of general education, without reference to any peculiar religious opinions, which you may have formed.'[3] On Phillippo's suggestion, a model teacher-training school was established in Spanish Town. When the Jamaican Assembly refused to provide the necessary funding, Sligo turned to the Colonial Office in London from which he extracted a grant of £500. Despite further appeals regarding 'the want of education or any effort to prepare the mind of the Negro for eventual freedom', little additional government funding was forthcoming.[4] He personally funded a school for black children beside Highgate which, as he recorded, 'I frequently visit to see what progress it is making.'[5]

Other than two suppers given in his honour in Spanish Town and Kingston and one visit to the race track, by personal choice and owing to the high cost of living on the island which, as he found, 'will draw over and above my allowances',[6] he and his family chose to live quietly at Highgate. Other than Dowell O'Reilly, his relation Captain Browne, a military secretary in his administration, and his secretary, Richard Hill, there were few with whom he felt at ease. Whatever friends he made on the island were among the more liberal wing of political life, missionaries and 'free coloureds'. The plantocracy derided him for filling offices in his administration with 'his missionary toadies' and 'his Sambo and Mulatto friends'.[7] But even his most determined enemies testified to his good humour, chivalrous manner and kindness and to his desire to ensure fair play for all. Jamaica's semi-tropical climate suited his rheumatic condition, and his health improved considerably. 'I like this place very much,' he wrote to his step-uncle, Peter Browne, 'and have not had a day's illness ... since I have been here.'[8]

In August his son Altamont arrived from England having completed his final year at Eton. The family numbers were further augmented on 6 August when Catherine gave birth to another son, Richard Howe, named after his great-grandfather. The difficulties associated with a Creole confinement were many, ranging from the intense heat and humidity to flies and disease. But the 'young Creole' survived his tropical beginnings and was baptised on 11 August at King's House by the Bishop of Jamaica. For Catherine, the birth of her child in a country where the mortality rates of infants were notoriously high brought an added measure of anxiety. When it became apparent that the baby and her younger children were unable to acclimatise, and mindful of the death of their infant son in Italy, in early 1835 they were returned to Ireland in the care of their nurses, leaving Altamont, nineteen-year-old Louisa, seventeen-year-old Elizabeth, thirteen-year-old Catherine, twelve-year-old Jem and eleven-year-old Thomas to remain in Jamaica with their parents.

With the exception of her weekly 'at homes' in King's House, Catherine kept her social engagements to a minimum. Attendance at Sunday service in the Anglican cathedral church of St James in Spanish Town, the first cathedral to be built in the West Indies, provided a break from the isolation of the family's mountain retreat. From the observations written about her and her children by those who made their acquaintance, 'the rare combination of amiable qualities they have exhibited in their domestic circle [served] to annihilate the vain customs and to correct the worst vices of colonial society'.[9] Daily life began at daybreak to take maximum advantage of the cool morning temperature. Hot coffee was followed by breakfast at eight, a second breakfast at noon and dinner between six and seven. Their daily diet was supplemented by the exotic and abundant produce of the island – mango, breadfruit, avocado pear, pomegranate, figs, guava, plantain, sweet potato, yam, ackee, cocoa nut milk, highly seasoned dishes such as jerk hog and chicken, crab pepper-pot, salt fish and 'bammy', a round flatbread made from grated cassava. Despite their isolation, they were seldom idle. As well as acting as their father's copyists, Catherine and her daughter Louisa, in conjunction with the missionaries working in the area, busied themselves in promoting literacy and other educational programmes among the black population, Catherine becoming a patron of schools and charitable institutions in the vicinity of Highgate. As a keen and knowledgeable gardener, she delighted in the diversity and profusion of the flora of her surroundings.

For her husband, however, opportunities for relaxation were rare. For the two parties affected by the provisions of the Abolition Act, 'ill will on one side generated ill will on the other'.[10] This was aggravated by Sligo's determination to impose, to the letter of the law, the controversial conditions of the Emancipation Act, objectionable to both sides but particularly to the powerful plantocracy. For Sligo it boiled down to a simple equation. Jamaica was an oligarchy where 333,000 enslaved inhabitants supported less than 20,000 white masters 'who effectively keep down the others', a situation he saw it his duty to ameliorate.[11] While admirable in its intent, it was, perhaps, a naive approach to what was a complex and ingrained system that would take time and a sea-change in mind and attitude to remedy. His methodology was further compromised by his personal dislike of planter society that, even in his official correspondence with the British government, he found difficult to sublimate. But 'abominable as are the characters of a great number of the Planters, more especially of those of the Assembly', initially he tried his best to make some allowance and to 'feel a bit for them who have been accustomed to the most despotic exercise of absolute power here over their dependants'. His hope was that the white minority would come to terms with the fact that from a position of absolute power, they were, as he wrote, 'mere ciphers now'. To allay their fears that their 'once flourishing island' would very soon be 'on the brink of destruction', with the resultant 'ruin of the cultivation and commerce of Jamaica', he also had to ensure that the former slaves continued to work their required hours.[12]

To this effect he instructed the Special Magistrates to punish any refusal to work. For male apprentices this included whipping, confinement to the stocks, the treadmill or to a penal gang – but with one significant difference. Each punishment could be enforced, after due investigation, only on the sole recommendation of a Special Magistrate and not, as hitherto, at the whim of the plantocracy-controlled local magistracy. This single issue was to become a lit fuse racing towards a powder keg that would explode and create a chasm between the governor and the House of Assembly.

Sligo also sought to improve other issues which he felt compromised the 'state of commerce and enterprise on the island'.[13] These included the exorbitant freight rates charged on exports of Jamaican produce to Britain by English-based ship-owners, merchants and agents, many of whom, through the bankruptcy of their former clients, were absentee plantation owners and thereby enjoyed an unfair commercial advantage. In such a fertile country the concentration on sugar, rum and coffee production, to the virtual exclusion of other crops, astounded him. 'What are the 3 ideas of Jamaica – Sugar, Rum & Coffee, nothing else … I ask why don't the planters extend the cultivation of cotton here, the answer is simple – Sugar pays.'[14] He also deplored the antiquated cultivation methods of hoe, bill and oxen-powered sugar mills and the fact that two million acres of arable land remained uncultivated. The lack of good husbandry, drainage, crop rotation and fertilisation of the soil and the disinterest of the planters in land reclamation led him to establish agricultural societies, of which he became patron. Although replete with the most lucrative hardwoods, lumber production in Jamaica remained largely undeveloped. To highlight the variety and versatility of Jamaican timber, Sligo personally commissioned an exquisitely crafted games console (on view in Westport House) made from every known hardwood on the island. The appalling state of the island's road network he considered a major impediment to economic development and he forced the Assembly to vote £15,000 from public funds towards their improvement.

The former slave and his master were mutually dependent for their economic survival. The sugar crop could not be harvested without the apprentice; the planter could not survive without the income from his crop. While initially aggrieved that the freedom they expected was compromised by a period of apprenticeship, the former slaves gradually became reconciled, as the governor noted, 'to give their master a fair proportion of their work' in the expectation that their 'old masters cannot now use them as they did'.[15] The Negro labourer, however, as Sligo also observed, tended to associate work with punishment and 'as inhabitants of very hot climates everywhere, being naturally indolent … very basic in their tastes and fancies and … most unsettled in their habits' found it difficult to work on a voluntary basis. 'If they gain a taste for luxuries it would give them a more personal incentive to do so.'[16] While it required an enormous leap of faith and an incredible shift in ingrained mutual incomprehension and suspicion between planter and former slave for apprenticeship to succeed, it became his moral as much as his political duty to ensure that it did.

The success of the apprenticeship system, he maintained, was dependent on the diligence and impartiality of the Special Magistrates. On their unheralded arrival at an estate, Sligo instructed them

> … not to go to the houses [of the apprentices] in the first instance but to state before the Overseer and other White people that many instances of neglect of people … having been reported and, if there are any, to see them and find out if they are properly and legally attended to …. I wish all questions to be put first to the Overseer, but before all the Apprentices and then if there is any concealment they will find occasion to appeal to the Special.[17]

Initially the work of the Specials, as Sligo enthusiastically reported, had a 'marvellous effect. It has diminished flogging one half in one month.' He was also aware that the Specials were susceptible to the influence of planters – 'Specials have to be watched, if not, much oppression could take place' – and dismissed those he found wanting.[18] Planters who continued to impose their will on their apprentices by use of force found themselves abandoned by their workforce or taken to task by the Specials. Similarly the apprentice was made to understand that if he did not give his former master the hours of labour required under the new system, he too would have to face the consequences.

As the 1834 Christmas holiday period loomed, an air of foreboding hung over the island. Prior to apprenticeship, the festive season was a watershed for unrest. Traditionally it was an opportunity for the slaves to escape the hardship of their existence and, through their *myals* or spirit mediums, to reconnect with the spirits of their remote African ancestors. They were permitted, even encouraged, by their owners to indulge in wild excesses and celebrations, to release the tensions that simmered beneath the surface of their daily existence. In a mix of African and colonial ritual, culture and symbolism, dance, masquerade – involving elaborate and colourful costumes, often caricatures of white society – drumming and singing, the festival John-Canoe (*Jankunu*) was celebrated by the African-Creole population in every town and plantation in Jamaica. Accompanied by feasting, drinking and often by sexual excess, the event was regarded by missionaries as superstitious and degrading, an affront to the cause of emancipation, and by successive governors as an occasion for general disorder.

Despite the momentous changes that had occurred, however, as Sligo reported, 'there has been this year by far less of the John Canoeing and the barbarous accompaniments which heretofore have been practised at this season'.[19] He personally invited several 'sets' of bands and masqueraders to perform at King's House, where they were 'kindly treated with handsome presents made to them by the Governor. The younger members of his family appeared to be highly amused at the novel scene presented to them and the several native airs played by the *musicianers*.'[20] The governor subsequently became a patron of the seminal work *Sketches of Character: An Illustration of the Habits, Occupation and Costume of the Negro Population, in the Island of Jamaica (1837–38)* by the Jamaican-born artist Isaac Mendes Belisario. In a series of twelve hand-coloured lithographs, the artist vividly captured the exuberance and diversity of *Jankunu* characters and celebrations. Sligo also commissioned a series of paintings of his Jamaican properties from Belisario. (These are preserved in the National Gallery of Jamaica.) To his immense relief, however, the plantocracy's much-vaunted prediction of 'lurking rebellion' during the 1834 festive season did not materialise and, to his great relief and satisfaction, the apprentices returned to their plantations without undue trouble.

His relief was, however, short-lived. Before the Assembly adjourned for the holiday period, he fell foul of the speaker. In October Barrett threatened to resign as Custos of St James parish, citing the usurpation of his functions by a Special Magistrate and his refusal 'to truckle to the puerile, mawkish and pseudo philanthropy which fosters idleness and feeds vice'.[21] Much to Barrett's surprise and anger, the governor accepted his resignation and that of his cousin, Samuel Moulton Barrett, Custos of St Ann's. Together with William Burge, the island's agent in London, through a vitriolic media campaign, in both Jamaica and England, they set out to have Sligo removed from office. An unexpected change of government in Britain gave an impetus to their efforts.

It was late December before despatches reached Jamaica with news that not only had the British houses of parliament literally gone up in flames in October, but also the Whig government, under Lord Grey, had resigned. A new Tory government under Sir Robert Peel was installed, with the Duke of Wellington as foreign secretary. The change in government and his previous contretemps with Wellington made Sligo, as he confided to Lord Holland, fear for 'the success of this grand experiment' and that, pressurised by vested interests in Jamaica and London, 'the Duke will confer on the local magistrates the power of corporal punishment and that the moment he does, bitter indeed will be the fate of the Negroes'.[22] As a Whig appointee, he immediately offered his resignation. Much to the disappointment of the Assembly, the new colonial minister, Lord Aberdeen, however, requested him to remain in office. The new minister also indicated that there would be no change in the powers previously conferred on the stripendary magistrates and that additional numbers were to be appointed to oversee apprenticeship. In the event, the new Tory government lasted a mere five months and was replaced by a Whig government under William Lamb, 2nd Viscount Melbourne. With their hopes for Sligo's recall thwarted, determined to make his position as intolerable as possible, the Assembly refused to pay his annual allowance, not from any motive of economy, as Sligo noted, but merely in retribution for his refusal to bend to their will.

The close monitoring of the apprenticeship system by the Special Magistrates gave the former slaves confidence to work for their one-time masters. Incidences of cruelty decreased. 'The masters,' as Sligo intimated, 'have seen that they must, as we call it in Ireland, "behave".'[23] The economic wipeout foretold by the planters failed to materialise. In a comparative analysis with the previous year's sugar production under slavery, as Sligo reported to the Colonial Office, 'there is now made nearly *twice as much sugar per hour* as there was during slavery'.[24] It was his belief that as much work could be extracted from the workforce by fairness than had been formerly by cruelty. The long-held white monopoly in the Assembly was breached in November 1835 with the election of the first coloured candidates, including the editor of *The Watchman*, Edward Jordan. Many opponents of abolition, these 'most insolent men', some of whom were also the governor's most outspoken adversaries, lost their seats, making those remaining, as Sligo hoped, 'begin to see … by the rapid strides made by liberal opinions … on what frail foundations their seats depend'.[25] Further progress was achieved when a new Police Bill and an act-in-aid of the Abolition Act was passed without murmur. Sligo also succeeded in gaining the Assembly's tacit agreement to transfer his proposed immigration scheme (to encourage more European workers to Jamaica) for consideration by the parliament in London. The Coloured or 'Town Party' became his ally in the Assembly, while the Baptist missionaries were supportive of his efforts to protect the rights of the apprentices. Even, as he noted, his 'Bête Noir; my John Jones, the Speaker ... was all complacency and good humour'.[26]

The greatest affront both to the power and pocket of the planters was the right granted to the apprentices to withdraw or charge for their labour after working the prescribed forty and a half hours weekly. The planters baulked at paying former slaves a wage of one shilling and eight pence per day. Access to a regular income enabled the apprentice to purchase his freedom and thereby contribute to future labour shortages. To the governor, however, the apprentice had the same right as any man to dispose of his labour as he pleased outside apprenticeship hours. Sligo's assertion that output on the estates had increased during the first year of apprenticeship was also challenged in the planter press:

> The Governor forgets or wishes to forget that the canes for *this* crop were planted and brought to maturity under the old system .... We *almost* wish that Lord Sligo might be here during the shipment of the next crop in order that he might see the futile attempt of bolstering up a system established by his Whig friends for the destruction of the West Indian Colonies.[27]

For every favourable report Lord Sligo forwarded to the Colonial Office, another reporting the uncooperativeness of the apprentices was presented by the plantocracy, through their agent in London. Where estate owners and managers abided by the terms of apprenticeship the new system was successful, albeit that the pro-planter press sought to claim otherwise. 'The labourers will not work and are becoming every day more insubordinate ... unless Lord Sligo is deaf as well as blind, he must assert and maintain the authority of the laws.'[28]

By early 1835, in contravention of the Abolition Act, local magistrates usurped the role of the Specials. Instances of flogging, confinement to the stocks and penal gang and 'dancing' the treadmill, for the most innocuous transgressions, became widespread. Absence from work through illness was punished by the withdrawal of the apprentice's 'free time'. Convicted apprentices were confined to the notorious house of correction, to which the Specials were denied access. Physical cruelty, including flogging, was also inflicted on females, often for refusing the sexual advances of their white masters in, as Sligo protested, the most palpable and barefaced violation of the Abolition Law. He sought to have an enactment passed 'to put an end to conduct so repugnant to humanity and so contrary to law'.[29] The response from the Assembly was that the flogging of female prisoners was allowable under a local 'Goal Act' and neither the governor nor the Special Magistrates had any right to interfere. The reaction from the Colonial Office in London to Sligo's subsequent appeal merely concluded that, since the British government deemed the flogging of females 'already illegal, it was of no use to pass any other enactments on the subject'.[30]

Throughout 1835 acts of cruelty and deception perpetrated against the apprentices, especially on the estates of absentee proprietors, increased. The apprentices were particularly incensed by the ruse employed by overseers to make them work longer than the required hours or, as they enunciated, 'to steal their time' by the device known as 'blowing the shell', the signal by which the apprentice measured the hours worked in his master's employ. They also accused their employers of attempting to 'take away their Fridays without pay', i.e. to deprive them of their free Friday half-day. It was in the planters' interest that the apprentices work eight hours daily from Monday to Thursday, with a half-day on Friday, to make up the forty-and-a-half-hour week stipulated under the apprenticeship system. Apprentices, on the other hand, preferred to work a nine-hour day, from Monday to Thursday, leaving them a full free day on Friday to tend their provision grounds in order to sell their produce at the Saturday market. Sligo accused the plantocracy of 'placing obstacles in the way of the apprentice's industry and self-sufficiency to prevent ... [them] from becoming settlers, because they would then be independent of the Planters'.[31] He erroneously presumed that the nine-hour system was established by the Emancipation Act and, without verification, had embodied it in his initial proclamation to the slaves on 1 August 1834. It was a mistake that left him open to public censure.

While abuses of the apprenticeship system could be laid at the door of the plantocracy, some apprentices also took advantage of their newly protected status. Victimised and conditioned for centuries by a cruel and demeaning system, craft, cunning, deception and lies became essential weapons to circumvent their situation. Their attitude to theft was ambivalent and 'depredations on the property of an owner were considered justifiable, only *crimes* when committed among themselves'.[32] Theft of sugar, rum and other provisions from their masters had a certain rationale. 'As sugar belongs to massa and myself belongs to massa, it all de same ting – dat make me tell massa me don't tief it; me only take it.'[33]

During 1835 widespread incidences of theft by apprentices were reported in the Jamaican press. Such accusations, while generally justifiable, had to be judged both in the context of the inherent custom where 'theft of a pan of sugar or a few canes once winked at by the Overseer or Bookkeeper, now constitutes a serious offence'.[34] Public notices were erected by the planters throughout the island, warning apprentices 'whereas Sugar canes, Sugar, rum and other Produce, in large quantities, are publicly exposed for sale by Apprentices ... without proper authority or right to do so, the Constables are strictly enjoined ... to seize upon all such Produce, together with the Parties offering same for sale, that they may be dealt with according to the law.'[35] The sudden change from what was once an unwritten privilege to a criminal offence was difficult for former slaves, with little understanding of such legal quibbles, to comprehend. While asserting that he would not condone theft from any quarter, to ensure an unbiased hearing the governor had each case of theft transferred to the Specials for consideration. When items of clothing were stolen from his own estate, the planter press went into overdrive. Mocking Irish speech inflection, Sligo is heard to upbraid his own apprentices:

> You are not satisfied with *staelin* from others but you must rob *me,* you spalpeens. You villainous *thaves* you ... who stole my Galligaskins [breeches]? Aye my Irish ones! My half dozen huckaback towels, my two pair of sheets, my two pillowcases ... least of all my best jacket and a pair of trousers which can fit nobody but myself.[36]

Before apprenticeship the provision grounds were the main source of food for the slave and his family. After apprenticeship, they became a potential source of his economic self-sufficiency and independence. It was Sligo's hope that by improving their personal circumstances beyond mere subsistence and by working voluntarily, the apprentices would eventually become independent freeholders in their own right and net contributors to the economy of Jamaica. To this effect, he promoted a scheme to establish a number of 'free' villages for liberated apprentices throughout the island. The first was erected in the hills near his own property at Highgate. Purchased with money pooled by free slaves, some twenty-five acres of land were laid out in regular-sized quarter-acre allotments, intersected by streets. Each allotment had a garden and a three-roomed cottage made of plastered wood or stone, with a thatched or wood-shingled roof, and were deemed 'superior to the tenancies of labourers in the rural districts of England'.[37] The first free slave village established was named Sligoville in his honour and led to the foundation of other 'free' villages throughout Jamaica and the West Indies. In 1996 the 11th Marquess of Sligo was invited by the community of Sligoville to unveil a plaque in the Phillippo Baptist church to the memory of his revered ancestor. 'Some things in life are worth fighting for,' Lord Sligo told the modern-day descendants of Sligoville's first black settlers, 'and above everything else, freedom is the most important thing of all.'[38]

The implementation of apprenticeship in Jamaica was further complicated by an anomaly that arose in relation to the Caymanas. A series of low-lying islands 350 miles to the west of Jamaica, they were once the haven of pirates, wreckers and runaway slaves. By 1835 the Caymanas had a population of some 2,000 whites, most descended from the original buccaneers, as well as 900 black slaves. Albeit a protectorate of Jamaica, the islands were left more or less to their own devices by successive governors. The passing of the Act of Emancipation gave rise to an anomalous situation regarding the status of the black population there. In order to access the compensation money offered by the British government, slaves had firstly to be registered by their masters. Either through an administrative oversight, or more likely their unwillingness to pay the required Capitation Tax, or to have their affairs, which included wrecking and the provisioning of illegal slave ships, come under scrutiny, the Caymanas owners neglected to register their slaves. The British government thereby determined that the slaves were to be granted immediate freedom, while their owners were deemed ineligible for compensation. The precedent posed a serious dilemma, as Sligo realised. 'It strikes me that much danger would arise to Jamaica and the other West Indian Islands from the discontent which would be occasioned when the Negroes hear that their comrades at the Caymanas have become absolutely free; they would, I fear, consider that similar advantages had been concealed from them by their proprietors.'[39] Sligo resolved to travel to the Caymanas and make the announcement of emancipation in person.

On the morning of 30 April he sailed from Port Royal, 'with great reluctance, I must confess tho' the object of it was to release

900 slaves. My reluctance arose from the feeling that the utter ruin of 1100 inhabitants would accompany it.'[40] Uncertain of the reaction of the white community to the loss of their slaves and of compensation, he was accompanied by a detachment of the Jamaican army. On his arrival, he remained on board ship and read the proclamation in his cabin to a delegation of white slave owners who came on board. They were, he noted, 'about the finest race of men I ever saw'.[41] Albeit heralding their economic ruin, they agreed without protest to comply with the new conditions. The following day the governor went ashore to deliver the news of emancipation to the slaves. In his address to the assembled population, both black and white, Sligo urged both former owner and slave to cooperate together under the new situation. 'Do not imagine that because you are now free you are independent of one another …. All experience has shown how one hangs on the other.'[42] The former slaves accepted their new status with the same equanimity as their masters, one former slave indicating to the governor that the change would not affect his remaining with his former master. Leaving behind a small military force, Sligo set sail for Jamaica, only to find himself 'as annoyed as any man ever was having been beaten up seven days in almost a calm … an intolerable bore for a man who has no idle time on his hands'.[43]

In Jamaica he was faced with a similar situation regarding the slaves belonging to the Maroons. The prospect of treating with the much-feared Maroons, who 'from time immemorial were most inimical to all other blacks', put him, as he wrote, 'on standby for squalls'.[44] In the event, however, on his meeting with a Maroon delegation in Kingston, arrangements were concluded without undue difficulty and, as he reported, 'they submitted to the manumission of all their apprentices without a murmur'.[45]

The squalls, however, were to materialise from another quarter. The lull in hostilities between the governor and the House of Assembly was merely a calm before a political storm that nature itself seemed to herald when, in July 1835, 'a sudden and violent tornado ... followed by severe shocks of earthquake' reverberated across Jamaica.[46] It was the wettest spring ever experienced on the island and was followed by a period of very dry weather, which badly affected the cane crop. The island agent, Joseph Burge, who was reported to be 'in high favour with the Duke of Wellington, Sir Robert Peel and the Earl of Aberdeen', was busily at work in London.[47] Rebutting the positive reports forwarded by the governor, Burge presented a picture of decreased sugar output, plantations on the brink of ruin, gross insubordination by the apprentices and 'the affectation of disbelief and of stupid blindness which have marked the administration of the Marquess of Sligo'.[48] Alarm bells began to ring in Britain among those with vested interests in the colony, from absentee proprietors to commercial stakeholders, many of whom were also Whig and Tory members of parliament. Through their agent, the Assembly bypassed the governor and corresponded directly with government ministers and officials in the Colonial Office. The planter press in Jamaica added to the criticism. 'The proprietors have been robbed of the fruits of their industry .... They are taxed with a supine and vicious population who lumber the land they refuse to till.'[49] Bruge orchestrated a campaign of misinformation against Sligo in London.

> It is quite clear to me that the cabinet has been greatly deceived, nay very much frightened, by the misrepresentations of that Arch Impostor Burge .... His want of truth is a proverb even amongst his best friends .... How is it possible that any government can have confidence enough in me to dispel from their minds the venom that is instilled into them by this mischief-maker?[50]

In November 1835 the situation reached breaking point when Burge leaked the contents of private correspondence between the governor and the former colonial minister, Lord Aberdeen.

The correspondence or 'Blue Book' sardonically referred to in the planter press as the 'SLY GO Book' was widely published in Jamaica. The governor's assertion that the black population was reconciled to the apprenticeship system, that sugar production was not adversely affected and that any diminution in hours worked by the apprentices was solely attributable to the oppression and deceit of the estate managers caused an outcry among the plantocracy. The governor's insistence that 'the perfect success of the new system during the continuance of the apprenticeship depends entirely on the conduct of the white people, and that if it fails, on them will rest the entire blame,' the planter press complained, cast 'a most wanton libel on every attorney, manager, overseer and bookkeeper in the island. Fie! Fie! And his lordship is a proprietor himself too!'[51]

The campaign to effect Sligo's removal from office intensified. Public meetings were held to repudiate the 'base insinuations' in the Blue Book. A policy of non-cooperation and the stonewalling of bills presented by the governor commenced. 'Members of the Assembly, remember our fate is in your hands and you are called upon not again to legislate a tyranny from which we have suffered so much. Reject the Act-in-Aid and leave the Abolition Law to its own devices.'[52] In a calculated mark of disrespect, the Assembly refused to make the traditional reply to the governor's speech at the opening of parliament.

The campaign was reinforced with insults, both personal and racist. The appearance of 'our fat friend at King's House' was constantly lampooned and ridiculed.

If flesh is grass, as Parsons say
Old Sligo would make a load of hay.[53]

The governor's corpulence and his dress (the oppressive heat made him resort to wearing loose-fitting clothes) became a target for his detractors. When meeting a delegation from the Assembly at King's House, 'in defiance of what we consider the usual etiquette, of meeting the representatives of Jamaica', the governor was accused of dressing in a 'wrapper which the humblest magistrate … would have thrown off to clothe himself *dacently*'.[54] In cartoons and caricatures the governor's sartorial style and physique were lampooned.

> The negroes of the West Indies … like to see their ruler pay some deference to *costume* and if we were to give an opinion *seriously* upon the subject … we would declare that Lord S. must have employed an Agent to purchase at a Rag fair in London the most misshapen garments he could procure in order to astonish the *lieges* of Jamaica! And the contrast between Lord Mulgrave and Lord Sligo has afforded many a hearty laugh to Quashie who likes to see 'Big Buckra' look like a gentleman.[55]

Another report observed how 'the cares of administering the Government of Jamaica has sadly reduced the corporation of our Noble Governor. When his Excellency arrived here he measured round about the skirts of his jacket 60 inches! But alas 54 and a half is the extent of his present dimensions. How he must have larded the lean earth as he went along.'[56] Sligo's nationality and fondness for food and drink were the subject of much satirical imagery and caricature.

Details of his youthful misdemeanours were searched out 'to give a few anecdotes of our worthy and amiable Governor, while at College'.[57] His concealment of the navy seamen on the *Pylades*, his trial at the Old Bailey and his imprisonment at Newgate were highlighted:

> We know Lord Glenelg [the colonial secretary] does not read history and for this reason we refer him to the Newgate Calendar of 1812 wherein he will find a confirmation … of Lord Sligo's veracity. It is also faithfully recorded in the

Naval Chronicle …. We have seen our kind friend with his St Patrick's chains on all previous occasions but we suppose that the clank may remind him of the *Ould* Bailey.[58]

His liaison with the courtesan Harriette Wilson was contrasted with his promotion of the moral and religious welfare of the black population:

> We are exceedingly shocked to hear that the proprietors of a certain Society here have imported a thousand copies of the memoirs of Harriette Wilson for the information of the negro children. It is quite clear that one of the members for our good city of Kingston must have perused that celebrated work, otherwise he could not have been aware of its moral tendency.[59]

The condition of his Irish tenants was contrasted with that of the Jamaican apprentices. 'We wish Lord Sligo exhibited as much affection towards his Irish tenantry as he does to Mr Quashie.'[60] It was the expressed hope of the editor of the *Jamaica Despatch* 'that when His Lordship is smoking his pipe, peeling his praties and taking his poteen in Ireland, he will some day remember our prophecy, that he would be sacrificed to the political views of his pretended friends'.[61] His 'maudlin kindness now shown to the blacks is so truly ridiculous that O'Connell has expressed his regret that his countrymen, as well as himself, are not black … and humanity might then be extended to his poor countrymen'.[62] His association with missionaries and Special Magistrates was also attacked. 'We are unfortunately cursed with the presence of agitators … who have no more regard for the interests of the negroes present or to come, then they have for the savages of Africa. Yet, unhappily, these very men are the PET magistrates of the Marquis of Sligo.'[63] He was accused of surrounding himself 'with persons of the same political views and sentiments as himself' and that 'all his advisors address him with the echo of his own opinions ... from the tittle-tattle of a gossiping Special Justice down to the trumped-up tale of a vagabond negro, nothing is amiss'.[64]

In March 1836 a committee in London, chaired by Sir Thomas Fowell Buxton, a leading anti-slavery campaigner, was established to enquire into the workings of the apprenticeship system. The committee members included O'Connell, Gladstone, Stephen Lushington and Lord Howick. The pro-planter press, both in Jamaica and England, accused the governor by the 'calumnies' expressed in his official despatches of influencing the committee and of being a tool of the Anti-Slavery Society in England. And, as is evident from his correspondence, there was some truth in the assertion. 'Unless you anti-slavery people make some stir it is impossible for me to get on here as I ought,' Sligo confided to Lord Suffield in July 1835.[65]

Confidential despatches between the governor and the government in London continued to be leaked by Burge to the Assembly. The Jamaican papers further accused the governor of misrepresenting the Assembly's attitude to the apprenticeship system, exaggerating the ill-treatment of apprentices, of being under the influence of Baptist preachers and of 'linking himself with Tinkers, Bakers, and Cobblers, merely for the evanescent roar of a few fanatics who delude our peasantry'.[66] The Special Magistrates were condemned for interpreting the law exclusively in favour of the apprentices on the personal order of the governor. Special magistrates whom the governor dismissed for doing the bidding of the planters were publicly lauded and financially rewarded.

Not all Jamaican press reports were negative.

It is admirable to see the silent but sovereign contempt with which our present noble and excellent Governor treats these daily philippics. Nor is it less gratifying to know how little his actions seem to be guided by their influence. And with the armour of his inherent honesty of purpose, he is invincible; and domiciled in the bosom of a large and happy family, the breath of slander is not felt.[67]

Sligo himself shrugged off the criticisms. 'No man has any business to be governor here for the remainder of the Apprenticeship, who minds any embarrassment of the sort or any insults.'[68] What his children thought about the unrelenting personal attacks on their father, as they cut and pasted the offending newspaper articles into family scrapbooks, is open to conjecture.

In autumn 1835 the political situation reached an impasse over the passage of a new act-in-aid of the Abolition Law intended to cover the full period of apprenticeship. While the bill was pending between the Council and the Assembly, on 1 February 1836, Sligo informed the Assembly that he intended to pass the bill in its original form and that in doing so he had the backing of the Colonial Office. The Assembly immediately accused him of a breach of privilege 'inconsistent with its [the Assembly's] own dignity or with due regard to its rights and privileges' and refused 'to proceed with any new business until reparation shall be made for the breach of privilege .... Gracious God! Are *we* slaves to be thus addressed ... or does Lord Sligo consider us to be *mere Irish* to be so dictated to.'[69] Suspecting that the Assembly's action was merely a smoke screen 'to make one grand stand against the great system [apprenticeship]', Sligo prorogued the house and summoned the Assembly members to the council chamber.[70] He enumerated a litany of bills which they had refused to pass: from repeal of the laws regulating the houses of correction, the education of Negro children, extending religious instruction throughout the colony, the illegal taxation of the property of apprentices to the 'whipping of females [which] you were informed by me officially was in practice and I called on you to make enactments to put an end … you have taken no step to put an end to the practice so repugnant to humanity and so contrary to law.'[71] Their refusal, he told them, left him no alternative but to prorogue the house for one month.

As Sligo realised, a breach of privilege was a serious charge. He immediately wrote to the Colonial Office to be 'acquitted of formally by the Government or … to be found guilty … and treated accordingly'.[72] He cautioned the British government, however, against being swayed by the Assembly into reversing the progress made under apprenticeship. 'Who are those people who are to be coveted at the expense of the great mass here. Not more probably than two or three thousand attorneys & proprietors and their subordinates & dependants …. All the Brownes, all the Blacks, even all the Jews are in opposition to these cart-whip gentry.'[73]

If the government attempted to 'under-evaluate these people again there will be the most unpleasant consequence, I dread. The real cause of my unpopularity here was my not shutting my eyes as all my predecessors had done.'[74] Reminding the colonial secretary that he had

> … long since predicted that I should find an insuperable objection in the minds of the members to re-enact the said acts …. At first you naturally concluded that I took an exaggerated view …. You thought they would not so soon forget the munificent gift of the British nation, nor their compact … for remedying the effects of the Abolition Law. My predictions however have not turned out to be speculative assertions; they have unfortunately been proved to be, in every instance, correct and much I lament it. The REMEDY, I say ADVISEDLY, must come from home.[75]

The British government appeared to agree and the controversial act-in-aid bill was removed from the Assembly for consideration by the British parliament. That the imperial parliament might legislate again over their heads was a prospect the Assembly dreaded and the campaign to have Sligo removed intensified.

The anti-slavery press in Jamaica, however, rowed in behind the governor. Rebutting Burge's accusation that the governor

> … was at war with all the island … surely Lord Sligo is not at war with 300,000 apprentices in Jamaica. Of course not. But they form no part of the island. They are not men, free men … but *things,* mere chattels. Is Lord Sligo at war with the free Black and Brownes? We say no. Is Lord Sligo at war with the white population? We say no. They are even divided. He is only at war with those who desire to have their own way to do as they please with the apprentices and to use the Special Magistrates as they did their drivers under the old regime.[76]

How any governor could be expected to endure 'the indignities and abuse to which the Marquis of Sligo is here subject was beyond the call of duty'. His problem, they maintained, stemmed from the fact that he was considered

> … too liberal in his political principles – because he discharges the duties of his high office with too much impartiality – because he will not allow the provisions of the Abolition Law to be infringed – because he is a friend of the ignorant and the oppressed …. A more noble, upright, accessible, laborious and liberal Governor than the Marquis of Sligo, we cannot have.[77]

Such praise from the pro-emancipation press, however, only fuelled the determination of the plantocracy to have him removed.

In response to the stalemate, the British government, while passing the act-in-aid bill, was careful to point out that it should not be interpreted as unnecessary interference with the local Jamaican legislature' or that the Legislature had been guilty of bad faith. At the same time, the colonial secretary, Lord Glenelg, privately informed Sligo that it was the government's opinion that by intervening in a bill that was pending, he was guilty of a breach of privilege and that reparation was due to the House of Assembly for the infringement, however unintentional, of their privilege. The governor was ordered to reconvene the Assembly. Showing a 'strong sense of duty and dignity', Sligo took the government's reprimand on the chin.[78] He reconvened the Assembly and apologised to the members 'having', as he told them, 'been informed by authority of more experience than his own, and to which it was his duty to submit'.[79]

His chastisement by the British government, however, cast aspersions on his judgement, impartiality and character and undermined his position as governor. His enemies were ecstatic. 'The moment the guns of Fort Charles announce his departure from Port Royal, although it will be a waste of powder, bonfires will be lighted to show him off the coast.'[80] Every packet that arrived from England was rumoured to carry orders for the governor's resignation. His every movement and that of his family were monitored for any indication of eminent departure. This appeared to be confirmed in April 1836 by the departure of the governor's eldest son.

Like the rest of his family, Altamont maintained a low profile during his residence in Jamaica. On 19 March he performed his only public duty when he laid the foundation stone for the first Roman Catholic chapel, St Patrick and St Martin's, on the island. From early morning thousands of people congregated at the designated site in Kingston. Accompanied by Captain Browne, the parish priest, Father Murphy and other dignitaries, Altamont arrived in a carriage bedecked with green and white flags and bearing emblems of the harp, shamrock, rose, thistle and crown. In the evening a celebration dinner was held in his honour at 'Miss Green's' in Kingston. Toasts were raised to 'the Marchioness and the Ladies Browne' to which the young Earl returned thanks:

In the name of my mother and sisters I thank you heartily
for the honour you have done them. The hospitality and
kindness they have received from the inhabitants of this
island, will never be effaced from their memory .... I have
only to add, what I am sure is their wish as well as my own,
that health and happiness may ever attend the inhabitants
of this beautiful country.'[81]

Even the pro-planter press admitted that Lord Altamont had 'won
all hearts ... by his gentle, courteous and dignified conduct ...
without the slightest evidence of pride or hauteur'.[82] A month later,
accompanied by his two younger brothers, Altamont left Jamaica
and, after a tour of America and Canada, sailed from New York to
Liverpool and from there to Ireland.

At the beginning of 1836 the powerful planter interest in
England, in collaboration with Sir George Grey, under-secretary
for the colonies, finally engineered Sligo's removal from office.
Realising that he was 'in such favour with the dissenters, who
are a powerful and influential body in Parliament', rather than
publicly dismiss him from office and thereby invoke the wrath of
the anti-slavery lobby, Grey instead sent him a despatch which,
as reported in the planter press, 'will ensure his resignation'.[83]
Some months previously, on the basis of what later transpired
to be misinformation given to him by some of his own advisors,
including Chief Justice Sir Joshua Rowe and his private secretary,
W.G. Nunes, the governor had ordered the transfer of Dr A.L.
Palmer, a special magistrate in the parish of St Andrew-in-the-Vale,
ironically for upholding a case taken by some apprentices against
their master. Palmer was an ardent supporter of the anti-slavery
movement and was married to a black woman. As a Special, he had
made unsubstantiated charges against overseers as well as against
some of his fellow magistrates. In June 1835 Sligo established
a formal enquiry to investigate Palmer's charges, to which the

magistrate refused to submit. Left with little option, the governor was forced to suspend him from duty. Inexplicably accusing the governor of intriguing with the plantocracy to have him removed from office, Palmer appealed the decision to the Colonial Office in London. To pacify the anti-slavery lobby, Lord Glenelg ordered his immediate reinstatement. Considering the government's decision as undermining his authority and, more disturbingly, reinforcing the belief among the Jamaican planters that he had lost the support of the government, Sligo insisted that if the Colonial Office did not back his decision, he had no option but to resign. According to one source, 'the Government gladly seized their opportunity and sent out a despatch directing the restoration of Dr. Palmer ... deliberately intended to procure Lord Sligo's resignation'.[84]

His authority impugned and deeming his position untenable, Sligo tendered his resignation to the king. 'In this instance, as well as in the difference with the Assembly,' as he curtly informed Lord Glenelg, 'I have not received from your Lordship that support which I, perhaps erroneously, considered myself entitled to .... I find my continuance in the administration of Jamaica incompatible with Dr. Palmer's holding the special commission in this colony.'[85] To resign from office on such a seemingly insignificant matter, from both a personal and professional perspective, seemed an impetuous call and one, in retrospect, which Sligo appeared to regret, when he attempted to withdraw his resignation.

His critics were jubilant. What neither the obdurate intransigence of the Assembly nor the ridicule of the planter press could achieve was accomplished by a pro-emancipation special magistrate, appointed by the governor. Sligo's brother-in-law, Clanricarde, cautioned that while both Melbourne and Glenelg were, as he tactfully wrote, 'less at variance in their opinions with the Assembly than yourself,'[86] they were nonetheless generally supportive of his decision to resign. His friend Lord Holland voiced concern for his reputation, despite Sligo's defiant assertion that he considered his 'unpopularity *an honour*, I feel it to be a proof that I have done my duty and that they [the planters] are galled at it'.[87] Rather than be unceremoniously recalled, and to protect his reputation, Clanricarde advised him 'to choose your time to talk of coming away whenever you can find a calm or a very successful moment to avoid ... misapprehension or even misrepresentation'.[95]

Disclosure of the Machiavellian way his opponents, both in London and Jamaica, had secured his resignation eventually came to light. On being made aware by a member of the Jamaican Legislative Council about the part played in the affair by some of his own staff, Sligo summoned his secretaries, Stewart and Nunes, to account but, with each one accusing the other, 'with contemptuous indignation I left them to cover their confusion as best they could'.[89] There were, however, other strands to the conspiracy. There was growing disillusionment with the apprenticeship system among the anti-slavery lobby. Sligo's protection of the apprentices and his adherence to the apprenticeship law, albeit well-intentioned, to some anti-slavery proponents merely prolonged a system they considered little removed from slavery.

The pro-planter press in Jamaica greeted Sligo's impending departure with unrestrained satisfaction: 'Oh! Lard Oh – Big Massa Da Go At Last Fo True' one newspaper headline parodied in black patois. 'May the accidental breezes speedily waft the Noble Marquess to Ireland, to administer a little food and the remnant of his black humanity among his starving tenantry .... A more mischievous governor never ruled this Colony ... we cannot even hint at one redeeming act of his administration.'[90] Regret, as well as fear, at his imminent departure, however, manifested itself in the pro-emancipation press and in numerous signed public addresses (one containing over 1,500 signatures and measuring six yards in length) he received from the coloured and black population, special magistrates and missionaries in parishes throughout the island.

> Your Excellency's resignation of the Government of this
> colony would have awakened our regret and apprehension
> at any time ... but your departure at the present crises
> ... we feel at a loss for suitable terms [with] which to
> convey our disappointment and concern. The shout of
> fiendish triumph that sends Lord Sligo from the shores of
> the colony – is the prelude to the acclamations that will
> hail him a DELIVERER *of the human race* – as a friend
> of suffering humanity – as one of the truest champions of
> liberty .... [91]

A subscription of over $1,000 was raised by the Jamaican
apprentices and entrusted to Joseph Sturge, a leading anti-slavery
campaigner, to purchase an appropriate testimonial. After his
return to London, Sturge and Rt Hon. Stephen Lushington MP,
accompanied by 'two gentlemen of colour', presented Sligo with
a silver, six-light candelabrum, made in London by goldsmiths
Green & Ward.[92] Elaborately embellished with allegorical black
figures symbolising freedom, it was inscribed:

> Presented to the Most Noble Howe Peter Marquis of Sligo
> by the Negroes of Jamaica in testimony of the grateful
> remembrance they entertain for his unremitting efforts to
> alleviate their sufferings and to redress their wrongs during
> his just and enlightened administration of the Government
> of the Island and of the respect and gratitude they feel
> towards His Excellent Lady and Family for their kindness
> and sympathy displayed towards them.

His successor, however, proved more difficult to find. Few were
willing to take on the fraught and arduous office. Sligo agreed to
the government's request to remain in office until a successor was
appointed, despite, as he wrote to Lord Holland, that 'in doing
this, however, I considered that I was making a great sacrifice, as my

administration could not be agreeable under so many indignities which I had no means of meeting.'[93]

In July he embarked by steamer along Jamaica's rugged and spectacular east coast to visit the Republic of Haiti. The first black independent country in the West Indies, Haiti represented a nightmare scenario to planter interests. Sligo's visit drew both condemnation and scorn from his critics. 'Where is the Governor gone? Old Sligo is going to see his friend Boyer of Hayti … to take a peep at the beautifully cultivated domain of the grand Haytian Potentate General *Sans Culottes*.'[94] Following a slave revolt and the assassination of Dessalines, Haiti's first president in 1806, the island was divided between a black-controlled north and a mulatto-controlled south. Plantations were carved into smallholdings, providing a subsistence existence for their new owners. For the former slaves, who merely wanted to be their own masters, it was sufficient for their needs. For the island's economy, however, it was a disaster resulting in the abandonment of all export-oriented production. In 1818, Jean-Pierre Boyer, the Paris-educated son of a wealthy mulatto family in Port-au-Prince, became president. To halt the country's downward spiral, he reunited both parts of the island and introduced the Code Rural, which forced black peasants to work by making them legally bound to a plantation. Boyer also inadvertently introduced social division by promoting the better-educated mulattos over their black counterparts. The code proved a failure, mirroring what it set out to replace. In 1825, on the payment of the enormous sum of 150 million francs' indemnity, which almost bankrupt the new state, France agreed to recognise Haitian independence.

Into this example of both the glory and disaster of emancipation, Sligo came to see how a former slave colony had adapted to self-government, as well as to negotiate the removal of trade barriers between Jamaica and Haiti. In Port-au-Prince he lodged with the British consul, who conveyed him to government house to meet

President Boyer. He found Boyer 'aged – quite emaciated ... like a skeleton dressed in a suit of clothes made for an obese man'.[95] All around lay the negative obverse of independence, from the ramshackle condition of Port-au-Prince to the wilderness of its surrounding hinterland, dotted with the ruins of plantation houses and uncultivated fields. The pro-emancipation press in Jamaica urged the governor, however, to look beyond 'the dreariness and desolation' which should not be laid at the door of emancipation, but instead on Boyer's 'faithless, flagitious and detestable attempt to re-impose the yoke which that decree had broken'.[96] The pro-planter press condemned his visit, intimating that 'there are people in this island who wish Jamaica to be in a similar state, and we prophesy, if they live 7 years, they will be fully gratified ... and that sugar will then be as scarce in this island as it now is in Hayti.'[97]

To Sligo, however, Haiti's desolation was a reaffirmation of the necessity to prepare the Jamaican apprentices for their eventual freedom: to help them maximise the benefits freedom endowed for their own material advantage and to encourage them to aspire to a life of more than mere subsistence. If, as in Haiti, the former slaves associated physical labour with slavery and if that attitude was reinforced during apprenticeship, 'why', he wrote, 'should they [the apprentices] labour further than is necessary to provide for their own sustenance .... Let them [the planters] recollect that unless they regain the confidence of those from whom alone free labour can be obtained, the year 1840 will be the unprofitable commencement of a series of still more unprofitable years'. Echoing sentiments he had expressed regarding Catholic Emancipation, it was better, he added, 'for the Jamaican proprietor to give liberally now, whilst he has it in his power to give, than wait for a reaction which, if once it takes place, will be terrible in its consequences'.[98]

Sir Lionel Smith, governor of Barbados, was eventually appointed as Sligo's sucessor. On 27 August Smith arrived at Port Henderson and was escorted to Spanish Town where Sligo received him at King's House with all due ceremony. At their subsequent meeting the governor-elect expressed his disappointment at being 'led to expect a much larger salary' and, to Sligo's embarrassment, expressed 'his regret at having come here at all and declared openly in the presence of everyone that he would send in his resignation by the next packet'. Pacifying his reluctant successor, despite a less than enthusiastic start, Sligo ensured he was made 'fully aware of what he has to meet with here'.[99]

Sligo's two years and five months as governor general of Jamaica was to prove a life-changing experience. Although middle-aged, he still retained, as one of his critics wrote, 'a good deal of the impetuosity of the young dilettante and adventurer who had been sent to cool his heels in Newgate'.[100] His reliance on the opinion of advisers, such as missionaries, who maintained an uncompromising and, at times, self-righteous antipathy to colonial society generally, tended to colour his judgement and diverted him from being 'able to command and be under the influence of a spirit and of a temper, cool, dispassionate and unprejudiced'.[101] His lack of political and administrative experience, coupled with a tendency to speak his mind, was not always appreciated. His inability to delegate and his propensity to become involved in every aspect of government, down to individual grievances, diluted his effectiveness. The reports and decisions he personally communicated to the Special Magistrates on thousands of individual cases were hugely time-consuming and, perhaps, unnecessary. His efforts to nurture a sense of political consciousness among Afro-Jamaicans were cut short by his sudden resignation.

Yet to someone whose heart tended to rule his head, whose sense of fair play and compassion led him to buck the system, both as a slave owner and as a member of the establishment who, as he himself admitted, tended to be 'too candid ... and a fool for being so', it was, perhaps, too much to ask that he could be anything else. Even his political opponents admitted that whatever he may have lacked in political intuititiveness, he more than compensated for in integrity and honour. 'He was a noble lord, humane and earnest in his purposes – clear and frank in his dealings; teeming with unwearied activities; plunging boldly into the middle of all business in the confidence of a just intention and writing like a man.'[102]

His entertainment of individual black complainants at King's House and Highgate (unheard of by a governor) as well as his accessibility to their spokesmen – the missionaries and Special Magistrates – infuriated as well as empowered his critics. The line of conduct he adopted towards the former slaves, while gaining their confidence, at the same time placed a barrier between him and the planters, while his promotion of a political 'coloured' class was seen (as it eventually became) as a threat to white supremacy on the island. As he prepared to leave Jamaica, in his last official despatch to the Colonial Office, he was steadfast in his opinion 'that the only difficulties Sir Lionel Smith will have to encounter will be from the hands of the planters and members of the Assembly'.[103]

The defects in his administration were not, however, all of his own making. Sligo was badly served by his British political masters, especially by the Colonial Office, whose advice was often at best contradictory and at worst unsupportive. Lord Glenelg, the colonial minister, undermined his authority and eventually made his position as governor untenable.

The 2nd Marquess of Sligo earned a respected place in the history of Jamaica and 'deserves the honour of having his name commemorated in Sligoville, the first free village'.[104] In 1838, together with other anti-slavery proponents such as Wilberforce, Buxton and Sturge, he was further honoured by an emancipation memorial medallion bearing his name, with the inscription 'their names shall be sacred in the memory of the just'.[105] His stance against slavery in Jamaica was closely monitored by the anti-slavery movement in North America and his efforts to end slavery in the West Indies influenced the struggle for emancipation, which was to continue until 1865, in the United States of America.

On a personal basis, his tenure as governor cemented his attachment to Jamaica. The climate too brought relief to the painful and debilitating symptoms of his arthritic condition: 'I am sorry to say that I have not had one moment's health since I left the shores of Jamaica.'[106] His salary as governor, however, did little to ease his indebtedness. During his term of office his income of £31,286 was all but negated by his expenses, which amounted to £31,261. But his experience on the island stayed with him for the rest of his life, drove his future work as a legislator and absorbed his energy, perhaps at the expense of his other commitments, especially those in Ireland.

On 2 September 1836 from the deck of the *HMS Belvidera*, with Catherine and his daughters by his side, Sligo watched the outline of Jamaica disappear below the skyline. With optimism, not totally chastened by his experience, he wrote:

> ... it is my pride and satisfaction to be able to say that I leave the administration of affairs in the hands of my successor in as easy a state as can well be imagined. The Negroes everywhere behave in the most orderly manner.[107]

As for the plantocracy and the Assembly with whom he endured such a stormy relationship, they made little effort to hide their relief as the *Belvidera* bore away their bête noir 'after doing all the mischief he could to this fine island'.[108]

Little could they realise that their battle with the 'great Leviathan of black Humanity' was far from over.

Chapter 16

Suivez Raison

What I began as a duty I continue from inclination as well
as a duty and Please God I always will.

Marquess of Sligo

Sailing from Jamaica, via Havana, Sligo and his family reached
New York on 29 September 1836 to visit the country in whose
history his maternal grandfather and grand-uncle had played a
significant role. In New York he held meetings with members
of the newly established American Anti-Slavery Society and
with evangelical clergymen at the forefront of the struggle for
emancipation. All who met him 'formed an exalted opinion of his
integrity and friendship for the poor'.[1] His efforts and opinions
on behalf of the apprentices in Jamaica were recorded in many
anti-slavery publications.

Proceeding along the east coast, he visited Boston and
Philadelphia, cities closely associated with the anti-slavery
movement, where he received and conversed with individuals and
delegations from the movement. Crossing the border into Canada,
he travelled on to Quebec, where in 1759 his great-granduncle,
Henry Browne, had fought under General Wolfe. As the Canadian
winter approached, in late November, he returned by steam packet
to England.

His house on Mansfield Street being leased to the exiled Princess da Beira, the eldest daughter of the king of Portugal and her son, the Crown Prince of Asturias, Sligo and his family returned to Ireland. His arrival provoked much excitement in Westport. The town was brilliantly illuminated, bonfires blazed on the hills and headlands 'and a crowd of upwards of 5,000 persons accompanied him through the demesne to Westport House'.[2] At a meeting of the inhabitants of the town, attended by the local gentry, a resolution 'to devise the best means of expressing the warmest approbation of the conduct of the Marquess of Sligo, whilst Governor of Jamaica' was passed.[3] A silver six-light candelabrum, costing £500, with depictions of Irish tenants and designed by the same London silversmiths as its Jamaican counterpart, was presented to him bearing the inscription:

> Presented to the Most Noble Howe Peter, Marquis of Sligo,
> the Emancipator of the Slaves, by the Inhabitants of the
> Town and Neighbourhood of Westport, 1838.

Of historic significance to Jamaica and to Ireland, the two candelabras were subsequently sold in 1983 through Sotheby's and were thought to have been acquired by a purchaser in the Middle East.

The air of excitement generated by Sligo's return was also mingled with much relief. During his absence, his agent, George Glendenning, had evicted many tenants who had fallen into arrears for rent, tithes and other dues. When one tenant, a widow, came to Westport to sell a few bushels of oats, as reported in the local press, she 'had her money taken from her on order of one of Mr Glendenning's drivers'.[4] After his return from Jamaica, a noticeable coolness developed between Sligo and his long-serving agent. 'With Glen's judgement I have differed and I dare say shall often differ.' His agent's actions against his tenants, especially on the Lehinch estate where, as he heard, 'great oppression took place … and the discovery that the bailiffs were driving for their lease money, pointed out to me the duty and necessity of every landlord looking after his own affairs and watching the misconduct of the drivers, and other numerous instances of their oppressive conduct, which I discovered in consequence.' When he discovered that Glendenning was charging him a higher rate of interest than was available elsewhere, which 'I considered it an injury to my children to continue paying', it further undermined their long-standing association. 'I hoped we should have both gone down to Mother Earth without any coolness of our mutual affection and I am deeply disappointed on having not.' His distrust of Glendenning extended to his son, Alexander, and also to George Glendenning junior, whom Sligo later opposed 'both publicly and privately' when the latter sought election to local public office and whom he later dismissed from his service.[5]

Following an alliance in 1835 between the Melbourne-led Whig government and Daniel O'Connell, which was to last until 1841, the violence and subterfuge associated with the anti-tithe and pro-Repeal struggle receded. The government initiated less draconian measures towards Ireland and installed a more sympathetic administration under Lord Mulgrave, Viscount Morpeth and the liberal under-secretary Thomas Drummond. Catholics and liberal Protestants were appointed to vacancies in the Irish administration and judiciary. An overhaul in the legal system, the magistracy, police and law courts commenced. Many of the magistrates, about whose conduct Sligo had been critical, were dismissed from office. The police and military were no longer involved in the collection of tithes, while measures suppressing faction fights and secret societies all contributed to a period of calm. The Orange Order and ultra-Protestant agitators, like 'the slave drivers of Jamaica', to Sligo's relief also fell victim to the new, more liberal winds of change.[6]

The defeat of his cousin John Browne at the polls, in his absence, combined with his estrangement from the government of Lord Melbourne, reduced Sligo's influence in Mayo. The under-secretary of state, Thomas Drummond, negotiated over his head with the parish priest of Newport, a determined proponent of Repeal and 'one of the most violent and ill-intentioned of the Catholic Priesthood', by promising '*him* the Government interest for the establishment of a Poor House'.[7] When the government, without consultation, appointed a new deputy lord lieutenant for Mayo, Sligo felt his authority impugned. It was through his efforts, he reminded Melbourne, that the cause of Repeal had been kept at bay in Mayo. 'Should you on reflection think I am unfit to hold the office in Mayo with which I was entrusted by Lord Grey, I would prefer being fairly informed of it, rather than have my authority and influence lowered in the County.'[8] On the death of Dr Oliver Kelly, with whom he had enjoyed a positive relationship and who had Sligo's coat of arms installed in the newly built Catholic cathedral in Tuam, Dr John McHale was appointed archbishop of Tuam. While courteous and moderately supportive of Sligo's endeavour to alleviate hunger and destitution, the new archbishop was far more outspoken and vehement in his criticisms of the landlord class *per se*, was actively pro-Repeal and was a determined opponent of the multi-denominational education favoured by Sligo.

Despite the lull in agrarian violence, the plight of Irish rural tenants and labourers continued. During his absence, the economic and social situation pertaining in Mayo had worsened. Emigration, a measure particularly favoured by his agent Glendenning, had commenced. In April 1833 *The Herald* left the port of Westport for America with a cargo of marble 'and 106 passengers, many highly respectable families'.[9] This outflow was destined to increase in the coming years and from 1845 was to become a flood. With its famous linen trade all but ended, Westport struggled commercially, its once busy port already showing signs of decay, as William Thackeray observed during a visit to the town in 1842. 'As for the warehouses ... these dismal mausoleums as vast as pyramids are the places where the dead trade of Westport lies buried.'[10] Despite Lord Melbourne's promise to Sligo, 'that you may depend on it I will not forget the Irish',[11] as Britain itself became immersed in an economic depression that was to continue for almost eight years, hopes of any significant improvement in Ireland diminished.

Estate matters and lawsuits over rents, including the long-standing issue of head rents on the O'Donel estate in Newport, which in 1829 was placed under the control of the Court of Chancery, absorbed Sligo on his return. In 1837 a dispute with Lord Lucan over ownership of lands at Ballygolan, as well as legal proceedings against Dominick Browne, recently created Lord Oranmore and Browne, and against Sir Samuel O'Malley, together with the administration of family trusts and annuities from the wills of his mother and aunt, combined with negotiations regarding his personal debts and taxes, involved much consultation with his lawyers in London and in Dublin. A return trip to Frankfurt am Main in May 1837 to attend a mineral thermal spa at Carlsbad was followed by a brief stay in Paris during the winter.

In June 1838 Sligo attended the coronation of Queen Victoria in Westminster Abbey. Pregnant with her thirteenth child, Catherine was excused from the nine-hour ceremony and was later presented to the queen at a levee in St James's Palace. The accession of the eighteen-year-old monarch heralded an age of remarkable development, especially in steam power, which promoted the rapid development of the railway system, as well as steam-powered ships. Despite the passing of the Reform Act in 1832, unemployment was rife, while the conditions of workers in the mines and factories throughout Britain were inhumane.

In Ireland the coronation of Queen Victoria was celebrated enthusiastically, with Daniel O'Connell publicly professing his loyalty. The divisive tithe issue was partly resolved by converting tithes into a rent charge of some 75 per cent of the old composition and payable by the head landlord, who passed on the charge to tenants. Tenants-at-will were exempt and all arrears were written-off. In 1838 the English Poor Law system was extended to Ireland, with the establishment of Poor Law Unions and the introduction of the dreaded workhouse. The Westport Workhouse, built in 1842 to accommodate a thousand paupers, was privately maintained by Lord Sligo owing to a lack of public funding.

On 30 July 1837 Sligo's family was further increased by the birth of a daughter, Hester Georgina, followed by the birth of another daughter, Augusta, in August 1838. 'Sitting beside Lady Sligo's bed,' as Sligo wrote, after the birth of his latest daughter, discussing the complexities of business and family affairs, illustrated the couple's contentment and closeness. Their family was outgrowing the living quarters at Westport House: 'I have such work in my house here for my numerous family to be accommodated.'[12] Despite the number of his children and 'their inadequate fortune', Sligo, nevertheless, still anticipated 'the probability of more'.[13] He displayed a critical honesty about his children's characters and capabilities, especially of his sons, and was determined that they would grow up well-grounded. 'Altamont is between 18 & 19, is a sharp, intelligent, good-natured lad, has seen a great deal of the world, has been his own master since he was ten years of age and is, *in consequence,* the most obedient and inculpable person I ever saw. His education has been rather of a European than of a Classical kind.' On his entrance to Cambridge, where it was expected 'he should fag very hard at his College courses,' his father engaged a tutor, 'not to place him in a state of tutelage as I was with Caldwell,' deeming such an arrangement unsuitable for 'a boy who has been travelling about a great deal'.[14] Mindful too of his own student days of debauchery and excess, Sligo ensured that his son and heir spent the summer months away from the high life of London, safely ensconced with his family and tutor at Westport House.

As 3rd Marquess of Sligo and heir to the family estates, George's adult life was blighted by the catastrophe of the Great Famine, which descended on Ireland shortly after he succeeded to the title in January 1845 and which was to have a disastrous effect both on his inheritance and on his personal life. 'He is the one owner of the House I am truly sorry for,' his descendant the 10th Marquess wrote of him in 1981. 'He inherited a large income and a sense of duty. Within months there was no income, but the sense of duty remained.'[15] What faced him, however, was by then beyond the capability of any single individual to remedy but duty nonetheless prevailed. 'We have 8,000 on outdoor relief and 1,000 in the Workhouse,' he recorded at the height of the hunger in January 1848.[16] Feeding those around him as best he could, shooting whatever could be salvaged on his estate, from wild duck to deer, he paid for shiploads of meal and grain and subvented the infirmary and workhouse from his own pocket, 'rather than the unhappy occupants should be expelled'.[17] He closed Westport House and, with his mother and sisters, took up residence in a town house in Westport, from where he did his best to manage the unfolding nightmare. With no rents forthcoming from the estate, he sold off many of his father's treasured heirlooms, including most of his racing trophies, as well as the portraits by Gainsborough of his great-grandparents, Admiral and Countess Howe.

In 1847, in a pamphlet entitled *Remarks and Suggestions on the Present State of Ireland*, the 3rd Marquess castigated the British government's attitude and lack of effort in 'the system of distributing relief ... the ruinous and useless works and other "ill-advised measures" adopted in the face of such calamity, being merely temporary and gratuitous.' He advocated the adoption of fundamental changes, including a 'system of Tenant Right contingent on improvement and allow equity of redemption to the owner', so that 'out of the present chaos a new creation may gradually arise, with order instead of anarchy, and prosperity instead of suffering'.[18] Disillusioned with Britain's laissez-faire attitude to the Famine, in 1854, on being offered the vacant ribbon of St Patrick, so prized by his father and grandfather, by Queen

Victoria, he replied: 'I have no desire for the honour.'[19] In 1868, on being asked 'to serve Queen Victoria as Lord-in-Waiting', he excused himself on the pretext 'that I am quite unfit in taste and habits for any such appointment'.[20]

Married firstly to Ellen Sydney, daughter of his father's friend Lord Strangford, both his wife and daughter died shortly after the Famine. In 1858 he married Julia Nugent, daughter of Anthony Nugent (later created Earl of Westmeath), a Catholic landowner from Pallas Castle, Tynagh, County Galway. The couple were refused permission to marry by Catholic rite in Ireland. On appeal to Rome, however, a dispensation was subsequently granted by the pope. Both his second wife and daughter died one year later in childbirth. In 1878 the 3rd Marquess married Isabelle de Peyronet, by whom he had no children.

Sligo's second son, James de Burgh, 'Jem', was less pliable than his older brother. Possessing, as his father implacably described, 'a slobbering character, want of energy, so different from the rest of his brothers and sisters', he was removed from Eton because of 'idleness and the careless extravagant habits he had got into there following the lead of others whose financial resources far exceeded his'. Jem's desire to join the army was resisted by his father, both out of concern for his health, delicate since childhood, and also that 'in times of peace the Army is only the profession of an idler or of a fool who *is capable of nothing else*'. For his father's initial choice of a career at the Bar, Jem showed 'neither talents nor application'. His propensity for laziness was initially circumvented by sending him with a modest allowance 'to a small and cheaper college [at Cambridge] – not as a Nobleman, but as a Commoner'.[21] While fulfilling his father's wishes by graduating from Cambridge in 1841, he eventually attained his preferred choice of career when, on the recommendation of the Duke of Wellington, he was granted a commission as a cornet in the 9th Lancers and in 1846 was promoted to lieutenant in the 10th Hussars. Inheriting his father's lack of social pretension, aboard the *Oriental* on his way to join his regiment in India he found some of his fellow passengers, as he wrote to his mother, to be 'such a snobbish set, especially the ladies ... whose chief occupation seems to be gossiping'.[22] He served in the first Sikh war and became aide-de-camp to Sir Hugh Gough at the Battle of Sobraon in 1846. While in India he read in a newspaper of the death of his 'dear sister Catherine', which occurred in July 1844. Invalided home, he died from dysentery aboard ship on 6 April 1847, aged twenty-four, and was buried at Suez.

Sligo's son Ulick, the future 5th Marquess, was educated at Rugby. During the famine in Ireland, as a youth, he recalled helping round up and shoot 600 deer in Mount Browne for distribution among the starving tenants. At sixteen, courtesy of his father's old college friend Sir John Cam Hobhouse, president of the Board of Control for India, he was offered a position in the Bengali civil service on completion of the required course at Haileybury. Coming 'very high on the list' in 1851, he travelled overland to Trieste from where he embarked for Egypt by caravan to the Red Sea and from there by ship to India. He pursued a successful career in the Indian civil service and took an active role in suppressing the Mutiny of 1857 and in alleviating famine in Orissa in 1866. His baptism in a racing cup at Westport House imbued him with a passion for horses and he was instrumental in reorganising the rules of horse racing in India.

His younger brother Richard Howe, born in Jamaica, was sent to Harrow. He joined the Royal Fusiliers and saw action in the Crimean War at Sebastopol, The Quarries and Redan. At the battle of Inkerman he was severely wounded. Presumed dead, he was thrown into a communal grave on the battlefield but was saved from being buried alive when his brother John, searching the battlefield with a burial party, found him alive. An engineer and mechanic, after his retirement from the army Richard became involved in tramway and underwater cable development in England, on the Continent and in South America.

Another son, John de Burgh, followed in the seafaring tradition of his family, being appointed to the Royal Navy aboard the *Cleopatra* in May 1839, rising to the rank of lieutenant. He was later elected MP for Mayo and succeeded as 4th Marquess of Sligo.

On 18 May 1839 the family celebrated the marriage of their eldest daughter, Louisa, to Charles Knox, eldest son of Colonel Charles Nesbitt Knox of Castle Lacken in north Mayo, and his wife Jane Cuffe, daughter and heiress of James Cuff, Lord Tyrawley. With an estate of some '10,000 acres quite unencumbered settled on him',[23] Louisa's husband also came into possession of the Cuff estate near Ballinrobe, including Cranmore House, situated on the outskirts of the town, where the couple came to reside. While a joyful social occasion, like all aristocratic marriages it was proceeded by many months of legal haggling over dowries, jointures, securities and, as especially specified by Lord Sligo, the provision of 'pin money of £250 per annum' for his daughter's personal use.[24] They were married in All Souls Church, Langham Place, in London and Mansfield House played host to a wedding celebration for family and friends. Louisa died at Carnmore in 1891 and is buried with her husband in St Mary's Church of Ireland in Ballinrobe, where one of the stained-glass windows is dedicated to their memory. Another daughter, Harriet, married a local landlord, Robert Lynch-Blosse of Castlecarra, as did her youngest sister, Marianne, who, in 1868, married Hugh Wilbraham, the son of the owner of the Old Head estate. In 1838 Hester Georgina married Francis Carew Shapland in London, while her sisters Elizabeth, Emily and Augusta remained unmarried.

Jamaica was to monopolise Sligo's remaining years. 'Whenever the interests of Jamaica are concerned, I shall always, I trust, be found at my post.'[25] His hope was for a new colonial structure where the sugar estate was manned by a free labour force, providing gainful employment for the former slaves, as well as contributing to the economy of Jamaica. His initial belief that the apprenticeship system was the way to achieve orderly change and provide time to establish stable social and economic patterns underwent a dramatic change. After his experiences in Jamaica, he wrote:

> In truth, there is no justice in the general local institutions of Jamaica: because there is no public opinion to which an appeal can be made. Slavery has divided society into two classes: to one it has given power, but to the other it has not extended protection. One of those classes is above public opinion and the other is below it; neither one therefore is under its influence.[26]

Based on evidence gathered by missionaries on the ground in Jamaica and from visiting anti-slavery representatives from Britain, such as Joseph Sturge and Thomas Harvey, the continued violence perpetrated by the plantocracy against the apprentices fuelled the growing lobby for the abandonment of the apprenticeship system in favour of total emancipation. Incidents of abuse, especially the flogging of female apprentices, which Sligo had endeavoured to abolish, fuelled an ever-growing repulsion, especially among the vocal anti-slavery female groups in both Britain and Ireland. Sligo attended many such anti-slavery meetings, including one at Exeter Hall on the Strand in London in 1841 which attracted a crowd of over 4,000 people. On the other hand, the plutocracy and other commercial interests, through Burge, continued to lobby the government and the Colonial Office, over which Lord Glenelg still presided, to counter the claims of anti-slavery proponents.

Sligo also kept abreast of developments in Jamaica through correspondence with individual special magistrates and missionaries, as well as with former officials in his administration. 'From the accounts I have received from all classes, planters, magistrates and members of the Legislature, all take one view and give a most gloomy account.'[27] Rather than protecting the rights of the apprentices, his successor Sir Lionel Smith, as Sligo noted, had introduced measures 'to conciliate the Planters and the Assembly … [and] to crush the Black and Browne interest'.[28] Even the Colonial Office agreed with his observations, considering Smith's policy of appeasement as 'serving to fill the planters with false ideas of their own importance … to aggravate the original difference [between enslaved and slaveholder] into an abiding system of hostility'.[29] Stung by his predecessor's involvement in the affairs of the island, Smith complained to London about 'that great Leviathan of black humanity Peter Howe of Sligo' and threatened that 'if Lord Sligo is to be Governor of Jamaica in England and Sir Lionel Smith his deputy Governor in Jamaica … I am too proud a man to endure it long.'[30]

During the latter part of 1837 Sligo set himself the task 'afforded me by a temporary retirement' to compile a report based on his experiences as governor.[31] *Jamaica under the Apprenticeship System, by a Proprietor*, published in January 1838, laid bare the inequalities and imperfections that existed in the governance of the island from the legal system, policing, punishment, Court of Chancery, education, crop cultivation, the inefficiencies and dishonesty of attorneys entrusted with the management of absentee-owned estates to the lack of investment in the island's infrastructure. He enumerated the 'many objectionable acts' of the Jamaican Assembly, which made the condition of the apprentices worse than when under slavery. Passages and views expressed in his pamphlet influenced the 'Great Debate' on slavery which took place in the Houses of Parliament in 1838. His pamphlet also formed part of Lord Brougham's famous speech on emancipation in the House of Lords on 20 February, a subject which, as Brougham noted, 'Lord Sligo's name is so honourably and now inseparably connected.'[32] The prime minister, Lord Melbourne, presented a copy of his pamphlet to Queen Victoria, while the Duke of Cambridge informed Sligo that he had 'read his pamphlet with great interest'.[33] His views were also published and quoted by numerous anti-slavery groups. 'We have met with no work on the system of Negro apprenticeship containing a more clear and temperate statement of facts .... We commend Lord Sligo's pamphlet to the serious examination of all who seek for authentic information on the momentous question that now agitates the country.'[34]

Sligo's experiences in Jamaica not only helped to hasten the end of slavery, it also had a profound affect on its author. As he told the anti-slavery advocate Joseph Sturge, it 'changed my mind from being a supporter of Apprenticeship to become the warmest advocate of full and immediate emancipation'.[35] It also, as he acknowledged, 'shocked him at ever having held a different opinion'.[36] On 22 March 1838, being, as he wrote, 'well aware that it would put an end to the [Slavery] System', he publicly announced in the House of Lords that, regardless of the government's decision, he intended to emancipate all his apprentices on his Jamaican estates on 1 August 1838.[37] 'I am confident that no person who is acquainted with the state of the West Indian Colonies and at the same time uninfected with colonial prejudices, will deny that the time is now come to effect a final arrangement to this question.'[38] His decision, made in such a public way, 'was justly considered as of vast importance towards the successful issue of the great enterprise, not only as a high moral example to other large proprietors ... but also its effects in the colonies themselves'.[39]

Despite bitter protests from the Jamaican Assembly, Sligo's decision was vindicated. On 1 August 1838 the British government revoked apprenticeship in favour of full and immediate emancipation. In Spanish Town the news was celebrated by a huge concourse of former slaves who marched in procession behind a hearse containing chains and shackles, the symbols of slavery, which were solemnly buried in a grave.

Emancipation, however, brought in its wake uncertainty and insecurity for both former master and former slave. Hitherto the slave had access to free subsistence and accommodation for which he had now to pay an onerous rent. Deprived of free slave labour, the planter, in turn, had to pay high wages to lure the former slave back to work. As a proprietor, as well as a proponent of emancipation, Sligo realised that having access to a labour market, at a fair rate, was vital to the economic viability and survival, not only of individual estates, but also of the Jamaican economy. In 1839 in a public letter to the colonial minister, the Marquis of Normanby, he recommended that the price 'of labour must be regulated by the price of provisions and of other commodities' as in other countries. As the current rates of pay being demanded in Jamaica exceeded those in England, they should be brought into line without delay. It was the actions of the Assembly, he maintained, comprised of attorneys and merchants 'whose profits have been acquired in times of slavery, whose livelihood depends on the employment they receive from the planting agents and absentee proprietors', who, through their harsh treatment, had alienated the former apprentices from returning to work on the plantations. 'Can such a body have any really liberal sentiments?' Sligo asked. 'Is it to be expected that they can legislate upon the principles which suit a free country? It is quite impossible.' As well as the introduction of a fair wage, he also recommended that 'grants of tracts of land, with Negro houses … might be devised' to relieve the newly freed apprentices from having to pay exorbitant rents. He also recommended the immediate suspension of the Jamaican Assembly, as 'one of the most auspicious events which could occur', and instead 'to enact in this country the laws which appear necessary for the constitution of a free state into which the act of this Parliament has converted the Colony', and that the seat of government on the island be removed from Spanish Town to Kingston, 'the real capital of the island'.[40]

While the power of the planters to exploit slave labour was officially outlawed, the malignant legacy of slavery endured.

The intransigence of the plantocracy alienated the former slaves and, as Sligo had warned, 'increased their hatred'.[41] Without education, which he had long advocated, or compensation for their enslavement, for many decades to come the majority of the former slaves were destined to endure a life of mere survival. For the planter, despite the compensation allocated them by the British government, by the end of the century emancipation had become a journey from wealth to ruin. Most of the great Jamaican estates were later abandoned or divided among their former slaves while, for many decades, life in Jamaica remained trapped by the repercussions and memories of slavery.

On his departure from Jamaica, Sligo had left the management of his estates in the care of an overseer named Willetts. After his return, he received information from his missionary contacts on the island that Willetts 'was behaving harshly to the people' and was 'combining to ruin me'.[42] Evidence of overcharging and the purchase of unnecessary provisions, equipment and furnishings for Kelly's great house, and of crops being planted for others at his expense, were brought to his attention by Dowell O'Reilly. Despite ordering the liberation of his apprentices on 1 August 1838, Willetts, as Sligo was informed, had deliberately 'kept my Negroes one month after receiving notification of my intention to liberate them'.[43] He immediately terminated Willetts's contract and leased his estates to Alexandre Bravo, a liberal member of the Assembly, 'a great friend to the new order of things, and remarkable for the successful and humane manner in which he manages his Apprentices'.[44]

A plantation and slave owner, Assembly member for the parish of St Dorothy and father of nine children, of Jewish descent, Alexandre Bravo was a supporter of Sligo's policies as governor. Both favoured the establishment of an independent tenantry from among the newly freed apprentices. The payment of a fair wage to the apprentice and a fair rent for estate cottages and provision grounds to the planter enabled the tenant to take his labour to market, while the owner enjoyed a reasonable rental and a local supply of labour for the cultivation of his estate. To put such a plan into practice, 'Lord Sligo has given directions for the building of 100 comfortable cottages on the estate [Kelly's] which are to be leased out to the labourers, with 1 acre plots of ground, so as to render them independent tenants.'[45]

Sligo's lease agreement with Bravo was 'for seven years at a quarter of the gross produce [of the estates] of sugar and rum'.[46] After the expiry of the agreement, it was Sligo's expectation that one of his own sons would take over management of the estates. The rising cost of sugar production, a severe drought and crop failure, followed in 1845 by 'a total failure of the springs' on the estate, together with a scarcity of labour, however, combined to make his property uneconomic. Having expended a sizeable outlay on 'this unfortunate estate' and having personally experienced 'a frightful fall from immense wealth to actual poverty', after a few years Bravo opted out of the lease.[47] Kelly's and Cocoa Walk gradually fell into decline. Kelly's great house became a ruin and was eventually blown to pieces by fireworks, courtesy of its last 'unofficial' resident. Thus 'the partial fulfilment of Sligo's ambitions for the apprentices was won at the cost of the dismemberance of his Jamaican inheritance'.[48] The loss of revenue from his Jamaican estates contributed to his later refusal of a dukedom because he lacked the financial means to support the title.

In autumn 1839, approaching his fiftieth birthday, Sligo applied to the government for the post of provincial governor in India. On being offered the governorship of Mauritius, he declined 'to go to an inferior place'.[49] Badly afflicted with rheumatism and grossly overweight, 'his carriage door' and, when he travelled by sea, 'the hatchway leading from the deck to the quarters he was to occupy below, had to be specially enlarged'.[50] Suffering from 'tremors in the hand', much to the consternation of recipients of his voluminous correspondence, symptoms of paralysis first appeared in the summer of 1839, which he blamed on his consumption of too large a quantity of 'Colchicum', taken to relieve his rheumatic condition. In the autumn of 1839, accompanied by Catherine, pregnant with their last child, he was sufficiently recovered to journey to Italy to spend the winter months in Naples.

Subsumed into the Kingdom of the Two Sicilies, Naples was ruled by King Ferdinand II and his second wife, Queen Marie Theresa of Austria. Despite an ongoing trade disagreement with Britain, as a peer of the realm and an intimate of the British royal family, Sligo was warmly received. In the benign climate of Naples, his rheumatic condition gradually improved, which enabled him, as he wrote, to undertake some trips 'to see some antiquities .... I walked a good deal and got into a great perspiration and then came home in my phaeton'.[51] He suffered also from what he referred to as 'a continual and great depression' regarding his financial situation.[52] The future welfare of his large family and ongoing lawsuits, especially his dispute with Lord Lucan over Ballygolan for which essential land deeds were mislaid, all played greatly on his mind. His last child, a daughter Marianne, was born on Christmas Day and was christened on 15 January at the British Chaplaincy in Naples.

With Catherine, he returned again to Naples in November 1840, this time accompanied by Altamont, his daughters Catherine and Louisa and his son-in-law Charles Knox. After journeying overland through France, at Genoa they embarked on a steam vessel, one of the first to operate in the Italian peninsula and placed at their disposal by the King of Naples. Sligo rented the Palais Scaletta Chica on the southern slopes of the Vomero Hill overlooking the bay, once a favourite residence of his friend Joachim Murat. On 4 February 1841, as the *Court Journal* reported, 'the Marquess and Marchioness of Sligo opened their splendid palace ... for the purpose of giving a ball ... to celebrate the coming-of-age of their eldest son, the Earl of Altamont'.[53] Attended by the

King and Queen of Naples, the Prince and Princess of Salerno and
the Infanta of Spain, in the large ballroom, lit by two hundred wax
lights, some two hundred guests were entertained. The royal party,
together with Sligo and his family and the British minister William
Temple, brother of Lord Palmerston, took supper in a private
room, while the rest of the guests enjoyed a 'standing supper' in
the ballroom. The party lasted until four in the morning and was
deemed 'one of the most splendid and gay fêtes given for some
time in the city of Naples'.[54]

Returning to Westport in May 1841, the tremors in Sligo's hands
became more intense. 'I can hardly shave myself or button my shirt
collars.'[55] A creeping paralysis began to affect both his walk and
his speech. Catherine had his carriage converted to accommodate
the chair on which he had to be carried 'and she sat by his side on
a cane chair without a back' to enable them to continue to travel
together.[56] His offer to retire from the lord lieutenancy of Mayo
in favour of his son George, in an effort, as he informed Prime
Minister Lord Melbourne, 'to reconcile our differences', was not
fulfilled.[57] The office was conferred instead on his political rival
Lord Lucan. Despite his alienation from the government, the
worsening state of his home county made him once more swallow
his pride to seek help from individual contacts in the government,
including Lord Goderich, who promised to forward his petition
for a scheme of relief works to the government. 'You at least have
the satisfaction of doing your duty ... I wish everyone who had
it in his power would do the same.'[58] While well-intentioned and
commendable, such individual interventions, however, could do
little to prevent the calamity that was about to engulf Ireland.

The benefit derived from his visit to a therapeutic spa in West
Cowes on the Isle of Wight in September 1843, which 'wonderfully
improved' his health, was short-lived. By early 1844 the paralysis
had spread to 'affect his intellect'.[59] The administration of his
complex affairs and estates fell to Lady Sligo and, following his

return from a visit to India in 1844, on his twenty-two-year-old heir. Calm, practical and steadfast, Catherine ensured her husband's comfort, from sourcing 'stout thick linen' for his shirts, 'which get such desperate hard usage', to looking after his many medical requirements, which included 'having to be lanced'.[60] In summer 1844 she organised the removal of the family and household from Mansfield Street, because 'the constant repairs and rates and taxes of such a large house are so heavy', to a smaller house in the spa town of Tunbridge Wells.[61]

From lawyers, bankers and moneylenders, estate agents and land stewards, to the educational and career requirements of her large family, in her neat and legible handwriting Catherine addressed her husband's business affairs in which, as his long-time trusted confidante, she was already well-versed. While acting in that capacity, however, she was at pains to ensure that her son Altamont, who had taken over at Westport House, was consulted and involved in all her decisions, expressing satisfaction that he showed 'so good a feeling towards the poor on his estate', a trait that was later to single him out as one of Ireland's most compassionate landlords during the Great Famine.[62]

To help her son's efforts to protect his tenants during the devastating years of the Great Famine, Catherine declined to accept her own marriage jointure, due to be paid on the death of her husband. As her grandson later recorded: 'Granny's jointure was not paid and some years after she refused to accept the arrears Uncle Sligo [her son] made her take them by a trick, making her sign a paper accepting them which she thought was a paper releasing the estate from the arrears.'[63] Conscious of the social stigma attaching to single women in society, Catherine also ensured that her two unmarried daughters, Elizabeth and Emily, were financially secure, bequeathing them dividends from her own life assurance policy, as well as jewellery, furniture and personal effects.

The death of their third daughter, twenty-two-year-old Catherine, in 1844, came as a terrible blow. 'I am fearful of the effect it may have on my father in his present state,' Jem wrote from his posting in India – he was to survive his sister by only three years.[64] Influenza hit the family hard during Christmas 1844 and was especially severe on the younger children, Hester, Augusta and Marianne. Their father escaped the worst and by January he was reported 'to be going on well'.[65] In the middle of January Altamont, accompanied by sisters Elizabeth and Harriet, sailed from Southampton to Lisbon. Catherine's hope 'that they will not have stormy weather in the Bay of Biscay' was not realised when, as on her own journey to Jamaica ten years previously, they too endured a terrifying storm at sea before eventually landing safely in Lisbon.[66]

Towards the end of January Sligo's condition began to deteriorate. On Sunday 26 January 1845, with his beloved wife, daughter Emily and his younger children by his side, he died at Tunbridge Wells. According to his wishes 'to be buried wherever I may die, either in England or any other country and that my funeral may be conducted in the plainest manner and with as much privacy as possible', his remains were conveyed by steam train to London.[67] On 3 February he was interred with his daughter Catherine in All Saints Cemetery, Kensal Green. 'The mournful ceremony was conducted in a very private manner in accordance with the expressed wish of the deceased peer and the funeral was attended by only a small circle of the lamented nobleman's family connections.'[68] A stone sarcophagus, adorned with two Grecian urns, bearing the inscription *To the memory of Howe Peter Browne Marquis of Sligo who died January 26 1845*, was later erected over his grave.

As news of his death trickled through to Westport and the surrounding hinterland, there was an outpouring of sadness and not a little apprehension at his passing. In the Catholic chapel, to which, as the parish priest Dean Bourke reminded the immense congregation who filled the interior 'almost to suffocation', he had been a generous donor, 'a better-hearted or kinder man ... seldom comes'.[69] As the dark clouds of famine and distress once more hovered over his west of Ireland home, the dean recalled how, in the previous disaster in 1831, Lord Sligo had worked with him over a continual period of six days, from eleven in the morning until six each evening, in his efforts to provide relief to those most affected in the locality.

After a dissolute and irresponsible youth, Sligo had, albeit belatedly, followed the advice given him by his father. In a society not noted for marital stability, he became a devoted husband and father. 'I have a perfect recollection of his great attention and love of his family,' William Ramsay wrote from Jamaica.[70] His trust in 'my beloved wife Hester Catherine Marchioness of Sligo' was reflected in his will.[71] Together with his brother-in-law, the Marquess of Clanricarde, his cousins Robert and George Browne and his steward, George Hildebrand, he appointed her executor of his estate and guardian and trustee of their children. Together with her marriage jointure, he bequeathed her the leasehold, furniture and contents of Mansfield Street, together with all his 'diamonds, jewellery and trinkets ... carriages and carriage horses'.[72]

Like his father, Sligo died relatively young and from a similar rheumatic condition. In an age where diet was dictated by little more than preference and means, he suffered the consequences by becoming a life-long 'martyr to gout', as well as developing an obese condition in latter middle age.

The 2nd Marquess of Sligo lived his relatively short lifespan with an energy and all-encompassing passion. While not always adhering to his family motto, *Suivez Raison* – instead, as he honestly admitted, 'my judgement is shaped by my feelings',[73] a characteristic that, at times, landed him in hot water. In his endeavours, both public and private, however, he invariably tried to do the right thing. As he admitted to his own faults, so he tended to forgive those he encountered in others and seldom held grudges, as he assured one agent who had embezzled his money: 'the idea of injury to any man for *dirty spite* never came across me'.[74] His upbringing, character and mindset were influenced and shaped in a cosmopolitan and more sophisticated European milieu. But that experience did not impinge negatively on his more claustrophobic role as an Irish landlord and as a Jamaican plantation owner. On the contrary, it enhanced, enlightened and shaped his attitude and endeavours on behalf of those less fortunate for whom he felt responsible.

From a youth of privilege and indulgence to liberal landlord, legislator, emancipator and colonial governor, Sligo made a significant, if forgotten, contribution to his time. In the past, Irish aristocrats were usually depicted as rapacious land-grabbers, tools of an evil empire. Because of their political, religious and cultural differences, a gulf more pronounced than the social divide existing between commoner and aristocrat in other countries consequently contributed to their dismissal from Irish historiography.

Enshrined in the history of Jamaica, however, as 'emancipator of the slaves' and in Ireland as 'the poor man's friend', the legacy of Howe Peter Browne, 2nd Marquess of Sligo, in the most difficult and abject of times, is all the more deserving of due recognition.

Family Tree

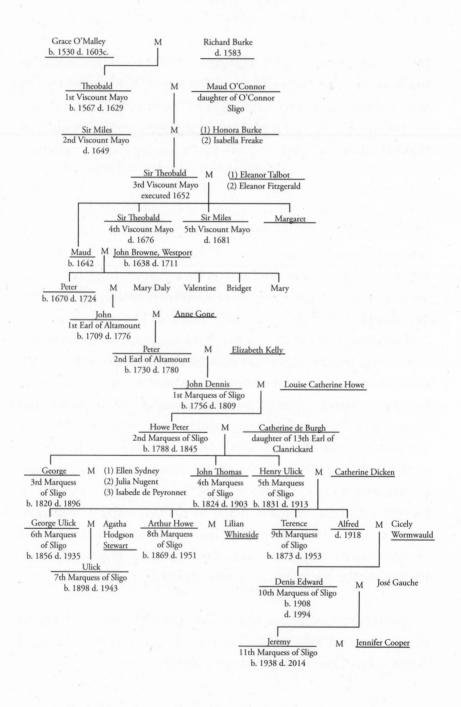

Grace O'Malley
b. 1530 d. 1603c.   **M**   Richard Burke
d. 1583

Theobald
1st Viscount Mayo
b. 1567 d. 1629   **M**   Maud O'Connor
daughter of O'Connor
Sligo

Sir Miles
2nd Viscount Mayo
d. 1649   **M**   (1) Honora Burke
(2) Isabella Freake

Sir Theobald
3rd Viscount Mayo
executed 1652   **M**   (1) Eleanor Talbot
(2) Eleanor Fitzgerald

Sir Theobald
4th Viscount Mayo
d. 1676   Sir Miles
5th Viscount Mayo
d. 1681   Margaret

Maud
b. 1642 **M** John Browne, Westport
b. 1638 d. 1711

Peter
b. 1670 d. 1724 **M** Mary Daly   Valentine   Bridget   Mary

John
1st Earl of Altamount
b. 1709 d. 1776   **M**   Anne Gone

Peter
2nd Earl of Altamount
b. 1730 d. 1780   **M**   Elizabeth Kelly

John Dennis
1st Marquess of Sligo
b. 1756 d. 1809   **M**   Louise Catherine Howe

Howe Peter
2nd Marquess of Sligo
b. 1788 d. 1845   **M**   Catherine de Burgh
daughter of 13th Earl of
Clanrickard

George
3rd Marquess
of Sligo
b. 1820 d. 1896 **M** (1) Ellen Sydney
(2) Julia Nugent
(3) Isabede de Peyronnet   John Thomas
4th Marquess
of Sligo
b. 1824 d. 1903   Henry Ulick
5th Marquess
of Sligo
b. 1831 d. 1913 **M** Catherine Dicken

George Ulick
6th Marquess
of Sligo
b. 1856 d. 1935 **M** Agatha
Hodgson
Stewart   Arthur Howe
8th Marquess
of Sligo
b. 1869 d. 1951 **M** Lilian
Whiteside   Terence
9th Marquess
of Sligo
b. 1873 d. 1953   Alfred
d. 1918 **M** Cicely
Wormwauld

Ulick
7th Marquess of Sligo
b. 1898 d. 1943

Denis Edward
10th Marquess of Sligo
b. 1908
d. 1994   **M**   José Gauche

Jeremy
11th Marquess of Sligo
b. 1938 d. 2014   **M**   Jennifer Cooper

Sources and Bibliography

Howe Peter Browne, 2nd Marquess of Sligo, was an inveterate letter-writer and correspondent. Some 15,000 eighteenth- and nineteenth-century documents, located in national and international archives, form the basis of this biography, in addition to other related archival material. (See notes for individual items.)

Primary Sources

Westport House (WH):
Browne Family manuscripts, facsimiles and artefacts
1st Marquess of Sligo – personal and official correspondence
3rd Marquess of Sligo – personal and official correspondence
2nd Marquess of Sligo – letter books (original and facsimile) containing copies of his personal and official correspondence, local, national and international, in his capacity as landlord, Custos Rotulorum, Privy Counsellor, Lord Lieutenant of County Mayo, West Indian plantation owner, Member of the House of Lords, Chairman of Mayo Magistrates and a founding member of the Irish Turf Club; diaries of his extensive travels in Europe; private and public correspondence in relation to his role as Governor General of Jamaica and in the cause of emancipation; correspondence relating to the political, social, religious, legal and commercial developments in Ireland between 1788 and 1845, with particular relevance to the west of Ireland.

National Library of Ireland (NLI): Collection List no. 78, Westport Estate Papers 1540–1993 (Westport Estate Papers); Historical Manuscripts Commission, various volumes

Yale University (YU): James Marshall and Marie-Louise Osborn Collection, Beinecke Rare Book and Manuscript Library, OSB MSS 74, The Levantine Correspondence of Howe Peter Browne, 2nd Marquess of Sligo (Levantine Correspondence)

British Library Manuscript Collection (BL): Add MSS 51816, Correspondence of Lord Holland, 1834–1840; Newspaper Department, Colindale, various newspapers

British Museum (BM): Department of Greek and Roman Antiquities, Correspondence with the 5th Marquess of Sligo, 1905

Trinity College Dublin (TCD): MS 6403, Miscellaneous Family and Political Correspondence of Howe Peter Browne, 2nd Marquess of Sligo, Governor of Jamaica (1815–39) (Sligo Papers)

Mayo County Library, Castlebar: Telegraph and Connaught Ranger; Connaught Telegraph; Mayo Constitution

Royal Archives, Windsor Castle (RA), by permission of Her Majesty Queen Elizabeth II: RA GEO/Main/22578-81 and RA GEO/Main/26714-5

Public Record Office, Northern Ireland (PRONI): Anglesey Papers D619 25–43

Durham University Library (DU): Archives and Special Collections, GB-0033-GRE-B: NRA 6228, Political and Public Papers of Charles, 2nd Earl Grey

West Sussex Record Office: Goodwood MSS nos. 1465 and 1470, Letters of the 5th Duke of Richmond

Eton College: Student attendance books

Jesus College, Cambridge: archives department

National Library of Jamaica (NLJ): Letter Books of Howe Peter Browne, 2nd Marquess of Sligo MS 228; Excerpts from the Letter Book of Howe Peter Browne, 2nd Marquess of Sligo, MS 59, Livingston Collection no. 4

National Library of Scotland (NLS): MS 169–09, Byron Letters, John Murray Archive (Byron Letters)

Quinnipiac University, Connecticut (QU): Arnold Bernhard Library – Ireland's Great Hunger Institute, Correspondence of Hester Catherine de Burgh, 2nd Marchioness of Sligo (Correspondence of Hester de Burgh)

Bibliothèque National de France (BNF): World Biographical Information System

Fondation Napoleon, Paris

Published Sources

Abrahams, Peter, *Jamaica: An Island Mosaic* (Jamaica, 1957)

Accounts and Papers Abolishing Slavery, vol. 33. part I, Jamaica 1833–1835 (2007)

Alde, *Catalogue*, Lot no. 72 (Paris, 1973)

Angelo, Henry, *Pic Nic or Table Talk, Including Numerous Recollections of Public Characters* (London, 1830)

Aspinall, Arthur (ed.), *Correspondence of George Prince of Wales, 1770–1812*, 8 vols (London, 1963–71)

——*The Letters of King George IV, 1812–1830*, 3 vols (Cambridge, 1938)

Barringer, Tim, Gillian Forrester, Barbaro Marinez-Ruiz, (eds), *Art and Emancipation in Jamaica: Isaac Mendes Belisario and His Worlds* (New Haven, 2007)

Beckett, J.C., *The Making of Modern Ireland* (London, 1966)

Binney, Keith R., *Horsemen of the First Frontier, 1788–1900* (Australia, 2005)

Blanch, Lesley (ed), *Harriette Wilson's Memoirs* (London, 2003)

Broughton, Lord (John Cam Hobhouse), *Recollections of a Long Life*, ed. Lady Dorchester, 6 vols (London, 1909–11)

Browne, Denis, *A Letter from the Right Hon. Denis Browne MP for Kilkenny to the Most Noble Marquess of Wellesley on the Present State of Ireland* (London, 1822)

Browne, William, *Diary of William Browne, 1822–1882*, facsimile (private source, Jamaica)

Burge, William, *Reply to the Letter of the Marquis of Sligo to the Marquis of Normanby* (London, 1839)

Burn, W.L., *Emancipation and Apprenticeship in the British West Indies* (London, 1937)

Burnard, Trevor, *Mastery, Tyranny and Desire* (Kingston, 2004)

Butler, Kathleen Mary, *The Economics of Emancipation: Jamaica and Barbados, 1823–1843* (Chapel Hill, 1995)

Buxton, Sir Thomas Fowell, *Memoirs of Sir Thomas Fowell Buxton, Baronet* (London, 1848)

Card, Tim, *Eton Established* (Eton, 2001)

Chambers, Anne, *At Arm's Length: Aristocrats in the Republic of Ireland* (Dublin, 2004)

Chambers, E.K., *Samuel Taylor Coleridge: A Biographical Study* (London, 1938)

Christie's, Manson and Wood, *Sale of Important Historical Manuscripts and Autographed Letters, Property of the Marquess of Sligo and Jasper Moore Esq.*, catalogue (6 October 1958)

Cleveland, Duchess of (ed.), *The Life and Letters of Lady Hester Stanhope, 1776–1839* (London, 1914)

Cochran, Peter, *Hobby-O: Lord Byron's Relationship with John Cam Hobhouse* (Cambridge, 2010)

— *The Levantine Correspondence of Howe Peter Browne, 2nd Marquess of Sligo, August–December 1810*, https://petercochran.files. wordpress.com/2014/12/sligo3.pdf

Cochran, Peter (ed.), *Hobhouse on the Continent: 1 January 1813–6 February 1814*, https://petercochran.files.wordpress. com/2009/12/12hobhouse-on-the-continent2.pdf

— *The Irish Avatar*, https://petercochran.files.wordpress. com/2009/03/the_irish_avatar.pdf

Colburn, H., ed., *Correspondence, Despatches and Other Papers of Robert Steward, Lord Castlereagh* (London, 1850)

Coleridge, E.H. and E. Rowland (eds), *The Works of Lord Byron* (London, 1898)

Copley, Esther, *History of Slavery and Its Abolition* (London, 1839)

D'Arcy, Fergus, *Horses, Lords and Racing Men* (Kildare, 1991)

David, Saul, *Prince of Pleasure: the Prince of Wales and the Making of the Regency* (London, 1999)

De Quincey, Thomas, *Autobiographical Sketches* (Edinburgh, 1853)

—, *Confessions of an English Opium-Eater* (London, 1997)

Edwards, Bryan, *The History, Civil and Commercial, of the West Indies*, vol. 4 (Jamaica, 2010)

Ellis, Kirsten, *Star of the Morning: The Extraordinary Life of Lady Hester Stanhope* (London, 2008)

Fraser, Flora, *Princesses: The Six Daughters of George III* (London, 2004)

—, *The Unruly Queen: The Life of Queen Caroline* (London, 1999)

Galt, John, *The Life of Lord Byron* (London, 2008)

Gell, William, *Itinerary of Greece with a Commentary on Pausanias and Strabo, and an Account of the Monuments of Antiquity at Present Existing in That Country* (London, 1810)

Geoghegan, Patrick M., *King Dan: The Rise of Daniel O'Connell, 1775–1829* (Dublin, 2008)

Gibb, Lorna, *Lady Hester: Queen of the East* (London, 2005)

Graham, P.W. (ed.), *Byron's Bulldog: The Letters of John Cam Hobhouse to Lord Byron* (Columbus, Ohio, 1984)

Gray, Arthur and Frederick Brittain, *Jesus College Cambridge: A History* (Cambridge, 1979)

Gurney, Joseph J., *Familiar Letters to Henry Clay of Kentucky Describing a Winter in the West Indies* (London, 1840)

Harrington, J.P. (ed.) *The English Traveller in Ireland* (Dublin, 1991)

Hibbert, Christopher, *George IV* (London, 1973)

Higman, B.W., *Montpelier Jamaica: A Plantation Community in Slavery and Freedom, 1739–1912* (Jamaica, 1998)

—, *Plantation Jamaica, 1750–1850: Capital and Control in a Colonial Economy* (Jamaica, 2005)

Jago, Lucy, *Regency House Party* (London, 2004)

Johnson, Paul, *Napoleon* (London, 2002)

Kieran, Brian L., *The Lawless Caymanas* (Cayman Islands, 1992)

Knighton, Lady, *Memoirs of Sir William Knighton*, 2 vols (London, 1838)

Laurent, Peter E., *Recollections of a Classical Tour* (London, 1821)

Leigh, Ione, *Castlereagh* (London, 1951)

Linnane, Fergus, *The Lives of the English Rakes* (London, 2006)

Longford, Elizabeth, *Wellington* (London, 1992)

Lynam, Shevawn, *Humanity Dick: A Biography of Richard Martin MP 1754–1834* (Dublin, 1975)

MacCarthy, Fiona, *Byron: Life and Legend* (London, 2002)

Macirone, Francis, *The Fall and Death of Joachim Murat* (London, 1817)

Madden, R.R., *A Twelvemonth's Residence in the West Indies, during the Transition from Slavery to Apprenticeship* (London, 1835)

Mansel, Philip, *Paris between the Empires, 1814–1852* (London, 2001)

Marchand, Leslie A. (ed), *Byron's Letters and Journals*, 13 vols (Harvard, 1973–82)

Masson, David (ed.), *The Collected Writings of Thomas De Quincey*, 14 vols (Edinburgh, 1889–1890)

Maxwell, Constance, *Country and Town in Ireland under the Georges* (Dublin, 1940)

Melvin, Patrick, *Estates and Landed Society in Galway* (Dublin, 2012)

Meryon, Charles Lewis, *Memoirs of Lady Hester Stanhope as Related by Herself in Conversation with Her Physician; Comprising Her Opinions and Anecdotes of Some of the Most Remarkable Persons of Her Time* (London, 1845)

—, *Travels of Lady Hester Stanhope, Forming the Completion of Her Memoirs Narrated by Her Physician , Charles Lewis Meryon* (London, 1846)

Moody, T.W. and F.X. Martin, *The Course of Irish History* (Cork, 1994)

Moore, Thomas (ed.), *Life of Byron: Letters and Journals of Lord Byron, with Notices of His Life*, 6 vols (London, 1830)

Morrison, Robert, *The English Opium Eater: A Biography of Thomas De Quincey* (London, 2009)

Mulloy, Sheila (ed.), *Victory or Glorious Defeat: Biographies of Participants in the Mayo Rebellion of 1798* (Westport, 2010)

Oldfield, T.H.B., *The Representative History of Great Britain and Ireland* (London, 1816)

Otter, Rev. William, *Life and Remains of Edward Daniel Clarke* (New York, 1827)

Ó Tuathaigh, Gearóid, *Ireland before the Famine, 1798–1848* (Dublin, 1979)

Parker, Matthew, *The Sugar Barons: Family Corruption, Empire and War* (London, 2011)

Phillippo, James M., *Jamaica, Its Past and Present State* (London, 1843)

Phillips, Peter, *Humanity Dick: The Eccentric Member for Galway* (London, 2003)

Price, Munro, *The Perilous Crown: France between Revolutions* (London, 2007)

Priestly, John B. (ed.), *A Selection from Thomas Moore's Diary* (Cambridge, 1925)

Prothero, Rowland E. (ed.), *The Works of Lord Byron with Letters and Journals,* 6 vols (1898–1904)

Ranson, Jackie, *Belisario: Sketches of Character: A Historical Biography of a Jamaican Artist* (Jamaica, 2008)

Robertson, James, *Gone Is the Ancient Glory: Spanish Town, Jamaica, 1534–2000* (Kingston, 2005)

Roche, Daniel, *France in the Enlightenment* (London, 2000)

Sligo, Denis, 10th Marquess, *Westport House and the Brownes* (Westport, 1981)

Sligo, Howe Peter, 2nd Marquess, *Jamaica under the Apprenticeship System, by a Proprietor* (London, 1838)

—, *A Letter to the Marquis of Normanby Relative to the Present State of Jamaica* (London, 1839)

Sligo, George, 3rd Marquess, *Remarks and Suggestions on the Present State of Ireland* (London, 1847)

Somerville-Large, Peter, *Dublin* (Dublin, 1981)

Stanley, A.M.W. (ed.), *The Letters of Lady Elizabeth Spencer Stanhope* (London, 1814)

Sturge, Joseph and Thomas Harvey, *A Reply to Letters to Joseph Sturge, Esq. by William Hankey* (London, 1836)

—, *The West Indies in 1837* (London, 1838)

Sweeney, Tony and Annie, *The Sweeney Guide to the Irish Turf from 1501–2001* (Dublin, 2002)

Thackeray, William M., *The Irish Sketch Book* (London, 1902)

The Founding of Sligoville: A Tribute to Howe Peter Browne, 2nd Marquess of Sligo, Governor of Jamaica and Friend and Protector of the Former Slaves of Jamaica (Jamaica, 1996)

The Late Elections: An Impartial Statement of All Proceedings (London, 1818)

Thorne, James A. and Joseph H. Kimball, *Emancipation in the West Indies: A Six Months' Tour in Antigua, Barbados and Jamaica* (New York, 1839)

Venn, J. and J.A. (eds), *A Biographical List of All Known Students, Graduates and Holders of Office at the University of Cambridge from Earliest Times to 1900* (Cambridge, 1922–53)

Whigman, B.W., *Plantation Jamaica: West Indies and Its Inhabitants, 1750–1850* (Jamaica, 2005)

White, Terence de Vere (ed.), 'A Lost Correspondence: Letters from Italy from 2nd Marquess of Sligo to Rt Hon. Lord Lowther', *Twentieth Century*, clxxiii (1958)

Wilson, A.N., *The Victorians* (London, 2002)

Wilson, Ben, *Decency and Disorder: The Age of Cant, 1789–1837* (London, 2008)

Wilson, Frances, *The Courtesan's Revenge* (London, 2003)

Wright, Paul, *Selected Poems of Lord Byron* (London, 2006)

Wright, Philip (ed.), *Lady Nugent's Journal of Her Residence in Jamaica, 1801–1805* (Jamaica, 2002)

Wright, Richardson, *Revels in Jamaica, 1682–1838* (Jamaica, 1986)

Newspapers, Journals and Periodicals

Annual Register
Cathair na Mart: Journal of the Westport Historical and Archaeological Society
Connaught Telegraph
Court Journal and Fashionable Gazette

Dublin Gazette
Eclectic Review
Edinburgh Review
Falmouth Post
Fraser's Magazine
Freeman's Journal
Jamaica Chronicle
Jamaica Despatch
Jamaica Despatch and Kingston Chronicle
Jamaica Herald
John Bull
Journals of the Galway Archaeological and Historical Society
Journals of the Kildare Archaeological and Historical Society
Kingston Chronicle
Kingston Despatch
Mayo Constitution
Morning Chronicle
Morning Post
Munchausen Journal
New York Times
Racing Calendar
Royal Gazette
Shrewsbury Chronicle
Sleator's Public Gazette
Society for Irish Latin American Studies, vol. 5 no. 3
Sotheby's Catalogue, 6 December 1983
St Jago de la Vega Gazette
Studies: An Irish Quarterly Review
Telegraph and Connaught Ranger
Thoroughbred Heritage, www.tbheritage.com
The Bury and Norwich Post
The Citizen's Resource, Understanding Slavery Initiative (USI), UK
The Court Journal

The Patriot
The Quarterly Theological Review and Ecclesiastical Record
The Sydney Gazette and New South Wales Advertiser
The Times
The Watchman

Notes

Chapter 1

1. Earl of Altamont to Ross Mahon, 6 November 1790, MS 41094/2, Westport Estate Papers, National Library of Ireland (NLI)
2. Henry Browne to John Browne, November 1759 (facsimile), WH
3. Dockets and Patents, Purchases and Sales of Edmund Kelly Deceased, 25 April 1720 (facsimile), WH
4. *Dublin Gazette*, 18 April 1752
5. Last Will and Testament of Dennis Kelly, 1 March 1754 (facsimile), WH
6. *Ibid.*
7. Lease of Cocoa Walk, Peter Browne and Elizabeth Kelly (MS), WH
8. *Sleater's Public Gazette*, 13 August 1752
9. Last Will and Testament of Peter Browne, Earl of Altamont, April 1752 (MS), WH
10. Thomas De Quincey, *Autobiographical Sketches* (Edinburgh, 1853), p. 366
11. Arthur Young, 'A Tour in Ireland' in J.P. Harrington (ed.), *The English Traveller in Ireland* (Dublin, 1991), p. 181
12. Anne Chambers, *At Arm's Length: Aristocrats in the Republic of Ireland* (Dublin, 2004), p. 74
13. Constance Maxwell, *Country and Town in Ireland under the Georges* (London, 1940), p. 17
14. Note, Matters of Recommendation to My Son, 1808, 1st Marquess of Sligo (facsimile), WH
15. De Quincey, *Autobiographical Sketches*, p. 57
16. MS 40911/1(2), Westport Estate Papers, NLI
17. Arthur Aspinall (ed.), *The Letters of King George IV 1812–1830* (Cambridge, 1938) vol. 3, p. 93
18. Christie's, Manson and Wood, *Sale of Important Historical Manuscripts and Autographed Letters, Property of the Marquess of Sligo and Jasper Moore Esq.*, catalogue (6 October 1958), p. 38

19. Aspinall, *Letters*, vol. 2, p. 220
20. *Ibid.*, Duke of Clarence to Prince George Augustus, 1790, p. 88
21. Queen Charlotte to Lady Howe, 1887 (facsimile), WH
22. Flora Fraser, *Princesses: The Six Daughters of George III* (London, 2004) p. 94
23. Earl Howe to Earl of Altamont, 1787, Christie's, Manson and Wood, p. 16
24. Fraser, *Princesses*, p. 94
25. Abstract of the Will of the Most Noble Marquess of Sligo, 1809 (MS), WH
26. De Quincey, *Autobiographical Sketches*, p. 225
27. MS 41058/8, Westport Estate Papers, NLI
28. David Masson (ed.), *The Collected Writings of Thomas De Quincey* (Edinburgh, 1889), vol. 2, p. 335
29. 2nd Marquess of Sligo to Louisa, Marchioness of Sligo, 5 December 1810, Levantine Correspondence of Howe Peter Browne, 2nd Marquess of Sligo, August–December 1810, MSS 74, Box 1, Folder 3, Beinecke Rare Book and Manuscript Library, Yale University (YU)
30. Last Will and Testament of Louisa Catherine, Marchioness of Sligo (facsimile), WH

Chapter 2

1. De Quincey, *Autobiographical Sketches*, p. 212
2. Earl of Altamont to Rev. Dean Peter Browne, 1801 (facsimile), WH
3. Thomas De Quincey, Diary, 1803, p.221, NLI
4. MS 41094/2, Westport Estate Papers, NLI
5. *Ibid.*
6. *Ibid.*
7. Admiral Howe to Earl of Altamont, 1793, in Christie's, Manson and Wood, p. 18
8. Peter Somerville-Large, *Dublin* (Dublin, 1981), p. 198
9. Admiral Howe to Earl of Altamont, 1793, in Christie's, Manson and Wood, p. 18
10. George III to Lady Howe, 2 July 1794 (facsimile), WH
11. Lady Mary Howe to Countess of Altamont, 2 July 1794 (facsimile), WH
12. *Ibid.*

13. Admiral Howe to Earl of Altamont, 1794, Christie's, Manson and Wood, p. 20
14. *Ibid.*
15. Earl of Altamont to Mr Cooke, 27 November 1796, SPO 620/26/82, London, p. 290 (facsimile), WH
16. Earl of Altamont to Thomas Pelham, 27 June 1796, SPO 620/26/82, London (facsimile), WH
17. Denis Browne MP to Thomas Pelham, SPO 620/26/82, London, p. 301 (facsimile), WH
18. Admiral Howe to Admiralty, 8 April 1797, Christie's, Manson and Wood, p. 21
19. Earl of Altamont to Rev. Dean Peter Browne, 1 December 1798 (facsimile), WH
20. De Quincey, *Autobiographical Sketches*, p. 205
21. *Ibid.*, p. 210
22. Countess of Altamont to Earl of Altamont, 28 June 1800, MS 40911/3, Westport Estate Papers, NLI
23. Lady Anne Mahon to Anne Browne, September 1798 (facsimile transcript), WH
24. Sheila Mulloy (ed.), *Victory or Glorious Defeat: Biographies of Participants in the Mayo Rebellion of 1798* (Westport, 2010), p. 64
25. De Quincey, *Autobiographical Sketches*, p. 202
26. Countess of Altamont to Earl of Altamont, 8 September 1799, MS 40911/3 (6), Westport Estate Papers, NLI
27. *Ibid.*
28. Tim Card, *Eton Established* (Eton, 2001) p. 87
29. Thomas De Quincey, *Confessions of an English Opium-Eater* (London, 1997), p. 50
30. Earl of Altamont to Rev. Dean Peter Browne, 21 November 1799 (facsimile), WH
31. *Ibid.*
32. 'The Invisible Muse of Don Juan', *New York Times*, 4 February 2010
33. Masson, p. 165
34. Countess of Altamont to Earl of Altamont, 4 June 1800, MS 40911/3, Westport Estate Papers, NLI
35. De Quincey, *Autobiographical Sketches*, p. 163
36. *Ibid.*, p. 167
37. *Ibid.*, p. 195

38. *Ibid.*, p. 196
39. *Ibid.*, p. 200
40. *Ibid.*
41. *Ibid.*, p. 182
42. *Ibid.*
43. Countess of Altamont to Earl of Altamont, 6 August 6 1800, MS 40911/3, Westport Estate Papers, NLI
44. Masson, p. 19
45. De Quincey, *Autobiographical Sketches*, p. 209
46. *Ibid.*, p. 212
47. *Ibid.*
48. Earl of Altamont to Rev. Dean Peter Browne, 30 December 1798 (facsimile), WH
49. De Quincey, *Autobiographical Sketches*, p. 218
50. *Ibid.*, p. 217
51. *Ibid.*, p. 220
52. *Ibid.*, p. 223
53. *Ibid.*
54. *Ibid.*, p. 224
55. Robert Morrison, *The English Opium Eater: A Biography of Thomas De Quincey* (London, 2009), p. 43
56. De Quincey, *Autobiographical Sketches*, p. 336
57. MS 40911/3, Westport Estate Papers, NLI
58. Marchioness of Sligo to Rev. Dean Peter Browne, 2 June 1800, MS 41058/8, Westport Estate Papers, NLI
59. *Ibid.*
60. *Ibid.*
61. De Quincey, *Confessions*, p. 169
62. *Ibid.*, p. 170

Chapter 3

1. E.K. Chambers, *Samuel Taylor Coleridge: A Biographical Study* (London, 1938), p. 78
2. Arthur Gray and Frederick Brittain, *Jesus College Cambridge: A History* (Cambridge, 1979) p. 152
3. Leslie A. Marchand (ed.), *Byron's Letters and Journals* (Harvard, 1973–82), vol. 1, p. 111

4. De Quincey, *Autobiographical Sketches*, p. 54

5. Marchand, vol. 1, p. 80

6. Marchioness of Sligo to Marquess of Sligo, 30 August 1803, MS 40911/6, Westport Estate Papers, NLI

7. Chambers, *Coleridge*, p. 79

8. MS 40911/6, Westport Estate Papers, NLI

9. Accounts of Rebellion in Ireland, Thomas Wilson Croker to Marquess of Sligo, 26 August 1803, MS 40911/2, Westport Estate Papers, NLI

10. Parliamentary Debates, King's Address to Parliament, 22 November 1803 (facsimile), WH

11. *Ibid.*

12. Henry Angelo, *Pic Nic or Table Talk, Including Numerous Recollections of Public Characters* (London, 1830), p. 536

13. Gray and Brittain, p. 143

14. E.H. Coleridge and E. Rowlands (eds), *The Works of Lord Byron* (London, 1898), vol. 1, p. 122

15. Rowland E. Prothero (ed.), *The Works of Lord Byron with Letters and Journals* (1898–1904), vol. 11, p. 117

16. Thomas Moore (ed.), *Life of Byron: Letters and Journals of Lord Byron, with Notices of His Life* (London, 1830), vol. 1, p. 113

17. Coleridge and Rowlands, vol. 1, p. 118

18. Lesley Blanch (ed.), *Harriette Wilson's Memoirs* (London, 2003), p. 237

19. *Ibid.*, p. 239

20. *Ibid.*, p. 240

21. Moore, vol. 1, p. 240

22. Frances Wilson, *The Courtesan's Revenge* (London, 2003), p. 68

23. Angelo, p. 161

24. Coleridge and Rowlands, vol. 1, p. 51

25. Lucy Jago, *Regency House Party* (London, 2004), p. 64

26. De Quincey, *Autobiographical Sketches*, p. 320

27. Duke of Bedford to Marquess of Sligo, October 1806 (facsimile), WH

28. Marquess of Sligo to Earl of Altamont, 1808 (facsimile), WH

29. Marquess of Sligo to Thomas Metcalf, London, 1808, MS 41080/27, Westport Estate Papers, NLI

30. Earl of Altamont to Rev. Dean Peter Browne, 31 December 1808 (facsimile), WH

31. *Morning Post*, 13 January 1809

Chapter 4

1. *The Bury and Norwich Post*, 8 March 1809
2. 2nd Marquess of Sligo to Marchioness of Sligo, 1809 (facsimile), WH
3. John Galt, *The Life of Lord Byron* (London, 2008), p. 42
4. Coleridge and Rowland, vol. 1, p. 171
5. Sligo to Marchioness of Sligo, 13 January 1810 (facsimile), WH
6. Sligo to George Glendenning, 10 December 1810, Levantine Correspondence, box 1, folder, YB
7. Fiona MacCarthy, *Byron: Life and Legend* (London, 2002), p. 90
8. *Ibid.*
9. Rev. William Otter, *Life and Remains of Edward Daniel Clarke* (New York, 1827), p. 549
10. *Ibid.*, p. 426
11. *Ibid.*, p. 400
12. *Ibid.*, p. 425
13. *Ibid.*, p. 502
14. *Morning Chronicle*, 21 December 1809
15. Sligo to Marchioness of Sligo, 5 January 1810 (facsimile), WH
16. A Journal of a Tour, December 1809–May 1810, 2nd Marquess of Sligo (facsimile), WH
17. *Ibid.*, 25 December 1809
18. *Ibid.*, 10 January 1810
19. *Ibid.*
20. *Ibid.*, 28 April 1810
21. Sligo to Marchioness of Sligo, 5 December 1810, Levantine Correspondence, box 1, folder 3, YB
22. A Journal of a Tour, WH
23. *Ibid.*, 6 February 1810
24. Charles Lewis Meryon, *Travels of Lady Hester Stanhope, Forming the Completion of Her Memoirs Narrated by Her Physician, Charles Lewis Meryon* (London, 1846), p. 18
25. Lorna Gibb, *Lady Hester: Queen of the East* (London, 2005), p. 62
26. Sligo to Marchioness of Sligo, 18 December 1810, Levantine Correspondence, box 1, folder 4, YB
27. Duchess of Cleveland (ed.), *The Life and Letters of Lady Hester Stanhope, 1776–1839* (London, 1914), p. 119
28. Sligo to Marchioness of Sligo, 28 March 1810, Levantine Correspondence, box 1, folder 3, YB

29. A Journal of a Tour, WH
30. *Ibid.*
31. *Ibid.*
32. *Ibid.*
33. *Ibid.*
34. 2nd Marchioness of Sligo to George Hildebrand, 20 March 1845, Correspondence of Hester Catherine de Burgh, 2nd Marchioness of Sligo, Ireland's Great Hunger Institute, Quinnipiac University, Connecticut
35. Sligo to Marchioness of Sligo, 6 June 1810 (facsimile), WH
36. Cleveland, p. 110
37. A Journal of a Tour, WH
38. *Ibid.*
39. Sligo to Marchioness of Sligo, 6 June 1810 (facsimile), WH
40. A Journal of a Tour, WH
41. *Ibid.*

Chapter 5

1. Otter, p. 485
2. Peter E. Laurent, *Recollections of a Classical Tour* (London, 1821), p. 163
3. A Journal of a Tour, WH
4. *Ibid.*
5. Sligo to George Caldwell, 16 November 1810, Levantine Correspondence, box 1, folder 5, YB
6. *Ibid.*
7. A Journal of a Tour, WH
8. Sligo to Marchioness of Sligo, 25 August 1810, Levantine Correspondence, box 1, folder 5, YB
9. A Journal of a Tour, WH
10. Sligo to Marchioness of Sligo, 3 August 1810, Levantine Correspondence, box 1, folder 5, YB
11. *Ibid.*
12. Marchand, vol. 2, pp. 7–8
13. Sligo to Marchioness of Sligo, 24 July 1810, Levantine Correspondence, box 1, folder 5, YB
14. Marchand, 29 July 1810, vol. 2, p. 5
15. Moore, vol. 1, p. 113

16. John B. Priestly, *A Selection from Thomas Moore's Diary* (Cambridge, 1925), p. 125
17. Sligo to Marchioness of Sligo, 3 August 1810, Levantine Correspondence, box 1, folder 5
18. Moore, p. 110
19. Marchand, vol. 2, p. 29
20. *Ibid.*
21. A Journal of a Tour, WH
22. Sligo to Marchioness of Sligo, 3 August 1810, Levantine Correspondence, box 1, folder 1, YB
23. Barthold to Marchioness of Sligo, 7 November 1810, MS 41008/1, Westport Estate Papers, NLI
24. Sligo to Marchioness of Sligo, 3 August 1810, Levantine Correspondence, box 1, folder 1, YB
25. MacCarthy, p. 127
26. Sligo to Marchioness of Sligo, 3 August 1810, Levantine Correspondence, box 1, folder 1, YB
27. *Ibid.*
28. *Ibid.*
29. A Journal of a Tour, WH
30. Sligo to Marchioness of Sligo, 3 August 1810, Levantine Correspondence, box 1, folder 1, YB
31. *Ibid.*
32. *Ibid.*
33. A Journal of a Tour, WH
34. Sligo to Marchioness of Sligo, 3 August 1810, Levantine Correspondence, box 1, folder 1, YB
35. *Ibid.*
36. *The Times*, 13 March 1905
37. Sligo to Marchioness of Sligo, 3 August 1810, Levantine Correspondence, box 1, folder 1, YB
38. Sligo to Trustees, 18 February 1905, Correspondence with the 5th Marquess of Sligo, Department of Greek and Roman Antiquities, British Museum
39. *Ibid.*
40. *Ibid.*
41. Sligo to Marchioness of Sligo, 15 September 1810, Levantine Correspondence, box 1, folder 2, YB

42. A Journal of a Tour, July 1810, WH
43. Sligo to Marchioness of Sligo, 3 August 1810, Levantine Correspondence, box 1, folder 1, YB
44. Sligo to George Caldwell and others, September 1810, Levantine Correspondence, box 1, folders 1–5, YB
45. *Ibid.*
46. *Ibid.*
47. *Ibid.*
48. Marchand, vol. 2, pp. 11–14
49. Moore, vol. 1, p. 81
50. MS 41088/1, Westport Estate Papers, National Library of Ireland, NLI
51. Sligo to Marchioness of Sligo, 25 August 1810, Levantine Correspondence, box 1, folder 1, YB
52. *Ibid.*
53. *Ibid.*
54. Kirsten Ellis, *Star of the Morning: The Extraordinary Life of Lady Hester Stanhope* (London, 2008), p. 166
55. Sligo to Marchioness of Sligo, 15 September 1810, Levantine Correspondence, box 1, folder 2, YB
56. Gibb, p. 61
57. Sligo to Marchioness of Sligo, 15 September 1810, Levantine Correspondence, box 1, folder 2, YB
58. Marchand, vol. 2, p. 14
59. Marchioness of Sligo to George Hildebrand, 5 January 1846, no. 30, Correspondence of Hester de Burgh, QU
60. Cleveland, p. 96
61. Marchand, vol. 2, p. 14
62. Sligo to George Caldwell, 24 September 1810, Levantine Correspondence, box 1, folder 5, YB
63. Arthur Aspinall (ed.), *Correspondence of George Prince of Wales, 1770–1812* (London, 1963–71), vol. 5, no. 3141, p. 90
64. Moore, vol. 1, p. 81
65. Sligo to George Caldwell, 20 September 1810, Levantine Correspondence, box 1, folder 5, YB
66. *Ibid.*
67. Galt, p. 126
68. *Ibid.*

69. Sligo to Byron, 5 November 1810, MS 169-09, Byron Letters, John Murray Archive, NLS
70. Sligo to Byron, 31 August 1813, Byron Letters, NLS
71. Galt, p. 125
72. Report, 8 December 1904, Cecil Sharp, British Museum
73. A Journal of a Tour, WH
74. Sligo to Marchioness of Sligo, 8 October 1810, Levantine Correspondence, box 1, folder 2, YB
75. *Ibid.*
76. *Ibid.*

Chapter 6

1. MacCarthy, p. 131
2. Sligo to George Caldwell, 24 December 1810, Levantine Correspondence, box 1, folder 5, YB
3. *Ibid.*
4. Sligo to George Glendenning, 6 December 1810, Levantine Correspondence, box 1, folder 6, YB
5. Sligo to Marchioness of Sligo, 26 November 1810, Levantine Correspondence, box 1, folder 2, YB
6. Sligo to Marchioness of Sligo, 15 October 1810, Levantine Correspondence, box 1, folder 2, YB
7. *Ibid.*
8. *Ibid.*
9. *Ibid.*
10. Charles Meryon, *Memoirs of Lady Hester Stanhope as Related by Herself in Conversation with Her Physician; Comprising Her Opinions and Anecdotes of Some of the Most Remarkable Persons of Her Time* (London, 1845), p. 48
11. Sligo to Byron, 10 December 1810, Byron Letters, NLS
12. Sligo to Marchioness of Sligo, 26 November 1810, Levantine Correspondence, box 1, folder 2, YB
13. *Ibid.*
14. Sligo to Byron, 10 December 1810, Byron Letters, NLS
15. Cleveland, p. 106
16. Sligo to Marchioness of Sligo, 14 November 1810, Levantine Correspondence, box 1, folder 2, YB

17. *Ibid.*
18. Sligo to Glendenning, 14 November 1810, Levantine Correspondence, box 1, folder 2, YB
19. Sligo to Marchioness of Sligo, 18 December 1810, Levantine Correspondence, box 1, folder 4, YB
20. Moore, vol. 2, p. 125
21. Cleveland, p. 110
22. *Annual Register*, Admiralty Sessions 1813, p. 282
23. Sligo to Marchioness of Sligo, 26 November 1810, Levantine Correspondence, box 1, folder 2, YB
24. Sligo to George Caldwell, 16 November 1810, Levantine Correspondence, box 1, folder 5, YB
25. *Ibid.*
26. Sligo to Marchioness of Sligo, 18 December 1810, Levantine Correspondence, box 1, folder 5, YB
27. *Ibid.*
28. Sligo to Byron, 10 December 1810, Byron Letters, NLS
29. Gibb, p. 68
30. Sligo to Marchioness of Sligo, 28 December 1810, Levantine Correspondence, box 1, folder 3, YB
31. *Ibid.*
32. *Ibid.*
33. Cleveland, p. 110
34. Sligo to Byron, 18 March 1811, Byron Letters, NLS
35. *Ibid.*
36. Cleveland, p. 110
37. Sligo to Byron, 18 March 1811, Byron Letters, NLS
38. *Ibid.*
39. Meryon, *Travels*, p. 72
40. Cleveland, p. 177
41. Sligo to Marchioness of Sligo, 18 December 1810, Levantine Correspondence, box 1, folder 4, YB
42. 2nd Marchioness of Sligo to George Hildebrand, 5 January 1846, no. 33, Correspondence of Hester de Burgh, QU
43. A Journal of a Tour, WH
44. *Ibid.*
45. Marchand, vol. 2, pp. 54–5
46. Sligo to Byron, 10 March 1811, Byron Letters, NLS

47. Sligo to Byron, June 1811, Byron Letters, NLS
48. Sligo to Byron, July 1811, Byron Letters, NLS
49. Gibb, p. 75

Chapter 7

1. Fortescue MS, vol. 10, p. 185, Historical Manuscript Commission (1927), NLI
2. Fergus D'Arcy, *Horses, Lords and Racing Men* (Kildare, 1991), p. 65
3. Sligo to Marchioness of Sligo, 15 January 1815, Sligo Papers, no. 21b, TCD
4. F. Ross Mahon, Memorandum, Levantine Correspondence, box 1, folder 7, YB
5. Sligo to Glendenning, 6 December 1811, Levantine Correspondence, box 1, folder 7, YB
6. Sligo to Marchioness of Sligo, 18 December 1810, Levantine Correspondence, box 1, folder 4, YB
7. Sligo to Byron, February 1812, Byron Letters, NLS
8. *Shrewsbury Chronicle*, 1 May 1812
9. Sligo to Marchioness of Sligo, 1 January 1815 (facsimile), WH
10. Moore, vol. 1, p. 240
11. Sligo to Marchioness of Sligo, 20 November 1813 (facsimile), WH
12. *Ibid.*
13. Marchand, vol. 3, p. 90
14. MS 41088/14, Westport Estate Papers, NLI
15. Moore, vol. 1, p. 240
16. *Ibid.*
17. Marchand, vol. 3, pp. 92–3
18. Sligo to Marchioness of Sligo, 20 November 1813, Sligo Papers, no. 18b, TCD
19. MS 40911/4, Westport Estate Papers, NLI
20. Sligo to Marchioness of Sligo, 20 November 1813, Sligo Papers, no. 20a, TCD
21. *Ibid.*
22. Sligo to Marchioness of Sligo, 31 July 1815, Sligo Papers, no. 16, TCD
23. Lord Sligo, World Biographical Information System, BNF, p. 6
24. Affidavit, Lord Sligo, 17 December 1812 (facsimile), WH
25. *Annual Register 1812* (London, 1813), p. 280

26. *Ibid.*, p. 282
27. *The Times*, 17 December 1812
28. *Annual Register 1812*, p. 282
29. *Ibid.*
30. Lord Sligo, World Biographical Information System, BNF, p. 6
31. *Mayo Constitution*, December 1812
32. *The Times*, 18 December 1812
33. 17 February 1813 in Peter Cochrane (ed.), *Hobhouse on the Continent: 1 January 1813–6 February 1814* (2009), p. 326
34. MS 41088/12, Westport Estate Papers, NLI
35. Marchand, vol. 3, p. 27
36. Sligo to Byron, March 1813, Byron Letters, NLS
37. Sligo to Byron, 31 March 1813, Byron Letters, NLS
38. Marchand, vol. 3, p. 9
39. *Ibid.*
40. *The Criminal Law Journal* (London, 1812), vol. 33
41. Terence de Vere White (ed.), 'A Lost Correspondence: Letters from Italy from 2nd Marquess of Sligo to Rt Hon. Lord Lowther', *Twentieth Century*, clxxiii (1958), p. 231
42. Marchioness of Sligo to Sir William Scott, 15 January 1816 (facsimile), WH
43. Sligo to Marchioness of Sligo, 16 July 1815, Sligo Papers, no. 16, TCD
44. Marchioness of Sligo to Sligo, 15 January 1815 (facsimile), WH
45. Sligo to Byron, 5 April 1815, Byron Letters, NLS

Chapter 8

1.   Moore, vol. 1, pp. 419–22
2.   Diary of the 2nd Marquess of Sligo, 1813–14 (facsimile), WH
3.   *Ibid.*
4.   *Ibid.*
5.   *Ibid.*
6.   *Ibid.*
7.   Fraser, *Princesses*, p. 178
8.   Diary of the 2nd Marquess of Sligo, 1813–14 (facsimile), WH
9.   *Ibid.*
10. *Ibid.*, December 1813
11. *Ibid.*

12. Peter Cochran (ed.), *Hobby-O: Lord Byron's Relationship with John Cam Hobhouse* (Cambridge, 2010), p. 244
13. Diary of the 2nd Marquess of Sligo, 1813–14 (facsimile), WH
14. *Ibid.*
15. *Ibid.*
16. *Ibid.*
17. *Ibid.*, August 1814
18. *Ibid.*
19. White, p. 231
20. Sligo to Dowager Marchioness of Sligo, September 1814 (facsimile), WH
21. White, p. 232
22. *Ibid.*
23. *Ibid.*
24. *Ibid.*
25. Lord Broughton (John Cam Hobhouse), *Recollections of a Long Life*, ed. Lady Dorchester (London, 1909), vol. 1, p. 231
26. *Ibid.*
27. Sligo to Marchioness of Sligo, 1 January 1815, Sligo Papers, no. 20a, TCD
28. White, p. 239
29. *Ibid.*, p. 232
30. *Ibid.*, p. 233
31. *Ibid.*
32. *Ibid.*, p. 237
33. *Ibid.*
34. Sligo to Marchioness of Sligo, 1 January 1815, Sligo Papers, no. 20a, TCD
35. *Ibid.*
36. White, p. 235
37. *Ibid.*, p. 243
38. *Ibid.*, p. 239
39. Sligo to Marchioness of Sligo, 1 January 1815, Sligo Papers, no. 20a, TCD
40. White, p. 234
41. Broughton, vol. 1, p. 132
42. White, p. 235
43. *Ibid.*, p. 234

44. H. Colburn (ed.), *Correspondence, Despatches and Other Papers of Robert Steward, Lord Castlereagh* (London, 1850), p. 309

45. A.M.W. Stanley (ed.), *The Letters of Lady Elizabeth Spencer Stanhope* (London, 1814), p. 254

46. White, p. 235

47. *Ibid.*, p. 238

48. *Ibid.*, p. 237

49. *Ibid.*, p. 236

50. *Ibid.*, p. 235

51. *Ibid.*, p. 238

52. *Ibid.*, p. 240

53. *Ibid.*

54. *Ibid.*

55. *Ibid.*

56. *Ibid.*, p. 241

57. *Ibid.*, p. 243

58. Sligo to Marchioness of Sligo, 1 January 1815, Sligo Papers, no. 20, TCD

59. *Ibid.*, no. 21b

60. White, p. 243

61. MS 41058/6, Westport Estate Papers, NLI

62. Foundation Napoleon, Paris

63. Caroline Bonaparte to Letizia Bonaparte, March 1815 in Alde, *Catalogue*, Lot no. 72 (Paris, 1973)

64. Caroline Bonaparte, Queen of Naples, to the Emperor, March 1815 (facsimile), WH

65. Elisa, Princess of Luca and Piombino, c. March 1815 (facsimile), WH

66. Sligo to Marchioness of Sligo, April 1815 (facsimile), WH

Chapter 9

1. Marchioness of Sligo to Sir William Scott, 16 January 1816 (facsimile), WH

2. Sligo to Marchioness of Sligo, 3 October 1815, Sligo Papers, no. 22, TCD

3. Sligo to Marchioness of Sligo, 15 January 1815, Sligo Papers, no. 5, TCD

4. Sligo to Marchioness of Sligo, 8 July 1815, Sligo Papers, no. 13, TCD

5. *Ibid.*

6.   William M. Thackeray, *The Irish Sketch Book* (London, 1902), p. 230

7.   *Cathair na Mart: Journal of the Westport Historical and Archaeological Society*, 2.1 (1982), p. 40

8.   MS 41058/6, Westport Estate Papers, NLI

9.   Sligo to Marchioness of Sligo, 22 July 1815, Sligo Papers, no. 19, TCD

10. *Ibid.*

11. Sligo to Marchioness of Sligo, 24 October 1815, Sligo Papers, no. 24, TCD

12. Sligo to Marchioness of Sligo, 19 July 1815, Sligo Papers, no. 9, TCD

13. Robert Browne to Marchioness of Sligo, 19 July 1815, Sligo Papers, no. 8, TCD

14. Sligo to Marchioness of Sligo, 31 July 1815, Sligo Papers, no. 16, TCD

15. Sligo to Marchioness of Sligo, 27 and 29 July 1815, Sligo Papers, nos. 13/14, TCD

16. Sligo to Marchioness of Sligo, 31 July 1815, Sligo Papers, no. 16, TCD

17. Sligo to Marchioness of Sligo, 12 August 1815, Sligo Papers, no. 17, TCD

18. Sligo to Marchioness of Sligo, 31 August 1815, Sligo Papers, no. 18, TCD

19. Sligo to Marchioness of Sligo, 22 October 1815, Sligo Papers, no. 24, TCD

20. Tony and Annie Sweeney, *The Sweeney Guide to the Irish Turf from 1501–2001* (Dublin, 2002), p. 80

21. Sligo to Marchioness of Sligo, 1 January 1815, Sligo Papers, no. 20a, TCD

22. *Racing Calendar* (London, 1814)

23. Thoroughbred Heritage, Historic Sires, Portraits: Waxy, www.ibheritage.com

24. Sligo to G.W. Chad, Norfolk, November 1816 (facsimile), WH

25. Keith R. Binney, *Horsemen of the First Frontier, 1788–1900* (Australia, 2005), p. 102

26. *The Sydney Gazette and New South Wales Advertiser*, 24 November 1832

27. *Ibid.*

28. Sligo to Marchioness of Sligo, 28 December 1815, Sligo Papers, no. 35, TCD

29. J.C. Beckett, *The Making of Modern Ireland* (London, 1966), p. 294

30. Sligo to Marchioness of Sligo, 15 October 1815, Sligo Papers, no. 20, TCD

31. MS40911/6, Westport Estate Papers, NLI
32. Sligo to Lord Strangford, 19 November 1815 (facsimile), WH
33. *Ibid.*
34. Sligo to James Caldwell, 15 November 1815, Sligo Papers, no. 26, TCD
35. *Ibid.*
36. *Ibid.*
37. Francis Macirone, *The Fall and Death of Joachim Murat* (London, 1817), p. 142
38. Sligo to Marchioness of Sligo, 19 November 1815, Sligo Papers, no. 27, TCD
39. Sligo to Marchioness of Sligo, 20 December 1815, Sligo Papers, no. 29, TCD

Chapter 10

1.   Frances Wilson, *The Courtesan's Revenge* (London, 2003), p. 168
2.   MacCarthy, p. 415
3.   Sligo to Marchioness of Sligo, 20 October 1815, Sligo Papers, no. 20, TCD
4.   Sligo to Marchioness of Sligo, Sligo Papers, no. 22, TCD
5.   Sligo to Marchioness of Sligo, Sligo Papers, no. 23, TCD
6.   *Ibid.*
7.   Browne family notes (facsimile), WH
8.   Sligo to George Caldwell, 31 January 1816, Sligo Papers, no. 39, TCD
9.   Marchioness of Sligo to Sligo, 5 February 1816, Sligo Papers, no. 42, TCD
10. Marchioness of Sligo to Lady Catherine de Burgh, 5 February 1816 (facsimile), WH
11. Marchioness of Sligo to Rev. Dean Peter Browne, 19 February 1816 (facsimile), WH
12. Marchioness of Sligo to Countess of Clanricarde, 5 February 1816 (facsimile), WH
13. Sir William Scott to Sligo, 5 February 1816 (facsimile), WH
14. Sligo to George Caldwell, 31 January 1816, Sligo Papers, no. 39, TCD
15. Sligo to George Caldwell, 5 February 1816, Sligo Papers, no. 43, TCD
16. Sligo to George Caldwell, 31 January 1816, Sligo Papers, no. 38, TCD
17. Sligo to George Caldwell, 4 February 1816, Sligo Papers, no. 40, TCD

18. Sligo to George Caldwell, 5 February 1816, Sligo Papers, no. 41, TCD
19. Sligo to George Caldwell, 4 February 1816, Sligo Papers, no. 40, TCD
20. MS41058/6, Westport Estate Papers, NLI
21. Marchioness of Sligo to Sligo, 16 January 1816 (facsimile), WH
22. *Ibid.*
23. Marchioness of Sligo to Sligo, 19 May 1816 (facsimile), WH
24. Sligo to Dowager Marchioness of Sligo, May 1817, Sligo Papers, no. 62, TCD
25. Marchioness of Sligo to Dowager Marchioness of Sligo, 3 March 1817, MS40911/4, Westport Estate Papers NLI
26. *Ibid.*
27. Sligo to Bloomfield, 20 June 1816, Geo/Main/26714-5, Royal Archives, Windsor Castle (RA)
28. Dowager Marchioness of Sligo to Sligo, 29 February 1817, Sligo Papers, no. 45, TCD
29. *Ibid.*
30. Sligo to Dowager Marchioness of Sligo, 2 May 1817, Sligo Papers, no. 47, TCD
31. Marchioness of Sligo to Dowager Marchioness of Sligo, 24 March 1817, Sligo Papers, no. 52, TCD
32. Sligo to Dowager Marchioness of Sligo, 28 March 1817, Sligo Papers, no. 56, TCD
33. Sligo to Dowager Marchioness of Sligo, 18 April 1817, Sligo Papers, no. 57, TCD
34. Marchioness of Sligo to Dowager Marchioness of Sligo, 15 April 1817, Sligo Papers, no. 58, TCD
35. Sligo to Dowager Marchioness of Sligo, 1 May 1817, Sligo Papers, no. 60, TCD
36. Sligo to Dowager Marchioness of Sligo, 18 April 1817, Sligo Papers, no. 59, TCD
37. Sligo to Dowager Marchioness of Sligo, 1 May 1817, Sligo Papers, no. 60, TCD
38. Sligo to Dowager Marchioness of Sligo, 18 April 1817, Sligo Papers, no. 59, TCD
39. Sligo to Dowager Marchioness of Sligo, 16 April 1817, Sligo Papers, no. 57, TCD
40. Will and Last Testament of Louisa Catherine, Dowager Marchioness of Sligo (facsimile), WH

41. *The Late Elections: An Impartial Statement of All Proceedings* (London, 1818), p. 486

42. *Ibid.*, p. 487

43. Denis Browne, *A Letter from the Right Hon. Denis Browne MP for Kilkenny to the Most Noble Marquess of Wellesley on the Present State of Ireland* (London, 1822), Pamphlets 668, no. 6, p. 9, NLI

44. T.H.B. Oldfield, *The Representative History of Great Britain and Ireland* (London, 1816), vol. 4, p. 276

45. *Ibid.*, p. 297

46. Sligo to George Glendenning, 26 December 1824, Sligo letter book (MS), WH

47. Sligo to His Royal Highness, The Duke of York, 12 June 1824, Sligo letter book (MS), WH

48. Browne family notes (facsimile), WH

49. *Ibid.*

50. Saul David, *Prince of Pleasure: the Prince of Wales and the Making of the Regency* (London, 1999), p. 400

51. Ione Leigh, *Castlereagh* (London, 1951), p. 334

52. Sligo to His Royal Majesty, George IV RA/Geo/Main 22578-81, RA

53. Sligo diary, 1821–22 (facsimile), WH

54. *Ibid.*

55. George Hildebrand to Marquess of Sligo, undated (facsimile), WH

56. Sligo diary, 1821–22 (facsimile), WH

57. *Ibid.*

58. *Ibid.*

59. Denis Browne to Sligo, 12 September 1822, Sligo Papers, no. 93, TCD

60. *Cathair na Mart: Journal of the Westport Historical and Archaeological Society* (1986), p. 48

61. Denis Browne to Sligo, 15 October 1822, Sligo Papers, no. 93, TCD

62. Peter Browne to Sligo, 12 September 1822, Sligo Papers, no. 90, TCD

63. Denis Browne to Sligo, 19 July 1822, Sligo Papers, no. 86, TCD

64. Denis Browne to Sligo, 29 July 1822, Sligo Papers, no. 90, TCD

65. Denis Browne to Sligo, 19 July 1822, Sligo Papers, no. 86, TCD

66. Denis Browne to Sligo, 26 August 1822, Sligo Papers, no. 91, TCD

67. *Ibid.*

Chapter 11

1. Denis Browne to Sligo, 26 August 1822, Sligo Papers, no. 91, TCD
2. *Telegraph and Connaught Ranger*, 9 April 1831
3. Sligo to Glendenning, 26 December 1824, Sligo letter book (MS), WH
4. Sligo to Gamy, Curtis & Co., Shipping Agents, London, 7 August 1825, Sligo letter book (MS), WH
5. *Morning Post*, 16 February 1816
6. Sligo to Messrs James Alan & Son, Glasgow, 30 July 1824, Sligo letter book (MS), WH
7. Sligo to Messrs Blackstock, Manchester, 3 March 1825, Sligo letter book (MS), WH
8. *Ibid.*
9. Sligo to Thomas Dillon, MD, 18 May 1824, Sligo letter book (MS), WH
10. MS41044/10, Westport Estate Papers, NLI
11. Sligo to Henry Goulburn, Chief Secretary for Ireland, 19 July 1825, Sligo letter book (MS), WH
12. Sligo to Henry Goulburn, March 1826, Sligo letter book (MS), WH
13. Sligo to Lord Chancellor of Ireland, 8 May 1824, Sligo letter book (MS), WH
14. Sligo to Mrs Carr, 22 January 1825, Sligo letter book (MS), WH
15. Sligo to Lord Chancellor of Ireland, 8 May 1824, Sligo letter book (MS), WH
16. *Ibid.*
17. Sligo to James Carr, 21 February 1825, Sligo letter book (MS), WH
18. *Telegraph and Connaught Ranger*, 11 January 1832
19. *Ibid.*
20. *Ibid.*
21. Sligo to Charles Fitzgerald Higgins, 9 June 1827, Sligo letter book (MS), WH
22. Sligo to Henry Goulburn, 20 November 1824, Sligo letter book (MS), WH
23. Sligo to Henry Goulburn, 6 August 1826, Sligo letter book (MS), WH
24. Sligo to Rev. T. Walker, 4 October 1826, Sligo letter book (MS), WH
25. *Ibid.*

26. *Ibid.*
27. *Ibid.*
28. *Mayo Constitution*, 27 December 1827
29. Elizabeth Mathews to Sligo, December 1823, Sligo Papers no. 96, TCD
30. Sligo to Lord Strangford, 20 September 1827 (facsimile), WH
31. MacCarthy, p. 534
32. Sligo to Lord Kilmaine, 17 January 1826, Sligo letter book (MS), WH
33. T.W. Moody and F.X. Martin (eds), *The Course of Irish History* (Cork, 1994)
34. Sligo to Henry Goulburn, 15 December 1824, Sligo letter book (MS), WH
35. *Ibid.*
36. *Ibid.*
37. House of Commons Debate, 10 February 1825, Right Hon. Denis Browne, MP (facsimile), WH
38. *Ibid.*
39. *The Quarterly Theological Review and Ecclesiastical Record*, vol. 2, p. 206
40. Sligo to Right Hon. Charles Wynne, 12 April 1826, Sligo letter book (MS), WH
41. Sligo to Metcalf, 17 November 1825, Sligo letter book (MS), WH
42. Sligo to Louisa Moore, 19 May 1826, Sligo letter book (MS), WH
43. Sligo to Henry Goulburn, 7 December 1825, Sligo letter book (MS), WH
44. Sligo to Louisa Moore, 18 June 1826, Sligo letter book (MS), WH
45. Sligo to John Knox, 25 August 1826, Sligo letter book (MS), WH
46. *Ibid.*
47. Sligo to Denis Bingham, 14 October 1824, Sligo letter book (MS), WH
48. Sligo to Henry Goulburn, 7 December 1825, Sligo letter book (MS), WH
49. Sligo to Major Edward Browne, 27 March 1827, Sligo letter book (MS), WH
50. Sligo to Harry Browne, 28 August 1825, Sligo letter book (MS), WH
51. Sligo to Major Edward Browne, 24 March 1826, Sligo letter book (MS), WH
52. Sligo to Daniel O'Connell, 27 January 1826, Sligo letter book (MS), WH

53. Sligo to George Browne, 13 March 1826, Sligo letter book (MS), WH

54. Sligo to Major Edward Browne, 25 May 1826, Sligo letter book (MS), WH

55. Sligo to Lord Kilmaine, 14 June 1826, Sligo letter book (MS), WH

56. Sligo to Archbishop of Tuam, 10 December 1827, Sligo letter book (MS), WH

57. *Ibid.*

58. Sligo to Denis Browne, 5 September 1826, Sligo letter book (MS), WH

59. Sligo to Rev. William Hamilton Maxwell, 20 July 1826, Sligo letter book (MS), WH

60. Sligo to Metcalf, 19 August 1826, Sligo letter book (MS), WH

61. Sligo to Charles FitzGerald Higgins, 16 December 1826, Sligo letter book (MS), WH

62. Sligo to Henry Goulburn, 7 September 1826, Sligo letter book (MS), WH

63. Sligo to George Glendenning, 20 October 1829, Sligo letter book (MS), WH

64. Sligo to Denis Browne, 8 August 1826, Sligo letter book (MS), WH

65. Sligo to Rev. Maxwell, 20 July 1826, Sligo letter book (MS), WH

66. Sligo to George Canning, 24 May 1827, Sligo letter book (MS), WH

Chapter 12

1. Sligo to Colonel Fitzgerald, 24 November 1826, Sligo letter book (facsimile), WH

2. Sligo to Mr Blake, 28 August 1827, Sligo letter book (facsimile), WH

3. Patrick M. Geoghegan, *King Dan: The Rise of Daniel O'Connell, 1775–1829* (Dublin, 2008), p. 241

4. Sligo to Lady Molyneaux, 1 June 1827, Sligo letter book (facsimile), WH

5. Sligo to Lord Strangford, August 1827, Sligo letter book (facsimile), WH

6. *Ibid.*

7. Philip Mansel, *Paris between the Empires, 1814–1852* (London, 2001) p. 121

8. Sligo to Lord Strangford, 22 November 1827 (facsimile), WH

9. Testimony of George Christie (undated) (facsimile), WH
10. Sligo to Lord Strangford, 22 November 1827 (facsimile), WH
11. *Ibid.*
12. *Ibid.*
13. Christopher Hibbert, *George IV* (London, 1973), p. 728
14. Sligo to Lord Strangford, 11 March 1828 (facsimile), WH
15. Sligo to Duke of Wellington, 30 July 1828, Sligo letter book (facsimile), WH
16. *Ibid.*
17. Elizabeth Longford, *Wellington* (London, 1992), p. 397
18. Sligo to Dr Oliver Kelly, Archbishop of Tuam, 28 August 1828, Sligo letter book (facsimile), WH
19. *Ibid.*
20. Sligo to John Browne, 12 July 1828, Sligo Papers, no. 130, TCD
21. Sligo to Dr Oliver Kelly, 17 March 1828, Sligo letter book (facsimile), WH
22. Sligo to Lord Strangford, 17 May 1831 (facsimile), WH
23. *Mayo Constitution*, 18 August 1828
24. Denis Browne to Sligo, 6 August 1828 (facsimile), WH
25. *Ibid.* (note in Sligo's hand)
26. Sligo to W. Pundon, 7 November 1831, Sligo letter book (facsimile), WH
27. Denis Browne, *Letter*, p. 16
28. *Ibid.*
29. Sligo to Henry Blake, 29 August 1826, Sligo letter book (MS), WH
30. Sligo to Lord Chancellor of Ireland, 13 September 1828, Sligo letter book (facsimile), WH
31. Sligo to Lord Strangford, 30 December 1828 (facsimile), WH
32. Sligo to Mrs Tuite, 20 November 1831, Sligo letter book (facsimile), WH
33. Family notes of 5th Marquess of Sligo (facsimile), WH
34. Sligo to George Browne, February 1829, Sligo letter book (facsimile), WH
35. *Mayo Constitution*, 19 March 1829
36. *Mayo Constitution*, 25 May 1829
37. *Ibid.*
38. *Mayo Constitution*, 8 June 1829
39. Sligo to George Browne, 23 September 1829, Sligo letter book (facsimile), WH

40. Sligo to Sir John Burke, 22 October 1829, Sligo letter book (facsimile), WH

41. Sligo to Sir John Burke, 19 December 1829, Sligo letter book (facsimile), WH

42. Sligo to John Puget, 17 January 1830, Sligo letter book (facsimile), WH

43. Sligo to George Browne, 30 October 1829, Sligo letter book (facsimile), WH

44. Sligo to George Browne, July 1830, Sligo letter book (facsimile), WH

45. *Ibid.*

46. *Telegraph and Connaught Ranger*, 19 January 1830

47. Sligo to Lord Strangford, January 1830 (facsimile), WH

48. *Telegraph and Connaught Ranger*, 30 December 1830

49. *Ibid.*

50. Sligo to Marquess of Anglesey, 25 December 1830, Sligo letter book (facsimile), WH

51. *Telegraph and Connaught Ranger*, 30 December 1830

52. Daniel O'Connell MP, House of Commons Debate, 21 March 1830 (facsimile), WH

53. Sligo to Sir Samuel O'Malley, 6 December 1830, Sligo letter book (facsimile), WH

54. Sligo to Lord Strangford, 17 May 1831 (facsimile), WH

55. Gearóid Ó Tuathaigh, *Ireland before the Famine, 1798–1848* (Dublin, 1979), p. 162

56. Sligo to Marquess of Anglesey, 25 December 1830, Sligo letter book (facsimile), WH

57. *Ibid.*

58. *Ibid.*

59. Sligo to Lord Strangford, 24 December 1830 (facsimile), WH

60. Sligo to Marquess of Anglesey, 25 December 1830, Sligo letter book (facsimile), WH

61. Marquess of Anglesey to Lord Holland, 20 April 1830, Anglesey Papers, D619/32, Public Records Office of Northern Ireland, PRONI

62. Sligo to Lord Strangford, 28 January 1831 (facsimile), WH

63. *Ibid.*

64. Sligo to E.G. Stanley, Chief Secretary for Ireland, January 1831, Sligo letter book (facsimile), WH

65. Sligo to Lord Strangford, 28 January 1831 (facsimile), WH

66. Lord Goderich to Sligo, 24 February 1831 (facsimile), WH
67. Sligo to Lord Strangford, 28 July 1831 (facsimile), WH
68. E.G. Stanley to Sligo, 4 March 1831, Sligo Papers, no. 181, TCD
69. Sligo to Prime Minister Lord Grey, Political and Public Papers of Charles, 2nd Earl Grey, NRA 6228 Grey; GRE-B52/7/5, Durham University Library, DU
70. *Ibid.*
71. Sligo to E.G. Stanley, 2 January 1831, Sligo letter book (facsimile), WH
72. *Telegraph and Connaught Ranger*, 9 April 1831
73. *Ibid.*
74. *Ibid.*
75. Lord Grey to Sligo, 6 June 1831, GBE/B52/7/4, DU
76. *Telegraph and Connaught Ranger*, 9 April 1831
77. *Ibid.*
78. Marquess of Anglesey to Lord Holland, 18 April 1831, Anglesey Papers, D 619/25–43, PRONI
79. *Telegraph and Connaught Ranger*, 9 April 1831
80. *Mayo Constitution*, 14 April 1831
81. Family papers (facsimile), WH
82. *Telegraph and Connaught Ranger*, 1 June 1831
83. Sligo to Viscount Morpeth, 15 June 1840, Sligo letter book (facsimile), WH
84. *Telegraph and Connaught Ranger*, 4 May 1831
85. Sligo to Lord Strangford, 17 May 1831 (facsimile), WH
86. Sligo to Richard Sharpe, 28 January 1831, Sligo letter book (facsimile), WH
87. Sligo Private and Confidential Report on the Magistrates of Mayo, November 1831 (facsimile), Lord Lieutenant letter book, WH (Lord Sligo was appointed Lord Lieutenant of County Mayo in September 1831)
88. *Ibid.*
89. Sligo to Colonel Jackson, 26 September 1831, Lord Lieutenant letter book (facsimile), WH
90. Sligo to G. N. Knox, 17 November 1831, Lord Lieutenant letter book (facsimile), WH
91. Sligo to Archbishop of Tuam, 26 November 1831, Sligo letter book (facsimile)

92. Sligo to E.G. Stanley, 23 November 1831, Lord Lieutenant letter book (facsimile), WH

93. Sligo to Rev. Patrick Gibbons, 10 October 1828, Sligo letter book (facsimile), WH

94. Sligo to George Glendenning, 20 October 1826, Sligo letter book (facsimile), WH

95. Sligo to Sir William Gosset, Chief Secretary of Ireland, 17 December 1832, Lord Lieutenant letter book (facsimile), WH

96. Sligo to Sir William Gosset, Chief Secretary of Ireland, 8 March 1833, Lord Lieutenant letter book (facsimile), WH

97. 'Frederick Cavendish and the Early Years of the *Connaught Telegraph*', *Connaught Telegraph*, 17 July 2012

98. *Telegraph and Connaught Ranger*, 3 October 1832

99. *Telegraph and Connaught Ranger*, 9 October 1832

100. Sligo to Sir William Brabazon, 24 September 1832, Sligo letter book (facsimile), WH

101. Sligo to Archbishop of Tuam, Dr Oliver Kelly, Sligo letter book (facsimile), WH

102. *Telegraph and Connaught Ranger*, 14 October 1832

103. *Telegraph and Connaught Ranger*, 5 and 12 September 1832

104. Sligo to Sir William Gosset, 17 December 1832, Lord Lieutenant letter book (facsimile), WH

105. Sligo to Colonel Jackson, September 1832, Sligo letter book (facsimile), WH

106. *Telegraph and Connaught Ranger*, 9 February 1845

107. Sligo to E.G. Stanley, 19 September 1832, Sligo letter book (facsimile), WH

108. Eneas MacDonnell to Sligo, 23 November 1823, Sligo Papers, no. 194, TCD

109. *Telegraph and Connaught Ranger*, 2 January 1833

110. Sligo to Marquess of Anglesey, 15 January 1833, Sligo letter book (facsimile), WH

111. *Mayo Constitution*, 12 December 1833

112. *Telegraph and Connaught Ranger*, 13 March 1833

113. Sligo to Sir William Gosset, 17 September 1832, Lord Lieutenant letter book (facsimile), WH

114. Sligo to Sir William Gosset, 22 January 1833, Lord Lieutenant letter book (facsimile), WH

115. Sligo to E.G. Stanley, 17 November 1832, Lord Lieutenant letter book (facsimile), WH

116. *Telegraph and Connaught Ranger*, 13 February 1833

117. Lord Teynham, House of Lords Debate, 18 March 1833 (facsimile), WH

118. Sligo, House of Lords Debate, 18 March 1833 (facsimile), WH

119. Grey, House of Lords Debate, 15 February 1833 (facsimile), WH

120. Sligo, House of Lords Debate, 18 March 1833 (facsimile), WH

121. Teynham, House of Lords Debate (facsimile), WH

122. *Mayo Constitution*, 1 July 1833

123. Sligo to W. Nickhalson, March 1833, Sligo letter book (facsimile), WH

124. Broughton, vol. 4, p. 315

125. *Telegraph and Connaught Ranger*, 4 April 1833

126. *Mayo Constitution*, 10 June 1833

127. Sligo to Marquis of Normanby, 24 January 1839, Sligo letter book (facsimile), WH

128. E.G. Stanley to Sligo, 8 August 1833, Sligo Papers, no. 202, TCD

129. Sligo to George Browne, December 1833, Sligo letter book (facsimile), WH

Chapter 13

1.   *The Citizen's Resource*, Understanding Slavery Initiative (USI) (2007)

2.   Kathleen Mary Butler, *The Economics of Emancipation: Jamaica and Barbados, 1823–1843* (Chapel Hill, 1995), p. 35

3.   Sligo to E.G. Stanley, Colonial Secretary 18 November 1833, Sligo letter book (facsimile), WH

4.   Sligo to Louisa Moore, 27 November 1833, Sligo letter book (facsimile), WH

5.   Sligo to E.G. Stanley, 11 January 1834, Sligo letter book (facsimile), WH

6.   Sligo to George Browne, November 1833, Sligo letter book (facsimile), WH

7.   *Ibid.*

8.   B.W. Higman, *Plantation Jamaica, 1750–1850: Capital and Control in a Colonial Economy* (Jamaica, 2005), p. 26

9.   W.L. Burn, *Emancipation and Apprenticeship in the British West Indies* (London, 1937), p. 37

10. Sligo to Lord Holland, 7 January 1836, Correspondence of Lord Holland, 1834–1840, Add. MS. 51816, British Library, BL

11. Sligo to Alex Bayley, 26 December 1830, Sligo letter book (facsimile), WH

12. Sligo to Gibbs & Bayley, 20 February, 1829, Sligo letter book (facsimile), WH

13. Sligo to William Clarke, 24 January 1826, Sligo letter book (facsimile), WH

14. Sligo to William Gregory, 11 June 1826, Sligo letter book (facsimile), WH

15. Attorney to 1st Marquess of Sligo, 1802, MS409111/1 (2), Westport Estate Papers, NLI

16. James M. Phillippo, *Jamaica, Its Past and Present State* (London, 1843), p. 156

17. Tim Barringer, Gillian Forrester, Barbaro Martinez-Ruiz(eds), *Art and Emancipation in Jamaica: Isaac Mendes Belisario and His Worlds* (New Haven, 2007)

18. Trevor Burnard, *Mastery, Tyranny and Desire* (Kingston, 2004)

19. Richardson Wright, *Revels in Jamaica, 1682–1838* (Jamaica, 1986) p. 126

20. *Ibid.*, p. 128

21. Burnard, p. 103

22. Philip Wright (ed.), *Lady Nugent's Journal of Her Residence in Jamaica, 1801–1805* (Jamaica, 2002), p. 81

23. A.N. Wilson, *The Victorians* (London, 2002), p. 12

24. Wright, *Lady Nugent*, p. 97

25. Burnard, p. 33

26. Sligo to George Browne, 28 December 1828, Sligo letter book (facsimile), WH

27. Sligo to Bayley and Phillips, January 1826, Sligo letter book (facsimile), WH

28. *Ibid.*

29. Sligo to Bayley and Phillips, 17 February 1826, Sligo letter book (facsimile), WH

30. Sligo to Bayley and Phillips, 12 February 1826, Sligo letter book (facsimile), WH

31. Kingston, 2 June 1836, Lord Sligo's newspaper scrapbook (MS), WH

32. Sligo to Alex Bayley, 19 May 1827, Sligo letter book (facsimile), WH

33. *Morning Chronicle*, 18 March 1839

34. 2nd Marquess of Sligo, *Jamaica under the Apprenticeship System, by a Proprietor* (London, 1838)

35. Sligo to Earl of Mulgrave, 10 November 1833, Sligo letter book (facsimile), WH

36. Burn, p. 149

37. Sligo to Rev. Peter Browne, 30 November 1833, Sligo letter book (facsimile), WH

38. Sligo to Messrs Stock & Co, Paris, 12 November 1833, Sligo letter book (facsimile), WH

39. *Ibid.*

40. Sligo to E.G. Stanley, 10 November 1833, Sligo letter book (facsimile), WH

41. Sligo to E.G. Stanley, 22 November 1833, Sligo letter book (facsimile), WH

42. Sligo to Holland, 14 February 1836, Correspondence of Lord Holland, BL

43. Sligo to E.G. Stanley, 23 November 1833, Sligo letter book (facsimile), WH

44. Sligo to George Browne, 9 November 1833, Sligo letter book (facsimile), WH

45. Sligo to George Browne, 23 November 1833, Sligo letter book (facsimile), WH

46. Sligo to King William IV, 10 August 1834, Excerpts from the Letter Book of Howe Peter Browne, 2nd Marquess of Sligo, MS 59, Livingstone Collection no. 4, National Library of Jamaica (NLJ)

47. Sligo to Captain Mason, January 1834, Sligo letter book (facsimile), WH

48. Family notes (facsimile), WH

Chapter 14

1. *Jamaica Despatch*, 17 April 1834

2. *Ibid.*

3. *Jamaica Despatch*, 9 February 1836

4. Sligo to Lord Holland, December 1835, Correspondence of Lord Holland, BL

5. Phillippo, p. 135

6. Sligo to Lord Holland, 20 June 1836, Sligo letter book (facsimile), WH

7. *Jamaica Herald*, 7 January 1836

8. Sligo to Lord Holland, January 1836, Correspondence of Lord Holland, BL

9. James A. Thorne and Joseph H. Kimball, *Emancipation in the West Indies: A Six Month's Tour in Antigua, Barbados and Jamaica* (New York, 1839), p. 329

10. Sligo to Cockburn, 31 August 1834, MSS 228, Letter Books of Howe Peter Browne, 2nd Marquess of Sligo, MS 228, vol. 5, NLJ

11. Peter Abrahams, *Jamaica: An Island Mosaic* (Jamaica, 1957), p. 89

12. Sligo to Lord Holland, 10 July 1834, Correspondence of Lord Holland, BL

13. Sligo, *Jamaica*, p. 32

14. Sligo to Lord Holland, March 1836, Correspondence of Lord Holland, BL

15. Sligo to Lord Holland, 7 January 1836, Correspondence of Lord Holland, BL

16. Sligo, *Jamaica*, p. 8

17. 2nd Marquess of Sligo, *A Letter to the Marquis of Normanby Relative to the Present State of Jamaica* (London, 1839), p. 7

18. Sligo to Lord Holland, 15 November 1835, Correspondence of Lord Holland, BL

19. R.R. Madden, *A Twelvemonth's Residence in the West Indies, during the Transition from Slavery to Apprenticeship* (London, 1835), p. 95

20. Lord Sligo's Jamaican newspaper scrapbook (MS), WH

21. Sligo, *Jamaica*, p. 31

22. Phillippo, p. 65

23. Robert Browne to Sligo, 27 July 1834, Sligo Papers, no. 211, TCD

24. Sligo to Thomas Spring Rice, Letter Books of Howe Peter Browne, MS 228, NLJ

25. Sligo to Lord Holland, 2 July 1834, Correspondence of Lord Holland, BL

26. *Ibid.*

27. Lord Sligo's Jamaican newspaper scrapbook (MS), WH

28. Burn, p.176

29. Sligo to Lord Holland, 10 July 1834, Correspondence of Lord Holland, BL

30. *Accounts and Papers Abolishing Slavery*, vol. 33. part I, Jamaica 1833–1835 (2007), p. 43

31. Sligo, *Jamaica*, p. vi

32. *Royal Gazette*, 22 August 1834

33. Sligo to Lord Holland, 14 February 1836, Correspondence of Lord Holland, BL

34. Sligo to Marquis of Normanby, Sligo letter book (facsimile), WH

35. Thorne and Kimball, p. 367

36. Sligo to Lord Holland, 3 November 1834, Correspondence of Lord Holland, BL

37. Sligo to Lord Holland, 10 July 1834, Correspondence of Lord Holland, BL

38. *Ibid.*

39. Sligo, *Jamaica*, p. 2

40. Phillippo, p. 170

41. Sligo to Spring-Rice, 17 August 1834, Sligo letter book (facsimile), WH

42. Lord Sligo's Jamaican newspaper scrapbook (MS), WH

43. Sligo to King William, 10 August 1834, Excerpts from the Letter Book of Howe Peter Browne, MS 59, vol. 3, NLJ

44. Sligo to Spring-Rice, 13 August 1834, Excerpts from the Letter Book of Howe Peter Browne, MS 59, vol. 3, NLJ

45. Sligo to Lord Holland, Correspondence of Lord Holland, BL

Chapter 15

1. Sligo to Lord Holland, 5 November 1834, Correspondence of Lord Holland, BL

2. Sligo to Lord Holland, 22 July 1835, Correspondence of Lord Holland, BL

3. Sligo to Rev. James Phillippo, 29 June 1835, Excerpts from the Letter Book of Howe Peter Browne, MS 59, vol. 1, NLJ

4. *Ibid.*

5. Sligo to Lord Glenelg, 20 February 1836, Excerpts from the Letter Book of Howe Peter Browne, MS 59, vol. 3, NLJ

6. Sligo to Lord Holland, 10 July 1834, Correspondence of Lord Holland, BL

7. Lord Sligo's Jamaican newspaper scrapbook (MS), WH

8. Sligo to Rev. Peter Browne (undated), Sligo letter book (facsimile), WH

9. Lord Sligo's Jamaican newspaper scrapbook (MS), WH

10. Burn, p.176

11. Sligo to Lord Holland, 7 January 1836, Correspondence of Lord Holland, BL

12. *Ibid.*

13. Sligo to Lord Holland, 25 March 1835, Correspondence of Lord Holland, BL

14. *Ibid.*

15. *Ibid.*

16. Sligo to Lord Holland, 20 May 1835, Correspondence of Lord Holland, BL

17. Instructions to Stipendiary Magistrates Ledger, July 1835, no.4245 (facsimile), WH

18. Sligo to Lord Holland, 24 May 1836, Correspondence of Lord Holland, BL

19. Barringer et al., p.129

20. *Kingston Chronicle,* 29 December 1834 (facsimile), WH

21. *Jamaica Chronicle,* 18 October 1834 (facsimile), WH

22. Sligo to Lord Holland, 28 December 1834, Correspondence of Lord Holland, BL

23. Sligo to Lord Holland, 7 January 1836, Correspondence of Lord Holland, BL

24. Sligo to Lord Holland, 15 May 1835, Correspondence of Lord Holland, BL

25. Sligo to Lord Holland, 7 January 1836, Correspondence of Lord Holland, BL

26. *Ibid.*

27. Lord Sligo's Jamaican newspaper scrapbook (MS), WH

28. *Ibid.*

29. Sligo, *Jamaica,* p. 27

30. *Ibid.,* p. 17

31. Sligo to Lord Holland, 28 December 1834, Correspondence of Lord Holland BL

32. Phillippo, p. 252

33. *Ibid.*

34. Lord Sligo's Jamaican newspaper scrapbook (MS), WH

35. *Ibid.*

36. *Ibid.*
37. Phillippo, p. 220
38. Personal notes of the 11th Marquess of Sligo, 1996
39. Brian L. Kieran, *The Lawless Caymanas* (Cayman Islands, 1992), p. 42
40. Sligo to Lord Holland, 10 May 1835, Correspondence of Lord Holland BL
41. *Ibid.*
42. Kieran, p. 61
43. Sligo to Lord Holland, 10 May 1835, Correspondence of Lord Holland, BL
44. *Ibid.*
45. Sligo, *Jamaica,* p. 60
46. Lord Sligo's Jamaican newspaper scrapbook (MS), WH
47. *Ibid.*
48. *Ibid.*
49. *Ibid.*
50. Sligo to Lord Holland, 13 December 1835, Correspondence of Lord Holland, BL
51. Lord Sligo's Jamaican newspaper scrapbook (MS), WH
52. *Ibid.*
53. *Ibid.*
54. *Ibid.*
55. *Ibid.*
56. *Ibid.*
57. *Ibid.*
58. *Ibid.*
59. *Ibid.*
60. *Ibid.*
61. *Ibid.*
62. *Ibid.*
63. *Ibid.*
64. *Ibid.*
65. Burn, p. 269
66. Lord Sligo's Jamaican newspaper scrapbook (MS), WH
67. *Ibid.*
68. Sligo to Lord Holland, 14 February 1836, Correspondence of Lord Holland, BL
69. Lord Sligo's Jamaican newspaper scrapbook (MS), WH

70. Sligo to Lord Holland, 14 February 1836, correspondence of Lord Holland, BL

71. Lord Sligo's Jamaican newspaper scrapbook (MS), WH

72. Sligo to Lord Holland, 24 May 1836, Correspondence of Lord Holland, BL

73. Lord Sligo's Jamaican newspaper scrapbook (MS), WH

74. Sligo to Lord Holland, 28 May 1836, Correspondence of Lord Holland, BL

75. Sligo to Lord Glenelg, 23 October 1835 (facsimile), WH

76. Lord Sligo's Jamaican newspaper scrapbook (MS), WH

77. *Ibid.*

78. *Ibid.*

79. *Ibid.*

80. *Ibid.*

81. *Ibid.*

82. *Ibid.*

83. *Ibid.*

84. W. Henry Stowell in *Eclectic Review* (London, 1864), p. 94

85. Burn, p. 243

86. Lord Clanricarde to Sligo, 1 May 1836, Sligo Papers, no. 222, TCD

87. Sligo to Lord Holland, 7 January 1836, Correspondence of Lord Holland, BL

88. Lord Clanricarde to Sligo, 27 March 1836, Sligo Papers, no. 220, TCD

89. Stowell, p. 92

90. Lord Sligo's Jamaican newspaper scrapbook (MS), WH

91. *Ibid.*

92. *Sotheby's Catalogue*, 6 December 1983

93. Sligo to Lord Holland, 7 January 1837, Correspondence of Lord Holland, BL

94. Lord Sligo's Jamaican newspaper scrapbook (MS), WH

95. *Ibid.*

96. *Ibid.*

97. *Ibid.*

98. Sligo, *Jamaica*, p. 108

99. Sligo to Lord Holland, 31 August 1836, Correspondence of Lord Holland, BL

100. Burn, p. 149

101. *Ibid.*
102. *Edinburgh Review,* vol. LXVI (1838)
103. Sligo to Lord Glenelg, 23 August 1836, Letter Books of Howe Peter Browne, MS 228, vol. 4, NLJ
104. *The Founding of Sligoville: A Tribute to Howe Peter Browne, 2nd Marquess of Sligo, Governor of Jamaica and Friend and Protector of the Former Slaves of Jamaica* (Jamaica, 1996)
105. Champion of the Slaves Exhibition, WH
106. Sligo to Alexander Holmes, 21 January 1837, Sligo letter book (MS), WH
107. *The Founding of Sligoville*
108. W.H.T. Lundie (Jamaica), letter to unknown recipient, 1 November 1836 (facsimile), WH

Chapter 16

1. Thorne and Kimball, p. 341
2. *Royal Gazette,* 25 February 1837
3. *Sotheby's Catalogue,* 6 December 1983
4. *Telegraph and Connaught Ranger,* September 1837
5. Sligo to J.D. Browne, 17 June 1837, Sligo letter book (MS), WH
6. Vassal Holland to Sligo, 29 January 1837 (facsimile), WH
7. Sligo to Marquis of Normanby, 23 September 1838, Sligo letter book (MS), WH
8. Sligo to Prime Minister Melbourne, 15 December 1838, Sligo letter book (MS), WH
9. *Telegraph and Connaught Ranger,* April 1833
10. Thackeray, p. 466
11. Prime Minister Melbourne to Sligo, 12 May 1837 (facsimile), WH
12. Sligo to Lord Ely, 11 June 1835, Sligo letter book (MS), WH
13. Sligo to Lord Ely, 3 November 1838, Sligo letter book (MS), WH
14. Sligo to Lord Ely, 11 June 1838, Sligo letter book (MS), WH
15. 10th Marquess of Sligo, *Westport House and the Brownes* (Westport, 1981), p. 49
16. MS41096/5, Westport Estate Papers, NLI
17. Sligo, *Westport House,* p. 49
18. 3rd Marquess of Sligo, *Remarks and Suggestions on the Present State of Ireland* (London, 1847)

19. Sligo, *Westport House*, p. 49
20. MS40913/1 (6), Westport Estate Papers, NLI
21. Sligo to Tutor, 3 November 1838, Sligo letter book (MS), WH
22. MS41096/2, Westport Estate Papers, NLI
23. Sligo, handwritten note, 17 January 1839 (facsimile), WH
24. *Ibid.*
25. Sligo to Dr [illegible], 26 January 1837, Sligo letter book (MS), WH
26. *Ibid.*
27. Sligo to Lord Holland, 17 January 1837, Sligo letter book (MS), WH
28. *Ibid.*
29. Barringer et al., p. 391
30. Burn, p. 323
31. Sligo, *Jamaica*, introduction
32. Lord Brougham, 20 February 1838, House of Lords Debate (facsimile), WH
33. Duke of Cambridge to Sligo, 20 March 1838 (facsimile), WH
34. *Eclectic Review*, April 1838, p. 84
35. Sligo to Joseph Sturge, March 1838, Sligo letter book (MS), WH
36. Sir Thomas Fowell Buxton, *Memoirs of Sir Thomas Fowell Buxton, Baronet* (London, 1848), p. 273
37. Sligo to Willam Ramsay, 9 December 1838, Sligo letter book (MS), WH
38. Lord Sligo, 20 February 1838, House of Lords Debate (facsimile), WH
39. Esther Copley, *History of Slavery and Its Abolition* (London, 1839), p. 168
40. Sligo, *A Letter to the Marquis of Normanby*, p. 21
41. Sligo to Alexandre Bravo, 14 August 1838, Sligo letter book (MS), WH
42. Sligo to Dowell O'Reilly, 30 December 1838, Sligo letter book (MS), WH
43. *Ibid.*
44. Sligo to Marquis of Aberdeen, 27 April 1835, Letter Books of Howe Peter Browne, MS 228, vol. 2, p. 300, NLJ
45. Joseph J. Gurney, *Familiar Letters to Henry Clay of Kentucky Describing a Winter in the West Indies* (London, 1840)
46. Sligo to J. Turner, 19 December 1838, Sligo letter book (MS), WH
47. Moses Bravo to 3rd Marquess of Sligo, 25 July 1854 (facsimile), WH

48. Barringer et al., p. 392
49. Sligo to Marquis of Normanby, May 1839, Sligo letter book (MS), WH
50. Sligo family notes (facsimile), WH
51. Sligo to Dr Dillon, 17 January 1840, Sligo letter book (MS), WH
52. Sligo to George Glendenning, 18 January 1840, Sligo letter book (MS), WH
53. *The Court Journal*, 27 February 1841, no. 618, p. 1017
54. *Ibid.*
55. Sligo to Dean Lyons, 1 July 1840, Sligo letter book (MS), WH
56. Sligo family notes (facsimile), WH
57. Sligo to Lord Melbourne, 14 June 1841, Sligo letter book (MS), WH
58. Lord Goderich to Sligo, 24 November 1841 (facsimile), WH
59. *Freeman's Journal*, 5 February 1845
60. Marchioness of Sligo to George Hildebrand, 4 January 1845, no. 20, Correspondence of Hester de Burgh, QU
61. Marchioness of Sligo to George Hildebrand, 11 November (facsimile), WH
62. Marchioness of Sligo to George Hildebrand, 14 January 1846, Correspondence of Hester de Burgh, QU
63. Sligo family notes (facsimile), WH
64. MS41096/2, Westport Estate Papers, NLI
65. Marchioness of Sligo to George Hildebrand, 4 January 1845, no. 30, Correspondence of Hester de Burgh, QU
66. *Ibid.*
67. Last Will and Testament of the Most Noble Howe Peter Browne, Marquess of Sligo, 7 September 1840 (MS), WH
68. *Freeman's Journal*, 6 February 1845
69. *Telegraph and Connaught Ranger*, 9 February 1845
70. William Ramsay to 3rd Marquess of Sligo, 5 March 1845 (facsimile), WH
71. Last Will and Testament of the Most Noble Howe Peter Browne, Marquess of Sligo
72. *Ibid.*
73. Sligo to Lord Plunket, Chancellor of Ireland, 5 October 1833, Sligo letter book (facsimile), WH
74. Sligo to William Ramsay, 1 June 1840, Sligo letter book (MS), WH

Index